Official Rules of Card Games

90th Edition
Printed in 2006

THE UNITED STATES PLAYING CARD COMPANY
Cincinnati, Ohio, U. S. A.

Canadian Subsidiary
INTERNATIONAL PLAYING CARD COMPANY LIMITED
Markam, Ontario

Joli Quentin Kansil, *Editor*

Tom Braunlich, *Associate Editor*

© International Copyright Reserved
Copyrighted, Printed and Published
1887, 1888, 1889, 1891, 1893, 1894, 1897, 1898, 1899, 1900, 1904, 1907, 1909, 1911, 1912, 1913, 1914, 1915, 1916, 1917, 1918, 1919, 1920, 1921, 1922, 1926, 1928, 1929, 1931, 1934, 1936, 1937, 1938, 1939, 1940, 1941, 1942, 1943, 1945, 1946, 1947, 1948, 1950, 1952, 1955, 1957, 1958, 1959, 1961, 1963, 1966, 1968, 1999, 2000, 2001, 2002, 2003, 2004, 2005, 2006

by
THE UNITED STATES PLAYING CARD COMPANY
CINCINNATI, OHIO, U. S. A.

ISBN: 1-889752-06-1

Library of Congress Catalog Card Number: 98-89680

Rules of Contract and Duplicate Bridge by permission of the American Contract Bridge League

Manufactured in Canada

Table Of Contents

Introduction

Today, when people think of card games, what immediately springs to mind? Grandma playing Solitaire on a Sunday night . . . tuxedoed gentlemen and elegantly attired ladies indulging in Baccarat in Monte Carlo . . . giggling children playing a boisterous round of I Doubt It or Slapjack . . . a Poker game on a Friday night in a smoke-filled room . . . more than two thousand people seated at hundreds of card tables, concentrating at a Duplicate Bridge tournament . . . a couple whiling away the time playing Gin Rummy on a crowded airline flight. . . .

All these scenarios share one thing in common. Since the late 1300s, people have been using an ordinary pack of playing cards to provide hours of stimulating enjoyment. Over the years, card playing has brought pleasure to millions of people, but it was not until 1887 that The United States Playing Card Company of Cincinnati, Ohio, issued the first edition of *The Official Rules of Card Games*. Since then, this book has been a primary source for rules and the arbiter of disagreements for hundreds of card games.

In this updated version, you will find rules for all of the classic favorites as well as some newcomers, including Spades, Bid Whist, Pai-Gow Poker, *Robert Abbott's* Eleusis, and the Editor's Bridgette and Joker Solitaire.

For the more prominent games, we are also featuring a chart which will enable you to see important details almost at a glance. An example is provided on the next page.

We hope you will be just as excited as we are with this latest in a long line of Official Rule Books. And now it is time to break out a fresh deck of Bicycle® cards and enjoy this edition.

The United States Playing Card Company

Game Chart

NUMBER OF PLAYERS	NUMBER OF CARDS	GAME PLAY	SKILL LEVEL
5-8 (2-14)	**52** (53)	◊ ◆ ◊ ◊ ◊ EASY → COMPLEX	◊ ◊ ◊ ◊ ◆ LUCK → SKILL

New feature provides important game information at a glance.

In this example for Poker, the reader can see the number of cards and players required, as well as the degree of skill and complexity. Note that for the number of players in this particular example, the game is best for five to eight participants, but as the numbers in parentheses indicate, Poker can be played by as few as two players, and in some versions, as many as fourteen can play. Similarly, the number of cards in the pack can vary. Thus, the 53 shown in parentheses in this example, indicates that a Poker deck is sometimes augmented with one more card – a joker.

The filled in diamond symbols show how the editors rank a game for skill and complexity. In this example, the diamond in the second position under Game Play means it is fairly easy to learn. The diamond in the fifth position under Skill Level is the highest ranking and means that Poker players need exceptional ability, not just luck.

About the Editors

Joli Quentin Kansil, Editor

In 1950, *Albert H. Morehead*, the Bridge editor of *The New York Times*, was appointed editor of *The Official Rules of Card Games*. He held this position for many years, until shortly before *Joli Quentin Kansil*, a fledgling game inventor, came to work for him as his personal assistant on card game books, Bridge articles, crossword puzzles and dictionaries. Now a full generation later, *Mr. Kansil* is gratified to follow in *Mr. Morehead's* footsteps as the editor of this current edition.

Tom Braunlich, Associate Editor.

The game chart innovation and the layout for the book were spearheaded by Tom Braunlich, long-time friend, associate, and agent of *Joli Quentin Kansil*. A Chess and Pente expert, *Mr. Braunlich* has had almost 20 years of experience in writing rules for all kinds of games.

Special thanks to Joann Shollenbarger, Kay Walker and Russ and Bridget Haggerty. Cover Design by Bev Furr.

A Brief
History of
Playing Cards

Did you know that at one time, the king of hearts represented Charlemagne, the king of diamonds was Julius Caesar, the king of clubs was Alexander the Great and the king of spades was King David from the Bible? These fascinating identities, along with special designations for the other court cards, were bestowed by the French who were instrumental in bringing the pleasures of card play to people in Europe and the New World.

The earliest playing cards are believed to have originated in Central Asia. The documented history of card playing began in the 10th century. The Chinese began using paper dominoes which they shuffled and dealt in new card like games. Four-suited decks with court cards evolved in the Moslem world and were imported by Europeans before 1370. In those days, cards were hand-painted and only the very wealthy could afford them, but with the invention of woodcuts in the 14th century, Europeans began mass production of playing cards.

It is from French designs that the cards we use today are derived. France gave us the suits of spades, clubs, diamonds and hearts, and the use of simple shapes and flat colors helped facilitate manufacture. French cards soon flooded the market and were exported in all directions. They became the standard first in England, and then in the British Colonies of America.

Americans began making their own cards around 1800. Yankee ingenuity soon invented or adopted practical refinements: double-headed court cards (to avoid the nuisance of turning the figure upright), varnished surfaces (for durability and smoothness in shuffling), indexes (the identifying marks placed in the cards' borders or corners), and rounded corners (which avoid the wear that card players inflict on square corners).

Americans also invented the Joker. It originated around 1870 and was inscribed as the "Best Bower," the highest card in the game of Euchre. Since the game was sometimes called "Juker," it is thought that the Best Bower card might have been referred to as the "Juker card" which eventually evolved into "Joker." By the 1880s, certainly the card had come to depict a jocular imp, jester or clown. Many other images were also used, especially as Jokers became vehicles for social satire and commercial advertising. Similarly, the backs of cards were used to promote ideas, products and services, and to depict famous landmarks, events — and even fads.

During this same period, cycling — on unicycles, bicycles and tricycles — was taking the country by storm. It was also in the latter part of the decade that Russell & Morgan, the forerunners of The United States Playing Card Company, decided to produce a line of cards of the highest quality. Employees were asked to suggest an attractive name for the new product, and a printer, "Gus" Berens, offered "Bicycle." His idea was enthusiastically accepted in 1885, and the Rider Back made its debut in 1887. Since then, while the Bicycle brand has featured dozens of different designs, the Rider Back has never gone out of production.

Today, people all over the world are familiar with the traditional red or blue back showing cupid astride a two-wheeler. The brand has become synonymous with playing cards and quality.

Choosing
Which
Games
To Play

I n selecting the game or games to play at a card party, there are several important considerations to be addressed: How many guests will be playing? How many know the games that are being considered? How difficult will it be to teach the rules to novices? Do the prospective guests want to play seriously or do they want to play casually, as an accompaniment to small talk?

The following guide is designed to help make an appropriate choice. The selected games are first grouped according to the number that can play at one table. Many can be played in one form or another by varying numbers of players, from two or three up to seven. Such games are not entered under every heading, but only under the numbers for which they will be most enjoyable.

Under each heading, the games are divided roughly into three categories: lighthearted, casual, and serious. Obviously this division is somewhat arbitrary. Lighthearted games can be played to the accompaniment of either children's chatter or adult small talk, whereas serious games either require close attention or skill or both. Finally, casual games can be contests of skill as well, but they are less disrupted by social conversation.

Games that are easiest for children are marked with an asterisk (*). (Games for children appear in Chapter IX.)

For Two Players

Lighthearted	*Casual*	*Serious*
Eights*	Canasta	Belotte
Concentration*	Cassino	Bezique
Crazy Eights	Cribbage	Bridgette
War	Forty-Five	California Jack
	Honeymoon Bridge	Domino Hearts
	Piquet	Gin Rummy
	Rummy*	Klaberjass
	Samba	Knock Rummy
	Two-Hand Euchre	Pinochle
		Russian Bank
		Sixty-Six
		Six Pack Bezique

For Three Players

Lighthearted	*Casual*	*Serious*
Eights*	Canasta	Auction Pinochle
Concentration*	Cassino	Continental Rummy
	Cribbage	Domino Hearts
	Cutthroat Bridge	Five Hundred
	Cutthroat Euchre	Five Hundred Rum
	Hearts	Knock Rummy
	Rummy	Schafskopf
	Seven Up	Six-Bid Solo
		Skat
		Towie

* Games for Children

For Four Players

Lighthearted	*Casual*	*Serious*
Fan Tan	Canasta	Cinch
I Doubt It	Euchre	Continental Rum
Michigan	Forty-Five	Contract Bridge
Napoleon	Hearts	Five Hundred
Pig	Pitch	Liverpool Rum
Red Dog	Poker Squares	Omnibus Hearts
Snip Snap Snorem*	Rummy	Partnership 500 Rum
	Seven Up	Partnership Pinochle
	Spades	Persian Rum
	Spoil Five	Poker
		Sixty-Six
		Skat
		Solo (Ombre)
		Whist

For Five or More Players

Lighthearted	*Casual*	*Serious*
Cancellation Hearts	Auction Euchre	Auction Hearts
Fan Tan	Black Jack	Bridge
I Doubt It*	Double-Ace Euchre	Eleusis
In-Between	Double Rum	Liverpool Rum
Michigan*	Five Hundred	Panguingue
Napoleon	Knock Poker	Poker
Pounce*	Oklahoma	
Red Dog	Pitch	
Spoil Five		

Banking Games

Baccarat	Faro
Black Jack	Pai-Gow Poker
	Pusoy

* Games for Children

General Rules
That Apply
to All
Card Games

Certain customs of card play are so well established that it is not necessary to repeat them as part of the rules for every game, unless otherwise stated. The following guidelines and formalities can be assumed to apply to any game, in the absence of any rule stating otherwise.

The Pack. The standard 52-card pack is used. It contains four suits, each identified by its symbol, or "pip": spades (♠), hearts (♥), diamonds (♦), and clubs (♣). There are thirteen cards of each suit: ace (A), king (K), queen (Q), jack (J), 10, 9, 8, 7, 6, 5, 4, 3, 2. Wherever a game is said to require 52 cards, reference is to this standard pack. A majority of card games use the standard pack, including some of the most popular games in the world, namely, Bridge, Gin Rummy, Hearts, Cribbage, Cassino, Fan Tan, and most versions of Poker.

The Joker. A fifty-third card – the joker – and a fifty-fourth card, which may be used as an extra joker, are usually furnished with the standard 52-card pack and may become part of the pack if the rules of the game require it. For example, a number of versions of Poker, including Pai-Gow, utilize the joker, and Canasta requires four jokers.

Other Packs. In addition to the standard pack and the pack that includes one or more jokers, other packs are used for a number of popular games. Below is a short list of some games and the kinds of decks that are required.

Canasta. Uses a double pack plus four jokers, making 108 cards. In assembling any of these double packs, it is usually desirable to use cards of identical back design and color.

Samba. Uses a triple pack plus six jokers, making 162 cards in all.

Pinochle. Uses two 24-card packs mixed together, with two each of the ace down to the nine in each suit. Thus there are 48 cards in all. There is also a 64-card Pinochle pack formed by mixing together two 32-card packs.

Spite and Malice. Two packs are used, but with a twist: The first pack is the standard 52-card pack, but the second pack has a different back design and comprises the standard 52 cards plus four jokers.

Black Jack. As played in many casinos, it is a six-pack game as six standard 52-card packs are shuffled together, making 312 cards in all. Some establishments use only one or two packs for Black Jack, and a few use four or eight packs.

Baccarat. This is an eight-pack game (416 cards), and Chemin de Fer, a close cousin of Baccarat, also uses eight packs. Games that use six or more packs invariably call for a "shoe," which is a container that houses several decks from which the cards are dealt one at a time.

Bridgette. A pack of 55 cards is used for this popular two-hand bridge game.Three extra cards, called colons, are added to the standard 52 cards. (Bridgette can be played with a standard 52-card pack to which modified jokers and another card are added.)

Euchre. This is one of many games that uses a "stripped deck," which is the standard pack systematically reduced, usually by removing the deuces, threes, and so forth. Euchre is commonly played with a 32-card pack – all of the cards from deuce through six are removed. Three other popular card games – Piquet, Skat, and Klaberjass – are also played with a 32-card deck.

Bezique. Uses two 32-card stripped decks, making 64 cards in all. The most popular version, Six-Pack Bezique uses half a dozen of these 32-card packs.

Five Hundred. Uses the 32-card pack just described, to which one joker is added, making 33 cards. In the six-player version, a special 62-card pack is used: the standard 52 cards plus an 11 and 12 in each suit, and a 13 in just the two red suits.

Sixty-Six. Uses an extremely stripped pack – only 24 cards. All of the cards below the nine are removed, so that each of the four suits contains only the A, K, Q, J, 10, and 9.

Panguingue or Pan. This game uses eight stripped packs. Each standard pack is stripped down to 40 cards by removing the eights, nines, and tens. Thus, the number of cards called for is 320.

The Draw. There are several methods for determining partnerships, seats at the table, right to deal first, and so on. The most common method is as follows: The pack is shuffled and then spread face down on the table, with the cards overlapping. Each player draws one card, but none of the four cards at each end of the pack may be drawn. The rank of the cards so drawn determines partnerships, and so forth. If two or more players draw cards of the same rank, in some games the rank of suits usually breaks the tie. Spades are ranked highest, followed by hearts, diamonds, and clubs. *For example,* a six of spades outranks a six of diamonds. In some card games, however, if two or more players draw cards of the same rank, suits do not apply, and the players must draw again.

Rotation. The right to deal, the turn to bid, and the turn to play all rotate clockwise–that is, from each player to his left-hand neighbor.

The Shuffle. Any player at the table has the right to shuffle the pack (and as a matter of common practice, this right remains even where special rules of a game designate one player responsible for shuffling). In most games, the dealer has the right to shuffle last, and this is the rule when no different provision is stated.

The Cut. Cutting is the act of dividing the deck into two packets and transposing the bottom packet to the top. The custom is for the dealer to present the pack, after shuffling, to his right-hand neighbor, who lifts a packet from the top and sets it down beside the bottom packet. The dealer completes the cut by placing the bottom packet on top of the other.

Each packet of the cut must contain a minimum of cards, which varies in different games, but is usually four or five.

First Player. This term refers to the left-hand neighbor of the dealer. The player in this position bids first in some games and plays first in most games.

The Deal. In most games, the first card dealt goes to the "first player," and the cards are distributed in clockwise rotation. The number of cards dealt at one time varies and is expressly stated for every game. The rule may be "one at a time," or "two at a time," or more at a time, but the same number of cards is dealt to every player in any one round. Sometimes the quota varies from round to round. For example, the rule to "deal 3-2" means, to deal a round of three cards at a time, then a round of two cards at a time.

Unless otherwise noted, all cards are dealt face down so that no player can see the face of a card dealt to another. If a card is found face up in the deck, it is usually a cause for declaring a misdeal.

Misdealing. It is a universal rule that when a player requests it, there must be a new deal by the same dealer if the customary or prescribed rules of shuffling, cutting, and dealing are breached in any way. Usually the request may no longer be made by a player who has looked at any of the cards dealt to him, or by any player after the prescribed deal has been completed.

Incorrect Pack. A pack is incorrect if it does not comprise exactly the number, rank, and suits of cards prescribed by the rules of a specific game. A deck will be incorrect if some cards have been dropped on the floor or have been gathered up in another pack, or if the pack contains some cards belonging to another pack. If the pack is found to be incorrect, the current deal is abandoned at once, even though it may have progressed through various stages of bidding or play. All scores made before that deal, however, stand without change.

Imperfect Pack. The term "imperfect" is used in a narrower sense, to mean an incorrect pack that cannot be rectified by the simple act of removing foreign cards or restoring cards that were originally included in it. The most common imperfection is when cards have become so worn and defaced that some are identifiable from the back. If a pack is found to be imperfect, but only through having an identifiable card, the current deal usually stands as if dealing has been completed, but the pack is then replaced prior to the next deal.

Chapter I

Bridge
and
Whist
Games

CONTRACT BRIDGE

NUMBER OF PLAYERS	NUMBER OF CARDS	GAME PLAY	SKILL LEVEL
4	52	◇ ◇ ◇ ◇ ◆ EASY ➔ COMPLEX	◇ ◇ ◇ ◇ ◆ LUCK ➔ SKILL

Since the 1930s, Contract Bridge has been one of the most popular card games in the world. Today, perhaps only Poker has more participants. Countless newspapers have daily Bridge columns, and there are more books about Bridge than any other game, except Chess. Bridge tournaments continue to attract thousands of players who compete with each other to become Life Masters.

The game of Whist appeared in England in the 1600s. The game developed into Bridge (1894), then Auction Bridge (1903), and finally the American form of Contract Bridge (1925). Whist and Auction Bridge still have followers, but Contract Bridge has become the most popular of these games.

Contract Bridge is an ideal game for entertainment because it is a partnership game. It is ideally adapted for social play at home or at clubs that meet weekly in groups of eight, 12, or more. Finally, the game is wonderful for tournament play among serious players.

A fascinating feature of Contract Bridge is that it is enjoyed equally by casual players, who do not want to take any game too seriously, and by scientific players who wish to study and master the intricacies of complex bidding techniques and card-play strategies.

The rules of Contract Bridge are presented here. These are condensed from *The Laws of Contract Bridge* copyright The American Contract Bridge League. For those who wish to learn the game on a more advanced level, there are hundreds of books and professional teachers.

Object of the Game. Each partnership attempts to score points by making its bid (or contract), or by setting (defeating) the opposing partnership's bid. At the end of play, the side with the most points wins, and the difference in points between the two partnerships is the margin of victory.

Preliminaries

Number of Players. Four people play, as partners, two against two. (Five or six people may take part in the same game by "cutting in"; that is, one or two players sit out for a set of deals while the other four are playing.) For ease of discussion, the positions of the four players at the table correspond to the compass points, North, South, East and West, with North and South playing as partners against East and West. In the scoring, partners share equally in every result so that only one score is kept for each side.

The Pack. The standard 52–card pack is used. Players usually have two packs with contrasting back designs. While one pack is being dealt, the dealer's partner shuffles the other pack for the next deal.

Rank of Suits. Spades (high), hearts, diamonds, clubs.

Rank of Cards. A (high), K, Q, J, 10, 9, 8, 7, 6, 5, 4, 3, 2.

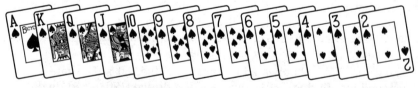

The Draw. Any player spreads a shuffled pack face down on the table and each player draws one card, but not one of the four cards at either end of the spread. (A player who exposes more than one card must draw again.)

The player drawing the highest card deals first. That player chooses his seat and the pack with which he will deal; the next highest card designates that player's partner who sits directly across the table. The two others take the remaining two seats. If two players draw cards of the same rank, such as ♥8 and ♣8, the rank of the suits determines the higher card; thus, in this example, the ♥8 would win the draw.

The Shuffle. The player to the dealer's left shuffles the cards and places them on the dealer's left. The dealer (after shuffling again, if he desires) sets the cards down on the right to be cut.

The Cut. The player at dealer's right must lift off a portion of the pack (not fewer than four cards nor more than 48) and set it down toward the dealer. The dealer completes the cut.

The Deal. The dealer distributes 13 cards to each player, one card at a time, face down, beginning with the player on his left.

Rotation. The turn to deal, to bid, and to play always passes to the left, from player to player. *For example:* If South is the dealer for the first hand, then West will deal next, then North, then East, and then South again. Likewise, in the play, if North leads a card, then East will play next, then South, and then West.

VANDERBILT'S CLAIM TO FAME

Many card games have evolved gradually, and no specific date can be given for the inception of some games. However, the invention of Contract Bridge can be dated with certainty: November 1, 1925. The inventor was the famous yachtsman *Harold S. Vanderbilt*, and he recorded the game's inception this way: "I compiled in the autumn of 1925 a scoring table for my new game. I called it Contract Bridge and incorporated . . . a number of new and exciting features; premiums for slams bid and made, vulnerability, and decimal system of scoring . . . . An ideal opportunity to try out my new game presented itself while I was voyaging . . . . on board the steamship *Finland* from Los Angeles to Havana via the Panama Canal."

The Bidding

Calls. Once the cards are dealt, each player picks up his hand. It is common for a player to arrange his hand into suits and further arrange each suit into descending order. Each player fans his hand to see all the cards, and keeps his fanned hand close enough to him so that no other player can see his cards. The auction or bidding then begins: Each player in rotation, beginning with the dealer, makes a call (pass, bid, double or redouble).

Passing. When a player does not wish to bid, to double, or to redouble, he says, "Pass." If all four players pass in the first round, the deal is "passed out," and the next dealer in turn deals a new hand.

Bidding a Suit. Each bid must name a certain number of tricks in excess of six (called "odd-tricks") that the bidder contracts to win, and a suit which will become the trump suit, if the bid becomes the final contract. Thus, One Spade is a bid to win seven tricks (6+1) with spades as trumps, and Four Diamonds is a bid to win 10 tricks (6+4) with diamonds as trumps. A bid may be made in Notrump, meaning that there will be no trump suit. The lowest possible bid is one, and the highest possible bid is seven.

Each bid must name a greater number of odd tricks than the last preceding bid, or an equal number but in a higher denomination. Notrump is the highest denomination, outranking spades. Thus, a bid of Two Notrump will overcall a bid of Two Hearts, and a bid of Four Clubs is required to overcall a bid of Three Notrump.

Doubling and Redoubling. Any player in turn may double the last preceding bid if it was made by an opponent. The effect of a double is to increase the value of the points at stake if the doubled bid becomes the contract. (See Scoring Table, page 10.)

Any player in turn may redouble the last preceding bid if it was made by his side and doubled by an opponent. A redouble again increases the scoring values.

A doubled or redoubled contract may be overcalled by any bid which would have been sufficient to overcall the same contract undoubled. Thus, if a bid of "Two Spades" is doubled and redoubled, it may still be overcalled by a bid of "Two Notrump," a bid of "Three Clubs," or by any other higher bid.

Final Bid and the Declarer. When a bid, double, or redouble is followed by three consecutive passes in rotation, the bidding is closed. The final bid in the auction becomes the contract. The player who, for his side, first bid the denomination named in the contract becomes the "declarer." If the contract names a trump suit, every card of that suit becomes a trump. The declarer's partner becomes the "dummy," and the opposing players become the "defenders."

The Play

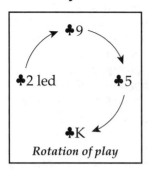

Rotation of play

Leads and Plays. A play consists of taking a card from one's hand and placing it, face up, in the center of the table. Four cards so played, one from each hand in rotation, constitute a trick. The first card played to a trick is a lead.

The leader to a trick may lead any card. The other three hands must follow suit if they can. If a player is unable to follow suit, he may play any card.

For the first trick, the defender on the declarer's left makes the first lead (the opening lead).

Facing the Dummy Hand. As soon as the opening lead has been made, the dummy then spreads his hand face up, grouped in suits, with each suit vertically arranged so that the other three players can easily view all 13 cards. The suits may be placed in any order as long as the trump suit (if any) is placed to the declarer's left. There is no particular order for placing the suits down in a Notrump bid.

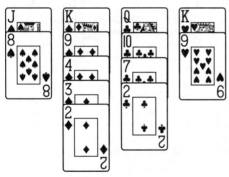

Dummy Hand

Winning of Tricks. A trick containing a trump is won by the hand playing the highest trump. A trick not containing a trump is won by the hand playing the highest card of the suit led. The winner of each trick leads next.

Declarer's Play. The declarer plays his own cards and the dummy's cards, but each in proper turn, since the dummy does not take an active part in the play.

Played Card. The declarer plays a card from his own hand when he places it on the table or when it is named as an intended play. When the declarer touches a card in the dummy hand, it is considered played (except when he is merely arranging the dummies cards). Alternatively, the declarer may name a card in the dummy and such a card must be played. A defender plays a card when he exposes it so that the other defender can see its face. A card once played may not be withdrawn, except to correct a revoke or other irregularity.

Taking in Tricks Won. A completed trick is gathered and turned face down on the table. The declarer and one of the defenders should keep all tricks won in front of them, and the tricks should be arranged so that the quantity and the order of the tricks played are apparent.

The Scoring

When the last (13th) trick has been played, the tricks taken by the respective sides are counted, and the points earned are then entered to the credit of that side on the score sheet. Any player may keep score. If only one player keeps score, both sides are equally responsible to see that the score for each deal is correctly entered.

The Scoring Table on page 10 indicates the point values, and a sample score sheet appears on page 9. The score sheet is ruled with a vertical line making two columns that are headed WE and THEY. The scorekeeper enters all scores made by his side in the WE column and all scores made by the opponents in the THEY column. A little below the middle of the score sheet is a horizontal line. Scores designated as "trick score" are entered below the line; all other scores are "premium scores" and and are written above the line.

Trick Score. If the declarer fulfills his bid by winning as many or more odd-tricks as the contract called for, his side scores below the line for every odd-trick named in the contract. Thus, if the declarer wins eight tricks and the bid is Two Hearts, the score for making "two" in a bid of hearts would be credited, as per the Scoring Table.

Overtricks. Odd-tricks won by the declarer in excess of the contract are called "overtricks" and are scored to the credit of his side as premium score.

Game. When a side has scored 100 or more points below the line, it has won a "game." To show this, the scorekeeper draws a horizontal line across the score sheet, below the score which ended the game. This signifies that the next game will begin. A game may be made in more than one deal, such as by scoring 60 and later 40, or it may be scored by making a larger bid and earning 100 or more points in a single deal. Once the next game begins, if the opponents had a score below the line for making a bid, such as 70, this score does not carry over, and each side needs the full 100 points to win the next game.

THE BARON PONDERS FOR TWO HOURS

Waldemar von Zedtwitz was considered by many to be the greatest player of the 1930s and '40s. "The Baron" was a very wealthy man, but he often wore the same light gray cotton cord suit for days at a time. As the declarer he was extremely slow in his card play, often tugging at his ear or a tuft of hair as he concentrated intensely. One day while dining alone in a fine restaurant in Manhattan, von Zedtwitz was pondering deeply about a Bridge hand that he had played some 35 years before. After some two hours, the check was still face down at his table, and the nearby waitresses were beginning to think that maybe this simply dressed man could not afford to pay the tab. Eventually, the employees took up a collection and one of the waitresses placed the money discretely on his plate on top of the check. The Baron finally snapped out of his stupor and put an equal amount of money on the plate– plus an exorbitant tip–and ambled out of the restaurant, still in deep concentration.

Vulnerable. A side that has won its first game becomes "vulnerable," and that side's objective is to win a second game and thus earn a bonus for the "rubber." When a side scores its second game, the rubber is over, and the scores are totaled. The winning partnership is the side with the most points. A vulnerable side is exposed to increased penalties if it fails to fulfill a future bid, but receives increased premiums for certain other bids that are fulfilled.

Honors. When there is a trump suit, the ace, king, queen, jack, and ten of trumps are "honors." If a player holds four of the five trump honors, that partnership scores 100 above the line; all five honors in one hand score 150. If the contract is in Notrump, a player holding all four aces scores 150 above the line for his side. Note that the points for honors are the same whether the side is not vulnerable or vulnerable, and that the defenders can also score for honors.

Slam Bonuses. Other premium scores are awarded for bidding and making a "small slam" (a bid at the six-level, such as Six Hearts) or a "grand slam" (a contract at the seven-level, such as Seven Spades or Seven Notrump).

Doubled or Redoubled Contract. When the declarer makes a doubled contract, a premium bonus is scored. Making a redoubled contract scores an even bigger premium bonus – this is a recent change in scoring. Note that doubling and redoubling do not affect honor, slam, or rubber bonus points.

Unfinished Rubber. If the players are unable to complete a full rubber and only one side has a game, that side scores a 300 bonus. If only one side has a part score, that side earns a 100 bonus.

Back Score. After each rubber, each player's standing, plus (+) or minus (–), in even hundreds of points, is entered on a separate score called the "back score." An odd 50 points or more count 100, so if a player wins a rubber by 950 he is +10, if he wins it by 940 the player is +9.

Bridge for Five or Six Players. When five people wish to play, the draw for deal establishes the order of precedence, and the player drawing the lowest card sits out for the first rubber. After the first rubber the fifth player joins the game, and the player who drew the fourth highest card sits out. After the next rubber, the player who just sat out re-enters the game, and the player who drew the third highest card now sits out, and so on until all players have sat out a rubber, after which the fifth player sits out again. The procedure is similar with six players, except that two sit out each rubber. Since a rubber can be any number of hands from two to twenty or more, a good variant is Four-Deal ("Chicago") Bridge, which is explained on page 12.

Illustration of Contract Bridge Scoring

WE	THEY
500 (h)	
750 (h)	
50 (d)	100 (g)
100 (b)	800 (g)
40 (b)	100 (d)
30 (a)	200 (c)
60 (a)	
40 (b)	
40 (e)	100 (f)
120 (h)	
1730	1300
1300	
+430	

a) WE bid Two Hearts and win nine tricks, scoring 60 points below the line (trick-score) for 2 tricks at hearts bid and made (30 each), and 30 points above the line (premium-score) for 1 over-trick at hearts. WE now have a part-score of 60 toward game.

b) WE then bid Two Clubs and make four-odd, scoring 40 points trick-score for 2 tricks bid and made (20 each), completing our game (100 points). So now, a line is drawn across both columns to show the end of first game of the rubber. WE also score 40 points for 2 overtricks at clubs (20 each), and 100 points for four honors in one hand (one of us held ♣ A K J 10). WE are now vulnerable.

c) WE bid Four Hearts, are doubled and set one trick as we make only 9 tricks. Our opponents score 200 for defeating our contract because WE are vulnerable.

d) The opponents bid Four Spades but win only 9 tricks; THEY are set 1. WE score 50 points, because THEY are not vulnerable and WE did not double. One of them held ♠A Q J 10, so THEY score 100 points for honors even though THEY did not make their contract.

e) WE bid and make One Notrump. This scores 40 points for us below the line. WE need only 60 points more to make a game

f) THEY bid and make Three Notrump, scoring 40 for the first trick, 30 for the second trick and 30 for the third trick over six (100 points below the line), and win a game. Another horizontal line is drawn across both columns, marking the end of the second game. Our part-score can no longer count toward a game. Now both sides are vulnerable.

g) WE bid Two Spades and are doubled. WE are set 3 tricks as WE won only 5 tricks, and the opponents hold 100 honors as well. THEY score 800 for the set and 100 for the honors.

h) WE bid and make Six Diamonds, a small slam, scoring 120 points trick-score (below the line), 750 bonus for a little slam, and 500 for winning the rubber as premium score above the line. Adding the score for both sides, WE have 1730 points, THEY 1300; WE win the rubber by 430. This gives us a 4-point rubber (see "Back Score," page 8).

SCORING FOR BRIDGE

VALUE PER TRICK	Undoubled	Doubled	Redoubled
IF TRUMP IS:			
Clubs or Diamonds (♣ ♦)	20	40	80
Hearts or Spades (♥ ♠)	30	60	120
NO TRUMP CONTRACT:			
1st trick over 6	40	80	160
Each additional trick over 6	30	60	120

Game is 100 Points
First side to win 100 points below line, in one or more hands, wins a game.
When a side wins two games, a rubber is concluded.

PREMIUM SCORE

	NOT VULNERABLE			VULNERABLE		
	Not Dbld.	Dbld.	Redbld.	Not Dbld.	Dbld.	Redbld.
Each overtrick	Trick Value	100	200	Trick Value	200	400
(Tricks made in excess of contract)						
Small Slam (12 tricks)	500	500	500	750	750	750
Grand Slam (all 13 tricks)	1000	1000	1000	1500	1500	1500

Two-Game Rubber. 700
Three-Game Rubber 500
Unfinished Rubber, One Game. 300
Unfinished Game, Part Score 100

Bonus for fulfilling any doubled contract. 50
Bonus for fulfilling any redoubled contract. 100

Honors (Scored above the line by either side)
Four of the five trump Honors (A, K, Q, J, 10) in one hand 100
All five trump Honors (A, K, Q, J, 10) in one hand. 150
All four Aces in one hand at notrump contract 150

UNDERTRICK PENALTIES

NOT VULNERABLE	Not Doubled	Doubled	Redoubled
One.	50	100	200
Two.	100	300	600
Three.	150	500	1000
For each additional undertrick	Add 50	Add 300	Add 600
VULNERABLE			
One.	100	200	400
Two.	200	500	1000
Three.	300	800	1600
For each additional undertrick	Add 100	Add 300	Add 600

Doubling and/or redoubling do not affect honor, slam or rubber points.
Vulnerability does not affect honor points or bonus points.
The side making the most points at the conclusion of the rubber (regardless
of games) is the actual winner of the rubber.

THE DUKE OF CUMBERLAND IS FLEECED FOR £20,000!

Bet You Didn't Know

NORTH
♠ ———
♥ 5 4 3 2
♦ 5 4 3 2
♣ 6 5 4 3 2

WEST
♠ J 10
♥ J 10 9 8 7 6
♦ 10 9 8 7 6
♣ ———

EAST
♠ A K Q
♥ A K Q
♦ A K Q J
♣ K J 9

SOUTH
♠ 9 8 7 6 5 4 3 2
♥ ———
♦ ———
♣ A Q 10 8 7

Final contract: Seven Clubs Redoubled, played by South
Opening lead: Jack of Hearts

This is likely the most famous hand in the history of bridge, although it was actually first reported in a game of Whist. The story has it that the Duke of Cumberland (son of King George III) some 200 years ago held the East hand. The wager from his opponents was that in spite of the duke's incredible hand, he would not win a single trick against a contract of Seven Clubs redoubled. The bet was some £20,000, and, alas, the duke lost his wager for the grand slam cannot be defeated if the declarer plays correctly.

Assuming that West's opening lead is a diamond or a heart, the declarer trumps, ruffs a spade in dummy, and then returns a club for a successful finesse against East. Now the declarer ruffs another spade in dummy, takes another successful trump finesse, and ruffs a third round of spades in dummy. His remaining spades are now established, and he returns to his hand by trumping a diamond or a heart. After cashing the ace of trumps, the declarer claims the rest of the tricks!

Four Deal Bridge
(Chicago)

This version uses the same rules and, with exceptions noted below, the same scoring as standard Contract Bridge. In a cut-in game with five or six players, a player who is "cut out" often has a long wait until the rubber ends and he can re-enter. By playing Four-Deal Bridge, a player seldom has to wait more than 15 or 20 minutes. The game is often called Chicago because it originated at the Standard Club in Chicago.

A round consists of four deals, one dealt by each player in turn. Vulnerability for a side is determined by which deal is being played, as follows:

First deal: Neither side is vulnerable.

Second and third deals: The dealer's side is vulnerable and opponents are not vulnerable. Even if the opponents previously made game, it does not matter.

Fourth deal: Both sides are vulnerable.

A passed-out deal is redealt by the same dealer. There is a bonus, scored immediately, of 300 for making game when not vulnerable and 500 when vulnerable. A part-score carries over as in Rubber Bridge and can help to make game in the next deal or deals, but it is canceled by any game score. There is a bonus of 100 for making a part-score on the fourth deal. After four deals have been played, the scores are totaled and entered on the back score, as in Rubber Bridge, and there is a new cut for partners, seats, and deal.

In one variation, played in certain regions, on the second and third deals the dealer's side is not vulnerable and the opposing side is vulnerable instead.

More points are usually scored in Four-deal Bridge than in the same number of deals at Rubber Bridge – estimates vary from 15 percent to 40 percent more. This is chiefly because at least one side is vulnerable in three deals out of four.

Standard Contract Bridge Bidding

The main parts in a game of Contract Bridge are the bidding and play. To bid correctly, a player should first determine the value of his hand and then state the bid consistent with that value. There are various systems of hand-valuation. The easiest and most popular one used in America is the "Point-Count System" advocated by *Charles H. Goren*, one of the great tournament champions and the player who is credited with popularizing Bridge in the 1950s. A modified outline of this system follows. It comprises the point-count method for hand-valuation and the requirements needed for various bids.

(A section on suggested leads in the play of the hand follows on page 21.)

Standard (Goren) Point-Count Table

High-Card Points

Ace	=	4 points
King	=	3 points
Queen	=	2 points
Jack	=	1 point

High-card points (usually called simply "points") are counted for nearly every bid. Distributional points, described below, are often added to high-card points to get a more accurate measure of just what a hand is worth.

Game and Slam Requirements Usually 26 points will produce a game, 33 points will produce a small slam, and 37 points will produce a grand slam.

Distribution Points

The Opening Bidder Counts –

Void suit (no cards in suit) = 3 points

Singleton (1 card in suit) = 2 points

Doubleton (2 cards in suit) = 1 point

Add 1 point for all 4 aces. Deduct 1 point for an aceless hand. Deduct 1 point for each unguarded honor. *Example:* Q-x, J-x, singleton K, Q, or J.

Opening Bid Requirements

One of a suit	14-point hands should be opened; 13-point hands may be opened if a good rebid is available (a rebiddable suit or a second biddable suit). A third-position opening is permitted with 11 points if hand contains a good suit. Minimum biddable suit: Q-x-x-x, or any five-card suit (x-x-x-x-x).
Two of a suit	25 points with a good 5-card suit; 23 points with a good 6-card suit; 21 points with a good 7-card suit.

Three, four, or five of a suit (preemptive bids)	Preemptive bids show less than 10 points in high cards and the ability to win within two tricks of the bid when vulnerable and within three tricks when not vulnerable. They should usually be based on a good seven-card or longer suit.
One Notrump	16 to 18 points (in notrump bidding only high-card points are counted) and 4-3-3-3, 4-4-3-2 or 5-3-3-2 distribution with Q-x or better in any doubleton.
Two Notrump	22 to 24 points and all suits stopped.
Three Notrump	25 to 27 points and all suits stopped.

Choice of Suits. Generally speaking, a player should bid his longest suit first. With two five-card suits, he should bid the higher ranking first. With two or more four-card suits, he should bid the suit immediately lower in rank to his short suit (doubleton, singleton, or void).

Five-Card Majors

In many rubber Bridge games and in standard American tournament play, an opening bid of 1♥ or 1♠ guarantees at least a five-card suit. This information is very helpful to the responder who can support the suit with as few as three small cards – or even a doubleton headed by a jack or better. With ample points for an opening bid and no five-card major or suitable holding for 1NT, the player opens 1♣ or 1♦, whichever minor suit is longer – even if there are only three cards in the suit. Even though the opening bidder bids a three-card suit, the contract will rarely be passed out at this low level, and if it is, it is probable that the opponents could have bid and made a higher contract of their own. An opening bid of 1♣ or 1♦ requests the partner to bid a major suit (hearts or spades) if he has one.

Responses

Any bid of a new suit by the responding hand is forcing on the opening bidder for one round. Thus, each time the responder bids a new suit, the opener must bid again. If responder should jump, the bid is forcing to game.

With fewer than 10 points, the responder should prefer to raise partner if the latter has opened in a major suit, and to bid a new suit himself at the one level in preference to raising a minor-suit opening bid. With 11 or 12 points, the responder can make two bids but should not force to game. With 13 points or more, the responder should see that the bidding is not dropped before a game contract is reached. With 19 or more points, he should make a strong effort to reach a slam.

Responses to Suit-Bids of One. *Raise.* When raising a partner's suit, count 5 points for a void, 3 for a singleton and 1 for a doubleton. To raise a partner's suit the responder must have adequate trump support. This consists of J-x-x, Q-x-x, x-x-x-x, or better for a non-rebid suit; and Q-x, K-x, A-x, or x-x-x for a rebid suit.

Raise partner's suit to two with 7 to 10 points and adequate trump support.

Raise to three with 13 to 16 points and at least four trumps.

Raise to four with no more than 9 high-card points plus at least five trumps and a short suit (singleton or void).

Bid of a new suit. At the one-level this bid requires 6 points or more. This response may be made on anything ranging from a weak hand, when a responder is just trying to keep the bidding open, to a very powerful one, when the responder is not sure where the hand should be played. At two-level a bid requires 10 points or more.

A jump in a new suit requires 17 points or more (the jump shift is reserved for hands when a slam is very likely. Responder should hold either a strong suit or strong support for the opener's suit).

Notrump responses (made with balanced hands). A 1NT response 6 to 9 points in high cards. (This bid is often made on an unbalanced hand if the responder's suit is lower in rank than the opening bidder's and the responder lacks the 10 points required to take the bidding into the two level.) A response of two – 2NT – requires 13 to 15 points in high cards, all unbid suits stopped, and a balanced hand. A response of three – 3NT requires 16 to 18 points in high cards, all unbid suits stopped, and very balanced distribution.

Responses to Suit-bids of Two. An opening bid of two in a suit (such as Two Hearts) is unconditionally forcing to game and the responder may not pass until game is reached. With 6 points or less the responder bids 2NT regardless of distribution. With 7 points and one sure trick, he may show a new suit or raise the opener's suit. With 8 or 9 high-card points and a balanced hand, the responder bids 3NT.

Responses to Preemptive Bids. Since the opener has overbid his hand by two or three tricks, the responder's high cards are the key factors to be considered when contemplating a raise. One or two trumps are sufficient support.

Responses to a One Notrump Bid. *Balanced hands.* Raise to 2NT with 8 or 9 points, or with 7 points and a good five-card suit. Raise to 3NT with 10 to 14 points. Raise to 4NT with 15 or 16 points. Raise to 6NT with 17 or 18 points. Raise to 7NT with 21 points.

Unbalanced hands. With fewer than 8 points plus any five-card suit, bid 2♦, 2♥, or 2♠. (Do not bid 2♣ on a five-card club suit.) With 8 points or more and a 4-card major suit, bid 2♣. (This is an artificial bid, asking the opener to show a four-card major if he has one. See section on rebids by opening 1NT bidder.) With 10 points and a good suit, bid three of that suit. With a Six-card major suit and less than 10 points in high cards, jump to game in the suit.

Responses to a Two Notrump Opening. *Balanced hands.* Raise to 3NT with 4 to 8 points. Raise to 4NT with 9 to 10 points. Raise to 6NT with 11 or 12 points. Raise to 7NT with 15 points.

Unbalanced hands. With a five-card major suit headed by an honor, or any six-card major, plus 4 points, bid the suit at the three-level.

Responses to a Three Notrump Opening. Show any five-card suit if the hand contains 5 points in high cards. Raise to 4NT with 7 points. Raise to 6NT with 8 or 9 points. Raise to 7NT with 12 points.

Rebids

Rebids by Opening Bidder. The opener's rebid is frequently the most important call of the auction. The opener now has the opportunity to reveal the exact strength of the opening bid and, therefore, whether a game or slam is contemplated. The opening is valued according to the following table:

13 to 16 points – Minimum hand
16 to 19 points – Good hand
19 to 21 points – Very good hand

After partner has raised the opening bidder's suit: Add 1 point for the fifth card in trump suit; add 2 additional points for the sixth and each subsequent trump. No four card is rebiddable; a five card suit is rebiddable if it is Q-J-9-x-x or better; any six card suit is rebiddable if it is x-x-x-x-x-x.

13 to 16 points. If partner has made a limited response (1NT or a single raise) the opener should pass, as game is impossible. If partner bids a new suit at the one-level, the opener may make a single raise with good trump support, rebid 1NT with a balanced hand, or, with an unbalanced hand, rebid the original suit or a new suit (if he rebid does not go past the level of two in the original suit).

16 to 19 points. If partner has made a limited response (1NT or a single raise) the opener should bid again, as game is possible if responder has maximum values. If the responder has bid a new suit, opener may make a jump raise with four trumps, or jump in his own suit if he has a six-card suit, or bid a new suit.

19 to 21 points. If partner has made a limited response (1NT or a single raise) opener may jump to game in either denomination, according to card strength and distribution. If the responder has bid a new suit, the opener may make a jump raise to game with four trumps, or jump to game in the original suit if it is strong. With a balanced hand and 19 or 20 points, the opener should jump to 2NT. With 21 points, rebidder should jump to 3NT. With 22 points and up, he should jump in a new suit (forcing to game and suggesting a slam).

Rebids by Opening Notrump Bidder. The Stayman Convention, populized by Bridge great *Samuel Stayman,* is an artificial set of bids that is very popular in both tournament and social play. When the responder bids 2♣, the opening bidder must show a four-card biddable major suit if he has such a suit:

With four spades, the player bids 2♠;

With four hearts, the player bids 2♥;

With four cards in each major, the player bids 2♠;

With no 4-card major suit, the player bids 2♦.

The opening Notrump bidder must pass: When the responder raises to Two Notrump and the opener has a minimum (16 points); when responder bids 2♦, 2♥, or 2♠, and the opener has only 16 or 17 points and no good fit for the responder's suit; when the responder bids 3 Notrump, 4♠, or 4♥.

Defensive Bidding

Overcalls. An overcall is a defensive bid (made after the other side has opened the bidding). Prospects for reaching game are not as good as they are for the opening bidder, in view of the opponent's bid strength. Therefore, safety becomes a prime consideration; overcalls are based not on a specified number of points, but rather on a good suit. Generally speaking, the overcaller should employ the same standards as a preemptor, with the ability to win in his own hand within two tricks of the overcall bid if vulnerable and within three tricks if not vulnerable.

One Notrump Overcall. An overcall of 1NT is similar to a 1NT opening bid and shows 16 to 18 points with a balanced hand and the opening bidder's suit well stopped.

Jump Overcall. Any jump overcall, whether it is a single, double, or triple jump, is preemptive and shows a hand weak in high cards but with a good suit that will produce within three tricks of the bid if not vulnerable and within two tricks if vulnerable.

Takeout Doubles. When a defender doubles and all the following conditions are present: a) his partner has made no bid, b) the double was made at the doubler's first opportunity, c) the double is of one, two, or three of a suit–it is intended for a takeout and asks partner to bid his best (longest) suit. This defensive bid is employed on either of two types of hand: 1) a hand of opening-bid strength where the doubler has no strong or long suit of his own but has good support for any of the unbid suits, or 2) where the doubler has a good suit and so much high-card strength that he fears a mere overcall might be passed out and a possible game missed.

Overcall in Opponent's Suit (cue-bid). The immediate cue-bid (*for example:* opponent opens 1♥; defender bids 2♥) is the strongest of all defensive bids. It is unconditionally forcing to game and shows approximately the equivalent of an opening forcing bid. It normally announces first-round control of the opening bid suit and is usually based on very fine support in all unbid suits.

Action by Partner of Overcaller. An overcaller's bid is based on a good suit; therefore, less-than-normal trump support is required to raise (Q-x or x-x-x). A raise should be preferred by the partner to bidding a suit of his own, particularly if the over-caller has bid a major. The partner of the overcaller should not bid for the sole purpose of keeping the bidding open. A single raise of a 1NT response should be made only in an effort to reach game. If appropriate values are held, a jump to game is in order, since a jump raise is not forcing.

Action by Partner of Takeout Doubler. In this situation, the weaker the hand, the more important it is to bid. The only holding that would justify a pass would be one that contained four defensive tricks, three in the trump suit. The response should be made in the longest suit, though preference is normally given to a major over a minor.

The doubler's partner should value his hand as follows: 6 points for a fair hand; 9 points for a good hand; 11 points for a probable game. A doubler's partner should indicate a probable game by jumping in his best suit, even if it is only four cards in length.

Since the partner of a doubler may be responding on nothing, it is a good policy for the doubler to subsequently underbid. while the doubler's partner should overbid.

Action by Partner of the Opening Bidder (when the opening bid has been overcalled or doubled). When an opener's bid has been overcalled, the responder is no longer under obligation to keep the bidding open; so a bid of 1NT or a raise should be based on a hand of at least average strength. Over a takeout double, the responder has only one way to show a good hand – a redouble. This bid does not promise support for the opener's suit but merely announces 10 points or more. Any other bid, while not indicative of weakness, shows only mediocre high-card strength.

Slam Bidding

When a partnership has been able to determine that they have the assets for a slam (33 points between the combined hands plus an adequate trump suit), they need only make sure that the opponents are unable to take two quick tricks. Various control-asking and control-showing bids have been employed through the years, but only three have stood the test of time: Blackwood, Gerber, and cue-bids (individual ace-showing). Blackwood is the most popular convention in Bridge. It was invented by *Easley Blackwood* in 1934.

Blackwood Convention. After a trump suit has been agreed upon, an immediate bid of 4NT asks partner to show his total number of aces.

Responses:

    5♣ – no aces or all four aces

    5♦ – one ace

    5♥ – two aces

    5♠ – three aces

After aces have been shown the 4NT bidder may ask for kings by now bidding 5NT.

Responses:

    6♣ – no kings

    6♦ – one king

    6♥ – two kings

    6♠ – three kings

    6NT – four kings

Gerber Convention. Invented by *John Gerber*, this convention is similar to Blackwood in that it asks for the number of aces. It is used when the partnership has agreed that the final contract will be played in Notrump. Its advantage is the fact that it initiates the response at a lower level. A sudden bid of 4♣ where it could not possibly have a natural meaning (*Example:* opener, 1NT; responder, 4♣) is Gerber and asks partner to indicate the number of his aces.

Responses:

    4♦ – no aces or all four aces

    4♥ – one ace

    4♠ – two aces

    4NT – three aces

If the asking hand desires information about kings, he bids the next higher suit over his partner's last response. Thus, if the responding hand has bid 4♥ over 4♣ to indicate one ace, a bid of 4♠ would now ask for kings, and the responder would now reply 4NT to signify no king, 5♣ to signify one king and so on.

Cue-bidding (Individual Ace-Showing). The Blackwood and Gerber conventions are designed to cover only a small number of potential slam hands. Many slams depend on the possession of a specific ace, rather than a wholesale number of aces. Cue-bids are employed in such cases. *For example:* Opener bids 2♠ and the responder bids 3♠; the opener now bids 4♣; this bid indicates the ace of clubs and invites the responder to signify an ace if he has one. The responder "signs off" by bidding the agreed trump suit.

Other Contract Bridge Bidding

Weak Two-Bids. In this system, an opening bid of 2♣ is artificial, not necessarily showing a club suit but showing a very powerful hand. It is forcing to game. The opener's partner must respond 2♦ if he has a weak hand. Any other response shows strength. An opening bid of 2♦, 4♥, or 2♠ is a "weak two-bid" – a preemptive bid, made on a fairly weak hand that includes a good five- or six-card suit but does not have 13 or more points.

Unusual Notrump. If a player bids 2NT after the opposing side has opened the bidding, and when his partner has not bid, this bid is a convention showing a two-suited hand (usually with five or more cards in each of the two minor suits). The partner of the 2NT bidder is required to respond in his best minor suit, even if it is a three-card or shorter suit.

Conventional Leads

Holding In Suit	Lead At Suit Bids	Lead At Notrump
A-K-Q alone or with others	K, then Q	K then Q
A-K-J-x-x-x-x	K, then A	A*, then K
A-K-J-x-x or A-K-x-x (-x)	K, then A	4th best
A-Q-J-x-x	A**	Q
A-Q-10-9	A**	10
A-Q-x-x(-x)	A	4th best
A-J-10-x	A**	J
A-10-9-x	A	10
A-x-x-x (-x)	A	4th best
A-K-x	K	K
A-K alone	A	K**
K-Q-J alone or with others	K then J	K
K-Q-10 alone or with others	K	K
K-Q-x-x(-x-x)	K	4th best**
K-Q alone	K	K
K-J-10 alone or with others	J	J
K-10-9-x	10	10
Q-J-10 or Q-J-9 alone or with others	Q	Q
Q-J-x or Q-J	Q	Q
Q-J-8-x (four or more)	Q	4th best
Q-10-9 alone or with others	10	10
J-10-9 or J-10-8 alone or with others	J	J
J-10-x or J-10	J	J
J-10-x-x or more	J	4th best
10-9-8 or 10-9-7, alone or with others	10	10
10-9-x-x (-x)	10	4th best
K-J-x-x (-x-x)	4th best	4th best
x-x-x-x (-x-x-x)	4th best	4th best
K-J, K-10, Q-10, A-x, K-x, Q-x, J-x, x-x-x-x-x	High card	High card
	Highest	Highest
A-J-x, A-x-x, K-J-x, K-x-x, Q-10-x, Q-x-x, J-x-x of partner's suit	Highest	Lowest

*The lead of the ace of an unbid suit at a no trump contract requests partner to play his highest card of the suit led, even the king or queen, unless dummy reveals that such a play might risk losing a trick.

**Usually not a good lead at this contract.

SUIT BREAKS IN CONTRACT BRIDGE

What are the odds on getting dealt a perfect 13-card suit? It is a long shot, as might be imagined: 1 in over 150 billion! As rare as this is, with all of the Bridge players in the world playing scores of hands daily, a 13-suiter should occur legitimately once a year. One of the greatest Bridge, gin rummy, poker, and backgammon players, *Oswald Jacoby*, played countless deals of Bridge for over 60 years and said he never had more than a 10-card suit – and that was just once in his life. Jacoby and others calculated the probabilities for all possible hand distributions, and they appear below. Note that the flattest distribution (4-3-3-3: a suit of four cards, and the other suits of three cards each) is not the most common holding. That distinction is reserved for the 4-4-3-2 shape which occurs a little more than 21% of the time.

Approximate Distribution (of Hand or Suit)	Approximate Probability 1 in –	Approximate Distribution (of Hand or Suit)	Approximate Probability 1 in –
4-4-3-2	5	8-2-2-1	500
5-3-3-2	7	8-3-1-1	850
5-4-3-1	8	7-5-1-0	900
5-4-2-2	10	8-3-2-0	900
4-3-3-3	10	6-6-1-0	1,400
6-3-2-2	18	8-4-1-0	2,500
6-4-2-1	21	9-2-1-1	5,000
6-3-3-1	28	9-3-1-0	10,000
5-5-2-1	31	9-2-2-0	12,500
4-4-4-1	33	7-6-0-0	16,500
7-3-2-1	50	8-5-0-0	33,000
6-4-3-0	75	10-2-1-0	100,000
5-4-4-0	80	9-4-0-0	100,000
5-5-3-0	100	10-1-1-1	350,000
6-5-1-1	140	10-3-0-0	500,000
6-5-2-0	150	11-1-1-0	5,000,000
7-2-2-2	200	11-2-0-0	10,000,000
7-4-1-1	250	12-1-0-0	333,000,000
7-4-2-0	275	13-0-0-0	159,000,000,000
7-3-3-0	400		

Bet You Didn't Know

Progressive Bridge
(Party Contract Bridge)

This version is played at Bridge parties when there are more than four players. It encourages sociability in that after several deals, players move to other tables to meet and play Bridge with other players. In some arrangements, partnerships change; in others, the partnerships remain set throughout the session.

Arrangement of Tables. The game is played at two or more tables of four players each. The tables are numbered consecutively from Table No. 1 to the highest number. The table numbers should be conspicuous for the convenience of the players, and each table should be provided with two decks of cards with different backs, one or more pencils, and a score pad showing the contract Bridge scoring table.

Tally Cards. Before play begins, the game director prepares individual tally cards, one for each player. Each tally card bears a table number and designates a position (North, South, East, or West) at the table.

PLAYER NUMBER			
ROUND	TABLE 1	TABLE 2	SCORE
1	1-6 vs. 2-5	3-8 vs. 4-7	
2	2-3 vs. 5-8	1-4 vs. 6-7	
3	1-8 vs. 3-6	2-7 vs. 4-5	
4	1-2 vs. 3-4	5-6 vs. 7-8	
5	1-7 vs. 2-8	3-5 vs. 4-6	
6	2-6 vs. 3-7	1-5 vs. 4-8	
7	2-4 vs. 6-8	1-3 vs. 5-7	
NAME			TOTAL

Two Table Progressive Bridge Tally

The tally cards may be drawn at random by the players or assigned by the game director, as he prefers. When play begins, each player takes the position assigned by his tally card.

Rounds. A round consists of four deals, one by each player. When all tables are through play, the game director gives a signal, and the players move to their positions for the next round according to the type of progression used. Each round should take about 20 minutes, and the average session of play is from six to seven rounds.

A Deal Passed Out. Only four hands are dealt at each table, one by each player. If a deal is passed out (that is, if all four players pass at their first opportunity to declare), the deal passes to the left, and both sides score zero for that deal.

Method of Progression. At the end of each round, the winning pair at Table No. 1 remains, and the losing pair moves to the last table. At all tables except Table No. 1, the losers remain, and the winners move up one table toward Table No. 1.

This is the standard method of progression, but it may be waived or altered to suit the wishes of the game director or the players. Special tallies may be arranged or obtained, assigning positions for each round in such a way as to give each player as wide a variety of partners as possible.

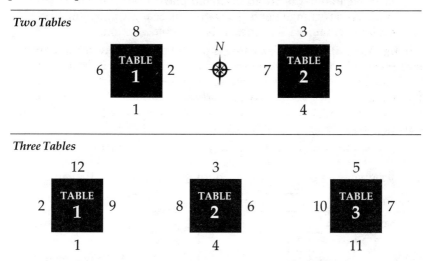

Selection of Partners. The four players at each table draw cards to determine partners at the start of each round. The two new arrivals at each table draw first, and the one drawing higher has choice of seats and is the first dealer. The one drawing lower sits at the left of the first dealer. The two players who remain at the table from the preceding round then draw. The higher becomes the partner of the dealer. Thus all players change partners after each round.

Since the chief function of Progressive Bridge is social, it is preferable to change partners at each round. However, if for some reason a pair contest is desired, the same partnerships may be retained throughout by simply progressing as described above without changing partners at the next table. Another method is to have the original North-South pairs remain in the same positions throughout the game, and to have the East-West pairs progress one table at a time until they reach Table No. 1, and then move to the last table. With this system, the progression is followed automatically, regardless of which pair wins at each table.

Draw for Deal. Unless the dealer has already been determined, the four players at a table draw for first deal. The player who draws highest is the first dealer and may select either deck.

Progressive Bridge Scoring. With the exceptions specifically mentioned below, the scoring for Progressive Bridge is exactly the same as for Rubber Bridge:

Each deal is scored and recorded separately, and no trick points are carried over from one deal to the next.

Game is 100 points for tricks bid and made in one deal. The game premium is 300 points, if not vulnerable, and 500 points if vulnerable, and is allowed only when a game is bid and made in one deal.

A premium of 50 points (some use 100 points) is scored for making any contract less than game (part-score). This premium is in addition to the value of the tricks made. Premiums for a small and grand slam are allowed only if they have been bid for.

A side may not score more than 1,000 points in a single deal, except in the case of a slam contract fulfilled.

Vulnerability. The first deal of each round is played and scored as if neither side were vulnerable.

The second and third deals of each round are played and scored as if the dealer's side were vulnerable and the other side not vulnerable.

The fourth deal of each round is played and scored as if both sides were vulnerable.

This is the most desirable method of determining vulnerability in Progressive Bridge and is in accord with the method used in Chicago Bridge.

Recording the Score. One of the four players at each table is appointed to record the score. He separately enters the result of each deal on the score pad and, at the end of the round, totals all the points made by each side.

The scorer enters on the individual tally of each player the points made by that player's side and also the points made by the opponents.

Correctly designed tallies provide spaces to record both "My Score" and "Opponent's Score." It is important that both scores be entered on the tally; otherwise the record would be meaningless.

Computing Total Scores. At the conclusion of the game, each player totals his score and also the opponents' scores, as recorded on his tally, and subtracts the opponents' total from his own. The difference, plus or minus as the case may be, is recorded in the space provided at the bottom of the tally.

Example: A player scores 2,460 points and the opponents score 1,520 points. This makes his net score +940 for the entire session. On the other hand, if a player scores only 1,650 points, and the opponents score 1,940 points, then his net score for the session is – 290 points. A player should not make the mistake of recording only plus scores, for that method gives false results and is likely to lead to improper doubling and redoubling.

Determining the Winner. The player with the largest plus score is the winner. Other players with plus scores rank in descending order, followed by the players with minus scores, the one with the largest minus being last.

Progressive Rubber Bridge

Progressive Rubber Bridge is a variation of the standard progressive game. It follows the same methods of progression and change of partners described in the preceding rules, but the scoring is somewhat different.

Under this arrangement it is preferable to play six or eight deals to a round, or to fix the length of a round by a definite time limit – 30 minutes for example. If the length of a round is determined by a time limit, any deal that has been started before time is up may be completed, but no new hand may be dealt.

Rubber scoring is used. As many rubbers as possible are completed during the allotted time. A rubber completed in two games carries a bonus of 700 points. A three-game rubber carries a bonus of 500 points. If a side has won one game toward a rubber and the other side has not won a game, 300 points are allowed for the single game won. If a rubber is unfinished and one side has made one or more part-score contracts in an unfinished game, but the other side has made no part-score, a side with a part-score adds 50 (or 100) points to its score.

Vulnerability is determined only by the state of the score. A side is vulnerable when it has won a game and remains vulnerable until the conclusion of that rubber. However, vulnerability lapses at the end of a round, and a new rubber is started at the beginning of each new round.

At the end of a round, each player enters on his tally only the net gain or loss–not the total score. At the end of the session these net gains and losses are totaled, and the player's final score, plus or minus as the case may be, is entered at the bottom of this tally.

Any time a player holds exactly 31, he may "knock" immediately, and wins the pot.

If a player knocks before the first round of exchanges have begun, the showdown occurs immediately, with no exchange of cards.

After the pot has been won, all the players put in chips for the next hand.

Proprieties in Bridge

The dealer should refrain from looking at the bottom card before completing the deal.

The other players should refrain from touching or looking at their cards until the deal is completed.

A player should refrain from:

1) Calling with special emphasis, inflection or intonation.

2) Making a call with undue delay which may result in conveying improper information to partner.

3) Indicating in any way approval or disapproval of partner's call or play.

4) Making a remark or gesture or asking a question from which an inference may be drawn.

5) Attracting attention to the score, except for his own information.

6) Calling attention to the number of tricks needed to complete or defeat the contract.

7) Preparing to gather a trick before all four hands have played to it.

8) Detaching a card from his hand before it is his turn to lead or play.

9) Watching the place in a player's hand from which he draws a card.

A partner's hesitation or mannerism should not be allowed to influence a call, lead, or play. It is proper to draw inferences from an opponent's gratuitous acts, but a player does so at his own risk.

It is proper to keep silent in regard to irregularities committed by a player's own side, but it is improper to infringe any law of the game deliberately.

It is improper to employ any convention whose significance is known to partner but has not been announced to the opponents.

DUPLICATE BRIDGE

NUMBER OF PLAYERS	NUMBER OF CARDS	GAME PLAY	SKILL LEVEL
8-100	52	◊ ◊ ◊ ◊ ♦ EASY → COMPLEX	◊ ◊ ◊ ◊ ♦ LUCK → SKILL

Duplicate Bridge is the only form of Bridge played in tournaments, but it is equally adapted to play in homes and clubs. It is considered the supreme test of skill among card games for the "luck of the deal" is eliminated to the extent that all of the competitors get to play the same cards.

Number of Players. Eight or more people may play a standard duplicate pair game, or an individual game, or a team-of-four match. (Four players in two partnerships may play Replay Duplicate, and the rules for this game follow on page 32.) There are four players to a full table, and the number of tables in a major tournament reach into the hundreds. For a local tournament, 20 to 25 tables (80 to 100 players) is fairly common.

Equipment. A "duplicate board" with one standard 52-card pack is needed for each table of four players. Each board (or "tray") is a device for holding intact the four hands of a deal so that once the hand is played, the cards can be used again in the next round with four other players playing the same duplicate hands. Each board is an aluminum or plastic tray about 11 inches long and 5 inches wide. *(See illustration next page).* It has four pockets, corresponding to the compass points, which are for holding the hands of the respective players. The face of each board is marked with an arrow pointing toward the "North" pocket, and the other three hands are marked East, South and West. The dealer (the player who gets the first turn to call) is also indicated, as well as whether a side is vulnerable or not vulnerable. When a set of two to four boards is to be played by the four players at a table, they must orient the boards so that they all point North, and usually one of the four walls in the room is designated as North.

There should be at least 16 boards, and each set of 16 is numbered consecutively, with the dealer and vulnerability marked as follows:

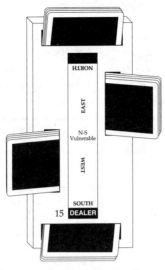

Typical Duplicate Board

Board No.	Dealer	Vulnerability
1	North	Neither side
2	East	North-South
3	South	East-West
4	West	Both sides
5	North	North-South
6	East	East-West
7	South	Both sides
8	West	Neither side
9	North	East-West
10	East	Both sides
11	South	Neither side
12	West	North-South
13	North	Both sides
14	East	Neither side
15	South	North-South
16	West	East-West

Boards numbered 17 to 32, 33 to 48, and so on, are marked the same as boards 1 to 16, except for the numbers themselves. Generally, the number of boards played by each pair is 24 to 30, and perhaps as many as 40 in a championship event.

Shuffle and Deal. Any player, in the presence of an opponent or the tournament director, prepares a board by thoroughly shuffling the pack of cards and dealing it, one card at a time face down, into four packets, each of which the player inserts in a pocket of the duplicate board.

The Bidding. Each player takes the hand from the pocket nearest him, and counts the cards to make sure there are thirteen. The player designated Dealer on the Duplicate tray calls first, and the auction proceeds as in standard Contract Bridge until the contract is determined. The only exception is that there is no redeal when a hand is passed out.

The Play. The opening lead, exposure of dummy, and subsequent play are the same as standard Contract Bridge except that after a trick is

---

"CONVENTION CARTE"

Before play begins in a Duplicate Bridge tournament, each partnership fills out a card with check marks and longhand remarks as to what conventions and special bids that partnership will be playing. The convention card is necessary so that the opponents will fully understand what a certain bid or card signal means when it occurs. Some convention cards used by long established partnerships can be quite lengthy. At one large tourney, the great Bridge veteran *Sam Stayman* was playing and before play began at a particular table, he picked up his opponents' convention card which was unduly long. Stayman sat in silence for almost five minutes, reading every single word. Then he handed the card back to his right-hand opponent and said, "I'll have the blue point oysters and the roast beef, medium rare."

---

completed, it is not gathered in. Instead, each player retains possession of his card and places it face down on the table directly in front of him, pointed lengthwise toward the partners who won the trick. The declarer plays dummy's cards by naming them, and the dummy player takes the card to show that it has been played and then turns it face down in front of him, also pointed lengthwise toward the side winning the trick. At the end of play, once the score is agreed on, each hand is carefully returned to its pocket in the tray, so the hand can be played again by other partners.

Scoring. The score of each board is independent of the scores of the other boards, and trick points scored on one board do not count toward game on a subsequent board. Thus, no rubber bonus is scored. Instead, the following premiums are used by the declarer's side when a contract is made:

	Not Vulnerable	Vulnerable
For making a contract of less than game	50	50
For bidding and making a game contract	300	500
For making a doubled contract	50	50
For making a redoubled contract	100	100

There is no premium for holding honors in one hand.

In other respects, the scoring of each board follows standard Contract Bridge, including the scoring change of 1993 which states that a side setting the contract doubled and not vulnerable, four or more tricks receives 100 extra points for the fourth and each subsequent undertrick, and 200 extra points for the fourth and each subsequent undertrick, if the contract is redoubled. This new scoring feature was added to prevent the non-vulnerable side from making ridiculously high sacrifice bids. Now such bids, when doubled or redoubled, earn a more reasonable undertrick penalty.

Determining the Winner. Match-point scoring is always used in individual games, is often used in pair games, and may be used in team-of-four games or replay games. Cumulative (or "total point") scoring may be used in pair games and team-of-four games.

(For complete Duplicate Bridge laws it is recommended that players refer to *The Laws of Duplicate Contract Bridge* by the American Contract Bridge League.)

Duplicate Bridge for Homes and Clubs

Replay Duplicate (for Four Players)

Replay Duplicate is a contest between two pairs of players. It is played in two sessions, called the original play and the replay. The players take places, one being designated North. The boards are shuffled and are played with the arrows pointing North. Any number of boards is feasible.

A separate score slip is kept for each board, and at the close of the session the boards and score slips are set aside where they will be undisturbed.

At some later time, the same four players take the same relative positions about the table. The boards are replayed but with the arrows now pointing East. Again, a separate score slip is kept for each board.

The scoring may be by match points or total points. If the match-point method is used, each deal is treated as a separate match. The pair having the better net score on a deal is credited with 1 point. The final scores are the totals of these match points.

If total-point scoring is employed, the two slips for each deal are compared, and the pair having the net plus score is credited with that amount. The net scores for all deals so determined are totaled, and the pair having the larger net total wins.

Replay Duplicate is popular as a home game among foursomes who meet weekly for social Bridge. It can easily be played in a continuous series of sessions; half the time in each session is devoted to original play of new boards, and half to the replay of old boards.

However, the game tends to become a test of memory rather than of Bridge skill. To check this tendency, the following measures are recommended:

1) Participants should not play the boards in consecutive order. They should choose the board to be played next at random from the stack.

2) Comment of any sort about the deal after its original play should be avoided.

3) At least a week should be allowed to elapse between the original play and the replay.

Some people prefer to make the game a test of skill in the play alone. In that case, the bidding during the original play is recorded, and for the replay the same bidding is read to fix the contract and declarer.

Individual Tournament Bridge *(for Eight or Twelve Players)*

In an individual game, each player plays once with every other person as a partner, and twice against every other person as an opponent.

The initial seating of the players in games for two or three tables is shown below:

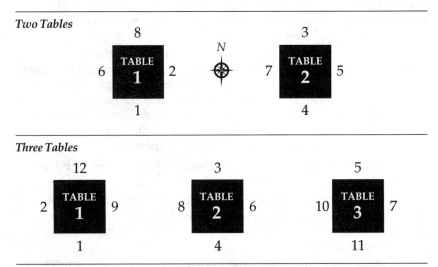

Two Tables

Three Tables

The game may be conducted without any guide cards as follows:

1) Players take places at random. The North position at Table 1 is reserved for the supervisor. This player is "anchor," retaining his seat throughout the game.

2) After the players are seated, each player is informed of his number and told who is the player of the next lower number.

3) After each round, all players except the anchor, progress by taking the seat vacated by the player with the next-lower number. (Player 1 stays, and all other players move as above.)

A new set of boards is played in each round. The set is played at all tables, the boards being circulated at convenience. The eight-player game requires seven rounds, with a total of 14, 21, or 28 boards. The twelve-player game requires eleven rounds, and the only feasible number of boards is 33.

Team-of-Four Contest *(for Eight Players)*

The Team-of-Four match between two teams has long been recognized as the best test of Bridge skill. The scoring is generally by International Match Points, which is described in the next section.

Two tables are provided, in different rooms if possible. One pair of Team 1 sits North-South at Table 1, and the other pair sits East-West at Table 2. The members of Team 2 take the remaining positions, its East-West pair playing at Table 1 and its North-South pair at Table 2.

The number of boards to be played should be a multiple of four. From 60 to 90 minutes are usually required for the play of 12 boards. The first fourth of the boards are placed on Table 1, and the second fourth on Table 2. These boards are shuffled, dealt, played, and scored.

The two tables then exchange boards, each replaying the ones played at the other table. Care must be taken to see that in every case the arrow points toward the North player. When the boards have been replayed, the two pairs of Team 2 exchange places, retaining the same partners but playing against the other pair of opponents. The remaining boards are divided equally between the two tables, to be shuffled, dealt, played, scored, exchanged, and replayed as explained above.

When all the boards have been replayed, the team whose members have a net plus score is the winner.

Team-of-Four contests for world and national championships are scored by "international match points" (IMP). On each deal, a team's net score is determined and is translated into international match points by the following schedule.

INTERNATIONAL MATCH-POINTS (IMP)					
0 - 10	0	320 - 360	8	1300 - 1490	16
20 - 40	1	370 - 420	9	1500 - 1740	17
50 - 80	2	430 - 490	10	1750 - 1990	18
90 - 120	3	500 - 590	11	2000 - 2240	19
130 - 160	4	600 - 740	12	2250 - 2490	20
170 - 210	5	750 - 890	13	2500 - 2990	21
220 - 260	6	900 - 1090	14	3000 - 3490	22
270 - 310	7	1100 - 1290	15	3500 - 3990	23
				4000 - & up	24

AUCTION BRIDGE

NUMBER OF PLAYERS	NUMBER OF CARDS	GAME PLAY	SKILL LEVEL
4	**52**	◇ ◇ ◇ ♦ ◇ EASY → COMPLEX	◇ ◇ ◇ ◇ ♦ LUCK → SKILL

There is no difference whatsoever between Auction Bridge and Contract Bridge except in the scoring. Whereas in Contract Bridge the declarer's tricks count toward game or slam only if he bid for them, in Auction Bridge the declarer's overtricks also count toward game or slam. Auction Bridge scoring is as follows:

Scoring. Provided the declarer has won at least the number of odd-tricks named in his contract, the declarer's side scores for each odd-trick won:

	Undoubled	Doubled	Redoubled
With no trump	10	20	40
With spades trump	9	18	36
With hearts trump	8	16	32
With diamonds trump	7	14	28
With clubs trump	6	12	24

Game and Rubber. When a side scores, in one or more hands, 30 points or more for odd tricks, it has won a game and both sides start fresh on the next game. When a side has won two games, it wins the rubber and adds 250 points to its score.

Doubles and Redoubles. If a doubled contract is fulfilled, the declarer's side scores 50 bonus points plus 50 points for each odd trick in excess of the contract. If a redoubled contract is fulfilled, the declarer's side scores 100 bonus points plus 100 points for each odd trick in excess of the contract. These bonuses are in addition to the score for odd tricks, but do not count toward game.

Undertricks. For every trick by which the declarer falls short of the contract, the opponents score 50 points; if the contract is doubled, 100 points; if it is redoubled, 200 points.

Honors. The side that holds the majority of the trump honors (A, K, Q, J, 10), or of the aces at notrump, scores:

For 3 honors (or aces)	30
For 4 honors (or aces), divided	40
For 5 honors, divided.	50
For 4 trump honors in one hand.	80
For 4 trump honors in one hand, 5th in partner's hand	90
For 4 aces in one hand at notrump.	100
For 5 honors in one hand	100

Slams. A side that wins 12 of the 13 tricks, regardless of the contract, scores 50 points for a small slam. A side that wins all 13 tricks, regardless of the contract, scores 100 points for grand slam.

Points for overtricks, undertricks, honors and slams do not count toward game. Only odd-tricks count toward game, and only when the declarer fulfills the contract.

Games Based on Bridge

Three-Hand Bridge

(Cutthroat)

Number of Players. Three people can play.

The Pack. The standard 52-card pack is used. (Two packs may be used as in Contract Bridge.)

Rank of Cards and Suits. As in Contract Bridge.

The Draw. Players draw for the deal and seats. High card deals.

The Shuffle and Cut. The player on the the dealer's left shuffles (the dealer may shuffle last), and the player on the dealer's right cuts.

The Deal. Four hands are dealt as in Contract Bridge. An extra or "dummy" hand is dealt between the players on the dealer's left and right.

The Bidding. The dealer bids first, and the bidding proceeds until any call is followed by two passes.

The Play. The highest bidder becomes the declarer. The other two players become defending partners for this deal, and the defender to the declarer's left makes the opening lead. The dummy is then spread out, face up, between the two defenders and play proceeds as in Contract Bridge.

Scoring. The Contract Bridge scoring table is used, although the game can be played utilizing Auction Bridge scoring. A separate score is kept for each player. If the declarer makes the contract, the points are scored to his credit. If the declarer is defeated, each of the opponents scores the full undertrick penalties. If either of the defenders hold honors, both defenders score for them. The rubber bonus in Three-Hand Bridge is as follows: The player winning two games receives 700 points if neither opponent has won a game, and 500 points if either opponent has won a game.

Settlement. Each player has his own scoring column, and each settles separately with the other two players, paying or collecting the difference in their scores rounded to the nearest 100 points, with 50 or more counting as 100.

Irregularities. During the auction, any improper double may be canceled by the player who is doubled, and thereafter neither opponent may double him at any contract. There is no penalty for any other improper call, which may be canceled by either opponent or condoned by agreement of both opponents. If a player improperly looks at any card in the dummy, he is barred from the auction thereafter. For the play of the hand, the rules and laws of Contract Bridge apply.

Trio

This variation was introduced by *George S. Coffin*.

Rank of Cards and Suits. As in Contract Bridge.

Players. The three players are designated as South, North, and East, and sit in those compass positions. South and North are partners against East and the dummy, which is in the West position.

Preliminaries. As in Three-Hand Bridge. After the deal the entire dummy hand is turned face up and is seen by all players during the bidding and play.

Bidding. South always bids first, then North, then East, and so on in rotation. Any player may become declarer, though East always plays the dummy.

Play. The player (which may be the dummy) on declarer's left makes the opening lead and play proceeds as in Contract Bridge.

Scoring. Score is kept as in Contract Bridge, with East and the dummy constituting one side and North-South the other. Hence, East wins or loses doubly, North and South each singly. After each rubber, the North player moves into the seat on his right and becomes South, and the previous South player becomes East.

Towie

This variation was introduced by *Leonard Replogle* of New York City.

Number of Players. Three people can play.

Rank of Cards and Suits. As in Contract Bridge.

Preliminaries. Four hands are dealt. The dealer then turns up six cards of the dummy hand opposite him.

Bidding and Play. The three players bid. High bidder becomes the declarer and after the opening lead (by the player on the declarer's left) the declarer turns up the rest of the dummy and places it opposite him. Play proceeds as in Bridge.

Scoring. Contract Bridge scoring may be used, but most players use special scoring in which down three, vulnerable, and doubled counts 1,000 (called a Towie). A separate scoring column is used for each player. If the declarer makes the contract, he scores the trick score plus 500 points for the game and 1,000 for the second (rubber) game. If the declarer is defeated, the other two players score the undertrick penalties.

Goulash. If a contract worth at least 100 trick-points is not reached, each player sorts his hand into suits. The hands are stacked; then the pack is cut, and the same dealer redeals the hands in three rounds, five, five, and three cards at a time. Six of dummy's cards are then turned face up, and the bidding begins again.

Two Notrump Doubled

This wild and amusing variation was suggested by Bridge great *Alfred Sheinwold* in his famous book "Five Weeks to Winning Bridge" (Simon & Schuster, 1959).

Number of Players. Three people can play.

Rank of Cards and Suits. As in Contract Bridge.

Bidding and Play. There is no bidding in this version. Each player in turn is the dealer, and the dealer is always the declarer at a contract of Two Notrump Doubled!

Scoring. The scores, of course, tend to run much higher than in regular Bridge. Each player has his own scoring column, and each settles separately with the other two players, paying or collecting the difference in their scores rounded to the nearest 100 points, with 50 or more counting as 100.

Tridge

Similar to Two Notrump Doubled, this equally wild variation of Bridge was devised by *Joli Quentin Kansil*.

Number of Players. Three people can play.

Rank of Cards and Suits. As in Contract Bridge.

Preliminaries. Each player in turn is the dealer, and four hands are dealt in a line without any one hand being assigned to any particular player. The dealer picks up the face-down hand of his choice and arranges it. The dealer then looks at the top four cards of each of the other three hands and picks one of these hands to be the dummy. The four cards of each of the other hands are not shown to any other player. The dealer then chooses which defender will get each of the two remaining hands. The other two players now sort their hands, and the play is ready to begin.

Bidding. There is no bidding. The dealer now selects the trump suit or notrump, and the final contract becomes three of that denomination redoubled!

The Play. The defender to the dealer's left makes the opening lead, the dummy hand is looked at and then spread by the dealer, and the play proceeds as in regular Contract Bridge.

Scoring. Each player has his own scoring column, and each settles separately with the two other players, paying or collecting the difference in their scores rounded to the nearest 100 points, with 50 or more counting as 100.

Honeymoon Bridge

(Two-Hand Bridge)

Number of Players. Two people can play.

The Pack. The standard 52-card pack is used.

Rank of Cards and Suits. As in Contract Bridge.

The Shuffle, Cut and Deal. Each player draws a card, and the player with the higher card deals first. Each player may shuffle, the dealer last, and the dealer's opponent must cut. The dealer gives each player 13 cards, one at a time, and places the remaining cards face down in the center of the table to form the stock.

The Play. The "receiver" (non-dealer) leads first. The opponent must follow suit, if possible. Play is at notrump, as in Contract Bridge. After each trick, each player draws a card from the stock, the winner of the previous trick drawing first and then leading to the next trick. Tricks won during this period have no scoring value.

Bidding and Final Play. When the last card of the stock has been drawn, the dealer may bid or pass. Bidding then proceeds as in Contract Bridge until a bid, double or redouble is followed by a pass. The player who does not make the final bid leads first, and thirteen tricks are played with or without a trump suit as determined by the final contract.

Scoring. Contract Bridge scoring is used, although the game can be played with Auction Bridge scoring.

BRIDGETTE

NUMBER OF PLAYERS	NUMBER OF CARDS	GAME PLAY	SKILL LEVEL
2	55	◇ ◇ ◇ ◆ ◇ EASY → COMPLEX	◇ ◇ ◇ ◆ ◇ LUCK → SKILL

Bridgette® was invented by *Joli Quentin Kansil* who was the protégé of *Albert H. Morehead*, the first Bridge editor of *The New York Times*. It is the only two-hand Bridge game that has been endorsed by many Bridge experts, and it has had a wide following since its introduction in 1970.

Number of Players. Two people can play.

The Pack. In addition to the standard 52 cards, there are three extra cards called "Colons." With the standard pack, the colon cards can be made by using two jokers and the display card that is often included with the deck. The more ornate joker serves as the "Grand Colon," the second joker as the "Royal Colon," and the display card as the "Little Colon." An indelible felt pen can be used to ink in colon designs on the three extra cards as follows: All of the colons are designed with two circles placed vertically, similar to the colon used in punctuation. The Grand Colon has both circles filled in plus an "A" in the center; the Royal Colon has one circle filled in and the other open (like a ring) plus "JQK" in the center; the Little Colon has both circles open plus "2 – 10" in the center.

Rank of Cards and Suits. As in Contract Bridge. The colons have no actual rank, but each matches with one of three "groups" of cards in the pack:

Aces (A) and the Grand Colon

Face Cards (J,Q,K) and the Royal Colon

Spot Cards (2 – 10) and the Little Colon.

The Shuffle, Cut and Deal. The turn to deal alternates. Each player picks a card from the pack spread face down on the table. The highest card deals first. If the cards are of equal rank, the rank of suits decides. If a colon is drawn, another card must be picked.

The dealer shuffles the cards thoroughly, and the receiver cuts. The dealer then completes the cut and deals 13 cards one at a time, face down, to each player, beginning with the opponent. The rest of the pack forms the stock, and it is placed face down on one side of the table, closest to the dealer who turns over the top card and places it next to the stock. This card is called the "upcard."

The players now pick up their cards and arrange them by suits. A colon may be placed in between any two suits or at either end of the hand.

The Exchange. Before the bidding begins, the dealer and receiver improve their original holdings by receiving extra cards which they can use to stack their hands offensively or defensively. The receiver is always given two cards first, face down, from the dealer. The upcard determines the number of extra cards that the dealer receives: Spot card or Little Colon – four cards; Face card or Royal Colon – eight cards; Ace or Grand Colon – 12 cards. *For example:* If the jack of diamonds is the upcard, the dealer gives two cards to the receiver before taking eight cards.

When the players take up their exchange cards, they should arrange them with their original 13 cards. The same number of cards are then discarded so that the players' hands are back to 13 cards before the bidding starts. The exchange discards are placed face down off to the side near the stock. After the exchange, each player should verify that his hand contains exactly 13 cards.

Before a player looks at his cards for his exchange, he has the option of taking the upcard into his hand by placing down the matching colon (capturing). Such a play has no effect on the number of cards the players exchange.

HOW FREQUENT IS A PERFECT 13-CARD SUIT IN BRIDGETTE?

Getting dealt a perfect 13-card suit in Bridge is 1 in 159,000,000,000, but in Bridgette, the odds are greatly reduced because of the exchange feature whereby a player can switch up to 12 cards after receiving his original hand of 13. It is an elaborate calculation, but with the Little Colon or a spot card as the upcard and a 4-card exchange for the dealer, the probability of being able to make a perfect 13-card suit is about 1 in 116,400,000 — a large proposition, but substantially better odds than receiving such a hand in Bridge. With an 8-card exchange for the Royal Colon or a picture card, the odds are about 1 in 1,361,500. Finally, with the full 12-card exchange for the Grand Colon or ace, the chances are about 1 in 53,000. Since the game's invention in 1960, no one has reported a 13-suiter, though two 12-card suits have occurred — both in hearts, and both in 1986!

Bet You Didn't Know

The Bidding. The turn to bid alternates. The dealer bids first and is required to open the bidding. His lowest possible bid is Zero Notrump. A contract to take six tricks, Zero Notrump ranks just below a bid of One Club and is the only exception to bidding for fewer than half the tricks.

One player may continue to bid even if the opponent passes, for the auction proceeds until the last bid has been followed by two consecutive passes. After a double, however, the bidding ends if it is followed by a pass. After a redouble, the auction ends immediately.

Bidding Requirement. To bid a suit, the player must have at least two cards of that suit; and if a player makes a "jump bid" (a bid higher than necessary to raise the previous bid), he must have at least four cards of that suit. For a bid in notrump, the player may not have any void suits; that is, there must be at least one card in every suit.

The Play. After the bidding ends, the declarer, not the defender, makes the opening lead by playing any card, and the defender then plays a card. The winner of the trick leads to the next trick, and play continues until all 13 tricks have been played.

Collecting Tricks. To make the hand go more quickly, the cards to each trick are not played to the middle of the table. Instead, the players play the cards in front of themselves (either holding the card or placing it on the table), and a card that wins a trick is placed face down to the player's left. The one that loses is placed face down to the player's right. A second advantage of this method is that both players' hands can be reassembled after the play for discussion or to see if any bidding requirements or other rules were violated.

The Colons. The three colons act mainly as defensive cards and add a very important element of skill to the play. Instead of following suit, a player may play the matching colon, that is, the colon from the same group as the card led. Played this way, the colon loses the trick, but it bars the opponent from leading the same suit on the next trick. That is, the opponent, on the next trick only, must lead a different suit (or one of the two other colons).

To illustrate: A player may discard the Grand Colon if the ace of hearts is led, whether or not the player has any hearts. For the next trick only, the other player may not lead a heart. (Of course, if the opponent has only hearts left, the colon play has no effect.) A player may discard one of the two non-matching colons only when the player has no cards in the suit led, and this play has no effect on the lead to the next trick. For example, if the queen of clubs is led and the other player discards either the non-matching Little Colon or Grand Colon, the opponent may continue leading clubs.

While a colon played to a lead always loses the trick, when a colon is led, it can win the trick. When a player leads a colon, the opponent may play any card. If the card is from the same group as the colon led (a matching card) or is any trump, the colon loses the trick; but if the player plays any non-matching card, including either of the other two colons, the colon led wins. A good time to lead a colon is on the last trick. If, for example, a player leads the Little Colon at Trick 13, and the opponent's last card is an ace or king, the Little Colon wins.

The Scoring. The score sheet is the same as for Contract Bridge, but instead of "WE" and "THEY," the players' actual names are written at the top of the respective columns. The scoring itself is the same except for these important differences:

1) Zero Notrump bid and made scores 10 points below the line with 30 above for each overtrick. (One Notrump is still 40: 10+30, etc.)

2) No points are awarded for holding honors.

3) The bonus for making a doubled contract is 100 points, and for making a redoubled contract, 250 points.

4) Five Notrump bid and made scores a "sub slam" bonus of 1000 points; Six Notrump scores 1300 points; Seven Notrump scores 1600 points; a small slam in a suit scores 900 points; a grand slam in a suit scores 1500 points. These bonuses are the same whether not vulnerable or vulnerable.

Six-Deal Scoring. Because beginners often find scoring for regular Bridge difficult, a simpler alternative scoring has been designed for Bridgette. This system also appeals to experienced players who want to play a quick match when time is limited, or who wish to play a lively game for a stake.

The score sheet has no center line, as part scores are not carried over to the next hand, and there is no vulnerability feature either. Six horizontal lines, one for the result of each deal, are drawn and there are two columns, one for each player. After each deal, one of the players will earn points, and the scorer writes the correct score in that player's column.

BRIDGETTE SIX-DEAL SCORING

Offensive Score

(Earned by declarer for making the bid)

BIT-SCORE : 0NT, 1♣, 1♦, 1♥, 1♠	150
PART-SCORE : 1NT, 2♣, 2♦, 2♥, 2♠, 2NT,	
3♣, 3♦, 3♥, 3♠, 4♣, 4♦	250
GAME-SCORE : 3NT, 4♥, 4♠, 4NT,	
5♣, 5♦, 5♥, 5♠	750

SLAM-SCORE:

Small Slam: 5NT, 6♣, 6♦, 6♥, 6♠	1,500
Grand Slam: 6NT, 7♣, 7♦, 7♥, 7♠	2,200
Super Slam: 7NT	2,500

EXACTO BONUS: _no overtricks, bid made exactly_

0NT to 5NT bid	250
Any 6-level bid	100
Any 7-level bid	0
TRIFECTA BONUS: _3 overtricks_	350
(No points are awarded for 1, 2, or 4 or more overtricks)	
Bonus for making any Doubled bid	400
Bonus for making any Redoubled bid	1,000

Defensive Score

(Earned by defender for setting the bid)

Down	Undoubled	Doubled	Redoubled
1	100	200	300
2	200	500	700
3	300	800	1,100
4	400	1,100	1,500
5	700	2,000	2,700
6+	1,000	3,000	4,000

As shown in the chart, there are several innovative features in
six-deal scoring. The standard part scores in Bridge are separated into
"part-scores" and "bit-scores" (scores entered for bids of less than One
Notrump). In Six-Deal Scoring, there is a bonus for making one's bid

"on the nose." This score is called an "exacto." It is worth 250 extra points. A bid at the six-level, however, scores only a 100 point exacto bonus, and, as expected, a seven-level bid scores no additional bonus.

There is no bonus for honors, and the only additional score for making overtricks is the "trifecta," exactly three overtricks which earns 350 additional points.

To illustrate the scoring, making Four Clubs Doubled with two overtricks scores 650 points (250 for part-score and 400 for making the doubled bid). Making Five Notrump Redoubled exactly scores 2,750: small slam (1,500), plus redoubled bonus (1,000), plus exacto bonus (250).

The scores for all of the deals are not added up until the match of six deals is over. If the match is tied, the player who dealt the first hand deals a tie-breaker seventh hand, and the score for that deal is recorded in the area below the sixth line entry. This scoring system is also adaptable for Contract Bridge.

Cue-Bids. In the advanced version of Bridgette there are cue-bids, which are special bids and calls that ask the opponent for information about his short suits and high cards. The opponent must either answer a cue-bid by giving the information with his response or evade by jump-bidding or cue-bidding back. The advanced rules are beyond the treatment of the game presented here.

OH PSHAW
(Oh Hell, Blackout)

NUMBER OF PLAYERS	NUMBER OF CARDS	GAME PLAY	SKILL LEVEL
4	52	◇ ◆ ◇ ◇ ◇ EASY ➔ COMPLEX	◇ ◇ ◇ ◆ ◇ LUCK ➔ SKILL

This is an amusing game that has a large following world wide. There are many variant rules, but the most popular way of playing is presented here.

Number of Players. Three to seven people can play. However, the game is best for four or five players. Each person plays for himself, regardless of the number of participants.

The Pack. The standard 52-card pack is used.

Object of the Game. The goal is to win exactly the number of tricks bid, neither more nor less.

The Deal. Each game comprises a series of deals. In the first deal, each player receives one card; in the second deal, two cards; and so on to the limit. With four players, there are 13 deals; with five players, 10 deals; with three players it is advisable to limit the game to 15 deals.

The Turn-Up. Having completed the deal, the dealer turns up the next card of the pack. The turn-up fixes the trump suit for that deal. When the last deal leaves no odd card to turn up, the deal is played at notrump.

The Bidding. Beginning with the the player to the left of the dealer (the first hand), each player in turn bids exactly the number of tricks that he expects to win. Thus, on the first deal the possible bids are "One" and "Zero." The total of all bids need not be equal to the number of tricks in play. After the dealer has bid last, it is a responsibility of the scorekeeper to announce "Over," or "Under," or "Even," according to how the total of bids compares with the number of tricks.

The Play. The first hand makes the opening lead. Each player must follow suit if possible. If a player cannot follow suit, he may trump or discard at will. A trick is won by the highest card of the suit led or, if it contains trumps, by the highest trump. The winner of a trick leads next. A player is entitled to be informed at any time how much any other player has bid, and how many tricks each player has won. Each player should keep his tricks arranged in an orderly fashion so that they may be easily counted.

Scoring. A scorekeeper must be appointed to record the bids and enter the results. A running account is kept of each player's cumulative score.

A player who takes more or less tricks than his bid scores nothing for the hand and loses nothing (though in many games, one point is scored for each trick taken). For making his bid exactly, a player scores 10 points plus the amount of the bid. (As yet there is no standard for scoring of "Zero" bids. In different localities the score is 10, 5, or 5 plus the number of tricks in the deal.)

The player with the highest cumulative score at the end of the game wins, and the winner gets a bonus of 10 points. Each player settles with every other player on the difference in their final scores.

Irregularities. There is no penalty for a bid out of turn, but such a bid must stand. The turn to bid reverts to the rightful player. A player may change his bid without penalty before the player on his left bids.

A lead or play out of turn must be retracted at the demand of any player, and the card played in error must be left face up on the table and played at the first legal opportunity. A card exposed in any way but by legal play in turn becomes exposed and is treated in the same way.

SPADES

NUMBER OF PLAYERS	NUMBER OF CARDS	GAME PLAY	SKILL LEVEL
2-5	52	◇ ◆ ◇ ◇ ◇ EASY → COMPLEX	◇ ◇ ◆ ◇ ◇ LUCK → SKILL

The game of Spades is comparatively new and has already attracted a large following. It is a trick taking game with the main feature being that the spade suit is always trump. While there are really no official rules for the game, the most popular conventions and variations are described below.

Number of Players. Two to five people can play as individuals or four in two partnerships. The rules below are for four individual players. The changes required for other player arrangements are presented later.

The Pack. The standard 52-card pack is used. In one variation, two jokers are added, the "Big Joker" and "Little Joker."

Rank of Suits. Unlike Bridge or Whist, the Spade suit is always trump.

Rank of Cards. A (high), K, Q, J, 10, 9, 8, 7, 6, 5, 4, 3, 2.

Object of the Game. To win at least the number of tricks bid.

The Deal. The first dealer is chosen by a draw for high card, and thereafter the turn to deal proceeds clockwise. The entire deck is dealt one at a time, face down, beginning on the dealer's left. The players then pick up their cards and arrange them by suits.

The Bidding. Each player decides how many tricks he will be able to take. The player to the dealer's left starts the bidding and, in turn, each player states how many tricks he expects to win. There is only one round of bidding, and the minimum bid is One. Every player must make a bid; no player may pass. No suit is named in the bid, for as the name of the game implies, spades are always trump.

The Play. The game is scored by hands, and the winner must make a certain number of points which is decided before the game begins. Five hundred points is common, but 200 points is suitable for a short game. The player on the dealer's left makes the opening lead, and players must follow suit, if possible. If a player cannot follow suit, he may play a trump or discard. The trick is won by the player who plays the highest trump or if no trump was played, the player who played the highest card in the suit led. The player who wins the trick leads next. Play continues until none of the players have any cards left. Each hand is worth 13 tricks. Spades cannot be led unless played previously or player to lead has nothing but Spades in his hand.

The Scoring. For making the contract (the number of tricks bid), the player scores 10 points for each trick bid, plus 1 point for each overtrick. For example, if the player's bid is Seven and he makes seven tricks, the score would be 70. If the bid was Five and the player won eight tricks, the score would be 53 points: 50 points for the bid, and 3 points for the three overtricks. (In some games, overtricks are called "bags" and a deduction of 100 points is made everytime a player accumulates 10 bags. Thus, the object is always to fulfill the bid exactly.)

If the player "breaks contract," that is, if he takes fewer than the number of tricks bid, the score is 0. For example, if a player bids Four and wins only three tricks, no points are awarded.

One of the players is the scorer and writes the bids down, so that during the play and for the scoring afterward, this information will be available to all the players. When a hand is over, the scores should be recorded next to the bids, and a running score should be kept so that players can readily see each other's total points. If there is a tie, then all players participate in one more round of play.

Partnership Spades

Partners sit across from each other, and the game is the same except that the partners' bids are added together to make a team bid (contract). For example, if a player bids Four and his partner bids Six, the team bid is Ten. It does not matter if, in the play, one partner wins eight tricks, and the other wins two tricks, since the combined score is ten and thus, the bid is fulfilled. In Partnership Spades, there is a minimum bid of two required of each player.

The partner who wins the trick leads next.

Spades for Two Players

The players draw for high card, and then the pack is placed in the middle of the table to form the stock. The first player picks the top card and looks at it. If he wants to keep the card, then the player picks the next card, looks at it, and discards it face down. If the player elects not to keep the first card, he discards it face down and picks the second card which he must keep. The other player now proceeds in the same way, and the turn to draw two cards and discard one continues alternately until the entire stock is exhausted. Each player will then have 13 cards and the game proceeds as described above, except that each trick is two cards, rather than four.

Spades for Three Players

This game is the same as the four-player game except that the deuce of clubs is removed from the pack, and 17 cards are dealt to each player. Thus, there are 17 three-card tricks to be made, and a bid can be from One to Seventeen.

Spades for Five Players.

In this version, the deuces of clubs and diamonds are removed, leaving 50 cards which are dealt 10 cards to each player. There are 10 five-card tricks, and a bid can be from One to Ten.

Spades with Jokers

There are many variations for Spades which allow even more skillful maneuvers, high scoring, and ruthless strategies. Some of these variations are presented below, and the favorite is Spades with Jokers.

When the two jokers are used, they are the highest-ranking trump cards. The spade suit is comprised of 15 cards: the Big Joker outranks the Little Joker which outranks the ace of spades. For the two- and four-player games, the deuces of clubs and diamonds should be removed; for the five-player game, all four deuces should be removed; and for the three-player game, no cards are removed, as 18 cards are dealt to each person and there are 18 tricks.

Bidding Options

Blind Bids. In this version, played with or without the jokers, a player who falls behind the high scorer by 100 or more points may bid before looking at his cards. Making the contract gives the player 20 points per trick bid (instead of 10), but no points are scored for any overtricks.

Nil Bids. This variation may be played with or without jokers and allows a player to bid Zero (to win no tricks), which is harder to accomplish than it sounds. If the player succeeds, he wins 100 points; but if the contract fails, 100 points are deducted from his score. Thus, a player can have a minus score at the end of a hand or game.

"Irregularities". A player (or partnership) not following suit when possible revokes "renigs" and cannot receive any points for making the contract.

WHIST

NUMBER OF PLAYERS	NUMBER OF CARDS	GAME PLAY	SKILL LEVEL
4	52	◇ ◆ ◇ ◇ ◇ EASY → COMPLEX	◇ ◇ ◆ ◇ ◇ LUCK → SKILL

Whist is the direct forerunner of Bridge and is of English origin. Before the days of auction bridge and contract bridge it was a very popular game indeed, but today Whist has been superseded by Bridge.

Number of players. Four people can play in partnerships of two against two.

The Pack. The standard 52-card pack is used. As in many bridge games, two packs of cards of contrasting back design are recommended. While one pack is being dealt, the other can be shuffled for the next deal.

Rank of Cards. A (high), K, Q, J, 10, 9, 8, 7, 6, 5, 4, 3, 2. (In drawing for partners and deal, however, ace is low.)

The Draw. Players cut or draw from a spread pack for partners. The two highest play against the two lowest. The player with the lowest card has his choice of cards and seats. The player with the highest card is the dealer.

The Shuffle and Cut. Any player may shuffle, the dealer last. The player on the dealer's right cuts.

The Deal. The dealer gives each player one card at a time, face down, beginning with the player on his left, until he comes to the last card. The last card is the trump card.

The Trump Card. The dealer places the last card of the pack face up on the table before him, and every card of its suit becomes a trump. When it is the dealer's turn to play to the first trick, he picks up the trump card and it becomes part of the dealer's hand.

Object of the Game. Each of the partnerships tries to score points by taking any trick in excess of six. The partnership with the most points at the end of play wins the game.

The Play. The turn to play is in clockwise rotation. The player on the dealer's left leads first and may play any card. Each player in turn plays a card, following suit if possible. If he cannot follow suit, a player may play any card. Four cards played (including the card led) constitute a trick.

A trick is won by the person who played the highest trump. Any trick not containing a trump is won by the person who played the highest card of the suit led. The winner of each trick leads next.

Scoring. Each odd trick (a trick in excess of six) counts one point for the side winning it.

BID WHIST

NUMBER OF PLAYERS	NUMBER OF CARDS	GAME PLAY	SKILL LEVEL
4	54	◊ ◊ ◊ ◆ ◊ EASY → COMPLEX	◊ ◊ ◊ ◆ ◊ LUCK → SKILL

Bid Whist is a comparatively new game of the Whist family. In certain regions, it has gained a considerable following. The original version was invented by *Hubert Phillips*. Since then, some of the rules have changed. The conventions that follow are based on *R. Wesley Agee's* booklet *How to Play Bid Whist*.

Number of Players. Four people play in partnerships of two against two, with partners sitting opposite each other. Partners may be chosen by mutual agreement or by drawing cards from a pack spread face down. The two highest cards are partners, and the person with the highest card deals first.

The Pack. The standard 52-card pack is used, plus the big and little jokers. As in many bridge games, two packs of cards of contrasting back design are recommended. While one pack is being dealt, the other can be shuffled for the next deal.

Rank of Cards. The cards rank either from ace (high) down to deuce or from ace (high) down to king. Herein lies the main characteristic of Bid Whist and one of the most original features of any card game. When Bid Whist is played in an "uptown" contract, the cards rank: ace (high), king, queen, jack, 10, 9, 8, 7, 6, 5, 4, 3, 2. When the contract is played "downtown," the cards rank in reverse, from ace (high), 2, 3, 4, 5, 6, 7, 8, 9, 10, jack, queen, king (low). Thus, aces are the best cards in either the uptown or downtown formats, which will be described later. In all trump contracts, the big joker ranks best, and the little joker is second best. In notrump contracts, the jokers are of no value.

Object of the Game. The goal of the bidders is to make the contracted bid. The object for the opponents is to defeat the bid. The partnership with the most points at the end of play wins the game.

The Deal. After the shuffle and cut, the dealer distributes 12 cards one at a time, face down, to each player, beginning with the opponent on his left. The dealer gets the last card. The remaining six cards (referred to as "the kitty") are placed in the center of the table face down. The player receiving one or both jokers should place the joker with the card suit which appears to be the strongest.

The Bidding. A bid is an offer to win a stated number of odd-tricks (tricks in excess of six). Thus a bid of One contracts for seven tricks, a bid of Two, for eight tricks, and so on. The highest possible bid is Seven (a contract to win all 13 tricks), and the lowest possible bid is One. (In some games, the lowest allowable bid is Three.) In addition to bidding a number from One to Seven, the bidder must specify whether the bid is trump or notrump and whether the cards will rank uptown or downtown if the bid is a trump bid. If the player bids a number only, it is presumed that there will be a trump and the cards will rank uptown.

Examples: A simple bid of Four means 10 tricks are contracted for, the cards will rank uptown (ace down to deuce), and there will be a trump suit. The trump suit is named only after the bidding ends and only if the highest bid was not notrump. A bid of Three-Low or Three-Downtown indicates nine tricks, with a trump suit to be named later, and that the cards will rank ace down to king. A bid of Four Notrump calls for 10 tricks to be won, and if it stands as the highest bid, the bidder will then state if it is high or low (uptown or downtown).

The player on the dealer's left starts the bidding and may bid a number from One to Seven or may pass. The bidding proceeds clockwise, and each player has only one turn to call. The dealer has the last bid or pass, and if all three players pass, the dealer must make a bid, and the auction ends.

Ranking of Bids. When a bid is announced, any succeeding bid must be higher than the last bid. A downtown bid outranks an uptown bid; thus a bid of Four-Low is higher than a bid of Four-High (or just Four). A notrump bid is higher than a suit bid; thus a bid of Four Notrump outranks Four-Low or Four-High. Finally, a bid of a higher number outranks any bid in a lower number; for example, a bid of Five-High, Five-Low, or Five Notrump is higher than any bid at the four-level.

The Kitty. The highest bidder names the trump suit or, if the bid is notrump, he states whether it is uptown or downtown. After these designations, the highest bidder is entitled to the six cards placed in the center of the table, the "kitty." These additional cards allow the highest bidder to exchange up to six of the cards in his hand for some or all of the cards in the kitty. After the exchange, the highest bidder should again hold 12 cards.

For a trump bid, the highest bidder customarily permits the other three players to see the six cards in the kitty before he exchanges. (This is commonly referred to as "sporting the kitty.") For notrump bids, the highest bidder does not sport the kitty, but a player who has a joker may play it when he cannot follow suit.

The Play. Each partnership tries to win tricks. A trick consists of four cards, one from each player in rotation, and the first card played to a trick is the lead. A player must follow suit if possible, and the highest card played in the suit wins the trick. When a player cannot follow suit, he may play any card. The highest trump card wins, if it is not a trump, it is merely a discard, and loses.

The highest bidder wins the kitty (classified in the play as the first trick) and leads first. The winner of a trick leads next. The play proceeds until all tricks are played.

When a side wins all 13 tricks, it is called a "Boston," but no extra bonus is awarded.

Scoring. The best method is to pick a point total, usually 5. A side can win if it wins this many odd tricks. *For example:* The partnership makes a five- or six-bid (referred to as "rise and fly") or, over the course of few deals, it accumulates a few lesser bids that add up to at least five, such as a two-bid, two one-bids, and another two-bid (6 points in this case). A partnership can also win if the opponents lose 5 points. A team loses points by bidding too high and then being set. *For example,* If a team bids Four and makes only eight tricks instead of the required 10, it loses 2 points. The partnership scoring 5 points first wins the game. If a partnership, over the course of one or more deals, loses 5 points, the opponents win the game. (In some games, the scoring process for a notrump bid doubles the number of tricks won. If the partners do not make their notrump bid, they are set for twice the number of tricks bid.)

BOORAY
(Bouré)

NUMBER OF PLAYERS	NUMBER OF CARDS	GAME PLAY	SKILL LEVEL
4-7	52	◊ ◊ ♦ ◊ ◊ EASY → COMPLEX	◊ ◊ ◊ ♦ ◊ LUCK → SKILL

This game combines features of both Bridge and Poker and is thus a good link between these two frequently played games. Booray is also related to an old card game called Écarté. Booray is popular in Louisiana and with French-speaking Canadians.

Number of Players. While the game can be played by two or three people, it is best played by more. Each player plays for himself.

The Pack. The standard 52-card pack is used.

Rank of Cards. A (high), K, Q, J, 10, 9, 8, 7, 6, 5, 4, 3, 2 in each suit.

The Ante. For each deal, players ante to a pot. The current dealer decides the amount that he and each other player pays, but usually a maximum is placed on the ante in advance.

The Deal. Players draw or cut for first deal. Thereafter, the turn passes to the player on the left. Only the dealer shuffles, and the player on his right cuts. Five cards are dealt to each player, one at a time, face down, beginning with the player on the left. The dealer then turns up the next card, which is designated the trump suit, and then he announces this suit.

Object of the Game. The goal is to win at least one trick and the primary object is to win each pot by taking the most tricks.

The Draw. After looking at his cards, any player may drop out of the hand and forfeit his ante by placing all five cards face down. Otherwise, a player may stay in and have a chance to win the pot, or he may sustain additional losses. Each active player, beginning on the dealer's left, now discards one to four cards and receives replacements from the deck, or stands pat. (In some games, a player is not allowed to draw more than three cards; in other games, the limit is five cards – a new hand.)

The Play. When the draw is completed, the player on the dealer's left leads and the cards are played out in tricks (one card from each player in turn). The leader must lead his highest trump if he has the ace, king, or queen. To each trick, a player in turn must:

1) Follow suit, if possible.

2) Play a higher card than any previously played, if possible.

3) Play a trump, if unable to follow suit.

4) Play any card, if unable to follow suit or trump.

Although a player who cannot follow suit must trump, he need not overtrump. A trick is won by the highest card of the suit led unless a trump is played, in which case the highest trump wins. The winner of a trick leads next. He may lead any card unless he holds the ace, king or queen of trumps, in which case one of these three cards must be led.

The Scoring. The player who wins the most tricks wins the pot. If two players win two tricks each, or if five players win one trick each, they divide the pot equally. A player who stays in the game but fails to win a trick must contribute an amount equal to the current pot. This is added to the next pot and not to the current pot.

Chapter II

Poker
and Its
Many
Versions

POKER

NUMBER OF PLAYERS	NUMBER OF CARDS	GAME PLAY		SKILL LEVEL	
5-8 (2-14)	**52** (53)	◇ ◆ ◇ ◇ ◇ EASY → COMPLEX		◇ ◇ ◇ ◇ ◆ LUCK → SKILL	

As early as the sixteenth century, Germans played a bluffing game which they called "Pochen." It later developed into a French version, called "Poque," which was eventually brought over to New Orleans and played on the riverboats that plied the Mississippi. In the 1830s, the game was refined further and became known as Poker. During the Civil War, the key rule about drawing cards to improve one's hand was added. A variation – Stud Poker – appeared at about the same time.

Today, Poker is truly an international game, enjoyed in virtually every country where card games are played. There are hundreds of versions of Poker, and the game is played not only in private homes, but also in countless Poker rooms at famous casinos. Poker can be played socially for pennies or matchsticks, or professionally for thousands of dollars. There is plenty of luck in Poker, but the game requires incredibly great skill as well, and each player is the master of his own fate.

As with Backgammon and Gin Rummy, the luck-to-skill ratio is hard to quantify, but with games such as these, a novice can win in a short session; however, over the course of playing for many hours, the better player will invariably prevail. *Herbert O. Yardley,* who wrote the classic book *The Education of a Poker Player in 1957*, said that he never lost at more than three consecutive sessions. Indeed, if a player constantly loses in more sessions than he wins, then such a player is not just unlucky; he is simply being outplayed. With the exception of Bridge, Poker demands more skill than any other card game. Some people would debate even this statement and say that Poker stands at the very apex of card games requiring skill.

General Rules of Poker

Number of Players. Any number of players from two to 14 may play in one of the various forms of Poker, but most experienced players consider five to eight players ideal. Everyone plays for himself. There are never any partnerships in Poker.

The Pack. The standard 52-card pack, sometimes with the addition of one or two jokers, is used. Poker is a one-pack game, but today, in virtually all games played in clubs and among the best players, two packs of contrasting colors are utilized in order to speed up the game. While one pack is being dealt, the other is being shuffled and prepared for the next deal. The procedure for two packs is as follows: While the deal is in progress, the previous dealer assembles all the cards from the pack he dealt, shuffles them, and places them to the left. When it is time for the next deal, the shuffled deck is passed to the next dealer. In many games in which two packs are used, the dealer's left-hand opponent, instead of his right-hand opponent, cuts the pack.

In clubs, it is customary to change cards often and to permit any player to call for new cards whenever he wishes. When new cards are introduced, both packs are replaced, and the seal and cellophane wrapping on the new decks should be broken in full view of all the players.

Object of the Game. The goal of each player is to win the pot which contains all the bets that the players have made in any one deal. A player makes a bet in hopes that he has the best hand, or to give the impression that he does. In most Poker versions, the top combination of five cards is the best hand.

Poker Hands. While Poker is played in innumerable forms, a player who understands the values of the Poker hands and the principles of betting can play without difficulty in any type of Poker game. Except in a few versions of the game, a Poker hand consists of five cards. The various combinations of Poker hands rank from five of a kind (the highest) to no pair or nothing (the lowest):

Five of a Kind. This is the highest possible hand and can occur only in games where at least one card is wild, such as a joker, the two one-eyed jacks, or the four deuces. Examples of five of a kind would be four 10s and a wild card or two queens and three wild cards.

Straight Flush. This is the highest possible hand when only the standard pack is used, and there are no wild cards. A straight flush consists of five cards of the same suit in sequence, such as 10, 9, 8, 7, 6 of hearts. The highest-ranking straight flush is the A, K, Q, J, and 10 of one suit, and this combination has a special name: a *royal flush* or a *royal straight flush.* The odds on being dealt this hand are 1 in almost 650,000.

Four of a Kind. This is the next highest hand, and it ranks just below a straight flush. An example is four aces or four 3s. It does not matter what the fifth, unmatched card is.

Full House. This colorful hand is made up of three cards of one rank and two cards of another rank, such as three 8s and two 4s, or three aces and two 6s.

Flush. Five cards all of the same suit, but not all in sequence, is a flush. An example is Q, 10, 7, 6, and 2 of clubs.

Straight. Five cards in sequence, but not all of the same suit is a straight. An example is ♣9, ♦8, ♦7, ♥6, ♣5.

Three of a Kind. This combination contains three cards of the same rank, and the other two cards each of a different rank, such as three jacks, a seven, and a four.

Two Pairs. This hand contains a pair of one rank and another pair of a different rank, plus any fifth card of a different rank, such as Q, Q, 7, 7, 4.

One Pair. This frequent combination contains just one pair with the other three cards being of different rank. An example is 10, 10, K, 4, 3.

No Pair. This very common hand contains "nothing." None of the five cards pair up, nor are all five cards of the same suit or consecutive in rank. When more than one player has no pair, the hands are rated by the highest card each hand contains, so that an ace-high hand beats a king-high hand, and so on.

Two hands that are identical, card for card, are tied since the suits have no relative rank in Poker. In such a case, the tied players split the pot. Note that if two hands contain the same high pair, then the ranking of the next card in the hands determines which one wins. *For example:* 9, 9, 7, 4, 2 beats 9, 9, 5, 3, 2. Likewise, two hands that have identical pairs would be decided by the fifth card. *For example:* Q, Q, 6, 6, J beats Q, Q, 6, 6, 10.

RANK OF POKER HANDS

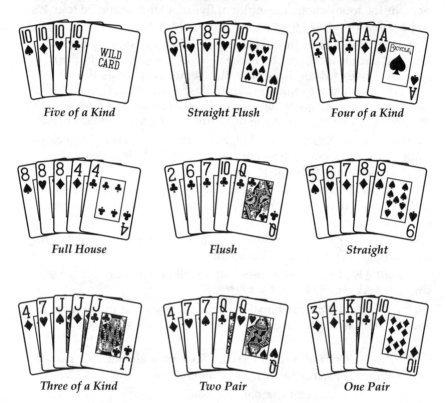

Five of a Kind   *Straight Flush*   *Four of a Kind*

Full House   *Flush*   *Straight*

Three of a Kind   *Two Pair*   *One Pair*

How the Betting Works. In the course of each Poker deal, there will be one or more betting intervals in which the players have an opportunity to bet on their hands. Betting is the key to Poker, for the game, in essence, is a game of chip management. Minimizing losses with poor hands and maximizing winnings with good hands is the underlying skill that Poker requires.

Before the cards are even dealt, the rules of the Poker game being played may require that each player put an initial contribution, called an "ante," of one or more chips into the pot, to start it off.

Each betting interval, or round, begins when a player, in turn, makes a bet of one or more chips. Each player to the left, in turn, must either "call" that bet by putting into the pot the same number of chips; or "raise," which means that he puts in more than enough chips to call; or "drop" ("fold"), which means that he puts no chips in the pot, discards his hand, and is out of the betting until the next deal.

When a player drops, he loses any chips he has put into that pot. Unless a player is willing to put into the pot at least as many chips as any preceding player, he must drop out.

A betting interval ends when the bets have been equalized – that is, when each player has either put in exactly as many chips as his predecessors or has dropped. There are usually two or more betting intervals for each Poker deal. After the final interval there is a "showdown," which means that each player who remains shows his hand face up on the table. The best Poker hand then takes the pot.

If a player makes a bet or a raise that no other player calls, he wins the pot without showing his hand. Thus, in Poker, there is a bluffing element, and the best combination of cards does not always win the pot! Bluffing is one of the key reasons why Poker is so popular.

If a player wishes to remain in the game without betting, he "checks." This means, in effect, that the player is making a "bet of nothing." A player may check provided no one before him in that betting interval has made a bet. If another player has bet, he cannot check but must at least call the bet or drop. A player who checks may raise a bet that has been raised by another player. This is called "sandbagging," which is allowed, unless it has been decided beforehand that this practice is forbidden. If all players check during a round of play, the betting interval is over, and all the players still in the pot remain in the game.

In each betting round, one player is designated as the first bettor, according to the rules of the game. The turn to bet always moves to the left, from player to player, and no one may check, bet, or even drop, except when it is his turn.

Knowing When to Bet. The ranking of Poker hands is based on mathematics. The less likely a player is to get a certain hand, the higher it ranks and the more likely it is to win the pot. For example, a player should not expect to be dealt a straight flush more than once in 65,000 hands, but he can expect to be dealt two pair about once in every 21 hands.

Unless a player is planning to bluff, he should not make a bet without holding a hand that he thinks may be the best. No Poker player can bet intelligently unless he knows what constitutes a good hand, a fair hand, and a bad hand. A table of the various Poker hands and the number of combinations of each in a pack of cards is provided. (See chart next page).

POSSIBLE POKER HANDS IN A 52-CARD PACK	
Straight Flush	40
Four of a Kind	624
Full House	3,744
Flush	5,108
Straight	10,200
Three of a Kind	54,912
Two Pairs	123,552
One Pair	1,098,240
No Pair	1,302,540
Total	**2,598,960**

The Kitty. By unanimous or majority agreement, the players may establish a special fund called a "kitty." Usually the kitty is built up by "cutting" (taking) one low-denomination chip from each pot in which there is more than one raise. The kitty belongs to all the players equally, and it is used to pay for new decks of cards or for food and drinks. Any chips left in the kitty when the game ends are divided equally among the players who are still in the game. Unlike the rule in some other games, such as Pinochle, when a player leaves a Poker game before it ends, he is not entitled to take his share of chips that comprised part of the kitty.

Chips. Poker is almost always played with poker chips. For a game with seven or more players, there should be a supply of at least 200 chips. Usually, the white chip (or the lightest-colored chip) is the unit, or lowest-valued chip, worth whatever the minimum ante or bet is; a red chip (or some other colored chip) is worth five whites, and a blue chip (or some other dark-colored chip) is worth 10 or 20 or 25 whites or two, four or five reds. At the start of the game, each player "buys in" by purchasing a certain number of chips. All of the players usually buy in for the same amount.

Banker. One player should be designated as the banker, who keeps the stock of chips and records how many have been issued to each player or how much cash the player has paid for his chips. Players should make no private transactions or exchanges among themselves; a player with surplus chips may return them to the banker and receive credit or cash for them, while a player who wants more chips should obtain them only from the banker,

Betting Limits. There are different ways of fixing a betting limit. Some limit is necessary; otherwise a player with a lot more money would have, or would be perceived to have, an unfair advantage. Once fixed, the limit should be unalterable throughout the game unless the players unanimously agree to change the stakes. Some popular limit systems follow:

Fixed limit. No one may bet or raise by more than a stipulated number of chips, for example, two, or five, or 10. Usually this limit varies with the stage of the game: In Draw Poker, if the limit is five before the draw, it might be ten after the draw. In Stud Poker, if the limit is five in the first four betting intervals, it is ten in the final betting interval (and often ten whenever a player has a pair or better showing).

Pot limit. Any bet or raise is limited to the number of chips in the pot at that time. This means that a player who raises may count as part of the pot the number of chips required for him to call. If there are six chips in the pot, and a bet of four is made, the total is 10 chips; it requires four chips for the next player to call, making 14; and the player may then raise by 14 chips. But even when the pot limit is played, there should be some maximum limit, such as 50 chips.

Table stakes. The limit for each player is the number of chips the player has in front of him. If the player has only 10 chips, he may bet no more than 10 and he may call any other player's bet to that extent. In table stakes, no player may withdraw chips from the table, or return chips to the banker, until he leaves the game. A player may add to his stack, but only between the deal just completed and the beginning of the next deal.

Whangdoodles, or Roodles. In a fixed-limit game, it is often agreed that following any very good hand – a full house or better, for example – there will be one deal by each player of Jackpots, in which everyone antes double, and the betting limit is doubled for these deals as well.

Poverty Poker. A maximum limit is put on the number of chips any player may lose. Each takes out one stack at the start; if he loses that stack, the banker issues the player another, without charging for it, and in many cases, the player can get still a third stack free before dropping out of the game. (Some limit should be placed on the number of free stacks so that a player will have the incentive to play carefully.)

No limit. In these sessions, the "sky's the limit," but such games are rarely played today.

Limits on Raises. In almost all games played today, there is a limit on the number of raises at each betting interval, and this limit is invariably three raises.

Draw Poker and Stud Poker

The main forms of Poker are Draw Poker and Stud Poker. In Draw Poker, all the cards are dealt face down to the players. In Stud Poker, some of the cards are dealt face up as the betting progresses, so that all of the other players get to see a part of each player's hands.

Unless the host, or the rule of a club, has already established the game, the players should first decide what form of Poker they will play. Two factors should influence their decision: the number of players, and whether the group has only experienced players or has some inexperienced players. The following selections are recommended:

Two, three, or four players. Stud Poker in any form. Usually, with so few players, only the very experienced play Draw Poker and they will often use a stripped deck, which is a pack with cards removed, such as all the deuces (twos) and treys (threes).

Five to eight players. Any form of Poker, either Draw or Stud.

Nine or ten players. Five-card Stud Poker.

More than 10 players. One of the games in which fewer than five cards are dealt, such as Three-Card Monte or Spit-in-the-Ocean. All of the Poker variations are described later in this chapter. Another alternative with so many players is to simply form two tables and organize two separate games.

Dealer's Choice. When the Poker session is Dealer's Choice, each dealer has the privilege of naming the form of Poker to be played and to designate the ante, wild cards (if any), and the maximum limit of chips that can be wagered during each round. However, the dealer may not require one player to ante more than another. If a game such as Jackpots is selected and no one opens the betting, the same dealer deals again and everyone antes again.

Wild Cards. While most Poker purists choose to play with no wild cards, in many games, especially Dealer's Choice, various cards may be designated as wild. A wild card is specified by the holder to be a card of any rank or suit, such as a fifth queen, or the card needed to combine with the other four in a player's hand to form a straight or a flush. Wild cards in a Poker game add variety, and of course, they greatly increase the chances of getting a rare combination such as a full house or a straight flush. The usual choices for wild cards are as follows:

The joker. Note that most packs of cards include two jokers for use in such games as Canasta. Poker players are increasingly adding one or both jokers as wild cards.

The bug. This is the joker, but its wildness is limited: It counts as an ace; or as a card of any suit for making a flush; or as a card of any rank and suit for making a straight or straight flush.

Deuces. "Deuces Wild" is a popular form of Draw Poker. Every two is wild. Sometimes the joker is included as a fifth wild card. Note that the number of wild cards in a hand does not diminish it in anyway; thus, with deuces wild, five of a kind comprised of 10, 10, 2, 2, 2 (five 10s) beats 8, 8, 8, 8, 2 (five 8s).

One-eyed cards. The king of diamonds and the jacks of spades and hearts show only one eye, whereas the other face cards all have two eyes. One-eyed jacks are sometimes designated as wild cards, but the king of diamonds is rarely selected to be wild.

Low hole card. In Stud Poker, each player's lowest "hole" card (that is, the lowest card that is dealt face down and not seen by the other players) is wild. In Draw Poker, the wild card would be the lowest card in a player's hand. When such a card is designated, it means that every card of that rank in that player's hand is wild, but the fact that a certain card is wild in one player's hand does not make that same rank of card wild in other players' hands.

Laws and Ethics. In every game, a written code of Poker laws should be used as the final arbiter for settling all questions. No Poker laws are universally followed – there are many local customs and preferences – but the Poker laws in this book embrace the latest customs of the most expert games and are recommended for adoption. (see "The Laws of Poker," p. 79). It is a tradition of Poker that any club or group of players may make special rules, called "house rules," to suit their personal preferences. Of course, any such house rules should be written down.

Time Limit. Before play begins, the players should set a time limit for when the game ends and stick to it. Violation of this principle could eventually turn pleasant sessions into unpleasant ones. Often when the time for quitting is approaching, the host or one of the players will say "three more deals" or "through Zane's deal," so that players will know how many deals are left and can gauge their strategies accordingly.

Draw Poker

Principal Forms. There are several methods of playing Draw Poker, and they differ mostly in the rules governing betting. The essential features of the game, common to all varieties, are as follows:

Each player is dealt five cards face down, one at a time in rotation, beginning on the dealer's left. After the deal, there is a betting interval. The player on the dealer's left has the first right or obligation to bet.

When the first betting interval has ended, each active player in turn, beginning with the player on the dealer's left, may discard one or more cards, and the dealer then gives him, from the top of the undealt portion of the pack, face down, as many cards as he discarded. This is the draw. A player may, if desired, "stand pat" (draw no cards). Unless otherwise stated, the maximum number of cards a player may draw is three or, if the player shows an ace to all the other players, he may draw four. (In some games, especially in casinos, a player may draw four cards without exposing an ace, or may draw five cards – a fresh hand.) Note that, unlike some other card games, the player must always discard before taking any new cards for his draw.

After the draw, there is another betting interval, followed by a showdown.

HENRY CLAY AT THE POKER TABLE

Bet You Didn't Know

The great U. S. Senator Henry Clay, who lost the presidency three times, was, nevertheless, a frequent winner at Pochen, the European forerunner of Poker. John Quincy Adams, who was to become the sixth U.S. President a decade later, reported in his lifelong diary that when he and Clay were diplomats in Ghent, Belgium, negotiating the end of the War of 1812, it was not uncommon for Clay to trudge up the stairs to their quarters at 4 a.m. after an all-night card game – just as Adams was waking up to write in his journal and start his day.

All games of Draw Poker fall into one of two classes, depending on the betting rules:

Pass and Out. Also called Pass Out or Bet or Drop. In this method, whenever it is a player's turn, and if there has been no bet before him, he must bet the minimum allowed or drop out. In most games, this rule applies only before the draw. After the draw, a player may check. In some games, however, each player must bet or drop out before and after the draw. This procedure is followed in casinos where the House runs the game.

Pass and Back In. At his first turn, a player may pass (check) rather than bet, provided no previous player has made a bet. The first player to make a bet is said to open. Once the pot is opened, each player in turn has another chance to stay in or drop out. After the draw, a player may check. This procedure is common in home games and other social games, and is the one used in the versions of Poker explained later in this chapter.

The Ante. The players must decide in advance which of two methods they will adopt for the ante: Either each player antes one chip before the deal or the dealer antes one chip for all the players in the game before dealing. Thus, if there are six players in all, the dealer's ante is six chips.

Special Hands. To create more playable hands and enliven the game, many players give special value to one or more hands that are not among the traditional Poker hands:

Skip straight (also called Dutch straight or Kilter). Five cards in an alternate sequence, such as Q, 10, 8, 6, 4, or K, J, 9, 7, 5. This hand beats three of a kind but loses to a straight.

Round-the-corner straight. A sequence such as 3, 2, A, K, Q. Note that the hand 5, 4, 3, 2, A beats 4, 3, 2, 1, A, K, which beats 3, 2, A, K, Q, and so on. When both skip straights and round-the-corner straights are played, the skip straight ranks higher.

Bobtail or Fourflush. A four-card flush or a four-card straight in sequence with "both ends open." An example of the latter is 8, 7, 6, 5, with the fifth card not in sequence; A,K, Q, J is not a bobtail, because only a single card, the 10, will fill it; 9, 8, 6, 5 is not, because only a 7 will fill it, this being called an "inside straight." The bobtail beats a pair but loses to two pair.

"I WASN'T BLUFFING – JUST DREAMING"

A famous story recounts a high-stakes no-limit, game in which a young man picked up the ♠A, K, Q, J and 10. The betting was fierce, and when the young man ran out of money, he asked to adjourn the game momentarily while he went to locate his father to get more. His hand, and that of the one opponent remaining, were sealed in separate envelopes; a short time later, the lad was back with his father who was told that the envelope contained a Royal Flush. The father brought enough cash to call the last bet and make a very big raise. The opponent, who held four 9s, realized that this could not be a bluff, and he threw in his cards. The son raked in all the chips and the envelopes were unsealed. The young man's hand was the ♣A, ♠K, Q, J and 10; he had misread his hand!

Standard Draw Poker

This game is played as described beginning on (p. 65), and the player who makes the first bet does not need any minimum hand in order to bet. In other words, he can open the betting without even a pair. Once the betting round is complete and players have drawn their cards, the second betting round begins and the first hand again has the opportunity to bet.

Some players vary this game slightly by playing a "blind opening", whereby the first hand must open the pot and (usually) the next player must raise. This game is played "pass and out" (described above) before the draw, but usually "pass and back in" after the draw. This is the form of Poker played in private clubs when Draw Poker is selected instead of Stud. A variant of the blind opening is English or Australian Poker, in which a player who raises can double the preceding bet. (Raising in this game is often called "doubling".)

Jackpots

Once all players have placed their antes and the deal is completed, each player in turn has the right to "open" (make the first bet) but may not do so unless he has a pair of jacks or better. If no one opens (that is, every player passes), everyone antes again, and the same dealer deals again. (In some games, the deal passes to the left, even when no one opens.)

If any player opens, the first betting interval has begun. Each other player in turn after him (including players who passed on the first round) must drop, call, or raise, until this betting interval ends. The game then continues as in standard Draw Poker.

In Jackpots, the player who opens must "show openers" before he can discard his hand. He need show only as many cards as will prove to the other players that he had the requirements. Of course, if this player is in the showdown, he must show his entire hand.

Progressive Jackpots

This is the same as Jackpots, except that if no one can open with jacks or better on the first deal, on the next deal queens or better are required to open. If two deals in a row are passed out and no one can open, kings or better are required, then aces or better. In some games, players will progress all the way up to two pair or better. Alternatively, they can return to jacks or better after aces or better.

Jacks or Bobtail to Open

Many players use a rule that the first player may open either on a pair of jacks or better, or on any bobtail.

Deuces Wild

This is a regular game of Jackpots, but with all four deuces wild. Naturally, Deuces Wild can be played in virtually any Poker version, but it is most common in the game of Jackpots.

Double Draw

This version features a second draw after the second betting round, and then there is a third (final) betting round. Obviously, because of the extra betting round, the pots will be bigger, and with two draws, the final hands of the players will invariably be better.

Straight Poker

This may be the original form of Poker. Each player is dealt five cards face down. The players bet, and then there is a showdown. There is no draw in this version.

Cold Hands

In this version of Straight Poker, each player puts up an agreed ante. Five cards are then dealt to each player one at a time, face up, and the highest hand takes the pot. There is no draw and there are no rounds of betting.

The Wild Widow

Five cards are dealt face down to each player. Before the last round of cards is dealt, a card is turned up in the center of the table; the other three cards of that rank are wild. There is a betting interval, then the draw, and then the final betting interval.

Spit in the Ocean

Only four cards are dealt to each player. The next card in the pack is turned face up in the center of the table and it is considered to be the fifth card in each player's hand. This card is wild, and the other cards of the same rank are also wild throughout the game. After a betting interval, there is a draw as in standard Draw Poker, except that each player draws to a four-card hand. A player may draw up to four cards. After a final betting interval, there is a showdown.

Cincinnati

Five cards are dealt to each player plus another hand of five cards face down on the table. These cards are turned up one at a time, and there is a round of betting each time a card is exposed. Each player selects a hand of five cards from among the cards in his own hand and the five on the table.

Cincinnati Liz

This game is the same as Cincinnati, but the middle card of the five table cards is wild, or the lowest card on the table is wild. The players must agree in advance which form of the game they are going to play.

Round the World

This version is the same as Cincinnati, except that each player is dealt four cards and there are four cards in the center of the table, face down. Each player selects a hand of five cards from among the four cards in his own hand and the four on the table.

Shotgun

Three cards are dealt to each player face down and there is a round of betting. Other rounds of betting follow the dealing of the fourth and fifth cards. Players still in the game draw to improve their hands, and there is a final round of betting.

Three-Card Monte

One card is dealt to each player face down and two cards face up. A round of betting follows the dealing of each card. The usual Poker rankings prevail, except that two pairs, a full house, or four of a kind are not possible. Straights and flushes do count, but they are comprised of three cards only.

Two-Card Poker

In this game only two cards are dealt to each player, and the highest possible hand consists of two aces. There are no straights or flushes in this version. The game is usually played as in Straight Poker, with no draw.

Indian Poker

This is one-card poker, with an interesting twist. A single card is dealt face down to each player. On a signal from the dealer, each player simultaneously lifts his card, placing it on his forehead so that all of the other players can see it, but the player cannot see his own. There is a single round of betting and then a showdown, which at times, can be quite hilarious. In some games the suits have rank – spades (high), hearts, diamonds, clubs – so that the ace of spades would be the highest card, the ace of hearts the next highest, and so on.

Lowball

This is one of the most popular versions of Draw Poker, especially in the western United States. It is ideal for players who constantly complain about being dealt poor hands because in Lowball, the lowest hand wins the pot! The ace is always low, so that two aces are the lowest pair. Straights and flushes do not count, so the lowest possible hand is 5, 4, 3, 2, A, regardless of suits. This hand is called a "wheel" or a "bicycle" – named after Bicycle® brand playing cards. In some games, 6, 4, 3, 2, A is the lowest hand possible, though the game really should be played with the "wheel" as the lowest.

There are no minimum requirements for opening the pot, and after the draw, a player may check. The betting for this round always begins with the active player nearest the dealer's left.

A satisfactory Lowball hand is 9-high (such as 9, 7, 5, 4, A), and a good low hand is 8-high. It is rare for a good player to have to draw two or three cards; most of the time, the winner will have stayed pat or drawn just one card.

Lowball can also be played as a version of Stud Poker.

THE DEAD MAN'S HAND

From New Orleans and the Mississippi riverboats, Poker spread to the West, and cowboys thoroughly embraced the game. Among the colorful enthusiasts the game attracted was Wild Bill Hickok, whose last residence was in Deadwood in the Dakota Territory. Hickok came to Deadwood to prospect for gold, and he spent his leisure hours playing Poker at a saloon. Wild Bill had killed 36 people; gunslingers considered him a challenge, and several made threats on his life. On August 2, 1876, Hickok and three other men were playing Draw Poker at Carl Mann's saloon. Author Frank Jennings Wilbach reports that "for the first time known, Wild Bill was sitting with his back to a door...Jack McCall, the assassin,...sauntered around to a point a few yards behind Wild Bill. He then swiftly drew a .45-calibre Colt and fired." Wild Bill Hickok died holding two pairs: aces over eights. This holding has come to be known as the Dead Man's Hand.

Bet You Didn't Know

Stud Poker

In Stud Poker, each player is dealt one or more hole cards, face down. The remainder of his cards are dealt face up. The two most popular standard Stud Poker games are Five-Card Stud and Seven-Card Stud. After each player is dealt at least one card face up (upcard), and after each subsequent deal, there is a betting interval before dealing is resumed. Stud Poker has cut into the popularity of Draw Poker because there are more betting rounds (and thus, bigger pots), and there is a fascination about seeing some of the opponents' cards and trying to fathom what the hole card or cards may be.

Five-Card Stud

Two to ten people may play, though the game is best for five to eight players. There is no ante in some Five-Card Stud games, but the players agree in advance on the minimum that must be bet.

The dealer gives each player one card face down, and then each one card face up. The player with the highest upcard makes the first bet of at least the agreed-on minimum. In any later betting interval, the first bettor and players after him may check, unless and until a bet is made.

The first bettor in each betting interval is the player with the highest card or the highest Poker combination showing. If two or more players are tied for highest, the one nearest the dealer's left is the first bettor.

Following the first betting interval, the dealer gives another card face up to each active player in rotation; there is another betting interval, another round of face-up cards to the remaining active players, another betting interval, and then a final round of face-up cards and a final betting interval. Thus, each active player who is still in the game at the last round will have one card face down and four cards face up.

If two or more players remain after the final betting interval, there is a showdown in which each player turns up his hole card. If a bet or raise goes uncalled in any betting interval by all the other remaining players, the pot is taken by the bettor.

A player who drops must immediately turn all of his cards face down.

It is the dealer's duty, after each round of cards is dealt, to designate the first bettor (as by saying, "First king bets," or "Pair of sixes bets"). Also, after the third and fourth face-up cards are dealt, the dealer should indicate holdings that may become straights or flushes, as by saying "Possible straight" or "Possible flush." A possible straight or flush in no way determines the first bettor, however, except that in some games players agree that a fourflush will beat a pair in the showdown, and in these games a fourflush showing in the final betting interval bets first against a pair showing.

In a very large game, if there are not enough cards left in the pack for a final round of dealing, the dealer may flash a card from the top of the pack (turn it face up on the table), and this card serves as the common fifth card for all the hands.

Last Card Down

This is regular Five-Card Stud, except that the fifth card dealt is face down instead of face up.

Last Card Optionally Down

This game is similar to standard Five-Card Stud Poker, except that the player may turn up his hole card before the last round is dealt and ask for the fifth card to be dealt face down.

Mexican Stud

In this version of Five-Card Stud the first two cards are dealt to each player face down. Players look at their cards and select one to be placed face up. The concealed card is then wild for each player. After a round of betting, another card is dealt around face down. Each player then decides which of the two concealed cards to turn face up, and which to keep in his hand for a wild card. Another round of betting follows. The process continues until each player has four cards exposed and one wild card concealed. This card is wild only for the player who holds it; also wild for that player are all other cards of the same rank as the concealed card. After the final round of betting, all players still in the game show their concealed cards and announce the value of their hands.

Seven-Card Stud

The game of Seven-Card Stud is extremely popular, especially where the version of High-Low Poker is played (see p. 74). In High-Low games, the highest hand and the lowest hand split the pot.

Two to eight people may play, though the game is best for at least five players. In the initial deal, each player receives two cards face down and then one card face up, all dealt one at a time in rotation. There is then a betting interval. Each active player receives three more face-up cards and one more face-down card, in that order, with a betting interval after each round of cards that is dealt. In the showdown, each player turns up all his hole cards and selects five of the seven cards as his hand. The player must separate these five cards from the other two, which he discards. The cards then speak for themselves, as in any other form of Poker, and the player may not reclaim his two discards upon finding that a better five-card combination could have been made. In other respects the procedure is the same as in Five-card Stud.

Seven-Card Flip

Four face-down cards are dealt to each player. After examining them. the player turns up any two of the four. There is a betting interval, then play proceeds as in regular Seven-Card Stud. Three more cards are dealt, two up and one down, and there is a betting interval following each.

In another version, each player first receives two cards, one up and one down, followed by a betting interval; then another two cards, one up and one down, and another betting interval; then two cards a third time and a betting interval; then a seventh card face down. Each player then discards one face-down card and one face-up card, leaving a hand of three concealed cards and two exposed cards. The final betting interval and showdown follow.

Baseball

In this version, all nines and threes are wild, but when a three is dealt face up, the player who gets it must either match the pot (put into the pot as many chips as are already in it) or drop. If a four is dealt face up, it entitles the recipient to an additional hole card, which the dealer immediately provides, face down from the top of the pack.

Football

The same as Baseball, except that sixes and fours are wild. A four requires a player to match the pot or drop, and a deuce entitles a player to an extra hole card.

Heinz

Fives and sevens are wild, but a player dealt one of these cards face up must match the pot or drop.

Woolworth

Fives and tens are wild. A player dealt a five face up must pay five chips to the pot or drop, and a player dealt a ten face up must pay 10 chips to the pot or drop.

Six-Card Stud

The first five cards are dealt as in regular Five-Card Stud, but after the fourth betting interval, each player receives a second hole card. Then there is a final betting interval, and each player selects five of the six cards as his final hand.

Eight-Card Stud

The game is identical to Seven-Card Stud, except that each player receives an eighth card, dealt either up or down, as the dealer may decide in advance.

High-Low Poker

The basic idea of High-Low Poker is that the best Poker hand and the worst Poker hand split the pot. The original purpose of High-Low was to give holders of poor cards a chance to play. The game was found to be so enjoyable that it now rivals regular Poker in popularity, and it is a staple in Poker clubs and gambling casinos having a Poker room.

Forms of High-Low. Any form of Poker may be played high-low, whether or not there are wild cards, but the most popular version for high-low games is Seven-Card Stud. In a high-low game, there are usually two winners, the player with the highest hand taking half the pot and the player with the lowest hand taking the other half. The high hand takes the odd chip if the pot will not divide evenly. In some cases there may be a single winner, as that player wins both the high hand and low hand (see explanation that follows). .

Declarations. Some people play a version of High-Low that includes declaring whether they are trying for high, for low, or for both. After the final betting interval, but before the showdown, each player must declare what he is trying for. There are various methods of declaring, and the players should agree in advance which will be used. The most common method is that before any hands are shown, each player decides mentally what he is trying for. If the player decides upon low, he places one chip in his hand without letting the other players see it. He places two chips in his hand if he opts for high, and three chips if he is going for both high and low. When all players have "declared" (decided), they open their hands to reveal how many chips they are holding. If all players have decided the same way; the best hand in that category takes the whole pot.

When playing for both high and low, a player mentally selects two five-card hands from among the cards that he holds. (This is the one exception to discarding two cards in Seven-Card Stud prior to the showdown.) If a player claims both high and low, and is tied or beaten on either, he loses any title to the pot. If no one wins in full accordance with his declaration, all declarations are disregarded and the active players divide the pot equally.

Rank of Low Hands. Since straights and flushes do not count, the lowest hand, as in Lowball, is 5, 4, 3, 2, A. However, in some high-low games, the ace is always ranked highest, and flushes and straights do count and would interfere with the low hand. In such a case, 7, 5, 4, 3, 2 would be the lowest possible hand as long as all five cards were not of the same suit. It is very important for players to agree on what the lowest hand will be in High-Low. It is strongly recommended to allow aces to be high or low and for flushes and straights not to count for low hand. Thus, the wheel or bicycle (5, 4, 3, 2, A) would be the lowest possible hand.

With wild cards in a high-low game, any wild card ranks as a "zero", and the lowest hand would be 4, 3, 2, A, "0" in a game where, if there had been no wild cards allowed, the wheel would ordinarily be the lowest hand. Again, it is necessary for players to agree on what the lowest hand will be before play begins. Many experienced players agree that wild cards are best suited for high-hand games only, rather than for games of Lowball or High-Low.

High-Low – Eight or Better. In this version, played in Poker parlors and some home games, a qualifier of eight or better is needed for a player to be in contention for the low half of the pot. That is, a player cannot declare for the low hand unless he has a hand no higher than 8, 7, 6, 5, 4.

Hold 'Em

In recent years, this game has become very high popular in casinos that have Poker rooms. It is considered to require more skill than any other version of Poker.

Each player receives two cards face down, and five cards are dealt face down to the center of the table. After the first betting interval, three of the five center cards are turned face up in the center. Then there is a second betting interval, followed by one more center card being turned up. Then there is a third betting interval, and the last center card is turned up. Then there is a final betting round. The player must use his best five cards, taken from the two in his hand and the five turned up in the center of the table.

Omaha

This game is similar to Hold 'Em, and it is also very popular in American casinos with a Poker room. Each player receives two cards face down and five cards are dealt to the center of the table. There is a betting interval, and the center cards are turned up one by one, with a betting interval after each card is exposed. All players still in the game must make hands of five cards using two cards from their own hand plus three from the five cards in the center. Generally in High-Low Omaha, a qualifier of eight or better is needed for a hand to be in contention for the low half of the pot.

Bull

Each player receives three cards face down. He arranges them in any order desired, but may not thereafter change the order. There is a betting interval. Then each player receives four face-up cards, one at a time, with a betting interval after each. Next, each player turns up his first face-down card, followed by a betting interval, and then his second face-down card, followed by the final betting interval. The last card is then turned up for the showdown.

Other Poker Variants

Knock Poker

This game is for three to five players. Each player antes one chip, and the dealer gives each player five cards as in Draw Poker. The undealt cards are placed in the center to form the stock. The player to the dealer's left draws the top card and then discards one card face up, and thereafter each player in turn may draw the top card of the stock or the last previous discard, as in various games of Rummy.

Any player, after drawing and before discarding, may knock. He does so by knocking on the table and discarding. Then each other player has one turn to draw and discard until play comes back to the knocker, who does not have another turn. Each player, after drawing, may either drop out, immediately paying the knocker one chip, or he may stay in.

When the last player before the knocker has drawn and discarded, there is a showdown among all who have stayed in. If the knocker has the high hand, everyone who stayed in pays him two chips. If another player ties the knocker, they divide the winnings except for chips paid to the knocker by the players who dropped out. If the knocker does not have the high hand, he pays two chips to every player who stayed in, and the player with the high hand gets the antes.

Bonuses are popular but they need not be used unless the players agree. If there is a bonus, everyone pays it, even a player who has dropped: two chips for knocking and winning without drawing a card; four chips for winning with a royal flush; two chips for winning with any other straight flush; one chip for winning with four of a kind.

In a similar version, many people play so that anyone may knock whenever it is his turn. There is then a showdown without further drawing, and the high hand wins the pot, which consists only of the antes. In another version, each player must put another chip in the pot every time he draws a card.

Whiskey Poker

After an ante from all players, the dealer gives five cards, face down, to each player and puts an extra hand ("widow") of five cards in the middle of the table. He must deal to each player in turn around to the left, one card at a time, then to the widow, then to himself last. Each player has the option of exchanging his hand for the widow, or keeping his hand as it is. If a player takes up the widow, his original five cards are placed face up on the table and become the new widow. Each player in turn has the option of taking up one card or all of the new widow and replacing it with cards from his hand. If a player wishes to play the original hand, he signals by knocking on the table, but he may not draw and knock at the same time.

The process of exchanging cards continues around the table until some player knocks. A knock means that this player will show the present hand as soon as it is his turn, so that each player has only one more chance to exchange cards. No player may draw if he has knocked. A player may knock before the widow is exposed, if desired.

If no one takes the widow until it comes around to the dealer, the dealer must either take up the widow or turn it face up on the table. Even if the dealer knocks, and does not take up the widow, he must spread it on the table for each player to see and draw once more. A player may pass at any turn – that is, decline either to exchange or to knock; however, he may not pass at two turns in a row. Having passed on the previous round, he must either exchange or knock.

After the knock and the final round of draws, all hands are shown, and the highest takes the pot. The lowest pays a "forfeit," or penalty in an amount of chips agreed upon beforehand. Some players prefer to have a round of betting before the showdown.

Red and Black

Strictly speaking, this game is not a form of Poker, but it is often played for variety during some social Poker games. Each player in turn, beginning on the dealer's left, places any bet up to the limit, and names "red" or "black." The dealer gives the player five cards face up. If three or more are of the color named, the dealer pays the bet; if three or more are of the opposite color, the dealer collects the bet. If all five cards are of the same color, double the bet is paid or collected.

In one other game called Red and Black, the cards are dealt as in Draw Poker, but the object is to make up hands of high or low point values. The point values are: king, queen, jack and ten – 10 each; ace – 1; other cards – their pip value. All red cards are plus values, and all black cards are minus values. Thus the hand, ♠K, ♦J, ♠8, ♣7, ♥3 would count minus 12. The high count and the low count divide the pot.

Other Poker Session Games

Many games played at social Poker sessions are not in the Poker family. A familiar one is Red Dog (also called In–Between), which is explained in Chapter III – Casino Games. Also appearing in that chapter is a game from Asia called Pai-Gow Poker, which is actually in the Poker family, but is, strictly speaking, a casino game, with a format on the order of Black Jack and other casino card games. Thus, this new game serves well as a link between Poker and casino games.

Laws of Poker

The following laws define correct procedure and the resolution of irregularities in Poker.

No penalties are assessed or proposed for breaches of law. A penalty can punish the offender but cannot restore the rights of a player who may have been damaged. In some cases, the players in a game decide on certain penalties to discourage persistent offenders.

The laws have three main sections: General Laws, applying to all forms of Poker; Draw Poker Laws; and Stud Poker Laws.

This section covers the pack of cards, the rank of hands, the shuffle, cut, and deal; the betting; and the showdown.

Number of Players. Poker may be played by two to 10 players and each plays for himself. No two players may play in partnership, and there may be no agreement between two or more players to divide a pot.

Object of the Game. The object of Poker is to win the pot, either by having the best Poker hand (as explained below), or by making a bet that no other player can meet.

The Pack. The standard 52-card deck is used. It consists of four suits: spades (♠), hearts (♥), diamonds (♦), clubs (♣). In each suit there are 13 cards: A, K, Q, J, 10, 9, 8, 7, 6, 5, 4, 3, 2. One or more jokers may be added to the pack. Each joker is a wild card.

Wild Cards. A joker or any other card or class of cards may be designated as wild by any of the following methods. The method must be selected in advance by the players in the game.

1) The wild card may be designated by its holder to represent any other card that its holder does not have.

2) The joker (in this case called the bug) may be designated by its holder to represent a fifth ace or any card needed to complete a straight, a flush, or any special hand such as a dog, cat and so on.

3) Any wild card may represent any other card, whether or not the holder of the wild card also has the card designated. (This permits double- or even triple-ace-high flushes, and the like). A wild card, properly designated, ranks exactly the same as a natural card.

Rank of Cards. A (high) K, Q, J, 10, 9, 8, 7, 6, 5, 4, 3, 2. The Ace is low only in the sequence 5, 4, 3, 2, A. Optional: the ace may rank low in Low Poker (Lowball) or in High-Low Poker when, by agreement, the ace is designated as low.

In Low Poker, the ace is always low, so that two aces is a lower pair than two 2s (deuces).

In High-Low Poker, the holder must designate the relative rank of the ace at the time that he shows his hand in the showdown, for example, by saying "aces high" (in which case two aces beats two kings for high), or "aces low" (in which case, two aces beats two 2s for low but loses to two 2s for high).

In any pot to be won by the high hand, the ranking goes from ace down to two so that, for example, 7, 6, 4, 3, 2 beats 7, 5, 4, 3, 2.

Seating. Players take seats at random unless any player requests before the game begins that the seats of the respective players be determined as provided in the next paragraph.

When any player requests a reseating, the banker has first choice of seats. The first dealer may either take the seat to left of the banker or participate with the other players in having his position determined by chance as follows: the dealer shuffles the pack, has the cards cut by the player on his right and deals one card, face up, to each player, beginning with the player to his left. The player dealt the highest-ranking card sits to the right of the banker, the player with the next-highest card at the right of that player, and so on. If two players are dealt cards of the same rank, the card dealt first ranks higher.

After the game begins, no player may request a reseating unless at least one hour has elapsed since the last reseating. A player entering the game after it begins must take any vacant seat. A player replacing another player must take the seat that player vacated. Two players may exchange seats after any showdown and before the next deal begins, provided no other player objects.

When there is no banker, the dealer has first choice of seats.

The Shuffle and Cut. Any player on request may shuffle the pack before the deal. The pack should be shuffled at least three times in all, by one or more players. The dealer has the right to shuffle last and should shuffle the pack at least once.

The dealer offers the shuffled pack to his right-hand opponent, who may cut it or not as he pleases. (When two packs are used, the dealer offers the pack to the left-hand opponent.) If this player does not cut, any other player may cut. If more than one player requests the right to cut, the one nearest the dealer's right cuts. Except in case of an irregularity that calls for a new cut, the pack is cut only once.

The player who cuts divides the pack into two or three portions. No portion can contain fewer than five cards. He completes the cut by placing the packet that was originally on the bottom on top. (If a card is exposed during a cut, the pack must be shuffled by the dealer and cut again.)

The Deal. At the start of the game, any player shuffles the pack and deals the cards face up, one at a time to each player beginning with the player on his left, until a jack is turned up. The player to whom the jack is dealt is the first dealer. Thereafter, the turn to deal passes from each player to the player on his left. A player may not voluntarily pass his turn to deal.

The dealer distributes the cards from the top of the pack, one card at a time to each player beginning with the player on his left and ending with himself.

Rank of Hands. Poker hands rank, from highest to lowest:

Straight Flush. Five cards of the same suit in sequence. The highest straight flush is A, K, Q, J, 10 of the same suit, called a royal flush. The lowest straight flush is 5, 4, 3, 2, A of the same suit. When there are two straight flushes in the same game, the one headed by the highest card wins. When any card has been designated as wild, a straight flush loses to five of a kind, which is the highest possible hand.

Four of a Kind. Four cards of the same rank. This hand loses to a straight flush but beats any other Poker hand. If two players have four of a kind, the four higher-ranking cards win. When there are wild cards, it is possible for two players to hold four of a kind of the same rank. In this case, the winning hand is the one with the higher-ranking fifth card.

Full House. Three cards of one rank and two cards of another rank. When two hands each have a full house, the one with the higher-ranking three of a kind is the winner. When there are wild cards, two players may have full houses in which the three of a kind holdings are the same rank; the higher of the pairs then determines the winning hand.

Flush. Five cards of the same suit. If two players have a flush, the one containing the highest card wins. If the highest cards are of the same rank, the higher of the next-highest cards determines the winning hand, and so on; so that ♦ A, K, 4, 3, 2 beats ♥ A, Q, J, 10, 8 and ♦ J, 9, 8, 6, 4 beats ♥ J, 9, 8, 6, 3.

Straight. Five cards, in two or more suits, ranking consecutively as 8, 7, 6, 5, 4. The ace is high in the straight A, K, Q, J, 10 and low in the straight 5, 4, 3, 2, A. If there are two or more straights, the one containing the highest card wins, so that 6, 5, 4, 3, 2 beats 5, 4, 3, 2, A.

Three of a Kind. Three cards of the same rank. If there are two or more hands each containing three of a kind, the one with the higher-ranking three of a kind wins. When there are wild cards, there may be two hands containing identical threes of a kind. In that case, the highest-ranking unmatched card determines the winner. If these cards are of the same rank, the higher-ranking fifth card in each hand determines the winner.

Two Pairs. Two cards of one rank and two cards of another rank, with an unmatched fifth card. If two or more hands each contain two pairs, the one with the highest pair wins. If the higher pairs are of the same rank, the one with the higher-ranking second pair wins. If these pairs are also of the same rank, the hand containing the higher of the unmatched cards is the winner.

One Pair. Two cards of the same rank, with three un-matched cards. If there are two or more one-pair hands, the one containing the higher pair wins. If two hands contain pairs of the same rank, the highest unmatched card determines the winner; if these are the same, the higher of the second-highest unmatched cards wins, and if these are the same, the higher of the lowest unmatched cards wins. For example, 8, 8, 9, 5, 3 beats 8, 8, 9, 5, 2.

No Pair. This loses to any hand having a pair or any higher-ranking combination. If there are two no-pair hands, the hand with the highest card wins; if these two cards are tied, the next-highest card decides, and so on, so that A, 8, 7, 4, 3 loses to A, 9, 7, 4, 3 but wins from A, 8, 7, 4, 2.

Two hands that are identical, card for card, are tied since the suits have no relative rank in Poker.

Betting. All the chips bet go into the center of the table to form a pot. The winner keeps the the pot.

The Ante. In many games, each player puts an equal amount of chips into the pot before any cards are dealt. This is called the ante. The amount of the ante is agreed upon before the game or is determined by the dealer.

Opening. After the deal, the beginning player announces whether he will pass, bet, or drop (throw in his cards). If a player drops, he loses any chips he has in the pot. If he passes and every player in turn, including the dealer, passes, there is a new deal by the next player on the left and the ante (if any) is repeated. If he bets, he is the first to bet, called "opening," and puts the number of chips he is betting into the pot. Next, each player in turn must either, check, call, raise or drop.

Sequence of Play. In each betting interval, the turn to bet begins with the player designated by the rules of the Poker version being played and moves to each active player on the left. No player may open, check, call, raise, or drop, except in his proper turn. A player may neither pass nor bet until the player on his right has put the correct number of chips into the pot or has dropped.

In Draw Poker, the first in turn before the draw is the player on the dealer's left. The first in turn after the draw is the player who made the first bet before the draw or, if he has dropped, the player on his left.

In Stud Poker, the first in each betting interval is the player whose exposed cards are higher than those of any other player. If two or more players have identical high holdings, the player on the dealer's left is first.

Check. Unless a bet has been made in that betting interval, an active player in turn may check, which means that he elects to remain an active player without betting. In some variations of Poker, checking is specifically prohibited.

If any player bets, each active player in turn after him (including players who checked originally) must either, call, raise, or drop.

Call. A call is a bet equal to the previous bet, that is, a matching number of chips. This amount must include any raises made during this betting interval. For example, a bet of five is "called" by the next player (also betting five); the next player "raises" two (betting seven). Any bet by the next player must be seven to call or more than seven to raise.

Raise. A raise is a bet greater than the previous bet.

Fold or Drop. A player in turn may drop even when he has the privilege of checking. Any time that a player discards his hand, or permits it to be mixed with any discard, he has dropped, and his hand may not be reclaimed.

The Showdown. When each player has either called the highest previous bet without raising or has dropped; or when every active player has checked; the full hand of every active player is placed face up on the table, and the highest-ranking hand wins the pot. If two or more hands tie for the highest rank, they divide the pot evenly, any odd chip going to the player who last bet or raised. It is customary for a player to announce the value of his hand. When there are wild cards, he must announce the value of his hand and may then claim no higher hand. Whenever only one active player remains because all other players have dropped, the remaining player wins the pot without showing his hand, and there is a new deal by the next dealer in turn.

Irregularities. *Redeal.* Any player, unless he has intentionally seen the face of any card dealt to him face down, may call for a new shuffle, cut, and deal by the same dealer if, before the dealer begins dealing the second round of cards:

1) A card was exposed in cutting

2) The cut left fewer than five cards in either packet

3) Two or more cards are face up in the pack

4) The pack is incorrect or imperfect in any way

5) A player is dealing out of turn.

If a player is dealing out of turn, and a redeal is called, the deal reverts to the proper player in turn. In a game in which every player antes, no one need ante again. Any other bet is left in the pot. If no redeal or misdeal is called within a time limit provided, the deal stands, and the player on the left of the out-of-turn dealer will be the next dealer.

Misdeal. A misdeal due to the dealer's error loses the deal if attention is drawn to it by a player who has not intentionally seen any face-down card dealt to him. The deal passes to the next player in turn. The misdealer's ante is forfeited to the pot. If all players have anted equally, their antes remain in the pot and no one need ante again. A blind bet or raise may be withdrawn.

A misdeal may be called by any player who has not intentionally seen any face-down card dealt to him:

1) If before the dealer begins the second round of cards he notices that the pack was not shuffled or offered for cut

2) By any player who receives two face-up cards in Draw Poker or any other form of closed Poker, provided he calls a misdeal immediately and has not contributed to the error

3) If the dealer gives too many cards to more than one player.

If the dealer mistakenly stops dealing before giving every player enough cards, due solely to his omission to deal one or more rounds, it is not a misdeal and the dealer is required to complete the deal whenever the irregularity is discovered. For example, if the dealer stops dealing after giving each player only four cards; or if the dealer gives the first five of seven players five cards each and the sixth and seventh players only four cards each, it is not a misdeal.

If the dealer deals too many hands, he shall determine which hand is dead, and that hand is discarded; but if any player has looked at any face-down card in any hand, he must keep that hand.

If the dealer deals too few hands, he must give his hand to the first omitted player to his left. Any other player who has been omitted and who has anted may withdraw his ante.

Exposed Card. If the dealer exposes one or more cards from the undealt portion of the pack after the deal is completed, those cards are dead and are placed among the discards. There is no penalty against any player for exposing any part of his hand, and he has no redress. A player who interferes with the deal and causes the dealer to expose a card may not call a misdeal.

Incorrect Pack. If it is determined, at any time before the pot has been taken in, that the pack has too many cards, too few cards, or duplicate cards, the deal is void; and each player withdraws from the pot any chips he contributed to it, any other laws of the game to the contrary notwithstanding; but the results of pots previously taken in are not affected.

Imperfect Pack. If the pack contains any card that is torn, discolored, or otherwise marked so it can be identified from the back, the pack must be replaced before the deal in progress or any other deal can be completed; but the play of the hand in progress is not affected if the deal has been completed.

Incorrect Hand. A hand having more or less than the correct number of cards in the Poker variation being played is foul and cannot win the pot. If every other player has dropped, the pot remains and goes to the winner of the next pot. Players may agree that a hand with fewer cards is not foul, in which case its holder may compete for the pot with the best poker combination he can make.

Irregularities in Betting. Chips once put in the pot may not be withdrawn except by a player who, after he has anted, is dealt out; or in jackpots, when another player has opened without proper openers (see False Openers p. 86); in Draw Poker, by the players who opened or raised blind, in case of a misdeal; or in Stud Poker, when the dealer has failed to deal a player any card face down.

Installment or String Bets. A player's entire bet must be put in the pot at one time. Having put in some number of chips, he may not add to that number unless the original number was insufficient to call, in which case he may add exactly enough chips to call. If, however, he announced before putting in any chips that he was raising by a certain amount and puts in an amount insufficient for such a raise, he must on demand supply enough additional chips to equal the announced amount of his bet.

Insufficient Bet. When a player in turn puts into the pot a number of chips insufficient to call, he must either add enough chips to call and may not raise, or he must drop and forfeit his chips already in the pot. When a player raises by less than the minimum permitted, he is deemed to have called, and any additional chips he put into the pot are forfeited to it.

Bet Above Limit. If a player puts in the pot more chips than are permitted by the limit, it stands as a bet of the limit and additional chips are forfeited to the pot. An exception is made in table stakes when a player's bet exceeds the number of chips an opponent has. In that event, the player may withdraw the excess and either bet it in a side pot, or, if no other players are willing or able to meet that bet in the side pot, restore those chips to his stack.

Announcement in Turn of Intention to Pass or Bet. If a player in turn announces that he passes or drops, his announcement is binding whether or not he discards his hand. If a player in turn announces a bet but does not put any chips in the pot, he is bound by his announcement and must, if possible, supply additional chips necessary to bring the bet up to the announced amount.

Announcement Out of Turn of Intention to Pass or Bet. If a player out of turn announces his intention to pass or drop when his turn comes, and then, does not actually discard his hand, or to make a certain bet but does not actually put any chips in the pot, his announcement is void; and he may take any action he chooses when his turn comes. Any other player who acts in reliance upon the announcement does so at his own risk and has no redress.

Bet Out of Turn. If a player puts any chips in the pot out of turn, they remain there, and the play reverts to the player whose turn it was. If any player to the offender's left puts chips in the pot, he has bet out of turn and is equally an offender. When the offender's turn comes, if the chips he put in were insufficient to call, the player may add enough chips to call. If the amount was exactly sufficient to call, he is deemed to have called. If the amount was more than enough to call, the player is deemed to have raised by the amount of the excess but cannot add chips to increase the amount of his raise. If no player before him has bet, he is deemed to have bet the number of chips he put in and any amount above the agreed limit is forfeited to the pot. If the chips he put in were insufficient to call, he may forfeit these chips and drop. However, the player may never add chips to raise or to increase his raise.

Pass Out of Turn. The pass (act of dropping) out of turn is among the most damaging of Poker improprieties, but there is no penalty except by prior agreement of the players. In any case, the offender's hand is dead and he cannot win the pot.

Irregularities in the Showdown. If a player in the showdown announces a hand he does not actually hold, the announcement is void if the error is discovered before the pot has been taken in by any player (including the player who miscalled his hand). "The cards speak for themselves."

Designation of Wild Cards. If, in the showdown, a player orally designates the suit or rank of a wild card in his hand, or implies such designation by announcing a certain hand, he may not change that designation (for example, an announcement of joker J, 10, 9, 8 as "jack-high straight" fixes the joker as a seven). A player may always show his hand without announcement and need not designate the value of a wild card unless another active player requests that he do so.

Concession of a Pot. A player who has discarded his hand after another player's announcement of a higher hand may not later claim the pot – even if the announcement was incorrect.

Laws of Draw Poker

The Draw. After each player has exactly called the highest previous bet without raising or has dropped, the first betting interval ends. The dealer picks up the undealt portion of the pack, and each active player beginning on his left may, in turn, discard one or more cards. Then, the dealer gives him that number of cards, face down, from the top of the pack. A player need not draw unless he so chooses.

If the dealer is an active player, he must announce how many cards, if any, he is drawing. At any time following the draw and before the first player in turn bets or checks in the final betting interval, any active player may ask any other active player how many cards he drew. The latter player must answer, but the questioner has no redress if the answer is incorrect. It is considered unethical, however, to give an incorrect answer intentionally.

The dealer may not deal the bottom card of the pack. If the pack exclusive of this card does not suffice for the draw, the dealer assembles all cards previously discarded, plus the bottom card of the original pack, shuffles these cards, and offers them for a cut. Then, he continues dealing. The cut is described in "The Shuffle and Cut" on p. ••, except that only an active player may cut. The opener's discards and the discards of any player yet to draw are excluded from the reassembled pack if they have been kept separate and can be identified.

Irregularities. Wrong number of cards. If the dealer gives a player more or fewer cards than he asks for, the error must be corrected if the player calls attention to it before he has looked at any of the cards. Unless a card has been served to the next active player in turn, the dealer must correct the error by supplying the missing cards or restoring the excess to the top of the pack, as the case may be. If the next player has been served, the player with the incorrect hand may discard the surplus cards. If he has already discarded and the draw is insufficient to restore his hand to five cards, his hand is foul. If the player has looked at any card of the draw and the entire draw would give him an incorrect number of cards, his hand is foul.

Card exposed. If any card is exposed in the draw, whether or not it was faced in the pack, the player must accept the first such card, but any additional exposed card is dead and is placed among the discards. After the dealer has served all other active players, he deals any additional cards due from the top of the pack.

Draw out of turn. If a player allows a player on his left to draw out of turn, he must play without drawing, or drop. If he has already discarded any card, his hand is foul.

A player may correct a slip of the tongue in stating the number of cards he wishes to draw, but only if the dealer has not yet given the player the number of cards he first requested.

If a player discards a number of cards that would make his hand incorrect after the dealer gives him as many cards as he asked for, his hand is fouled.

Showing openers. The player who opens must prove that he held a legal hand of five cards including the strength (if any) required to open. If the player is in the showdown, he must show his entire hand face up. In any other case, before discarding his entire hand, he must show his openers face up and his remaining cards, if any, face down.

Splitting openers. The player who opened may split his openers (discard one or more cards essential to them) and need not announce that he is doing so. He may put his discard in the pot, face down, for reference later. For example, having opened with ♦Q, ♥Q, J, 10, 9, he may discard the ♦Q and draw one card.

False openers. If it is determined at any time that a player opened without proper openers, or that his hand contains too many cards, the player's hand is foul, and all chips he has bet are forfeited to the pot.

If false openers are discovered before the draw, any other player in turn to the offender's left (excluding those who passed in their first turns) may open, and play continues; but any player except the offender may withdraw from the pot any chips he put in after the pot was falsely opened. If no one can open, the rest of the pot remains for the next deal.

If false openers are discovered after every player but the offender has dropped, the other players may withdraw from the pot any chips they put in after the pot was falsely opened.

If false openers are discovered after the draw, and if any player remains active, play continues; and the pot goes to the highest hand at the showdown, whether or not any player had openers. (If there is no hand at the showdown that is not foul, the pot remains and goes to the winner of the next pot. Regardless of other circumstances, a hand that has dropped can never win a pot.)

Laws of Stud Poker

Betting in Stud Poker. In each betting interval the player with the highest exposed combination has the right to bet first. In most games in the first interval, this player must bet at least the minimum established for the game. In any subsequent betting interval, the player may check.

If, in any betting interval, every active player checks, the interval ends. Another round of cards is dealt, or there is a showdown, as the case may be. If one player bets in any round, each active player after him must at least call the highest previous bet or drop.

At the start of each betting interval the dealer must announce which player bets first and identify the highest exposed holding, for example, "Pair of eights bets" or "First ace bets." The dealer should also announce, after the third and fourth face-up cards are dealt, any player's combination that, when combined with his hole card, may make a one-card draw to a flush or straight announced by saying "Possible flush" or "Possible straight."

Incomplete hands. For the purpose of establishing the first bettor in any interval, exposed cards rank from highest to lowest as follows:

Four of a kind: between two such hands, the four higher-ranking cards are high.

Three of a kind: if there are two such hands, the higher-ranking three of a kind is high.

Two pair: when two such combinations are showing, the highest pair determines the high hand, and if the highest pairs are the same, the higher of the two lower pairs.

One pair: between two such hands, the higher pair is high. If two hands have the identical pair, the highest unmatched card determines the high hand, and if these are identical, the higher of the two other cards.

The highest card: if two players tie for highest card, the next-highest card in their respective hands determines the high hand, and so on.

If there are two holdings that are identical card for card, the one nearest the dealer's left is high for purposes of betting but has no superiority over the other holding in the showdown.

Flush and straight combinations of four or fewer cards rank no higher, for determining the first bettor, than any other holdings including no pair except when a fourflush (four cards of the same suit) is played to beat a pair; in that case a fourflush showing bets ahead of a pair.

If, through the dealer's or his own error, all a player's cards are exposed, all are taken into consideration for establishing the first bettor. If, at the start of the final betting interval, that player has a straight, flush, full house, or straight flush showing, his hand outranks any combination of exposed cards that it would beat in a showdown.

Irregularities. At any time before the dealer begins dealing the second round of cards, a player who has not looked at a card dealt face down to him may call for a new shuffle, cut, and deal if the player notices that:

1) The pack was not shuffled or cut

2) A card was exposed in cutting, or the cut left fewer than five cards in either packet

3) Two or more cards are face up in the pack

4) The pack is incorrect or imperfect in any way

5) A player is dealing out of turn.

When there is a redeal, the same dealer deals again unless he was dealing out of turn, in which case the deal reverts to the proper player.

If the dealer deals too many hands, he shall determine which hand is dead and that hand is discarded. However, if a player has looked at the hole card of any hand, he must keep that hand.

If the dealer deals too few hands, he must give his own hand to the first omitted player to his left.

If the dealer gives a player two face-down cards instead of one during the first round of dealing, he turns up one of the cards and then omits that player on the second round of dealing (unless the rules of the game require two hole cards, as in Seven-Card Stud). The player who received the two cards may not look at them and then turn one of them up.

If the dealer gives a player more than two cards on the first deal, that player may require a redeal before the second round begins. If the error is not noted until later, his hand is dead.

If, in dealing any round of face-up cards, the dealer omits a player, he moves the cards one place backwards, so as to give each player the face-up card he would have had if no error had been made. However, if the error is not noticed before the first bet is made, the hand of the player who was omitted is dead.

Exposed card. If the dealer gives any player a hole card face up, the player must keep that card and receive his next card face down. The player has no redress, except to receive his next card face down, unless the dealer repeatedly fails to correct the error until the player has four cards. At that point, if the dealer has never given him a face-down card, the player may drop out and withdraw all his chips from the pot. If the player stays for his fifth card, and the fifth card is dealt face up, the player may withdraw his chips from the pot or may remain in the game and play with an exposed hand.

Dead cards. A card found face up in the pack during a round of dealing must be dealt to the appropriate player. If a card at the top of the pack is exposed during a betting interval, either because it is face up in the pack or prematurely dealt, it is discarded. In dealing the next round of face-up cards, the dealer skips the player who would have received that card and deals in rotation, ending with the player who would have received the exposed card. In each subsequent round, the dealer deals in the normal rotation.

Impossible call. If the last player to speak in the final betting interval calls a bet when his five cards, (whatever his hole card may be) cannot possibly beat the four showing cards of the player whose bet he calls, the call is void and the chips may be retracted, provided that a player calls attention to the error before the hole card of any other active player is shown.

Error in Valuing the Hand. If the dealer errs in calling the value of a hand or in designating the high hand, no player has any redress. If the player incorrectly designated makes the first bet, it is not a bet out of turn.

Hole Card Irregularity. The dealer does not have the option of dealing a player's first card up and his second card down intentionally. A player may not turn up his hole card and receive his next card face down. If he turns up his hole card, he must play the round with his cards exposed.

Poker Ethics

The only safe guiding principle in Poker ethics is, "When in Rome, do as the Romans do." In some games, a player may do anything to fool the opponents as long as he does not cheat. It is considered part of the skill of the game to do so, and by no means unsportsmanlike. In some games, it is considered unethical, or at least "sharp practice," to check while holding a good hand in the hope that someone else will bet and the player can raise him. Since card playing is a social pastime, a player is best advised to follow the standards of the other players.

Bluffing. To bluff in Poker is to make a bet on a hand the player knows, or believes, is not the best, in the hope that other players will believe his cards are strong and will drop out. Bluffing is so much a part of Poker that the game would be no good without it. But some players believe their opponent should not support the bluff by making remarks he knows are untrue, such as announcing his hand has improved in the draw when it has not.

Intentionally Breaking the Rules. In most circles it is not considered ethical to announce, out of turn, an intention to bet, raise, or drop, if there is no intention of doing so when the player's turn comes. Although such false announcements are not formally penalized, regard for the other players should rule them out when they conflict with the code of ethics followed in the game. It is always considered unethical to intentionally break the rules.

Splitting Pots. In all Poker circles it is considered unethical, and close to cheating, to split a pot rather than have a showdown.

Betting Blind. When a player announces that he is betting (or checking) "blind," (that is, without looking at his hand), it is considered unethical if the player has, in fact, seen his hand.

CHANCES OF IMPROVING A HAND ON THE DRAW

Drawing Four Cards to an Ace

Result	Approximate Probability 1 in –
A pair of aces or better	4
Two pairs or better	12

Drawing Three Cards to a Pair

Result	Approximate Probability 1 in –
Two pairs	6
Three of a kind	9
Full house	100
Four of a kind	350

Drawing Two Cards to a Pair and an Ace Kicker

Result	Approximate Probability 1 in –
Two pairs	6
Three of a kind	13
Full house	120
Four of a kind	1100

Drawing Two Cards to Three of a Kind

Result	Approximate Probability 1 in –
Full house	16
Four of a kind	23

Drawing One Card to Three of a Kind

Result	Approximate Probability 1 in –
Full house	15
Four of a kind	47

These tables are adopted from "The Complete Guide to Winning Poker" by Albert H. Morehead (1967, Simon & Schuster).

Chapter III

Casino
Games

Virtually all the card games that are played in a casino can be played at home, though sometimes it is necessary to vary the rules slightly. The main equipment needed for home play is a large table that can seat at least six players, ample packs of playing cards, a plentiful supply of chips of different colors, and a table cloth so that cards and chips can be handled easily.

PAI-GOW POKER
(Asian Poker)

NUMBER OF PLAYERS	NUMBER OF CARDS	GAME PLAY		SKILL LEVEL	
2-7	**53**	◊ ◊ ◆ ◊ ◊ EASY → COMPLEX		◊ ◊ ◆ ◊ ◊ LUCK → SKILL	

This new and fascinating game has taken the world by storm. Technically, Pai-Gow is a variation of Poker, but everything about it is stamped "gambling casino game." Indeed, since 1986, Pai-Gow Poker has made its way into Poker parlors in California, as well as many of the big casinos in Las Vegas, Atlantic City, and elsewhere. Pai-Gow Poker is even displacing tables previously used for Black Jack and Baccarat.

The game is derived from the Asian game of Pai-Gow, which is widely played in Southeast Asia, including Macao and the Philippines.

The actual game of Pai-Gow is played with domino-like black tiles. Each player receives four tiles and has to decide how to arrange them to make up two "hands" of two tiles each. Should the player go all out and try to win on both hands? Or should he play it safe and win on one hand for sure, and likely lose on the other so as to break even and avoid losing on both hands? This type of decision-making is at the heart of Pai-Gow Poker. The difference in Pai-Gow Poker is that cards are used instead of tiles, and instead of exotic Pai-Gow arrangements, Poker-hand combinations are featured.

Number of Players. Up to seven people can play: one dealer against up to six players, who play for themselves. In casino play, the dealer remains standing and the players are seated. In a home game, everyone is seated.

The Pack. The standard 52-card pack is used, plus a joker, which serves as a "bug." It can be used as an ace, or a fifth card needed to fill a straight, flush, or straight flush. (In Philippine casinos, the joker not only stands for an ace, but is also any J, Q, or K, too.)

In addition to the playing cards, three standard dice are required.

Object of the Game. The goal is to to form two winning Poker hands from the seven cards that are dealt: a hand of five cards, called the "back" hand, and a hand of two cards, called the "front" hand. To win the bet, both of a player's hands must beat both of the dealer's hands. If both hands lose to the dealer, the player loses the bet. If one hand wins and one hand loses, it is a standoff, and no chips are paid out or collected.

Poker Rankings. A basic knowledge of Poker is required to play Pai-Gow Poker. The hands rank as in regular Poker, from five aces down to no pair. One exception is that while A, K, Q, J, 10 is the highest straight, A, 2, 3, 4, 5 is the next highest straight, beating K, Q, J, 10, 9. This straight is often made with the joker, which is why it ranks so high. For the two-card hand, straights and flushes do not count. Thus, the highest "front" hand is a pair of aces, and the lowest is three-high (3,2); a pair of deuces ranks just ahead of A, K.

PAI-GOW RANK OF STRAIGHTS

Highest ranking straight

Second-highest ranking straight

Third-highest ranking straight

Betting. The players buy chips for cash, and each makes a bet by placing one or more chips in a designated area in front of him. At the casino table, this area is a circle about the size of a coaster. The minimum and maximum bets are established by the casino, or in a home game, by all the players.

The Shuffle and Cut. The dealer shuffles the cards thoroughly and selects one player for the cut. That player separates the pack into two parts, and the dealer completes the cut.

The Deal. The dealer deals seven hands in a line in front of himself, one card at a time, face down, until seven hands of seven cards each are dealt. (In some casinos, an electronic device shuffles the cards thoroughly and deals the hands in groups of seven cards at a time until seven hands are dealt.) The remaining four cards left in the pack are counted by the dealer and then stacked face down against a clear, L-shaped plastic shield in the discard area near the dealer's racks of chips.

Positioning of the Hands. The dealer selects one of the players to throw the three dice, which are used to randomly choose which player gets which hand of seven cards. The total of the numbers on the dice determines who will get the first hand. If these numbers add up to 1, 8, or 15, the dealer gets the hand, and the player to his right gets the second, and so forth around the table, counterclockwise. If the numbers are 2, 9, or 16, the first player to the right gets the first hand, the next player gets the second hand, and so forth. If the numbers are 3, 10, or 17, the second player to the right gets the first hand, and so forth. The dealer simply counts his position as "one," the player to his right as "two," the next player as "three" and so on, to determine how the hands are distributed. If there are fewer than six players against the dealer, the absent positions still get hands, just as if players were sitting in the vacant seats, but after all the hands are distributed, any absent hands are taken away (still face down) and placed in the discards.

Sometimes a shaker is used to mix the three dice, and the dealer removes the lid on top of the shaker to reveal the three dice. (The electronic card shuffler/dealer also incorporates a random-number generator with the same odds as three dice thrown manually, and the digital number displayed on the device similarly indicates which player will get the first hand, with the remaining hands distributed counterclockwise around the table.)

Setting the Hands. Each player picks up his hand and arranges it to make two poker hands, keeping in mind that the hand of five cards must outrank the hand of two cards. When a player is satisfied with his arrangement, he places the "back" hand (five-card hand) face down, farthest from the dealer in the vertical rectangle provided on the table's layout. The "front" hand (two-card hand) is placed face down horizontally in the horizontal rectangle, which is in front of the vertically-placed hand.

Each player at the table is responsible for setting his hands, and no one, except the dealer may touch the cards of that player. If requested by the player, the dealer may assist the player in setting his hands. Also, each player must keep the seven cards in full view of the dealer at all times. Once the player has placed his back and front hands accordingly in the vertical and horizontal rectangles, he is not permitted to touch the cards again.

Dealer's Setting. The dealer takes his cards, and spreads them face up on the table, and proceeds to make a hand of five cards and a hand of two cards. The procedure for the dealer is according to a prescribed set of rules known as "The House Ways." Often the dealer, by the rules of play, must separate two pairs, so that instead of having the "back" hand be two pairs, this hand would instead be one pair, with the lower pair being used for the "front" hand.

Settlement. With the dealer's five- and two-card hands in view of all the players, the dealer, beginning with the player to the right, exposes the front and back hands of each player and pays out or collects on each. For standoffs ("pushes"), the dealer usually knocks on the table or otherwise signals that there is no payout or collection. In that case, a player may either remove the bet he made or keep it there for the next round of play. Once all bets are settled, the dealer gathers in the cards and prepares them for the next round.

Decision-Making. Often, it is a player's strategy to split pairs, or if he is able to make a full house, to use three-of-a-kind for the back hand and the pair for the front hand. When a player has three pairs in the seven cards dealt, the correct strategy is to use the two smallest pairs to make the back hand, and the largest pair to make the front hand. For example, with two kings, two jacks, and two 7s, and a 5, most experienced players would make up the back hand of two jacks, two 7s and a 5; and the front hand of two kings. In this situation the two-pair hand is likely to be a winner no matter what it is headed by, and the little hand of two kings is virtually unbeatable.

The skill and the fun of Pai-Gow is in deciding whether to make two fairly good hands to go for a win on both, or whether to try to just make a winner out of one hand, with the second one a likely loser, so as to give the maximum chance of not losing on both hands. It is important to note, though, that the back hand must be better than the front hand. If this rule is violated, the player's hands are fouled, and the bet is automatically lost.

The Joker. The "bug" is obviously a very valuable card, as it will often help to make a straight or a flush, or a second ace for two aces, or even a third ace for three aces. Many times, having the joker will make a hand of just ace high for the front hand, which is the difference between winning and losing. *Example:* With a holding such as joker, ♣4, ♣5, ♠5,

♣6, ♥7, ♠7, a player could use the bug to make a straight (joker, 7, 6, 5, 4), but the little hand, comprised of 7, 5, would be a sure loser. A better arrangement would be to make two pairs for the big hand (7, 7, 5, 5, 4) and ace-high for the little hand (joker, 6). Now there is a good chance to win with both sets of cards.

Dealer's Edge. When a player wins, the amount paid out is the bet made, less a commission. No commission is paid to the dealer when the player loses or when there is a standoff.

The commission is one of only two advantages the dealer has. The other is that if the dealer's back or front hand exactly matches the corresponding hand of a player, the dealer wins. Thus, if both the dealer and a player have K, 8 for their little hands, the dealer's little hand prevails, just as if he had K, 9 or A, 8 or better.

Rotating Dealer. In some games, a player is allowed to "deal"–that is, he banks the game. The casino dealer still handles the cards and chips, but the player acts as the bank. He plays against the other players as well as the dealer, who acts as a player, betting the last amount that the player-banker bet on the previous hand. In some games, the chance to be dealer can occur only every other hand, and then only if one of the players is interested in banking the hand. If two or more players wish to bank, the casino dealer chooses one of them; and the other players, in turn, get the chance to bank the game later. The player as banker must have enough chips in front of him to cover all of the wagers made by the other players.

Home Game

In the home game, each player can be the banker, deal the cards, and handle payouts and collections for an agreed-upon number of deals, say, twice around the table. The next player to the dealer's right would then get the opportunity. In home play, the dealer does not get a commission when a player wins, but he does win when his back or front hand is identical with another player's.

PUSOY
(Piat-Piat, Pepito)

NUMBER OF PLAYERS	NUMBER OF CARDS	GAME PLAY		SKILL LEVEL	
4 (2, 3)	**52**	◊ ◊ ♦ ◊ ◊ EASY → COMPLEX		◊ ◊ ◊ ♦ ◊ LUCK → SKILL	

A relative of Pai-Gow Poker, this game is played in private gambling casinos in the Philippines and in one or two public casinos in Manila. Pusoy (pronounced "poo-soy") is also played in home games in both the Philippines and Hawaii. It is loaded with action and requires more skill than Pai-Gow. In fact, it is such a good game that it really deserves worldwide attention. Unlike Pai-Gow, where tied hands are frequent, in Pusoy no result between a player and dealer can end in a standoff – there is always a payoff.

Number of Players. An unusual feature of this gambling game is that it is inflexible as to the number of players – exactly four are required for casino play. Two or three persons, however, can play in a home game.

Object of the Game. A player's goal is to form two or three winning Poker hands from the 13 cards that are dealt. There is a hand of five cards, called the "back" hand, another hand of five cards, called the "middle" hand, and a hand of three cards, called the "front" hand. To win the bet, two out of three of a player's hands must beat the three hands of the dealer. If all three hands beat the dealer's three hands, the player wins double the bet. If only one hand wins, the player loses the bet. If all three hands lose to the dealer, the player loses double the bet. A loss or win of double the bet is called a "pusoy," which in the main language of the Philippines means "zero," since one side wins none of the three hands played.

Poker Rankings. A basic knowledge of Poker is needed to play Pusoy. The hands rank as in Poker, from a royal straight flush down to no pair. While A, 2, 3, 4, 5 is the second highest straight in Pai-Gow, it has no special standing in Pusoy because no joker is used. Thus, it is the lowest ranking straight. For the three-card hand, straights and flushes do not count. Thus, the highest "front" hand is three aces, and the lowest is four-high (4, 3, 2).

Betting. The players buy chips for cash, and each player bets by placing one or more chips in a designated area in front of him. The minimum and maximum bets are established by the casino, or in a home game, by all the players.

The Shuffle and Cut. In the home game, each player picks a card from a shuffled pack spread face down. The highest card deals first (Ace is highest). Thereafter, the turn to deal passes to the left. The dealer shuffles the cards thoroughly and selects one player for the cut. That player separates the deck into two packets, and the dealer completes the cut.

The Deal. The dealer deals out the entire deck out one card at a time, face down, clockwise, beginning with the player to his left. The players will have 13 cards each.

Setting the Hands. Each player picks up his hand and arranges it to make three poker hands: the "back" hand of five cards must outrank the "middle" hand of five cards, which must outrank the "front" hand of three cards. When a player is satisfied with his arrangement, he places the "back" (five-card) hand face down farthest from the center of the table. The "middle" (second five-card) hand is placed next face down, and the "front" (three-card) hand is placed closest to the table's center.

All players at the table, including the dealer, are responsible for setting their hands, and no other player may assist. Once any player has placed all three hands, he is not permitted to touch the cards again.

Settlement. When all four participants have finished setting up and placing their hands as detailed above, the dealer turns up his three hands, and the players do likewise. Beginning with the player to the left, the dealer compares that player's three hands to his own by mentioning the poker hands for each and indicating who has won two out of the three hands, or three out of three. The dealer then collects or pays off single or double accordingly. The dealer does this for the next player to the left and then for the last player. If one of the player's hands and the dealer's corresponding hand are exactly tied, the dealer wins. For example, if both the "middle" hands are A, A, 10, 9, 6, the dealer wins that hand.

Once all bets are settled, the cards are gathered by the dealer and prepared for the next round. If the deal rotates, as in the home game, the cards are collected, and handed over to the next dealer for preparation.

Decision-Making. Often it is a good strategy to split two pairs. If there is a chance to make a full house, a player should use three-of-a-kind for a five-card hand and the pair for the other five-card hand or for the three-card hand.

The skill and the fun of Pusoy is similar to Pai-Gow: Should the player make two fairly good hands and one relatively poor one? Or, should he make one outstanding hand and two fair ones to try and eke out a second winner? Or, should the player make three reasonably good hands and hope to win on two somehow, or at least not lose on all three? It is important to note, though, that the back hand must be better than the middle hand, which must be better than the front hand. If this rule is violated, the participant's hands are fouled (called "totyo" in the Philippines), and the player at fault automatically loses double the bet.

Variations. Two popular variations of Pusoy are often played, and participants should decide before the session begins whether either or both options will be used:

Surrender. In this variation, a player or dealer who thinks he has poor cards may concede and pay the single bet. This avoids the possibility of a "pusoy"– paying double the amount bet for losing on all three hands. If the dealer is considering surrender, he should make no sign of it until the players have indicated their intentions. Once a player has placed his three hands, it is too late to surrender. When a player does surrender, the dealer immediately collects that player's bet, and the player's cards are left unseen. When the dealer surrenders, he pays only those players who have not surrendered–that is, only those participants still in the game.

Royalties. In this delightful variation, a player who is dealt an unusually good combination may expose it before the settlement period begins and immediately win "royalties" or single the bet. The combinations that fit into this category are: a straight flush, four-of-a-kind, or six pairs. Note that the player does not have to declare royalties. Instead, he may continue to play by setting up the three poker hands and possibly earning double the bet by winning on all three.

Caribbean Stud

Based on Poker, the game of Caribbean Stud is a comparatively new casino gambling game that has been growing in popularity. It was invented by *David Sklansky*, a Poker expert from Las Vegas.

Number of Players. The basic game is played by up to seven players, plus the dealer, and participants are seated at a table similar to the one used for Black Jack

The Pack. The standard 52- card pack is used.

The Play. After each player makes a bet (antes), the dealer gives five cards face down, one at a time, to each player and to himself. The dealer's last card is turned face up. Each player examines his hand and has the option of either deciding to fold, forfeiting his ante, or to play, whereby he places a bet equal to the ante. No player may show his hand to another player or communicate about his hand in any other way.

The dealer can play only with a hand of ace, king or any pair, or better. If the dealer does not qualify, each player still in the game wins his ante, and the hand is over. If the dealer does have A, K, x, x, x or better, the game continues and each player, in turn, reveals his hand of five cards. A player wins the additional bet made if his hand is better than the dealer's. He is paid a higher amount for a hand of two-pair and higher, (*see chart.*)

CARIBBEAN STUD PAYOFF ODDS	
1 pair	1 to 1
2 pair	2 to 1
3 of a kind	3 to 1
Straight	4 to 1
Flush	5 to 1
Full House	7 to 1
4 of a kind	20 to 1
Straight Flush	50 to 1
Royal Flush	100 to 1

Let It Ride Stud

This game is based on Poker, and is played in some casinos.

Number of Players. The game can be played by up to seven players, plus the dealer, at a table similar to the one used for Black Jack. The layout has three circled areas for each player, who places three equal bets.

The Pack. The standard 52-card pack is used.

LET IT RIDE STUD PAYOFF ODDS	
Pair of 9s or worse	Player loses
Pair of 10s or better	1 to 1
3 of a kind	3 to 1
Straight	5 to 1
Flush	8 to 1
Full House	11 to 1
4 of a kind	50 to 1
Straight Flush	200 to 1
Royal Flush	1000 to 1

The Play. The dealer gives three cards to each player, face down, one at a time. Two cards are then placed face down in front of the dealer, who does not receive a hand of three cards. The players do not play against the dealer. Their objective is merely to get a good poker hand by using their three cards plus the dealer's two face-down cards. At no time may a player show his hand to any of the other players.

After looking at the three face-down cards, the player may ask for his first bet back or may elect to "let it ride." One of the dealer's face-down cards is then turned up. The player may then ask for his bet back or, again, may "let it ride." The dealer's second face-down card is now turned up, and the players expose their cards. The dealer then pays out all winning hands according to the chart above.

BLACK JACK
(Twenty-One, Vingt-et-Un)

NUMBER OF PLAYERS	NUMBER OF CARDS	GAME PLAY	SKILL LEVEL
2-8	52	◊ ◆ ◊ ◊ ◊ EASY → COMPLEX	◊ ◊ ◆ ◊ ◊ LUCK → SKILL

With the exception of Poker, Black Jack is the most popular gambling card game. Equally well known as Twenty-One, the rules are simple, the play is thrilling, and there is opportunity for high strategy. In fact, for the expert player who mathematically plays a perfect game and is able to count cards, the odds are sometimes in that player's favor to win. But even for the casual participant who plays a reasonably good game, the casino odds are less, making Black Jack one of the most attractive casino games for the player.

While the popularity of Black Jack dates from World War I, its roots go back to the 1760s in France, where it is called Vingt-et-Un (French for 21). Today, Black Jack is the one card game that can be found in every American gambling casino. As a popular home game, it is played with slightly different rules. In the casino version, the house is the dealer (a "permanent bank"). In the home game, all of the players have the opportunity to be the dealer (a "changing bank").

Black Jack with a Permanent Bank

Number of Players. Up to eight people can play. The dealer plays against up to seven players who play for themselves. In casino play, the dealer remains standing, and the players are seated. The dealer is in charge of running all aspects of the game, from shuffling and dealing the cards to handling all bets.

The Pack. The standard 52-card pack is used, but in most casinos several decks of cards are shuffled together. The six-deck game (312 cards) is the most popular. In addition, the dealer uses a blank plastic card, which is never dealt, but is placed toward the bottom of the pack to indicate when it will be time for the cards to be reshuffled. When four or more decks are used, they are dealt from a shoe (a wooden box that allows the dealer to remove cards one at a time, face down, without actually holding one or more packs).

The Layout. The casino Black Jack table is semicircular. There is ample space for each player to keep his chips. On the green felt surface of the table each player has a circular area about the size of a coaster for placing a bet. There is another rectangular area for each player, where the dealer places the cards as they are dealt.

Object of the Game. Counting any ace as 1 or 11, as a player wishes, any face card as 10, and any other card at its pip value, each participant attempts to beat the dealer by getting a count as close to 21 as possible, without going over 21.

The Shuffle and Cut. The dealer thoroughly shuffles portions of the pack until all the cards have been mixed and combined. He designates one of the players to cut, and the plastic insert card is placed so that the last 60 to 75 cards or so will not be used. (Not dealing to the bottom of all the cards makes it more difficult for professional card counters to operate effectively.)

Betting. Before the deal begins, each player places a bet, in chips, in front of him in the designated area. Minimum and maximum limits are established on the betting, and the general limits are from $2 to $500.

The Deal. When all the players have placed their bets, the dealer gives one card face up to each player in rotation clockwise, and then one card face up to himself. Another round of cards is then dealt face up to each player, but the dealer takes his second card face down. Thus, each player except the dealer receives two cards face up, and the dealer receives one card face up and one card face down. (In some games, played with only one deck, the players' cards are dealt face down and they get to hold them. Today, however, virtually all Black Jack games feature the players' cards dealt face up on the condition that no player may touch any cards.)

Naturals. If a player's first two cards are an ace and a "ten-card" (a picture card or 10), giving him a count of 21 in two cards, this is a natural or "black jack." If any player has a natural and the dealer does not, the dealer immediately pays that player one and a half times the amount of his bet. If the dealer has a natural, he immediately collects the bets of all players who do not have naturals, (but no additional amount). If the dealer and another player both have naturals, the bet of that player is a stand-off (a tie), and the player takes back his chips.

If the dealer's face-up card is a ten-card or an ace, he looks at his face-down card to see if the two cards make a natural. If the face-up card is not a ten-card or an ace, he does not look at the face-down card until it is the dealer's turn to play.

Drawing. The player to the left goes first and must decide whether to "stand" (not ask for another card) or "hit" (ask for another card in an attempt to get closer to a count of 21, or even hit 21 exactly). Thus, a player may stand on the two cards originally dealt him, or he may ask the dealer for additional cards, one at a time, until he either decides to stand on the total (if it is 21 or under), or goes "bust" (if it is over 21). In the latter case, the player loses and the dealer collects the bet wagered. The dealer then turns to the next player to his left and serves him in the same manner.

The combination of an ace with a card other than a ten-card is known as a "soft hand," because the player can count the ace as a 1 or 11, and either draw cards or not. For example with a "soft 17" (an ace and a 6), the total is 7 or 17. While a count of 17 is a good hand, the player may wish to draw for a higher total. If the draw creates a bust hand by counting the ace as an 11, the player simply counts the ace as a 1 and continues playing by standing or "hitting" (asking the dealer for additional cards, one at a time).

Dealer's Play. When the dealer has served every player, his face-down card is turned up. If the total is 17 or more, he must stand. If the total is 16 or under, he must take a card. He must continue to take cards until the total is 17 or more, at which point the dealer must stand. If the dealer has an ace, and counting it as 11 would bring his total to 17 or more (but not over 21), he must count the ace as 11 and stand. The dealer's decisions, then, are automatic on all plays, whereas the player always has the option of taking one or more cards.

Signaling Intentions. When a player's turn comes, he can say "Hit" or can signal for a card by scratching the table with a finger or two in a motion toward himself, or he can wave his hand in the same motion that would say to someone "Come here!" When the player decides to stand, he can say "Stand" or "No more," or can signal this intention by moving his hand sideways, palm down and just above the table.

Settlement. A bet once paid and collected is never returned. Thus, one key advantage to the dealer is that the player goes first. If the player goes bust, he has already lost his wager, even if the dealer goes bust as well. If the dealer goes over 21, he pays each player who has stood the amount of that player's bet. If the dealer stands at 21 or less, he pays the bet of any player having a higher total (not exceeding 21) and collects the bet of any player having a lower total. If there is a stand-off (a player having the same total as the dealer), no chips are paid out or collected.

Reshuffling. When each player's bet is settled, the dealer gathers in that player's cards and places them face up at the side against a clear plastic L-shaped shield. The dealer continues to deal from the shoe until he comes to the plastic insert card, which indicates that it is time to reshuffle. Once that round of play is over, the dealer shuffles all the cards, prepares them for the cut, places the cards in the shoe, and the game continues.

Splitting Pairs. If a player's first two cards are of the same denomination, such as two jacks or two sixes, he may choose to treat them as two separate hands when his turn comes around. The amount of his original bet then goes on one of the cards, and an equal amount must be placed as a bet on the other card. The player first plays the hand to his left by standing or hitting one or more times; only then is the hand to the right played. The two hands are thus treated separately, and the dealer settles with each on its own merits. With a pair of aces, the player is given one card for each ace and may not draw again. Also, if a ten-card is dealt to one of these aces, the payoff is equal to the bet (not one and one-half to one, as with a black jack at any other time).

Doubling Down. Another option open to the player is doubling his bet when the original two cards dealt total 9, 10, or 11. When the player's turn comes, he places a bet equal to the original bet, and the dealer gives him just one card, which is placed face down and is not turned up until the bets are settled at the end of the hand. With two fives, the player may split a pair, double down, or just play the hand in the regular way. Note that the dealer does not have the option of splitting or doubling down.

Insurance. When the dealer's face-up card is an ace, any of the players may make a side bet of up to half the original bet that the dealer's face-down card is a ten-card, and thus a black jack for the house. Once all such side bets are placed, the dealer looks at his hole card. If it is a

---

CARD COUNTING TO THE LIMIT

Bet You Didn't Know

Many years ago, when dealers did not shuffle the cards until the pack ran out, there is a story – how true it is no one knows for sure – of a brilliant Black Jack player who, counted all the cards perfectly until there were just four left. On this particular hand, only he and the dealer were left, and the player had a king and a queen for a total of 20. The dealer's upcard was a 10, and the player knew that the remaining four cards plus the dealer's hole card were comprised of three aces and two ten-cards. Since the dealer, after looking at his hole card, did not reveal that he had a black jack, the player knew for sure that he must have one of the ten-cards, and thus a total of 20. Throwing all caution to the wind, the card counter asked for a hit, and an ace was turned up. That was enough for the player, who was paid off. The pit boss was then summoned, and the expert player was politely asked to leave. It is not often that a player with 20 on the first two cards takes a hit!

ten-card, it is turned up, and those players who have made the insurance bet win and are paid double the amount of their half-bet – a 2 to 1 payoff. When a black jack occurs for the dealer, of course, the hand is over, and the players' main bets are collected – unless a player also has black jack, in which case it is a stand-off. Insurance is invariably not a good proposition for the player, unless he is quite sure that there are an unusually high number of ten-cards still left undealt.

Basic Strategy

Winning tactics in Black Jack require that the player play each hand in the optimum way, and such strategy always takes into account what the dealer's upcard is. When the dealer's upcard is a good one, a 7, 8, 9, 10-card, or ace for example, the player should not stop drawing until a total of 17 or more is reached. When the dealer's upcard is a poor one, 4, 5, or 6, the player should stop drawing as soon as he gets a total of 12 or higher. The strategy here is never to take a card if there is any chance of going bust. The desire with this poor holding is to let the dealer hit and hopefully go over 21. Finally, when the dealer's up card is a fair one, 2 or 3, the player should stop with a total of 13 or higher.

With a soft hand, the general strategy is to keep hitting until a total of at least 18 is reached. Thus, with a an ace and a six (7 or 17), the player would not stop at 17, but would hit.

The basic strategy for doubling down is as follows: With a total of 11, the player should always double down. With a total of 10, he should double down unless the dealer shows a ten-card or an ace. With a total of 9, he should double down only if the dealer's card is fair or poor (2 through 6).

For splitting, the player should always split a pair of aces or 8s; identical ten-cards should not be split, and neither should a pair of 5s, since two 5s are a total of 10, which can be used more effectively in doubling down. A pair of 4s should not be split either, as a total of 8 is a good number to draw to. Generally, 2s, 3s, or 7s can be split unless the dealer has an 8, 9, ten-card, or ace. Finally, 6s should not be split unless the dealer's card is poor (2 through 6).

Black Jack with a Changing Bank
("Pontoon")

With a few variations in the rules, Black Jack can be a wonderfully entertaining game to play at home. The objective is the same as in the casino version: to get 21 or as close to it as possible. Depending on the region, there are a number of Pontoon versions, but in all of them, every player gets the opportunity to be the dealer.

Number of Players. While two to 14 people can play, the game is best for up to seven participants.

The Pack. The standard 52-card pack is used. (A single pack is always used.) As in the casino game, an ace is worth 1 or 11 at the holder's option, and any face card is worth 10. All other cards count their pip value.

Determining First Banker. Any player picks up the pack and deals the cards in rotation, face up, until a jack of spades or jack of clubs falls to one of the players. That player becomes the first dealer.

The Shuffle and Cut. The dealer shuffles the pack, and any other player may cut. The dealer then turns up the top card of the pack, shows it to all players, and places it face up, at the bottom of the pack. This is called "burning a card." After each hand, the discards are gathered up and placed face up under the burned card. When the burned card is reached during a deal, there is a new shuffle and cut before the game continues.

Betting. Each player places a bet, which may not be less than one chip nor more than the betting limit established for the game, usually no more than five chips.

Dealing. The dealer gives one card face down to each player in rotation, including himself. He then deals a second round of cards face up in the same order.

Naturals. If the dealer has a natural (ace, and face card or ten), every player pays him double the amount of his bet. If the dealer and a player both have naturals, the player pays just the amount of his bet, not double. When a player has a natural and the dealer does not, the dealer pays that player double the amount of his bet.

Drawing Cards. When the dealer does not have a black jack, he starts with the player to the left and gives each player in turn as many cards as that player requests, one at a time, until that player goes over 21 and pays, or stands. If a player goes bust, he declares so and turns up the hole card. The dealer collects the bet that was made.

When all players have stood or gone bust, the dealer turns up his face-down card and may draw cards until he wishes to stand. The dealer is not bound by the rules to stand on or draw to any total. If the dealer goes over 21, he pays all players who have stood. If the dealer stands on a total of 21 or less, he pays all players who stood with a higher total and collects from all players who stood with a lower total or the same total – "ties pay the dealer."

As in the casino game, a player against the dealer may split a pair or double down, and the dealer does not have this option.

Bonus Payment. Any player who forms one of the following combinations collects immediately from the dealer, and cannot later lose the bet he made, even if the dealer has a higher total:

A player who has five cards that total 21 or under (often called a "Five-Card Charlie"), collects double the bet made. With six cards totaling 21 or under, he collects four times the bet made, and so on, doubling for each additional card.

A player who makes 21 with three 7s receives triple the amount of the bet made.

A player who makes 21 with an 8, 7, and 6 receives double the amount of the bet made.

The dealer does not collect more than the amount of the players' bets for making any one of these combinations, nor does he necessarily win with five or more cards that total 21 or under.

Changing the Bank. The player who is the dealer continues in that capacity until another player is dealt a black jack and the dealer has no natural. When this happens, the player who had the natural becomes the next dealer, after all bets in the current deal have been settled. If two or more players have naturals and the dealer has none, the one nearest the dealer's left becomes the next dealer. A player entitled to deal may, if he wishes, give or sell the privilege to another player.

RED DOG
(High-Card Pool)

NUMBER OF PLAYERS	NUMBER OF CARDS	GAME PLAY		SKILL LEVEL	
2-10	**52**	◆ ◇ ◇ ◇ ◇		◇ ◆ ◇ ◇ ◇	
		EASY ➤ COMPLEX		LUCK ➤ SKILL	

A gambling game that depends a lot on luck, Red Dog is not popular in casino play, but is often played at home just for fun – the stakes are meaningless. *Note:* The game below should not be confused with In-Between or Acey-Deucey, which is often called Red Dog, and which is described in the next section.

Number of Players. From two to 10 people can play.

The Pack. The standard 52-card pack is used.

Rank of Cards. A (high), K, Q, J, 10, 9, 8, 7, 6, 5, 4, 3, 2.

Object of the Game. The goal is to be the player with the most chips at the end of the game.

The Ante. Chips are distributed to the players, and each player places one chip in the center of the table to form a pool or pot.

The Draw. Any player deals the cards one at a time, face up, to the players in turn and the player with the highest card deals first.

The Shuffle, Cut and Deal. Any player may shuffle, the dealer shuffles last, and the player to the dealer's right cuts the cards. The dealer gives five cards, one at a time, face down, to each player in turn, beginning with the player on his left. (Some deal only four cards to a player. This is necessary if there are more than eight players.)

The Betting. After looking at his cards, the player on the dealer's left may bet any number of chips up to the number of chips in the pot at the time. A player who does not wish to bet may forfeit one chip to the pot. No bet may exceed the number of chips already in the pot.

When the player has placed his bet, the dealer turns up the top card from the remainder of the pack. If the player who bet has a card of the same suit and of higher rank, he shows the card and takes back the amount of his bet, plus an equivalent amount from the pot. If he has no card that beats the card shown, he must show his entire hand, and the amount of his bet is added to the pot. The next player in turn then places a bet, another card is turned, and the same procedure is followed until all players, including the dealer, have bet.

If at any time the pot has no more chips in it (because a player has "bet the pot" and won), each player again puts in one chip to restore the pot.

When every player has had a chance to bet, the turn to deal passes to the player on the dealer's left.

IN-BETWEEN
(Acey-Deucey, Red Dog)

NUMBER OF PLAYERS	NUMBER OF CARDS	GAME PLAY		SKILL LEVEL	
2-10	**52**	♦ ◊ ◊ ◊ ◊ EASY ➔ COMPLEX		◊ ♦ ◊ ◊ ◊ LUCK ➔ SKILL	

The game of In-Between or Acey-Deucey is often referred to as Red Dog, but its rules are very different from the Red Dog game previously described. In-Between is not very popular at casinos, but is often played in home Poker games as a break from Poker itself. The rules below are for the home game, which is easily adaptable for casino play.

Number of Players. From two to 10 people can play.

The Pack. The standard 52-card pack is used.

Rank of Cards. A (high), K, Q, J, 10, 9, 8, 7, 6, 5, 4, 3, 2.

Object of the Game. The goal is to be the player with the most chips at the end of the game.

The Ante. Chips are distributed to the players, and each players puts one chip in the center of the table to form a pool or pot.

The Draw. Any player deals one card face up, to each player in turn, and the player with the highest card deals first.

The Shuffle, Cut, and Deal. Any player may shuffle, and the dealer shuffles last. The player to the dealer's right cuts the cards. The dealer turns up two cards and places them in the middle of the table, positioning them so that there is ample room for a third card to fit in between.

The Betting. The player on the dealer's left may bet up to the entire pot or any portion of the number of chips in the pot, but he must always bet a minimum of one chip. When the player has placed a bet, the dealer turns up the top card from the pack and places it between the two cards already face up. If the card ranks between the two cards already face up, the player wins and takes back the amount of his bet plus an equivalent amount from the pot. If the third card is not between the face-up cards, or is of the same rank as either of them, the player loses his bet, and it is added to the pot. If the two face-up cards up are consecutive, the player automatically loses, and a third card need not be turned up. If the two face-up cards are the same, the player wins two chips and, again, no third card is turned up. (In some games, the player is paid three chips when this occurs.)

"Acey-Deucey" (ace, 2) is the best combination, and a player tends to bet the whole pot, if he can. This is because the only way an ace-deuce combination can lose is if the third card turned up is also an ace or a deuce.

After the first player has finished, the dealer clears away the cards and places them face down in a pile. The next player then places a bet, and the dealer repeats the same procedure until all the players, including the dealer, have had a turn.

If at any time, the pot has no more chips in it (because a player has "bet the pot" and won), each player again puts in one chip to restore the pot.

When every player has had a turn to bet, the deal passes to the player on the dealer's left, and the game continues.

BACCARAT
(Punto Banco)

NUMBER OF PLAYERS	NUMBER OF CARDS	GAME PLAY	SKILL LEVEL
2-12	**416**	◆ ◇ ◇ ◇ ◇ EASY → COMPLEX	◆ ◇ ◇ ◇ ◇ LUCK → SKILL

Baccarat was once one of the most often-played games in French casinos. Today, it has almost been replaced by Chemin de Fer which is an offspring.

Perhaps the most glamorous of all casino games, Baccarat's trappings are what made it so popular. The lure of the game? It requires no skill – it is a game of pure luck! Baccarat is played for very high stakes, and the gaming table for it is placed in a special alcove, blocked off from the masses and the rest of the casino action. Also, in American casinos, Baccarat tends to be played with real cash – lots of $100-bills are spread all around. European casinos use chips, but the high-denomination chips are oblong "plaques," which make the game look just as exciting as the American version when they are stacked in front of a winning player.

Number of Players. From two to 12 people can play.

The Pack. Eight 52-card packs are shuffled together and dealt by the croupier (dealer) from a dealing box, called a shoe, which releases one card at a time, face down. In some games, six packs are used.

The Layout. The very large Baccarat table has 12 seats, six on either side of the dealer, who only banks the game and does not otherwise participate. Green felt covers the entire table, and the numbers 1 to 12 are marked on it. These numbered areas are where the players keep their money (or chips, as the case may be). A player may bet on the Bank or the Player, and the layout indicates where such bets are placed. Baccarat is known in some areas as Punto Banco. The only difference is that the word "Bank" is replaced by "Banco," and the word "Player" is replaced by "Punto."

While in most casino games, the dealer stands, in Baccarat, the dealer is seated between players "1" and "12."

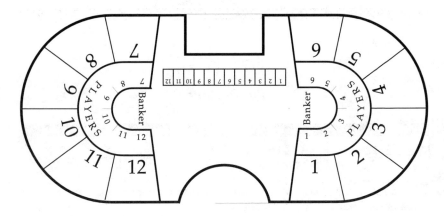

Typical Baccarat Table Layout

Object of the Game. The participants attempt to form, in two or three cards, a combination as close to 9 as possible. Face cards and 10s count zero. Aces count 1, and other cards count their pip value. Counts of 10 are disregarded in the total; thus, a 5 and a 6, totaling 11, count merely as 1.

The Deal. The dealer (or croupier) prepares the cards by thoroughly shuffling them and, after they are cut by any player, places them in the shoe. While the dealer does not participate in the game, he assists the players in making and settling their bets, and advises them on proper procedure. The shoe usually starts with the player in seat No. 1, who is the first to act as the Bank.

When all bets are placed, the player acting as the Bank distributes two cards face down, alternately, to the player who made the largest bet and to himself. The procedure for looking at, announcing, and displaying the hands is somewhat elaborate, but this only adds to the mystique of the game. The player making the largest bet faces the two cards and passes them back to the dealer, who announces the total. The hand is placed on the section of the layout marked "Player Hand." The Banker then faces his hand and passes the cards to the dealer, who announces this total as well and displays the cards on the position marked "Bank Hand."

Naturals. If either participant has a count of 8 or 9 in his first two cards, it is a natural. If only the player acting as Bank has a natural, all participants who bet on the Bank hand win. If only his opponent has a natural, the player acting as Bank pays all bets that were placed on the Player hand. A natural 9 beats a natural 8. Two naturals of the same number are a stand-off, in which case all bets are withdrawn, and the next deal begins.

RULES FOR DRAWING OR STANDING IN BACCARAT

Player Rules

Having	Action
0, 1, 2, 3, 4 or 5	Draws
6 or 7	Stands
8 or 9	Natural – cards are turned up

Bank Rules

Having	Draws after having given player–	Stands after having given player–
0, 1 or 2	1, 2, 3, 4, 5, 6, 7, 8, 9 or 10	–
3	1, 2, 3, 4, 5, 6, 7, 9 or 10	8
4	2, 3, 4, 5, 6 or 7	1, 8, 9 or 10
5	4, 5, 6 or 7	1, 2, 3, 8, 9 or 10
6	6 or 7	1, 2, 3, 4, 5, 8, 9 or 10
7	–	1, 2, 3, 4, 5, 6, 7, 8, 9 or 10
8 or 9	–	Natural – cards are faced

Having	When Player has stood
0, 1, 2, 3, 4 or 5	Bank must draw
6 or 7	Bank must stand
8 or 9	Natural – cards are turned

Rules of Drawing. If neither the player acting as Bank, nor his opponent has a natural, then either stands or draws one card only, according to the chart below. Note that the rules for standing or drawing are inflexible.

The Player goes first, and if, according to the chart, the Player must draw, the Bank deals a third card face up, which is placed alongside the two other cards that were originally dealt. If the Bank must draw, the third card is placed alongside the Bank's original two cards. The dealer then announces the result, such as "Bank wins 7 against 3," and settles all the bets. If the Bank is nearer 9 than the Player, those who bet on the Bank win. If the Player is nearer 9, those who bet on the Player win. If the two hands have the same total, all bets are a stand-off and are withdrawn. (When either player has a natural, the hand is always over, and the other side does not get to draw a card.)

Note that a hand can become much less favorable in the draw. *To illustrate:* Having a total of 3 and drawing a 7 would give a total of zero, (because counts of 10 are disregarded. This is called a "baccarat," and is the worst of all hand possibilities.)

House Edge. Winning bets on the Player are paid out at even money, but on winning Bank bets, the house takes a commission of five per cent, which is how the casino makes its profit. The cut for the house is traditionally taken out at the end of the shoe, which can comprise many rounds of play. However, if a player retires from the game, he must settle with the house at that time. Small boxes in the middle of the layout are for tokens that show how much each player owes on winning Bank hands.

The actual edge for betting on the Bank is just slightly above five per cent, so whether the participant bets on the Player or the Bank, the game is still a fairly even one.

CHEMIN DE FER

NUMBER OF PLAYERS	NUMBER OF CARDS	GAME PLAY	SKILL LEVEL
2-8	416	♦ ◊ ◊ ◊ ◊ EASY → COMPLEX	♦ ◊ ◊ ◊ ◊ LUCK → SKILL

Chemin de Fer (which literally means "railroad" in French) is a variation of Baccarat. The main difference is that there is some decision-making involved for the participants. The scoring of the cards is the same as in Baccarat, but the chart governing the game is different in that there are three situations (as noted in the chart below) when there is an option of whether to draw or stand.

Number of Players. From two to eight people can play.

The Pack. Eight standard 52-card packs are shuffled together and placed in a dealing box called a "shoe" which releases one card at a time, face down.

In addition to the three options for standing or drawing, the distinctive feature of Chemin de Fer is that the players bet against each other, as opposed to Baccarat, where it makes little difference whether a player backs the Player hand or the Bank hand. Thus, in Chemin de Fer, the player acting as the Bank, in dealing out the cards from the shoe, is actually the banker – that is, the amount he puts up governs how much the other players can wager against him. If one or two players match this amount, the remaining players do not get to bet for that round.

As in Baccarat, the casino makes its profit by taking five per cent from all winning Bank hands. This cut for the house is taken out immediately, rather than at the end of the shoe.

The Layout. Usually up to eight people play, though in some games, the number can go up to nine or even 12. A game is normally not begun until there are five or six players available. In the middle of the French layout is a square marked "Banque," which is for the banker's bet, if any. Another square marked "Reliquat" is for that part of the banker's bet (if any) that is not covered by all the other players.

Banking the Game. The player to the right of the dealer (or croupier) is the first banker and places the number of chips he is prepared to wager in front of him. Any player who wants to bet against this player calls out, "Banco!" and matches the same amount. If there is more than one such

RULES FOR DRAWING OR STANDING IN CHEMIN DE FER

Player Rules

Having	Action
0, 1, 2, 3 or 4	Draws
5	Option: Draws or Stands
6 or 7	Stands
8 or 9	Natural – card are turned up

Bank Rules

Having	Draws after having given player–	Stands after having given player–	Optional
0, 1 or 2	1, 2, 3, 4, 5, 6, 7, 8, 9 or 10	–	
3	1, 2, 3, 4, 5, 6, 7 or 10	8	9
4	2, 3, 4, 5, 6 or 7	1, 8, 9 or 10	
5	5, 6 or 7	1, 2, 3, 8, 9 or 10	4
6	6 or 7	1, 2, 3, 4, 5, 8, 9 or 10	
7	–	1, 2, 3, 4, 5, 6, 7, 8, 9 or 10	
8 or 9	–	Natural – cards are faced	

Having	When Player has stood
0, 1, 2, 3, 4 or 5	Bank must draw
6 or 7	Bank must stand
8 or 9	Natural – cards are turned up

challenger, priority is given to the player nearer to the dealer's right. If no one calls, "Banco!" two or more players may cover parts of the Bank, and the player placing the most money down gets the privilege of playing the hand. (There are other features of betting that are very detailed and which are played primarily in the European game.)

The Deal. As in Baccarat, two cards are dealt face down, one at a time, to the player and the banker. If the player has a natural (a total of 8 or 9), he turns over the cards immediately. If the player must draw a card, or with a total of 5 chooses to do so, he says, "Carte," but does not turn over the two initial cards. since exposing the cards would be to the dealer's advantage. The third card, though, is dealt face up for the players or for the dealer, whenever such a card is drawn.

Object of the Game. The goal is to form, in two or three cards, a combination that counts as close to 9 as possible. Face cards and 10s count 10 or zero, aces count 1, and other cards their pip value. Tens are disregarded in the total, thus, a 5 and a 6, totaling 11, counts as 1.

If a player has a count of 8 or 9 in his first two cards, he has a "natural," and shows his hand immediately. If only the dealer has a natural, the dealer wins all the bets. If only the opponent has a natural, the dealer pays all the bets. A natural 9 beats a natural 8. Two naturals of the same number are a stand-off. When this happens, cards are tossed in, all bets are withdrawn, and players place their bets for the next deal (called a "coup").

If neither the dealer nor his opponent has a natural, the opponent, according to the chart, may receive a third card, which is dealt face up. The dealer, also according to the chart, may draw a third card face up. (*Variation:* In some games, the dealer and any player who bancos are allowed to use their own judgment as to whether or not to draw a third card, regardless of mathematical advisability.)

When both players have stood or withdrawn, all cards are shown. If the dealer is nearer 9 than his opponent, he collects all the bets. If his opponent is nearer 9, the dealer pays all the bets. If the dealer and his opponent have the same total, all bets are a stand-off and are withdrawn.

Changing the Bank. Once the house settles all wagers, the next coup (deal) begins. The dealer remains dealer as long as he wins or has a stand-off. When he loses a coup, the player to his left becomes the dealer.

The new dealer announces the amount of his bank, bets are placed, and the deal continues as before. The cards are not removed from the shoe and reshuffled until only a few cards are left in it.

FARO

NUMBER OF PLAYERS	NUMBER OF CARDS	GAME PLAY	SKILL LEVEL
2-20+	52	◇ ◆ ◇ ◇ ◇ EASY → COMPLEX	◇ ◆ ◇ ◇ ◇ LUCK → SKILL

Faro is a very old card game. Introduced in France in the court of King Louis XIV, its name is derived from the picture of an Egyptian Pharaoh on one of the cards in the French deck. It was once the most widely played gambling game in England. Faro was also very popular in America, and during the 19th century, many referred to it as "the national card game." It is of historical interest to note that during the Civil War era there were more than 150 gambling houses in Washington D.C., and Faro was the principal attraction at every one of them. Today, with the advent of Black Jack and the dice game called Craps, Faro has almost vanished from casinos except in Nevada.

Number of Players. Any number of people can play. All bets are placed against the dealer (banker). The banker is usually selected by auction – that is, the player who agrees to put up the largest stake as the amount of his bank, becomes the banker.

The Pack. The standard 52-card pack is used, plus 13 spades from another pack which are used for the layout.

The Layout. The complete spade suit, either pasted to a board or enameled on felt, is placed on a table. Players indicate their bets by placing chips on any card on the layout. (The spade suit is selected arbitrarily–all suits are equivalent; only the ranks of the cards are relevant.)

The Deal. The cards are shuffled by the dealer and cut by any player. After bets have been placed against the dealer (banker), as described below, the dealer turns up the top card of the pack and places it to his left. This card is called "soda" and has no bearing on bets. The dealer then turns up the next card and places it face up on his right. He then turns up a third card and places it on top of soda, to his left. The dealing of these three cards constitutes a turn.

Betting. The first card turned up in any turn (except soda) always loses. The second card wins. Before the turn begins, the players may place their bets on cards in the layout. Chips placed on any card are a bet that the card will win unless a copper (penny or similar disc) is put on top of the chips. In this case, the player is betting that the card will lose. Any bet is settled the next time that a card of the indicated rank is turned up. For example: A player puts a chip on the ♠6 in the layout. The dealer turns up two cards, neither of which is a six, so the player's bet remains on the layout, unsettled. But on the next turn, the first card turned by dealer is the ♥6; this means that the six loses, and the dealer takes the player's bet. If the player had bet on the six to lose (by coppering his bet), the dealer would have paid him; or if the ♥6 had been the second card in that turn, instead of the first, the player would have won.

After each turn, all bets settled at that turn are paid and collected. Other bets remain on the layout or may be withdrawn, and new bets may be placed. In many regions, other types of bets are permitted.

As the deal progresses, all the cards that lose form one pile, and all cards that win form another pile.

Splits. If two cards of the same rank come up on the same turn, so that a bet on that rank both wins and loses, it is called a split, and the dealer takes half of all bets on that rank. This is the dealer's only advantage in the game.

Calling the Turn. A record of all cards turned is kept on a "casekeeper" which is similar to an abacus. Each spindle has four counters which are moved when each of the four cards of a denomination (ace through king) are played. By using a casekeeper, players always know which cards remain undealt. When only three cards remain, a player may bet on the exact order in which those cards will come up, and the dealer pays off the player's bet at 4 to 1 if he is correct. This is referred to as "calling the turn." There are six ways in which the cards may come up, so the actual odds against the player are 5 to 1. If two of the last three cards are a pair, it is called a "cat-hop," and the dealer pays only 2 to 1.

Stuss

The rules are the same as for Faro, except there are no elaborate side bets and no soda card. The dealer simply turns up two cards at each turn. Also, when there is a split, the dealer receives the full amount of the bet, rather than half.

Trente et Quarante

This game is popular at the famous casino in Monte Carlo. Trente et Quarante (which means 30 and 40 in French) is also played in Nice, on the French Riviera.

Number of Players. Any number of people can play, though more than 20 participants at the table can get somewhat cumbersome. Usually, a casino will open up another table when there are more than 20 players.

The Pack. Six packs of the standard 52-card pack are used. These are shuffled together.

The Play. The croupier (dealer) always deals. Any one of the players cuts the cards after the croupier has prepared them, and then the croupier places the cards in a shoe (dealing box). Before the deal begins, a player may bet on "rouge" (red), "noir" (black), "couleur" (color) or "inverse" (reverse).

Aces count 1, face cards count 10, and all other cards are equal to their pip value. Once the bets have been made, the croupier lays out a row of cards, announcing the cumulative total as each card is dealt, until the total hits 31 or more. This row of cards represents "noir." Below the first row, a second row is then dealt in the same way, and represents "rouge."

Settling. A bet on noir or rouge wins if the row of that designation counts nearer to 31. A bet on "couleur" wins if the first card dealt in a rouge or noir row is of the color designating that row. *For example*, a diamond is dealt first for the rouge row. If this first card is of the alternative color, the "inverse" bet wins.

When both rows total the same number, it is a "refait" or stand-off, and all bets are called off. However, when the same number for each row is 31, the house takes half of all the bets that have been made; this represents the house advantage, which is only a little more than one per cent because a refait of 31 occurs only about once in 40 coups (deals).

Chapter IV

Rummy
Games

GIN RUMMY
(Gin)

NUMBER OF PLAYERS	NUMBER OF CARDS	GAME PLAY					SKILL LEVEL				
2 (3-4)	**52**	◇	◇	♦	◇	◇	◇	◇	◇	♦	◇
		EASY	→		COMPLEX		LUCK		→		SKILL

"Gin" is a modern classic that has superseded all other rummy games in popularity. The game suddenly hit its stride in the 1930s when Hollywood celebrities took it up. They realized that Gin Rummy was not only simple and fast, but made an excellent wagering game, too. Although much luck is involved, the skill required far outweighs the chance factor, and Gin ranks as one of the most demanding of all card games.

Number of Players. Two people can play, though three may participate, usually with one sitting out while the other two play. Four or more, in pairs up to almost any number, may play a partnership game (see p. 129), but this is done by playing separate two-hand games and combining scores.

The Pack. The standard 52-card pack is used. Two packs should be used, so that while one player deals, the other shuffles for the next deal.

Rank of Cards. K, Q, J, 10, 9, 8, 7, 6, 5, 4, 3, 2, A. (Aces are always low.)

Value of Cards. Face cards, 10 points each; ace, 1; other cards, their pip values.

The Shuffle and Cut. One pack is shuffled and spread, and each player draws a card; if he draws one of the four cards at either end, the player must draw again. If the cards drawn are of the same rank, the suits decide the higher rank in this order: spades (high), hearts, diamonds, and clubs. The player drawing the high card has the choice of cards and seats. The other player, having picked the low card, deals first. Either player may shuffle, with the dealer having the right to shuffle last, and the opponent then cuts the pack.

The Deal. The dealer completes the cut, and then deals 10 cards, face down, one at a time, alternately, to each person, beginning with the opponent. The next card, called the "upcard," is placed face up in the center of the table to form the beginning of the "discard" pile; the "stock" (the remaining cards) are placed face down beside it. Many players spread the stock slightly so that cards can be more easily drawn from it.

Once the cards are dealt, each player takes up his hand, fans it, and if desired, arranges the cards into groups of "melds" (either sets of cards of the same denomination or sequences of cards of the same suit), so that it will be easier and faster to plan the strategy and play.

Object of the Game. Each player tries to form "matched sets," which consist of three or four cards of the same rank, or "sequences," which are three or more cards of consecutive rank in the same suit (such as the 6, 5, 4 of spades). A second objective is to reduce the count of the unmatched cards in a player's hand to less than the count of his opponent.

Group (set or book)

The Play. The non-dealer plays first, and the turn to play alternates thereafter. At each turn, a player must take either the upcard (top card of the discard pile) or draw the top card of the stock and then discard one card face up on the discard pile. When a player has elected to take the upcard, he may not discard it at the same turn.

Sequence (run)

On the first play of the hand, if the non-dealer does not wish to take the upcard, he must announce this, and the dealer may have the first turn by taking the upcard. If the dealer does not want the upcard, the opponent draws the top card from the stock, and play proceeds.

Players must decide at the start of the game whether anyone may look through the discard pile while playing. Most experts allow this practice. If the players agree that no one may look at previous discards, then the discard pile should be kept squared up so that only the top card shows.

Scoring or "Ginning". There are three ways to score points toward victory in Gin Rummy: ginning, knocking, and undercutting. A player who "gins" is able to meld out his entire hand, without any "deadwood" (unmatched cards). Usually, the hand will consist of one meld of four cards, and two melds of three cards each. A rarer gin hand is two sequences of five cards each.

When a player gets gin, he discards one card face down (instead of face up, as usual), says "Gin!" and then spreads the hand of 10 cards, assorted into melds, on the table. The score for gin is 25 points plus t he deadwood in the opponent's hand. After the gin is announced and spread, the opponent turns his hand face up into melds, and the unmelded cards remaining count against him. *For example:* If the deadwood left is K, 8, 3, A (of whatever suits), the count would be 22 points, which would be added to the winner's 25 points for gin, making a total of 47 points for the ginning player.

TYPICAL "GIN" HAND

3-Card Meld (Kings)   3-Card Meld (8s)   4-Card Meld (Sequence)

Knocking. A player may choose to "knock" instead of going for gin, but the value of the unmatched cards in his hand (after he discards) cannot exceed 10 points. Naturally, the player does not have to knock when able to do so; instead, he may play on for gin and the 25 point bonus. Having knocked, he discards one card down and spreads the hand of 10 cards, arranged into melds and unmatched cards.

The opponent then spreads his hand, removing from it any unmatched cards, and then is permitted to "lay off" whatever cards he has that match the knocker's matched sets. This helps to reduce the deadwood count in the opponent's hand, and is a reward for holding on to cards that the opponent is quite sure the knocker needs. An example of laying off: The knocker goes down with ♥10, 9, 8, 7, four deuces, a 5, and a 4. The opponent is able to spread two melds and the deadwood is comprised of ♥J, 6, and two threes. In this case, the opponent can lay off the jack and six of hearts onto the knocker's heart meld, to reduce his count from 22 points to only 6 points! Note that a player is not permitted to lay off any cards on the unmatched cards in the opponent's hand.

After a player knocks and the opponent attempts to lay off, the point values of the two players' unmatched cards are compared, and if the player who knocked has a lower point-count, he scores the difference in the counts. Thus, if the knocker has 6 points, and the opponent 17, the knocker would score 11 for the hand.

Note that when a player gins, the opponent may not lay off cards on the gin hand. That is one advantage in going for a gin.

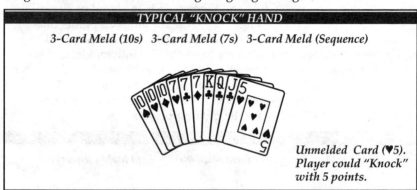

TYPICAL "KNOCK" HAND

3-Card Meld (10s)   3-Card Meld (7s)   3-Card Meld (Sequence)

Unmelded Card (♥5). Player could "Knock" with 5 points.

Undercutting. When a player knocks, and the opponent's deadwood total is the same or less than the knocker's, the opponent "undercuts" and scores a bonus of 20 points, plus the difference in the counts for the two players' unmatched cards. *For example:* If the opponent is able to reduce his count to only 6, compared with the knocker's count of 9, the difference is 3, plus the undercut bonus of 20, for a total of 23. If the players' counts are exactly even, it is still an undercut, but the undercutting player would score only 20 points! (In some games, the undercut bonus is 25, the same as for a gin.)

End of a Hand. Play continues until a player gins or knocks, or until there are only two cards left in the stock. If the latter event occurs, the hand is over, and ends in a tie. (No points are scored.) The same dealer deals a new hand.

A running total of each player's score is kept, with a line drawn under his score every time he wins a hand. *For example:* A player wins the first hand by 11 points; he scores 11 and draws a line under it. The same player wins the next hand by 14 points; he writes down 25 and draws another line.

The loser of each hand deals next.

Game. The player who first scores 100 points or more wins the game. (Some players may prefer to play to 150, 200, or 300 points.) The winner adds to his score a 100-point game bonus. (If the opponent has not won a hand during the game, then he doubles his entire score, including the game bonus. This is called a shutout or "schneider.") Each player then adds to his score 25 points for every hand he has won, a bonus called a line or a box. (In some games, an extra box or two is credited when a player scores a gin or an undercut.) The two players' total scores are then determined, and the player with the higher score wins the difference between his score and the opponent's. The winner has the choice of cards and seats for the next game, and the losing player deals the first hand.

Hollywood Scoring. The Gin Rummy score sheet is divided into six columns, and the names of the two players alternate at the top of each column. In this version, almost every hand is scored as though the players were playing three different games. The result of the first hand each player wins is scored once, and credited toward Game 1. The result of the second hand won by a player who has already scored in Game 1 is scored twice, and credited to him as a second score in Game 1 and as his first score in Game 2. The winning score of the third hand, if it is won by a player who has already scored in Games 1 and 2 is scored to his credit in all three games. Each subsequent hand won by that player is scored to his credit in all three games.

When a player reaches 100 points in any game, he wins that game, but play continues until all three games have been decided, and subsequent scores are entered only in the remaining game or games.

Each game is scored independently, and each player receives all bonuses to which he is entitled for that game. A player who was shut out (schneidered) in one game enters his first score in the game or games still uncompleted.

Straight Gin

This version for two players is simply Gin Rummy without knocking. Both players must go for gin, and the winner is the player who gins first. Some players agree to play a series, in which case the first player to go gin four times is the winner; the maximum number of games for the series would be seven, which would be played in the event that each player has won three games and needs a fourth win to claim victory.

In Straight Gin, an alternative to turning the twenty-first card as the upcard is for the dealer to give his opponent an eleventh card. The opponent then discards to start the game.

Celebes Rhum

In this Straight Gin version played in Southeast Asia and elsewhere, 54 cards are needed: the standard pack plus two jokers, which are wild. Two people play, each is dealt 13 cards, and the next card is turned up as the upcard. The procedure is the same as for Gin Rummy, with the following exceptions:

1) Only the dealer's opponent, whose turn comes first, may take the first upcard.

2) There is no knocking. To win, the player must meld his hand. The most common set of groupings is a sequence of four cards and three other melds of either matched sets or sequences. A joker can be played as any card but only in one of the three-card melds; it may not be used in the four-card meld, which must be a natural sequence of the same suit. Instead of melding in a 4-3-3-3 pattern, two other arrangements are possible: 5-5-3 and 5-4-4. If either of the latter two is chosen, a natural sequence meld of four or five cards is needed; the remaining two melds are comprised of either kind of meld, and one or both may contain a joker.

3) The joker may be used for a matched set of five-of-a-kind, since a suit need not be specified when a matched set is made.

OKLAHOMA GIN

NUMBER OF PLAYERS	NUMBER OF CARDS	GAME PLAY	SKILL LEVEL
2 (3, 4)	**52**	◇ ◇ ◆ ◇ ◇ EASY → COMPLEX	◇ ◇ ◇ ◇ ◆ LUCK → SKILL

This very popular version of Gin Rummy is just like the original except for one key rule that requires even more skill of the player: The rank of the upcard fixes the maximum number of points with which a player may knock in that deal. Thus, if the upcard is a five, the knocker must have 5 points or less. Face cards count 10. When an ace is the knock card, neither player may knock with a count of 1 point; instead, each must play for a gin hand. An additional rule, often played, is that when the upcard is a spade, all scores accruing from that deal are doubled.

If the upcard is not taken by either player, it is usually set aside near the stock, so that both players can refer to it during play. If the upcard is taken by either player, the opponent may, at any time, ask what the upcard was, and the other player is required to give this information.

THE TWO GREATEST GIN PLAYERS OF ALL TIME?

Top experts play Oklahoma Gin more often than the standard Gin Rummy, and two of the greatest players of all time were Oswald Jacoby and John Crawford. Jacoby and Crawford often got together for a very high stakes game at Manhattan's chic Regency Club. Both men also ranked among the greatest bridge, poker, and backgammon players as well, for they had great powers of concentration and each was supremely gifted at games. Jacoby was a brilliant mathematician who could multiply two four-digit numbers in his head, and he could memorize the order of all 52 cards of a randomly shuffled deck after looking at the cards for less than a minute! Crawford's edge was that he had a certain table presence that was cunning and at the same time intimidating. It was this trait that led Jacoby to admit that Crawford was an even better Gin player than he was.

Bet You Didn't Know

Strategy

In John Crawford's *"How to Be a Consistent Winner in the Most Popular Card Games,"* he gave many valuable pointers for winning at Oklahoma Gin. Among them were the following:

1) Always remember the knock card number.

2) The first object is to get on score (so there is no chance of being schneidered).

3) With a high knock card (10, 9, or 8), play for two melds and a quick knock.

4) With a low knock card (5, 4, 3 or 2), aim for three melds.

5) With a low knock card, discard a lot more freely.

6) On a must-gin hand, remember kings and aces are the least valuable cards.

7) With a low knock card it often pays to block your opponent by breaking up your hand.

Gin Rummy for Three Players

There are two methods for playing three-hand Gin Rummy in which two players are active and one is inactive in each hand. In another method, all three players may be active in every hand.

First method. Each player cuts the deck. The player with the lowest card sits out the first hand; the player with the next deals. At the end of each hand, the loser goes out and the idle player takes his place. The score sheet should have three columns, since each participant plays for himself, and winning hands are credited to individual scores. The idle player may not advise either of the active players. The game ends when a player reaches 100 points or more; after game and box bonuses have been added, each player pays the difference in scores to each player having a higher score. If one player is shut out, he pays an additional 100 points to the winner.

Second method. Each player draws a card; the high player is "in the box," and the two others play as partners against him throughout the game. The partner drawing the second-highest card deals the first hand, and the other partner sits out but may consult on the play, with the active partner having the final decision. When the active partner loses a hand, the idle partner takes his place. One score is kept for the player in the box, another for the partnership; if the player in the box wins, he collects in full from each opponent. If the partners win, each collects in full from the player in the box.

Third method. All three players participate. Each player draws a card. The player with the highest card deals, and the player with the next-highest card sits on the dealer's left. Ten cards are dealt to each of the three players. The player to the left of the dealer plays first; if he refuses the upcard, the player to his left may take it. Thereafter, each player in turn may draw either of his opponents' previous discards, unless one of them has already been taken.

An individual score is kept for each player. The winner of each hand scores the difference between his count and the combined counts of the other two players.

There is no undercut bonus; if the knocker is tied, the player who ties him wins the hand, and 20 points are deducted from the knocker's score.

The other two players may lay off cards only on the knocker's hand, and only on the original matched sets. *For example:* If the knocker has ♥9, 8, 7, and one opponent lays off ♥6 on it, the other opponent may not lay off ♥5. The bonus for going gin is 40 points. When only three cards remain in the stock and no one has knocked, the hand ends in a draw, and there is no scoring.

The game ends when a player reaches 200 points, after which bonuses are added as in two-hand Gin Rummy, and each player pays the difference in scores to any player having a higher score.

Partnership Gin Rummy *(for Four Players)*

The players draw for partnerships. The holders of the the two highest cards each play a two-hand game against the players with the two lowest cards. Partners sit opposite each other at the table. One member of each side cuts for deal, and both members of the side with the lowest card deal the first hand. Thereafter, the winners of each hand deal next.

Each dealer deals to the opponent on his right for the first hand and thereafter, the players alternate opponents.

Only one score is kept for each partnership, so that if one member wins his hand by 12 points and the other member loses his by 10 points, that side wins the hand by 2 points and will eventually receive a box bonus when the game is over.

When one member of a partnership knocks, either player in the opposing partnership may delay play until he learns how many points were scored. When one hand is finished, the idle player may advise his partner (after the partner's opponent has knocked) as to the best way of matching the hand, or laying off.

Drawn hands are not replayed. The game does not end until one side reaches 125 points, but all other scoring is the same as in regular Gin Rummy.

For Six or More Players *(in Even Numbers)*

Half the players form one partnership against the other half. All partners sit on one side of the table, and each plays against the opponent facing him, never changing opponents during the game. One partner draws for deal on each side, and all members of the side drawing the lower card deal the first hand. Thereafter, all members of the winning side deal the next hand.

Each player plays a regular two-hand game against the player facing him and the results of all these two-hand matches are added up for each side and then compared to determine the winning side of each deal.

The game ends when:

1) A partnership of 3 or 4 players reaches 150 points.

2) A partnership of five players reaches 175 points.

3) A partnership of six or more players reaches 200 points.

A player whose hand is finished may advise any of his teammates, but only if he has not seen the hand of any opponent.

Drawn hands are not replayed.

Round-The-Corner Gin Rummy

Round-The-Corner may be played as a version of Gin Rummy, but with the following differences:

The ace may rank high or low in a sequence, and sequences may go around the corner (A, 2, 3, A, K, Q, K, A, 2). As an unmatched card, an ace counts 15 points.

"Round-the-Corner" sequence

Unlike other Gin Rummy versions, if a knocker goes gin, the opponent is allowed to lay his cards off, and if the opponent can reduce his own count to zero, neither player scores on that hand.

The game ends when one player reaches 125 points. In any partnership game, it takes 25 points more to end the game than when regular Partnership Gin Rummy is played with the round-the-corner features.

Players may at all times inspect the previous discards.

RUMMY
(Rum)

NUMBER OF PLAYERS	NUMBER OF CARDS	GAME PLAY	SKILL LEVEL
2-6	**52**	◇ ◆ ◇ ◇ ◇ EASY → COMPLEX	◇ ◇ ◇ ◆ ◇ LUCK → SKILL

Rummy is still one of the best-known card games in the United States, though in many regions it has been superseded by Gin Rummy and Oklahoma Gin. Rummy works better than Gin Rummy when there are more than two players. A pleasing feature of the game is that it is so simple to play and has many variations.

Number of Players. Two to six people can play, and each person plays individually. More than six players should play Double Rum, 500 Rum, or Contract Rummy.

The Pack. The standard 52-card pack is used.

Rank of Cards. K (high), Q, J, 10, 9, 8, 7, 6, 5, 4, 3, 2, A. (In many forms of Rummy, the ace may rank either high or low.)

The Shuffle and Cut. The players draw or cut for deal and the player with the lowest card deals first. Each player may shuffle, the dealer last, although it is customary for the dealer alone to shuffle. The player on the dealer's right cuts.

The Deal. The dealer gives one card at a time, clockwise, face down, beginning with the player on his left. When two people play, each person gets 10 cards. When three or four people play, each receives seven cards; when five or six play, each receives six cards. The remaining cards are placed face down on the table, forming the stock. The top card of the stock is turned face up and becomes the upcard. It is placed next to the stock to start the discard pile.

When two people play, the winner of each hand deals the next. When more than two play, the deal passes to next the player on the left.

Object of the Game. Each player tries to form matched sets consisting of groups of three or four of a kind, or sequences of three or more cards of the same suit.

The Play. Each player in turn, beginning with the player to the left of the dealer, either draws the top card of the stock or takes the top card of the discard pile and adds it to his hand. The player may also lay down on the table, face up, any meld (matched set). If the player does not wish to lay down a meld, he discards one card, face up, onto the discard pile. If the player has drawn from the discard pile, he may not discard the same card on that turn.

Laying off. A player in turn may add one or more from his hand to any matched set already shown on the table. Thus, if threes are showing, he may add the fourth three; if ♥10, 9, 8 are showing, he may add ♥J, or ♥Q, J, ♥7, or ♥7, 6.

Going out. When a player gets rid of all his cards, he wins the game. If all his remaining cards are matched, the player may lay them down without discarding on his last turn. This ends the game and there is no further play (see scoring).

If the last card of the stock has been drawn and no player has gone out, the next player in turn may either take the top of the discard pile, or may turn the discard pile over to form a new stock (without shuffling it) and draw the top card. Play then proceeds as before.

Scoring. Each player pays to the winner the pip value of the cards remaining in his hand, whether the cards form matched sets or not. Face

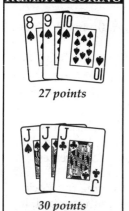

27 points

30 points

cards count 10 each, aces 1 each, and every other card its pip value.

A player goes "rummy" when he gets rid of all cards in his hand at once, without previously having put down or laid off any cards. In this event, every other player pays him double – twice what his opponents would otherwise owe.

Queen City Rum

This version is the same as regular Rummy except that seven cards are dealt to each player and the following special rules are observed:

A player may not meld until he can go rummy. When the player goes out, he may meld seven or eight cards, so that he need not discard (unless the discard helps him to go out.)

The winner collects the point value of his hand from every opponent. He does not collect the value of his opponents' hands, and is never paid double.

Boat House Rum

The rules are as in regular Rummy except that each player in turn may draw two cards from the stock or, before drawing those cards, two cards from the top of the discard pile. Then he discards only one card. Play does not end until a player can lay down his entire hand at once.

An ace counts either high or low in a sequence, and sequences may go round the corner as in K, A, 2, or A, K, Q.

In scoring, a player pays only for cards in his which does not form matched sets. He pays the pip value of all unmatched cards, with the ace counting as 11 points.

Kaluki
(Caloochi, Kaloochi, Kalougi)

This game is best for two, three, or four people, each playing individually. The rules are the same as for regular Rummy with the following exceptions.

Two standard 52-card packs plus four jokers are shuffled together to make a 108-card pack. Each person is dealt 15 cards (with five players, 13 cards; with six, 11 cards). Aces count 15 points each, face cards 10 each, and other cards their pip value. A player's first meld must count 51 or more. The ace is high or low, so A, 2, 3 or A, K, Q is a valid meld but not 2, A, K.

A player may not take the top discard, or lay off, until he has made his first meld. However, a player may take the discard if he uses it immediately to make his first meld. Jokers are wild. A joker used in a meld counts the same number of points as the card it represents. Before melding or discarding, a player may trade the appropriate natural card for a melded joker in any other player's meld and then use the joker as he wishes.

The player who goes out scores all the points remaining in his opponents' hands. A joker left in a hand counts as 25 points.

Double Rum

In this version, the rules of regular Rummy apply except for the following:

Two standard 52 card packs plus two jokers are shuffled together to form a 106-card deck.

Ten cards are dealt to each player.

An ace may count either high or low in sequences.

A matched set may be formed from any three or more cards of the same rank, such as ♠K, ♠K, ♦K. A joker is wild in any matched set or sequence.

In laying off on a sequence that contains a joker, a player may move the joker if it falls at the end of the sequence, but not if it lies within the interior of the sequence. Thus, if ♥7, ♥6, joker are on the table, either ♥8 or ♥5 may be added (but not ♥4); if ♥7, joker, ♥5 are on the table, only ♥8 or ♥4 may be added. (A joker can be moved only once.)

In scoring, a player is charged 15 points for each joker and 11 for each ace in his hand. The other cards count as in regular Rummy.

Knock Rummy
(Poker Rum)

Number of Players. Two, three, four, or five people can play.

The Pack. The standard 52-card pack is used.

Rank of Cards. K (high), Q, J, 10, 9, 8, 7, 6, 5, 4, 3, 2, A.

The Deal. The players draw for deal, and the player with the lowest card deals first. When two people play, each is dealt ten cards; when three or four play, seven cards; when five play, six cards.

Card Values. Each face card counts 10 points; each ace counts 1 point; other cards count their pip values.

The Play. The players either draw or take the upcard, and then discard as in Rummy, but they do not meld cards on the table or lay off on each other's melds. Any player, before discarding, may knock, ending the hand. He then discards, separates his melds from unmatched cards, and announces the count of the unmatched cards. Each opponent then separates his melds from unmatched cards and announces his count as well.

Scoring. The player with the lowest count wins the difference in counts from each opponent plus 25 points if he goes rummy. If any other player ties the knocker for low count, that player wins instead of the knocker. If the knocker does not have the lowest count, he pays a penalty of 10 points plus the difference in counts to the player with the lowest count, who wins the hand.

Tunk
(Tonk)

This version of Knock Rummy is played several different ways. ("Tunk" or "Tonk" means "knock.")

Number of Players. Two to five or more people can play.

The Pack. Two to four players use a standard 52-card pack. Five or more use a double pack.

The Deal. Seven cards are dealt to each player. All remaining cards become the stock pile and the top card is drawn and placed face up next to it. This is the first card (upcard) of the discard pile.

The Play. Deuces are wild. Each player in turn must either draw from the stock or take the top discard, followed by discarding. Only the player on the dealer's left, whose turn comes first, may take the first upcard. Before discarding, the player may "tunk" (knock) if his unmatched cards count 5 or less. The player then spreads his hand, separating matched and unmatched cards. A matched set may have no more than four cards and must include two natural cards. A sequence may be three cards or more. Each other player then has one turn to draw, take the discard, meld, lay off on the tunker's melds, and discard. (If all the tunker's cards were matched, no one may lay off on his hand.)

After each player has had his turn, the count of each player's unmatched cards is scored against him. (A deuce counts only 2 points.) If the tunker does not have the lowest count, he is charged double his count. When a player's score reaches 100, he is out of the game. Play continues until there is only one player left, who is the winner.

If the stock is exhausted, the hand is redealt and there is no score.

Continental Rummy

This game is one of the most popular Rummy pastimes for large groups. It is played in many different forms, but always with the same basic requirements.

Number of Players. Two to 12 people can play.

The Pack. Two or more standard 52-card packs plus one joker per pack are shuffled together. Five or fewer players use a double pack, six to eight players a triple pack, nine to 12 players a quadruple pack.

Rank of Cards. A, K, Q, J, 10, 9, 8, 7, 6, 5, 4, 3, 2, A. (Aces may be high or low.)

The Shuffle and Cut. If a double pack is used, the dealer shuffles. If a triple pack or quadruple pack is used, the dealer and one other player each shuffle a portion of the pack, the dealer having the right to shuffle each portion last, and the portions are then combined. The player on the dealer's right cuts.

The Deal. Each player receives 15 cards, dealt three at a time. The winner of each deal becomes the next dealer. Note: When the pack is too thick for the dealer to handle, he may take the top portion and deal as far as it will go and then resume dealing with the remaining portion, as necessary.

Object of the Game. Each player tries to go out by forming sequences in accordance with the following requirements:

A player may not lay down any cards until he can go out all at once with five 3-card sequences, or three 4-card and one 3-card sequence, or one 5-card, one 4-card, and two 3-card sequences. Two or more of these sequences may be in the same suit, but a sequence may not "go round the corner." Matched sets do not count in Continental Rummy, only sequences do.

The Play. Each player in turn draws either the top card of the stock or the top card of the discard pile, and then discards, as in Rummy, until one player goes out. Any joker is wild and may represent any card its holder designates. (Many play with deuces also as wild cards.)

Scoring. The winner of the game collects from all the other players: 1 point (or chip, or similar counter) for game, 2 points for each joker used in the winner's hand, and 1 point for each deuce used as a wild card (if deuces are wild).

Variations. There are many variations, both in play and in scoring, including the following bonus payments, which are used in some localities: for going out right away without drawing a single card, 10 points; for going out after drawing only one card, 7 points; for going out without using a joker or wild deuce, 10 points; for having all 15 cards of the same suit, 10 points.

Irregularities. *Going down illegally.* If a player lays down a hand that does not conform to the requirements stated above, he must leave his hand face up on the table, and play proceeds with his hand exposed. Any collections he has made are returned. Any other player who has exposed his hand may pick it up.

CONTRACT RUMMY
(Shanghai Rummy, Liverpool Rummy, Joker Rummy)

NUMBER OF PLAYERS	NUMBER OF CARDS	GAME PLAY	SKILL LEVEL
3-8	**105** (158)	◇ ◇ ◆ ◇ ◇ EASY ➤ COMPLEX	◇ ◇ ◆ ◇ ◇ LUCK ➤ SKILL

One of the most popular Rummy games for three or more persons playing individually. There are many forms of the game, differing in minor details but all are alike in one essential respect: A series of four, five, or more deals is played, with a different requirement for going out in each deal. One of the most popular versions is given here.

Number of Players. Three to eight people can play. Each plays individually.

The Pack. For three or four players, a double pack with one joker is used (105 cards in all); five or more players use a triple pack with two jokers (158 cards in all). All the cards are shuffled together.

Rank of Cards. A, K, Q, J, 10, 9, 8, 7, 6, 5, 4, 3, 2, A. (Aces are high or low.)

Card Values. Ace, joker, and other wild cards, if any, count as 15 points; each face card counts 10; each other card counts its pip value.

The Shuffle and Cut. If a double pack is used, the dealer shuffles; if a triple pack is used, the dealer and one other player each shuffle a portion of the pack, the dealer having the right to shuffle each portion last, and the portions are then combined. The player to the dealer's right cuts.

The Deal. The players draw for deal from a spread pack. Low card has the first deal, ace being low in the draw. Each game consists of seven deals, the turn to deal passing from player to player to the left. Cards are dealt clockwise face down, one at a time beginning on the dealer's left. Note: When the pack is too thick for the dealer to handle, he may take the top portion and deal as far as it will go, and then resume dealing with the remaining portion, if necessary.

In each of the first four deals, each player receives 10 cards.

In each of the last three deals, each player receives 12 cards.

The remainder of the pack is put in the center as the stock, and the top card is turned face up to begin the discard pile next to the stock.

Two Matched Sets

One Matched Set and One Sequence

Object of the Game. Each player tries to get rid of all his cards by laying down matched sets of three or more (regardless of suit) and sequences of four or more cards of the same suit, in accordance with the "Basic Contract" rules of the deal.

Basic Contracts:

First deal: Two matched sets (sometimes called books), which a player must lay down at the same time before he can lay off any other cards.

Second deal: One matched set and one sequence (sometimes called a run).

Third deal: Two sequences, or runs.

Fourth deal: Three matched sets, or books.

Fifth deal: Two matched sets and one sequence.

Sixth deal: One matched set and two sequences.

Seventh deal: Three sequences, but no cards may be laid down until one player can lay down his entire hand, matched in sets, to form the basic contract. The game ends after the seventh deal.

It should be noted that the basic contract in the first deal requires six cards, in the second deal seven cards, and so forth, increasing by one card each time.

When two or more sequences are required, they must be in different suits (or, if in the same suit, not in consecutive order, such as ♥2, 3, 4, 5, 7, 8, 9, 10; but not ♥2, 3, 4, 5, 6, 7, 8, 9, which counts as only one sequence).

The Play. Beginning with the person to the dealer's left, each player must draw either the top of the stock or the top card of the discard pile, and then discard. Just before discarding, provided he has laid down the basic contract, the player may lay off any cards that match a set already on the table, but may not lay down any more matched sets.

If the player does not want the top of the discard pile, any other player, in order of rotation to his left, may claim that card and must also draw the top card of the stock, as a penalty card, without discarding. The original player then draws the top card of the stock and play proceeds.

As the ace counts as either high or low, it may be laid off as a low card on a sequence that already includes the ace as high card, and vice versa.

For example: A, 2, 3, 4, 5, 6, 7, 8, 9, 10, J, Q, K, A – would be a 14-card sequence. A sequence cannot contain more than 14 cards.

Wild Cards. A joker may be used to stand as any card in a matched set or a sequence. When a joker has been laid down as part of a sequence, any other player (provided he has laid down the basic contract) may take the joker into his hand by substituting the card it represents. If more than one player is able to do this, the one with the next turn to play has precedence.

When a joker has been used in a sequence, any card not already in that sequence may be laid off on it, and the wild card moves to either end. *For example:* if ♦9, joker, ♦7, ♦6 are shown, the ♦8 may be added and the joker moved to either end.

Scoring. In each deal, play ends when any player gets rid of his last card. Each other player is then charged the pip value of each card remaining in his hand. The player having the lowest score at the end of the seventh deal is the winner.

Conquian
(Coon-Can)

This was the original type of Rummy played in the United States.

Number of Players. Two people play.

The Pack. A standard pack of 52 cards with all the tens, nines and eights removed, leaving a total of 40 cards in the deck.

Rank of Cards. The jack and seven are considered to be in sequence. The rank of an ace is low only so that the sequence A, 2, 3 can be formed, but not A, K, Q.

The Deal. Each of the two players is dealt 10 cards. The remaining cards form the stock; no upcard is turned.

The Play. After the deal is completed, the non-dealer turns up the top card of the stock. He does not put it into his hand but must immediately meld it, along with cards from his hand, or discard it. Melds ("spreads") are as in regular Rummy – matched sets of three or four or a sequence of three or more cards of the same suit. Each player in turn thereafter must either take the top discard and meld it (placing the meld face up on the table), or turn up the top card of the stock and meld or discard it. When the player takes and melds a discard, he must then discard from his hand. If a player is able to add the discard to one of his previous melds, the opponent may require him to do so, and then discard.

After turning up the top card of the stock, and before discarding it, a player may meld or lay off from his or her hand if he wishes.

A player may shift his own melds around as long as only valid melds remain. *For example:* If he previously melded ♥J, 7, 6 and the ♥5 is drawn or discarded, he may add it to the sequence, remove the jack, and meld three jacks.

The game ends when a player has melded exactly 11 cards. Therefore, a player may have no card left in his hand but still continues to play because he needs another melded card to go out. Each deal is a separate game, and if the stock is exhausted before either player has melded 11 cards, the next game counts double.

500 RUM
(Pinochle Rummy)

NUMBER OF PLAYERS	NUMBER OF CARDS	GAME PLAY	SKILL LEVEL
3-5 (2, 6-8)	**52** (104)	◊ ◊ ◆ ◊ ◊ EASY ➤ COMPLEX	◊ ◊ ◊ ◆ ◊ LUCK ➤ SKILL

The game of Canasta and several other games developed from this popular form of Rummy. The distinctive feature of 500 Rum is that each player scores the value of the sets he melds, in addition to the usual points for going out and for cards caught in other players' hands. 500 Rum is one of the finest games in the Rummy family, and it deserves to have an even bigger following than it does.

Number of Players. Two to eight persons may play, but the game is best played with three, four, or five people. Four may play as partners (see Persian Rummy, p. 142).

The Pack. A standard 52-card pack is used. Five or more players should use a double pack.

Rank of Cards. Ace (high or low), K, Q, J, 10, 9, 8, 7, 6, 5, 4, 3, 2, A.

Card Values. An ace counts as 15 points, except in the sequence 3, 2, A, when it counts as 1. Face cards count as 10 points each. Other cards count their pip value.

The Shuffle and Cut. The players draw for deal, low dealing first. Ace is the lowest card in the draw. The dealer shuffles, and the player to the right cuts

The Deal. The dealer completes the cut and deals seven cards to each player (except in the two-hand game, in which each player receives 13 cards).

Object of the Game. To score points by laying down and laying off cards as in regular Rummy, in matched sets of three or four, and in sequences of three or more cards of the same suit.

The Play. The undealt portion of the cards, placed face down, forms the stock; the top card is turned face up and is placed beside the stock as the upcard to start the discard pile. The discard pile should be slightly spread, so that players can readily see all the cards in it. Each player in turn, beginning with the player to the left of the dealer, may draw either the top card of the stock or any card from the discard pile. There are two conditions when drawing a card from the discard pile: 1) the player must take all the cards above the selected card and 2) the card so drawn must immediately be used, either by laying it down in a set or by laying it off on a set already on the table. The remaining cards taken with the discard may be melded in the same turn or simply added to the player's hand.

Each player in turn, after drawing but before discarding, may lay down any matched set or may lay off any card that matches a set already on the table. Cards that are laid off are kept on the table in front of the player.

Sequences may not "go round the corner"; thus, A, K, Q or A, 2, 3 may be melded, but not K, A, 2.

Scoring. When any player gets rid of all his cards, the play immediately ends. Each player's score is then figured as follows: The player is credited with the point value of all cards that he has showing on the table. From this figure is subtracted the point value of all cards remaining in his hand. The difference is added or subtracted from his score, as the case may be. *For example:* If the cards he has shown total 87 points, and the cards left in his hand total 90 points, 3 points are subtracted from his previous net score.

The first player whose score reaches +500 wins the game and collects from each opponent the difference between their final scores. If two or more players reach 500 on the same hand, the one with the highest score is the winner.

When a player lays off a card, he keeps it on the table in front of him for convenience in scoring later, but must state to what showing combination it is being added. Thus, if ♦J, 10, 9 are on the table, along with the set ♠Q, ♥Q, ♣Q, a player putting down the ♦Q must state to which set it belongs: If the player makes the queen part of the diamond sequence, any player may later add ♦K to that sequence.

Partnership 500 Rum

Four play, two against two as partners, with partners facing each other across the table. The rules are exactly as in 500 Rum, except the partners may play off on each other's matched sets and sequences in an effort to go out as quickly as possible. When any player goes out, the play ends and the score of each partnership is figured as a unit. The game is over when either side reaches +500.

Persian Rummy

The game is the same as Partnership 500 Rum with the following exceptions.

The pack is 56 cards: the standard 52 cards plus four jokers.

Each joker counts as 20 points, and jokers may not be used in sequences or as wild cards, but only in groups of three or four jokers. Any meld of four, laid down all at once, counts double its face value. Thus, four jokers laid down together count 160; three jokers laid down count 60, and the fourth joker when added counts only 20 more. Four 6s put down together count 48, but three 6s count only 18, and the fourth 6 adds only 6 points. If a player gets rid of all his cards, his side scores a bonus of 25.

A game ends after two deals. The side with the best score receives a bonus of 50 points and wins the difference between its final score and the opponents' score.

Michigan Rum

This game is played the same as 500 Rum, except for the following:

Melds are scored as they are put on the table. The player who goes out first is the winner. The cards left in the hands of the other players are not subtracted from their scores. Rather, the winner is credited with the total of all the points remaining in the opponents' hands.

CANASTA

NUMBER OF PLAYERS	NUMBER OF CARDS	GAME PLAY	SKILL LEVEL
4 (2, 3, 5, 6)	**108**	◇ ◇ ◇ ◇ ◆ EASY → COMPLEX	◇ ◇ ◇ ◆ ◇ LUCK → SKILL

Canasta, a game of the Rummy family was the most popular American game in the early 1950s. It originated in Uruguay about 10 years earlier, spread rapidly to Argentina and the rest of Latin America, and reached the United States about 1948. It is still played by millions. The word canasta means "basket" in Spanish, and the game was probably named for the tray used to hold the discards. The rules given below are the official rules, which very serious players use; however, many players have adopted one or more other versions, such as Bolivia, Samba and Chile, which are described later.

Number of Players. Four people, in two partnerships, can play. (Canasta may also be played by two, three, five, or six players. The rules for these forms are described later.)

The Pack. Two standard packs of 52 cards are used, plus four jokers, all shuffled together, giving a total of 108 cards.

Wild cards. Jokers and deuces are wild. A wild card is melded only with natural cards and then becomes a card of that same rank.

All 2s and Jokers are wild

The Draw. Partnerships may be determined by drawing cards from the deck. The player drawing the highest card has choice of seats, plays first in the first deal, and has the player drawing the second-highest card as his partner. In drawing, the cards rank: A (high), K, Q, J, 10, 9, 8, 7, 6, 5, 4, 3, 2. Jokers are void. Only for the draw, suits rank: Spades (high), hearts, diamonds, clubs. Players drawing equal cards or jokers must draw again. A player drawing more than one card or one of the four cards at either end of the deck, must draw again. Partners sit opposite each other.

Canasta Rank of Suits (only for the draw)

The Shuffle and Cut. The first hand is dealt by the player to the right of the person who drew the highest card. Thereafter the turn to deal rotates clockwise. Any player who wishes may shuffle the deck, and the dealer has the right to shuffle last. After the shuffle, the deck is cut by the player to the dealer's left.

The Deal. The dealer gives 11 cards face down to each player, one at a time, clockwise, beginning with the opponent on his left and ending with himself.

The undealt remainder of the pack is placed face down in the center of the table, becoming the stock, and the top card is turned face up beside it. If the upcard is a joker, deuce or three, one or more additional cards must be turned upon it until a "natural" card (a four or higher) appears.

Red Threes. A player finding a red three in his hand must, on his first turn, put it face up on the table and draw a replacement from the stock. A player who draws a red three from the stock also lays it on the table face up and draws a replacement. Finally, a player who takes the discard pile and finds a red three in it must place the three face up on the table but does not draw a replacement.

Each red three has a bonus value of 100 points, but if one side has all four red threes, they count 200 each, or 800 in all. The value of the red threes is credited to a side that has made a meld, or debited against a side that has made no meld, when the hand ends.

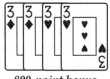

100-point bonus for each red 3 *800-point bonus for all red 3s*

Object of the Game. The principal object of play is to form melds – combinations of three or more cards of the same rank – with or without the help of wild cards. (Sequences are not valid melds.)

The Play. The player to left of the dealer plays first. Thereafter, the turn to play rotates clockwise (to the left). Each turn comprises a draw, a meld (optional) after drawing, and a discard, which ends the player's turn.

When his turn comes, a player is always entitled to draw the top card of the stock. Or, if the player wishes, he may instead (subject to restrictions under "Taking the Discard Pile" – see p. 148) take the top card of the discard pile to use it in a meld; having done so, he must take the rest of the discard pile.

The discard is always one card from the hand (never from a meld). All discards are placed in one pile beside the stock (on the upcard, if it is still there), and the discard pile must be kept squared up, except as noted later.

Melds. A meld is valid if it contains at least two natural cards of the same rank – aces down to fours inclusive – and not more than three wild cards. Jokers and deuces may never be melded apart from natural cards. A set of three or four black threes (without wild cards) may be melded only when a player goes out.

To count plus, a meld must be laid on the table face up during a person's turn to play. All cards that are left in the hand when play ends, even though they form melds, count minus.

A player may meld as many cards as he pleases, of one rank or different ranks, forming new melds or adding cards to previous melds. (But see restrictions on "Going Out".) All the melds of a partnership are placed in front of either partner. A partnership may meld in a rank already melded by the opponents, but may not make two different melds of the same rank.

A player may add additional cards to a meld by his side, provided that the melds remain valid (having no more than three wild cards). He may not add cards to the opponents' melds.

Meld examples

Canastas. A meld comprising seven or more cards, including at least four natural cards (called a "base"), is a canasta. In addition to the point values of the cards, a canasta earns a bonus of 500 for a natural or "pure" canasta (one that has no wild card), and 300 for a mixed canasta (one that has one to three wild cards).

A completed canasta is squared up with a red card on top to indicate a natural one and a black card on top to indicate a mixed canasta. Additional cards may be added to a canasta to score their point values, but these do not affect the bonus – except that a wild card added to a natural canasta reduces it to a mixed canasta (and a black card replaces the red card that was previously on top).

Natural Canasta

Mixed Canasta

Minimum Count. Every card has a fixed point value, as follows:

Each joker 50

Each deuce 20

Each ace 20

Each K, Q, J, 10, 9, 8 10

Each 7, 6 ,5, 4, and black 3 5

A partnership's first meld (its "initial" meld) must meet a minimum count requirement that depends on the accumulated score of that side at the time, as follows:

Accumulated Score (at beginning of the deal)   *Minimum Count*

Minus 15

0 to 1,495 50

1,500 to 2,995 90

3,000 or more 120

The count of a meld is the total point value of the cards in it. To meet the minimum, a player may make two or more different melds. If he takes the discard pile, the top card but no other may count toward the requirement. Bonuses for red threes and canastas do not count toward the minimum.

After a side has made its initial meld, either partner may make any valid meld without reference to any minimum count.

Freezing the Discard Pile. The discard pile is frozen against a side before that side has made its initial meld. The initial meld unfreezes it for both partners, provided that it is not frozen again as described below.

The discard pile is frozen when a red three is turned as an upcard or if a wild card or a black three is turned as an upcard or discarded. (The lowermost freezing card of the pile is turned sidewise to indicate the freeze.)

Unfreezing the Discard pile. A frozen discard pile is unfrozen only by being taken. When the discard pile is topped by a wild card or a black three, at least one natural card must be discarded on top of the pile before the pile may be taken. Then, a player may take that card (and the pile) only with a natural pair of the same rank from his hand. Before touching the discard pile, the player should show the pair (together with any additional cards if needed to meet the minimum count of an initial meld).

Taking the Discard Pile. When the discard pile is not frozen against his side, a player may take it: a) with a natural pair matching the top card as above; or b) by melding the top card with one matching natural card and one wild card from his hand; or c) by adding the top card to a meld he already has on the table.

Having taken and melded the top discard as described, the player takes the rest of the pile into his hand and may then meld some or all of the additional cards as he pleases.

The discard pile may never be taken when its top card is a wild card, a black three, or a red three.

Information. A player may:

1) Examine the discard pile during his first turn before he discards.

2) Call attention to the correct minimum count needed if his partner is making an initial meld.

3) Remind his partner to declare red threes or draw replacements.

4) Turn the sixth card of a meld crosswise to indicate that only one more card is needed to complete a canasta.

CANASTA AND OTHER FADS

By the late 1940s, a Latin American game named Canasta had spread like wildfire to the United States. Soon it was played everywhere, from beach resorts at the Jersey Shore to fashionable clubs in California. The game became the biggest fad since Mah-Jongg in the 1920s and crossword puzzles in the 1930s.
Albert H. Morehead has pointed out that Canasta and Mah-Jongg are much alike, in that both are Rummy-type games, and that "each had its boom period a few years after a World War." In the early 1950s, Canasta surpassed even Contract Bridge in popularity, and it is still one of the most widely-played card games in the country. The next game to reach fad proportions was Backgammon in the 1970s.

When its his turn to play, a player is entitled to be informed of a) the minimum count requirement or score (at the beginning of the hand) of either side; b) the number of cards held by any player; and c) the number of cards remaining in the stock. If a player's hand is reduced to one card, he may announce this fact.

Going Out. A player goes out when he gets rid of the last card in his hand by discarding or melding it, provided that his side has melded at least one canasta or he completes a canasta while going out. Failing this requirement, he must keep at least one card in his hand. When a player goes out, the hand ends and the results on both sides are scored.

A player need not make a discard in going out; he may meld all his remaining cards.

A player with only one card left in his hand may not take the discard pile if there is only one card in it.

Permission to Go Out. If a player sees that he is able to go out, before or after drawing, the player may say "Partner, may I go out?" The partner must answer "Yes" or "No," and the answer is binding. Before responding, the partner may obtain the information specified under "Information" (see above).

A player may not ask "Partner, may I go out?" after having melded any card or having indicated the intention to take the discard pile. However, he may go out without asking permission.

Concealed Hand. A player goes out "concealed" when he melds his entire hand in one turn, including at least one canasta, without having made an earlier meld and without previously having added any card to melds that his partner has made. If his partner has not made an initial meld, the player must meet the minimum count (without the canasta bonus) if he has taken the discard pile, but need not do so if he has drawn from the stock.

Exhausting the Stock. If a player draws the last card of the stock and it is a red three, he reveals it. The player may not then meld or discard, and play ends.

If the last card of the stock is not a red three, play continues as long as each player in turn takes the discard, and he must do so if it matches a meld on his side and the pack is not frozen. (The only exception is that a one-card hand may not take a one-card discard pile). A player does not have to take the discard to form a new meld. The play ends when a player cannot take the discard or legally refuses to take it.

Scoring a Deal. A partnership's base score is determined by totaling all applicable items in the following schedule:

For each natural canasta	500
For each mixed canasta	300
For each red three	100

(All four red threes count 800)

For going out	100
For going out concealed (extra)	100

A partnership's score for the hand is the values of all cards that were melded, minus the values of the cards left in both hands. In other words, the final score of a side for a deal is the net of its base and point scores. (It may be minus.)

Scoring a Game. The score should be recorded on a sheet of paper divided into two columns, one for each side. (Customarily, the columns are marked WE and THEY.) Each entry should show the scores of the previous deal, together with the accumulated totals (which determine the initial meld requirement).

The side that first reaches a total of 5,000 wins a game. The final deal is played out even though it is obvious that one or both sides have surely reached 5,000. There is no bonus for winning a game; the margin of victory is the difference of the final totals.

Canasta Customs. The discard pile is called "the pack" (or, by some players, "the deck") and taking it is called "taking the pack." A player who can find no safe discard is said to be "squeezed."

The partner who melds first keeps the melds and red threes for his side throughout the deal.

When a game ends, each side reckons its total score to the nearest hundred, counting 50 or more points as 100. The winners then receive the difference between these net scores.

Two-Hand Canasta

The standard Canasta rules apply, except as follows.

Each player receives 15 cards. A draw from the stock comprises two cards instead of one, but only one card is discarded in a turn. A player must have two canastas to go out. The penalties for red cards and insufficient melds do not apply.

Cutthroat Canasta *(for Three Players)*

Cutthroat Canasta is played in the same way as standard Canasta, but in this version, two sides are formed during the play, two against one, and the following rule changes apply.

The Draw. In drawing from the stock, a player takes two cards, but discards only one.

Lone Hand. The player who first takes the discard pile becomes the "lone hand." The other two players join in partnership against the lone hand, combining their melds and otherwise aiding each other. If a player goes out before the discard pile has ever been taken, he becomes lone hand and the other two score as a partnership.

Initial Meld. The initial meld requirement for a player depends on his own score. Thus, one partner can have a higher requirement than the other.

Scoring. A red three counts only for the owner, plus or minus depending on whether or not his side has melded. The base scores of the partners therefore differ if they have not drawn an equal number of red threes.

All other scores made by the partnership are totaled, and each partner receives the total, plus or minus his own red threes. Game is 7,500. The score sheet is divided into three columns, and each player's name is placed at the top of a column.

Stock Exhausted. If no one goes out, play ends with the discard of the player who drew the last card of the stock. If the discard pile was never taken, each player scores for himself.

Five-Hand Canasta

One side has three players, who take turns sitting out while the other two play the deal against the opponents. A regular four-hand game is played. The player sitting out may not give any advice to his teammates, and may not call attention to irregularities except in scoring after the play is completed.

Six-Hand Canasta *(Three-Pack Canasta)*

The rules of standard Canasta apply, except as follows:

There may be two partnerships of three players each, seated A, B, A, B, A, B (each player seated between two opponents), or there may be three partnerships of two players each, seated A, B, C, A, B, C.

A triple pack is used – three standard 52-card packs plus six jokers, shuffled together. Thirteen cards are dealt to each player. When there are three partnerships, game is 7,500. When there are two partnerships, game is 10,000; and when a side reaches 7,000, it needs 150 to make its initial meld. Four red threes count only 100 each; five red threes, 1,000 in all; six red threes, 1,200 in all. A side needs two canastas to go out. Six-hand Canasta has been largely superseded by Samba and other later forms of Canasta described in the following pages.

Variations of Canasta

In the years since Canasta first became popular, several variations have arisen, some of which have made the game just as exciting, or even more so, according to devotees. Other versions are regarded by many as having ruined the game.

Even in the original game of Canasta, two variations are generally played:

1) A player may not take the top discard to add to a completed canasta of his side, even if the pack is not frozen.

2) A player always needs a natural matching pair to take the pack for a meld, but he may take an unfrozen pack and add the top card to a meld that is less than a canasta.

Many versions, the first of which was Samba but which later came to include Bolivia, Chilean, Cuban, and Brazilian Canasta, to name a few, incorporate the two variations stated above, plus one or more of the following:

3) Three packs plus six jokers are used.

4) Sequences may be melded and a seven-card sequence ranks as a canasta.

5) Wild cards may be melded, and a seven-card meld of wild cards ranks as a canasta and scores a higher number of points.

6) In drawing from the stock, a player takes two cards and discards only one.

7) A side needs two canastas to go out.

Many of these variations are included in the versions of Canasta described next.

SAMBA

NUMBER OF PLAYERS	NUMBER OF CARDS	GAME PLAY	SKILL LEVEL
4	162	◇ ◇ ◇ ◇ ◆ EASY → COMPLEX	◇ ◇ ◇ ◆ ◇ LUCK → SKILL

As with the original Canasta game, Samba became a fad for a number of years. Its big novelty is that three packs of cards are used; when the game's popularity was at its height, a number of card manufacturers sold triple decks of cards in one package expressly for playing Samba.

Number of Players. Four people play in two partnerships as in Canasta.

The Pack. Three standard 52-card packs plus six jokers for a total of 162 cards.

The Deal. The dealer distributes 15 cards to each player. When drawing from the stock, a player takes two cards and discards one. The discard pile may be taken only with a natural matching pair or, when it is not frozen, the top card can be added to a meld that is less than a canasta (including a "sequence meld" — *see next section*). The top card may not be taken to start a sequence meld or combine with a card from the hand in adding to a sequence meld.

Samba Sequence Meld

Samba Sequence Canasta

Sequence Meld. Three or more cards of the same suit in sequence (ace high, four low) may be melded. Cards may be added until there are seven cards, at which point the meld becomes a "samba," or sequence canasta, ranking as a canasta but receiving a bonus of 1,500.

Wild Cards. Wild cards may not be melded separately, and no regular meld may contain more than two wild cards, and no sequence meld may contain any wild card.

Canastas. A side needs two canastas (mixed, natural, or samba) to go out. A side may have two canastas in the same rank and may combine its melds in the same rank at any time.

Scoring. Initial meld requirements are as follows: 15 with a minus score; 50 with a score of 0 to 1,495; 90 with 1,500 to 2,995; 120 with 3,000 to 6,995; 160 over 7,000. Game is 10,000, and there is a 200-point bonus for going out. No bonus is awarded for a concealed hand. Red threes are 100 each unless one side holds all six, in which case they count 1,000 for all, plus or minus. (Red threes count 100 minus against a side that has not completed two canastas.)

Bolivia

This is the same game as Samba with the following changes.

Wild Cards. Three or more wild cards may be melded. There is no distinction between deuces and jokers. A canasta of seven wild cards, called a "bolivia," counts 2,500. When the discard pile is topped by a wild card, it may not be taken.

Game. Game is 15,000. The initial meld requirement stays at 150 from 7,000 points up.

Going Out. At least one of the two canastas must be a sequence canasta, which in this game is called an "escalera" rather than a samba.

Black Threes. A black three left in the hand when any other player (including a partner) goes out counts minus 100 points. Black threes melded in going out count 5 points each.

Brazilian Canasta

This is the same as Bolivia but with some changes in the initial-meld requirements and scoring as follows:

Initial Meld. Game is 10,000. From 7,000 to 7,995 the initial meld must be a canasta (mixed or better); from 8,000 to 8,995 the canasta must be worth at least 200 points; from 9,000 to game it must be a natural canasta or better.

Discard Pile. The discard pile may not be taken for the initial meld.

Canastas. A wild-card canasta counts 2,000. A melded sequence of less than five cards costs a side 1,000 points when the hand ends. In going out, one may add to the ends of an escalera (sequence canasta).

Red Threes. One to four red threes count 100 points each, five count 1,000 in all, six count 1,200 in all. They count plus if a side has melded at least one canasta, minus if it has not.

Going Out. Before going out, a player must always ask permission of his partner. Going out is permitted if his side has melded any two canastas.

Chile

This is a three-pack version of Canasta (162 cards, including six jokers). Either sequences or wild-card melds are permitted, but not both.

Thus, players must agree which kind of meld is valid for that game. The draw from the stock is one card only, and only one canasta is required to go out. All other rules are the same as in standard Canasta.

Cuban Canasta

In this version, the standard 108-card pack for Canasta is used, but 13 cards are dealt to each player, rather than 11. Players draw one card at each turn. The discard pile may be taken only by matching its top card with a natural pair from the hand. Canastas may not contain more than seven cards, and only one canasta is required to go out. The scoring differences are as follows:

Game is 7,500. From 5,000 up, the initial meld must be 150.

Red threes count 100 points for one, 300 for two, 500 for three, 1,000 for all four. They count minus points unless a side has at least one canasta.

Black threes may not be discarded on the first round. Any black threes in the pack when the pack is taken are discarded and are put out of play, counting 5 points each for the side that took them. All four black threes together, whether discarded or melded, count 100.

Wild cards may be melded, and a canasta of wild cards counts as follows: 4,000 for seven deuces; 3,000 for four jokers and three deuces; 2,000 for any other combination of seven wild cards. Sequences may not be melded. A discard pile topped by a wild card may not be taken.

Going out earns a 100-point bonus.

Uruguay

Uruguay follows the rules of Canasta except for the following:

Three or more wild cards, up to seven, form a valid meld. A canasta of wild cards counts 2,000.

The discard pile may be taken only by matching its top card with a natural pair from the hand.

Mexicana

The basic rules of Canasta are followed (sequences and wild cards may not be melded; only one card per turn is drawn from the stock), plus the following special rules:

A triple pack is used with six jokers (a total of 162 cards). Each player is dealt 13 cards. When a player makes the initial meld for his side, this player draws the top 13 cards of the stock and adds them to his hand.

A canasta of sevens (natural or mixed) counts 1,000. The discard pile may not be taken when it is topped by a seven.

To go out, a side must have two canastas, plus at least as many red threes as it has canastas.

PENNIES FROM HEAVEN

NUMBER OF PLAYERS	NUMBER OF CARDS	GAME PLAY	SKILL LEVEL
6	216	◇ ◇ ◇ ◆ ◇ EASY → COMPLEX	◇ ◇ ◇ ◆ ◇ LUCK → SKILL

This Canasta version is for six players, playing in three partnerships. Lots of cards are used – even more than for Samba: four decks plus eight jokers (a total of 216 cards). One of the special features of Pennies from Heaven is that sevens play an unusual role.

The Deal. Partners sit A, B, C, A, B, C around the table. Players are dealt 13 cards one at a time, and then are dealt a packet of 11 cards face down. After completing the first canasta, a player takes the 11 cards into his hand.

The Play. Two cards are drawn from the stock and one card is discarded. Sevens may not be discarded until each side has completed a mixed or natural canasta of sevens. A seven may not be discarded in going out, and a canasta must not contain more than seven cards.

If all eight red threes are held by a side, that partnership receives a 1,000-point bonus. Otherwise, red threes score 100 points each. Red threes are subtracted from the score of a side that has not made a canasta of sevens.

Wild cards may be melded together. Other restrictions on wild cards follow the basic Canasta rules.

Going Out. Game is played to 20,000 points. To go out, a side must have a set of four canastas, but the four must be made up of one of each of the following: natural, mixed, seven, and wild.

Minimum Count. There are differences in minimum count as well as bonus values. *(See chart next page.)*

Accumulated Score *(at beginning of the deal)*

Minimum Count

Minus	15
0 to 495	50
500 to 995	90
1,000 to 1,495	120
1,500 or more	150

Bonus Values

Canasta	*Points*
Sevens	1,500
Wild Cards	1,000
Natural	500
Mixed	300

PANGUINGUE
(Pan)

NUMBER OF PLAYERS	NUMBER OF CARDS	GAME PLAY	SKILL LEVEL
6 – 8 (10 – 15)	**320**	◇ ◇ ◇ ◇ ◆ EASY → COMPLEX	◇ ◇ ◆ ◇ ◇ LUCK → SKILL

The game of Panguingue is the rage in areas of California and Southern Florida. It is a product of the Rummy family, but it is a gambling game, too. Imagine large round tables that seat up to 15 players, plus 320 playing cards, and hundreds of betting chips! Pan has a lot of action and a lot of devotees.

Number of Players. Any number of players, up to about 15 people can play, but the game is best played with six, seven, or eight people.

The Pack. Eight standard 52-card packs are used with the eights, nines and tens removed from each pack. (In some localities, as few as five packs are used.) Chips are used for settlement.

Rank of Cards. The cards in each suit rank: K (high), Q, J, 7, 6, 5, 4, 3, 2, A. The jack and seven are considered to be in sequence.

The Draw. A portion of the pack is shuffled and spread face down. Each player draws a card. The lowest card deals the first hand and has the choice of seats; if two or more players tie for low, they draw again. Other players take seats at random.

Rotation. The rotation of dealing and playing is to the right, not to the left as in most games. The first hand is therefore the player on the dealer's right. The winner of each hand becomes the first hand for the next, and the opponent on his left deals and deals first to that player.

The Shuffle. The player on dealer's left shuffles. Before the first deal, the eight packs are shuffled together thoroughly. After each hand, the discards are shuffled with a packet from the "foot" (bottom of the stock), to which they are then restored.

The Deal. The dealer gives each player 10 cards, in two rounds of five at a time, beginning with the first hand. For the deal, he should take from the top of the pack only such cards as he needs as nearly as can be estimated, taking more if needed or returning any excess to the top of the pack. After all hands are complete, the rest of the pack is placed face down on the table to form the stock, which is usually cut in two portions; the "head" is used in play, and the "foot" is set aside to be used if the head becomes exhausted. The top card of the stock is turned face up and set beside it to start the discard pile.

Going on Top. Before play begins, each player, starting with the first hand, declares whether he will stay in the play or retire. If he retires, he pays a forfeit, usually two chips. The player who retires is said to "go on top" because the forfeits are by custom stacked on the foot of the pack. Hands discarded by retiring players are not returned to the stock, but are kept separate, so that they may not be drawn in play. The "tops" (chips thus deposited) go to the player who goes out.

Object of the Game. The goal is to be the first player to meld all 11 cards in his hand.

The Play. Each player in turn, to the right, either must take the top card of the discard pile or the top card of the stock. A player may take from the discard pile only if the card 1) was drawn from the stock by the preceding player, and 2) can be immediately melded with the cards in the taker's hand. When a player draws from the stock, he must immediately meld the card or discard it (he may not put it in his hand and discard another unless the drawn card matches a meld of his right-hand opponent who has already melded 10 cards). To complete his turn, a player discards one card face up on the pile.

After drawing and before discarding, a player may meld as many sets as he holds or may add to his existing melds.

Melds. Each meld (or spread) must comprise at least three cards and may consist of as many as 11. The melds may be classified for convenience as sequences and matched sets, or just "sets." (Sequences are often called "stringers" or "ropes.")

Sequence. A sequence is a run of any three cards of the same suit, as ♥Q, J, 7.

Set. A set is three cards of the same rank and of different suits, as ♠4, ♥4, ♣4, or all of the same suit, as three ♣Q. In addition, any three aces or any three kings form a valid set regardless of suit, as ♦A, ♦A, ♣A. (Aces and kings are called "non-comoquers.")

Pan Set Examples

Pan Sequence Examples

Conditions. Certain melds are called "conditions." On melding a condition, the player immediately collects chips from every other player. All threes, fives, and sevens are "valle" (pronounced "valley") cards, that is,"cards of value." Cards of other rank are non-valle. The conditions are:

1) Any set of valle cards not in the same suit collects 1 chip from every player.

2) Any set of valle cards in the same suit collects 4 chips in spades, 2 chips in any other suit.

3) Any set of non-valle cards in the same suit collects 2 chips in spades, 1 chip in any other suit.

4) Any sequence of 3, 2, A in the same suit collects 2 chips in spades, 1 chip in any other suit.

5) Any sequence of K, Q, J in the same suit collects 2 chips in spades, 1 chip in any other suit.

Increasing. A player may add one or more cards to any of his melds, provided that the character of the meld is preserved. He may add a card of the same rank to a set of different suits or to a set of the same suit, another card of the same suit and rank. When cards are so added to a condition, the player collects the value of the original condition for each additional card except that for addition to a set of three valle cards in the same suit the payment is only 2 chips for spades, 1 chip for any other suit.

Through the addition of cards, one meld may be split into two, provided that each new part forms a valid meld in itself. *For example:* ♦J, 7, 6, 5 may be made into two melds by the addition of ♦Q, 4. If splitting a meld creates a condition, payment is duly collected. A player may take a card from one of his melds to complete a new meld, provided he leaves a valid meld. *Example:* From ♣7, 6, 5, 4, either the 7 or 4 may be borrowed, but not the 6 or 5.

Forcing Cards. If the top of the discard pile can be added to a meld of a person playing in turn, he is forced to take the card and meld it if another player demands that he do so.

Going Out. When any player shows 11 cards in melds, he collects 1 chip from every other player and also collects all over again for each condition in his cards. (In some games, a hand that has made no meld when another wins must pay 2 chips.)

When a player has melded 10 cards and needs only to pick up one card and meld it to bring his meld up to 11 cards, the player on his left may not discard a card that can be added to any of his melds, thereby putting his opponent out – unless the player on the left holds no safe card.

Any time a player holds exactly 31, he may "knock" immediately, and he wins the pot.

If a player knocks before the first round of exchanges have begun, the showdown occurs immediately, with no exchange of cards.

After the pot has been won, all the players put in chips for the next hand.

Irregularities. *Wrong number of cards.* If a player finds that he has more or less than ten cards before drawing for the first time, the dealer must withdraw any extra cards and put them with the discarded hands of retired players, or he deals the short hand right number of additional cards from the center of the pack. If, after a player's first draw, his hand is found to be incorrect, he must discard and retire from that deal, return all collections he has made for conditions, but continues to make payments due to others for conditions and winning.

Foul meld. If a player lays down any spread not conforming to the rules, he must make it valid on demand. If he cannot do so, any collections must be returned because of the improper spread and then legally proceed with his turn. If the player has already discarded, he must return all conditions made on that hand, and then he must discard his hand and retire from the play until the next deal. He must nevertheless continue to make payments due to others for conditions and winning. Exception: If the player has made the meld valid before attention is called to it, there is no penalty.

Chapter V

Hearts
and Other
Trick-Taking
Games

HEARTS
(Black Lady)

NUMBER OF PLAYERS	NUMBER OF CARDS	GAME PLAY	SKILL LEVEL
4 (3, 5-7)	**52**	◇ ◆ ◇ ◇ ◇ EASY → COMPLEX	◇ ◇ ◇ ◆ ◇ LUCK → SKILL

M any trick-taking games are not directly related to Bridge or Whist. Perhaps the foremost one is Hearts, which is truly one of the greatest card games ever devised for four players, each playing individually. The game is fairly easy to play, yet there is plenty of scope for high strategy.

Number of Players. Three to seven people can play, but the game is absolutely best for four, each playing for himself. Two players may play Domino Hearts; more than seven should play Cancellation Hearts. These versions are described later.

The Pack. The standard 52-card pack is used.

Rank of Cards. A (high), K, Q, J, 10, 9, 8, 7, 6, 5, 4, 3, 2.

The Draw, Shuffle and Cut. Each player draws one card from a shuffled pack spread face down. The highest card deals first, and thereafter the deal passes to the left. After the shuffle, the player on the dealer's right cuts.

The Deal. The dealer completes the cut and distributes the cards one at a time, face down, clockwise. In a four-player game, each is dealt 13 cards; in a three-player game, the ♦2 should be removed, and each player gets 17 cards; in a five-player game, the ♦2 and ♣2 should be removed so that each player will get 10 cards. For the six-player game, the ♦2, ♦3, ♣3 and ♣4 are removed, so that each player gets eight cards. Finally, with seven players, the ♦2, ♦3 and ♣3 are removed so that each player gets seven cards. However, if you have more than five players it is best to have two tables of 3 for six players and a table of 4 and a table of 3 for seven players.

Keeping The Black Maria Or Letting Her Go

Since the queen of spades counts as 13 points against the player taking that trick containing it, a player should be very careful when dealt this card. Most experts will pass the queen with three supporting spades or less. If the queen has four or more supporting spades, it is safe to keep her. The ace or king of spades requires at least three additional supporting spades to hold it. Any spade lower than the queen should never be passed.

The Pass. After looking at his hand, a player selects any three cards and passes them face down to the player on the left. The player must pass the three cards before looking at the cards received from the right. There is a passing rotation of left, right and across. With more than four players the passing rotation should be left and then right. A recent popular passing variation is to designate the fourth hand of every deal as a keep or hold hand where no cards are passed.

Object of the Game. The goal is to avoid winning in tricks any heart or the ♠Q (called Black Lady or Black Maria). Or, to win all 13 hearts and the ♠Q (referred to as "Shooting the Moon"). Ultimately, the object of the game is to have the lowest score when the game ends.

The Play. The player holding the ♣2 after the pass makes the opening lead. If the ♣2 has been removed for the three handed game, then the ♣3 is led. This is now the standard rule. Each player must follow suit if possible. If a player is void of the suit led, a card of any other suit may be discarded. However, if a player has no clubs when the first trick is led, a heart or the queen of spades cannot be discarded. The highest card of the suit led wins a trick and the winner of that trick leads next. There is no trump suit. The winner of the trick collects it and places it face down to form a neat "book" or stack of cards. Hearts may not be led until a heart or the queen of spades has been discarded. The queen does not have to be discarded at the first opportunity. The queen can be led at any time.

Scoring. A separate column on a score sheet is kept for each player. At the end of each hand, players count the number of hearts they have taken as well as the queen of spades, if applicable. Hearts count as one point each and the queen counts 13 points.

Each heart:	1 point
The ♠Q:	13 points

The point totals are then entered in each player's column. The aggregate total of all scores for each hand must be a multiple of 26. *Note*: The number of tricks a player wins does not count per se; the scoring is based solely on who wins tricks containing hearts and/or the queen of spades.

The game is usually played to 100 points (some play to 50). When one player hits the agreed upon score or higher, the game ends; and the player with the lowest score wins.

"Shooting the Moon." One of the great thrills of the game, shooting the moon or making a "slam", is when a player takes all 13 hearts and the

THE EVOLUTION OF THE GAME OF HEARTS

George S. Coffin, who was a bridge expert and the inventor of Trio (a bridge game for three players), reported that the game of Hearts evolved from Reversé, a card game played in the mid-1700s in Spain. In that game, the ♥J was called the *quinola grande*, "big quinola" and the ♥Q was the *quinola pequeña*, "little quinola." These cards scored negative points in a player's tricks, and that rule became the basis for the game of Hearts. Only in the last century or so has Hearts added rule variations, which are now standard to the game: shooting the moon, no leading a heart until the suit is broken, the mandatory ♣2 lead on the first trick, and no discarding a heart or the ♠Q on that trick. As Coffin pointed out, "Various embellishments have enlivened many card games, and so the variation of yesterday becomes the standard of today."

Bet You Didn't Know

queen of spades in one hand. Scores will differ dramatically. Instead of losing 26 points, that player scores zero and each of his opponents score an additional 26 points.

Scoring Variations.

1) Instead of a score sheet, chips are used. Each player pays one chip for each heart, thirteen chips for the ♠Q, and the lowest score for the deal takes all. Players who tie split the pot, leaving any odd chips for the next deal.

2) In this version called Sweepstakes, each player pays one chip for each heart and 13 chips for the ♠Q. If one player alone scores zero, he takes the pot; if two or more players make zero, they split the pot. If every player earns 1 point or more, the pot remains for the next deal, or until it is eventually won.

Irregularities. *Misdeal.* If the dealer exposes a card in dealing, or gives one player too many cards and another player too few, the next player in turn deals.

Play out of turn. A lead or play out of turn must be retracted if another player demands it before all have played to the trick. After everyone has played, a play out of turn stands without penalty.

Quitted tricks. Each trick gathered must be placed face down in front of the winner, and tricks must be kept separate. If a player so mixes his cards that a claim of revoke cannot be proved, he is charged with all 26 points for the deal, regardless of whether the alleged revoke was made by him or another player.

Revoke. Failure to follow suit when possible, or to discard the ♠Q at the first opportunity (when this variant rule is in force), constitutes a revoke. A revoke may be corrected before the trick is turned and quitted. If not discovered until later, the revoke is established, play is immediately abandoned, and the revoking hand is charged with all 26 points for the deal. If a revoke is established against more than one player, each is charged 26 points. However, the revoke penalty may not be enforced after the next deal has started.

Incorrect hand. A player discovered to have too few cards must take the last trick, and if his hand is more than one card short he must take in every trick to which he cannot play.

Omnibus Hearts

This version adds two features to standard Hearts whereby a player may actually score plus. The play of the cards takes on heightened interest, since it combines "nullo" play (to avoid gathering hearts and the ♠Q) with positive play to win plus points.

Number of Players. Four to six people can play. The game is best for four participants, each person playing for himself.

The Pack. The standard 52-card pack is used.

The Plus Card. The hearts and the ♠Q are minus cards, as in standard Hearts. In addition, the ♦10 counts plus 10 for the player who wins it. (In some localities, ♦J instead of ♦10 is the plus card.)

Slam. When a player wins all fifteen counting cards – the thirteen hearts, ♠Q, and ♦10 – it is called a slam and he scores 26 plus (instead of 16 minus).

Cancellation Hearts

Number of Players. Seven to ten people can play.

The Pack. Two standard packs of 52 cards are shuffled together.

The Deal. The cards are dealt around as far as they will go evenly. Any remaining odd cards are placed face down for a widow.

The Play. No cards are passed before the play. The player to the dealer's left makes the opening lead, and the rules of play are the same as in Four-Hand Hearts, with the following additions:

1) The widow is added to the first trick.

2) Cancellation: Two cards of the same rank in the same trick cancel each other, and neither can win the trick. If all cards played to a trick are paired, the trick goes to the winner of the next trick.

Hearts Without Black Lady

Hearts may be played without scoring ♠Q as a counting card, so that there are 13 points in play. In this version, players do not pass off three cards to each other, but play their original hands. Settlement is usually by the Howell method: For each heart taken, the player puts up as many chips as there are players besides himself; he then removes as many chips as the difference between 13 and the number of hearts he took. *Example*: In a four-hand game, a player who won seven hearts puts in 21 chips and takes out six.

Domino Hearts

Number of Players. Two to seven people can play.

The Pack. The standard 52-card pack is used.

The Deal. Each player receives six cards, dealt one at a time. The remainder of the pack is placed face down in the center of the table, forming the stock.

The Play. The player to the dealer's left leads first. The rules of play are the same as for Four-Hand Hearts, except that a player who cannot follow suit to the lead must draw cards from the top of the stock until he can play. After the stock is exhausted, a player unable to follow suit may discard. The game continues until all cards have been won in tricks, with each player dropping out as his cards are exhausted. If a player wins a trick with his last card, the turn to lead passes to the first active player on his left. The last survivor must keep all the cards remaining in his hand.

Scoring. The same as in Four-Hand Hearts, except that the ♠Q is usually not scored.

Auction Hearts

This game is the same as Hearts Without Black Lady, except that players bid after the deal for the privilege of naming the suit to be avoided. In bidding, a player names the number of chips he will put up as a pot, if allowed to name the suit. Bidding begins with the first hand dealt and rotates to the left, each player being allowed to bid only once. A player must either bid higher than the preceding bid or pass.

The highest bidder puts up his chips and names the suit. He leads first, and thereafter play proceeds as in the regular game.

The Play. When the hands are played out, each player adds one chip to the pot for each card he has taken of the forbidden suit. The player taking no cards of the forbidden suit wins the pot; if two players score no minus points, they divide the pot. If an odd chip remains, it is left for the next pot. If more than two players take no cards of the forbidden suit, or one player takes all 13, or each player takes at least one, no player wins; the deal passes, and the successful bidder on the original deal names the suit to be avoided, without bidding. The play then proceeds as before, and at the end of the hand, each player puts up a chip for each card of the forbidden suit he has taken. If no player wins on this deal, a new deal ensues, and so on, until the pot is won.

Joe Andrews, author of "Win at Hearts," and founder of the American Hearts and Spades Players' Association (AHSPA), has generously added to portions of the Hearts section. Card players interested in joining AHSPA and who would like to enjoy a good game of Hearts in their city, or on the Microsoft Hearts Game Zone at www.zone.com, may E-mail Mr. Andrews at heartsmoon@aol.com.

LOO

NUMBER OF PLAYERS	NUMBER OF CARDS	GAME PLAY	SKILL LEVEL
5-9	**52** (32)	◊ ◊ ◊ ◊ ◆ EASY → COMPLEX	◊ ◊ ◊ ◆ ◊ LUCK → SKILL

Two or three centuries ago, Loo was the leading card game in England, "a favorite alike of the idle rich and industrious poor," reported Albert H. Morehead. He went on to say that Loo is mentioned in English literature more than any other card game, although since then, Whist, Bridge, and Poker have largely displaced it. Loo takes its name from the French lanterlu, a refrain from a popular 17th-century song.

Number of Players. Though the game can be played by more or less people, Loo is best for five to nine participants. Each person plays for himself.

The Pack. The standard 52-card pack is used. However, if fewer than five people play, a stripped deck is used. It consists of 32 cards with the sixes down through deuces removed.

The Draw, Shuffle and Cut. Any player takes a shuffled pack and deals it around. The first player receiving a jack is the first dealer, and thereafter, the deal rotates clockwise. The dealer has the right to shuffle last, and the pack is cut by the player to his right.

The Deal. The dealer completes the cut and deals three cards to each player, one at a time, face down, beginning with the player to the left.

Stakes. The dealer antes three chips into the pot, and, at times, the pot is increased by units of three chips at a time. Thus, it can always be divided evenly into three parts, one for each trick. A deal that begins with only three chips in the pot is called a "single"; with more chips in the pot, it is a "double."

The Play. The player to the dealer's left leads. Players must follow suit if possible, and must play a higher card in the suit. If he has no cards of the suit led, the player may trump, and must trump higher if a previous player has trumped. The winner of a trick leads next. *Note*: The cards of a trick are not gathered together; each is left face up in front of the owner.

Single Pot. Should all hands fail to follow suit to each of the three leads, no trump suit is fixed. However, the first time any player fails to follow suit, the current trick is completed, and then the top card of the pack is turned up to fix the trump suit; that trump is in effect for the trick just played as well as for subsequent tricks.

Settlement. One-third of the pot is collected for each trick won. If a player fails to win one of the three tricks, it is called "loo," and that player must put three chips into the next pot, thereby making it a "double."

Double Pot. For a round with a double pot, an extra hand, called the "miss," is dealt to the right of the dealer. After the deal, the next card is turned up for trump, and prior to the opening lead, the dealer asks each player in turn to state his intentions. Each player must pass, stand, or take the "miss."

If a player passes, he is out for that deal, and his hand is placed immediately face down under the pack. A player who "stands" remains in the game. A player who takes the "miss" (and thus commits to standing), places his original hand under the pack. If all other players pass except either the dealer or a player who has taken the "miss," the lone player takes the pot and the cards are abandoned for that round. If only one player ahead of the dealer stands, the dealer must either stand and play for himself, or must take the "miss" and "defend the pot."

In the double-pot game, the leader to each trick must lead a trump if he can, and must lead the ace of trumps at the first opportunity, or the king, if the ace was turned up.

Settlement. All players who did not pass participate, and the pot is divided into three parts, one for each trick. When there is a loo, the player looed pays three chips to the next pot; and when the dealer is forced to "defend the pot," he neither collects nor pays, since settlement is made only by his opponent.

Flush. A hand of three trumps is a flush and wins the entire pot without play. If two or more players hold flushes, the hand closer to the dealer's left is the winner. Flushes are announced after the dealer has declared, and all hands of players who have stood (or taken the "miss") are looed.

PREFERENCE

NUMBER OF PLAYERS	NUMBER OF CARDS	GAME PLAY	SKILL LEVEL
3 (4+)	**32**	◇ ◇ ◆ ◇ ◇ EASY ➜ COMPLEX	◇ ◇ ◇ ◆ ◇ LUCK ➜ SKILL

Preference is played in parts of Europe, including summer resorts in Russia and the Ukraine. There are several versions of the game.

Number of Players. Three people can play this version.

The Pack. The standard 52-card pack is stripped to remove the sixes down through the deuces, leaving a 32 card-deck.

Rank of Cards. A (high), K, Q, J, 10, 9, 8, 7.

Rank of Suits. Hearts is the highest suit, followed by diamonds, clubs, and then spades which is low. Hearts is known as the "preference suit."

The Draw, Shuffle, and Cut. From a shuffled pack spread face down, each player draws a card. The highest card deals first, and thereafter the deal passes to the left.

Any player may shuffle, the dealer last. The player on the dealer's right cuts.

The Deal. The dealer completes the cut and distributes the cards clockwise in packets of three, face down, clockwise, to each player. The dealer then deals a widow of two cards, face down, to the center of the table. Finally, the dealer deals each player a packet of four cards and another packet of three cards. Each player should have a hand of 10 cards, so that along with the two-card widow, all 32 cards are distributed.

Object of the Game. Each player attempts to make the highest bid and then fulfill it.

Stakes. Chips are used and the players must agree beforehand how many chips will be placed in the pot, how many chips will be paid from the pot to the successful bidder, and finally, how many will be paid to the pot by a bidder who fails to fulfill his contract.

Bidding. The bidding in this game is only for the right to name the trump suit, not for the number of tricks expected to be won.

Starting with the player to the dealer's left, each player either bids a suit or passes. A player bids the suit he would prefer to use as trumps in order to make at least six tricks. Players bid only once, and any subsequent bid must be in a higher-ranking suit. If all the players pass on the first round, there is a second round of bidding. For this extra round, a player either passes or, in turn, places extra chips in the pool. The person who puts in the highest number of chips wins the bid and names the trump suit. The winning bidder then has the option of discarding two cards and picking up the two-card widow to add to his hand. (When a bid is made on the first round, the widow is left unused.)

The Play. The player to the left of the winning bidder leads first. A player must follow suit if possible. If not, he may trump or discard. The highest trump or the highest card of the suit led wins the trick. The winner of a trick leads next. When all 10 tricks have been played, the players settle their scores.

Settlement. If the bidder fulfills his bid by taking six or more tricks, he receives the agreed-upon amount of chips from the pot. If the player fails to take at least six tricks, he puts an agreed-on number of chips into the pot.

FIVE HUNDRED

NUMBER OF PLAYERS	NUMBER OF CARDS	GAME PLAY	SKILL LEVEL
2-6 (7, 8)	**33-63**	◇ ◇ ◇ ◆ ◇ EASY → COMPLEX	◇ ◇ ◇ ◆ ◇ LUCK → SKILL

In the early part of this century, Five Hundred was the favorite social game of the United States. It was finally eclipsed by Bridge but is still played worldwide by millions, particularly in Australia. It was devised and introduced in 1904 by the United States Playing Card Company, which held the copyright for 56 years but never charged anyone for its use. Five Hundred can be thought of as a combination of Euchre and Bridge.

Number of Players. Two to six people can play. The three-hand game is particularly interesting. Four people can play in two partnerships, or with three active players plus one player (the dealer) who sits out each game. Five people can play in two partnerships, three against two, or can cut to decide which three or four play the first game while the other sits out. Six people can play in two partnerships of three each.

The Pack. The size of the pack varies with the number of players. For two or three players, it is 33 cards – A, K, Q, J, 10, 9, 8, 7 in each suit, plus a joker. Four players use a 43-card pack: ace (high) to 5 (low) in each suit, plus the ♥4, ♦4 and the joker. Five players use 53 cards: the standard 52-card pack plus a joker. Six players use a special 62-card pack that includes spot cards numbered 11 and 12 in each suit, and 13 in each of two suits; 13 hearts and 13 diamonds. By agreement, the joker may or may not be included.

Rank of Cards. The joker is always the highest trump. Second best is the jack of trumps ("right bower"); third best is the jack of the other suit of the same color as the trump ("left bower"). The rank in trumps is: Joker (high), J (right bower), J (left bower), A, K, Q, 10, 9, down to the lowest card. In each plain suit, the rank is A (high), K, Q, J,10, 9, down to the lowest card.

The bidding denominations rank: No trump (high), hearts, diamonds, clubs, spades.

Drawing. Each player draws a card from a pack spread face down. The player with the lowest card deals first. In drawing for deal only, ace ranks low, below the deuce, and the joker is the lowest card of the pack.

Rank of Cards in Trump Suit

Rank of Cards in Plain Suits

Shuffle and Cut. Any player may shuffle. The dealer has the right to shuffle last. The pack is cut by the player on the dealer's right. The cut must leave at least four cards in each packet.

The Deal. Each player is dealt 10 cards, face down, clockwise, starting with the player on the dealer's left. In distributing the cards, the dealer gives each player three cards at a time, then deals a widow of three cards (two cards, if the joker is not used), then deals each player four cards at a time, followed by a final packet of three cards at a time.

Bidding. Each player in turn, beginning with the player on the dealer's left, has one opportunity to bid. A player may pass or bid. A bid must name a number of tricks, from six to 10, together with a denomination, which will establish the trump suit (such as, "Six Spades"). If there has been a previous bid, any subsequent bid must be higher. A player must bid more tricks, or the same number of tricks in a higher-ranking denomination. (*Optional rule*: If the Original or Inverted schedule is used, as shown in the table, a bid tops the preceding one if its scoring value is higher, or if it requires a greater number of tricks with the same scoring value.)

"Nullo" Bid. Some rules permit the bid Nullo, which is a contract to lose all the tricks at no trump. The nullo bid has a scoring value of 250. On the Avondale schedule it overcalls a bid of eight spades or lower and it is outbid by eight clubs or higher. If nullo becomes the contract in a partnership game, the contractor's partner or partners abandon their hands and the contractor plays alone against the others. If the contractor wins a trick, the penalty is to be set back the 250 points, and each opponent scores 10 for each trick the contractor takes.

Passing. If all players pass, the deal is abandoned without a score. *Optional rule*: A passed deal may be played as no trump, and each player plays for himself. The player to the left of dealer leads first. Each trick won counts 10 points. Since there is no contract, there is no setting back.

The Play. The high bid becomes the contract. In three-hand play, the two other players combine in a temporary partnership against the contractor.

The contractor takes the widow into his hand, without showing it, then discards any three cards face down without showing them.

The contractor leads, and may lead any card at any time. The other players must follow suit if they can. If unable to follow suit, a player may play any card. A trick is won by the highest trump, or if a no-trump card is played, it is won by the highest card of the suit led. The winner of a trick leads next. All of the contractor's opponents take in and keep the tricks they win.

The Joker. When there is a trump suit, the joker belongs to that suit, and it becomes the highest trump card. It must be played if necessary to follow suit, and it may be played only when a card of the trump suit can legally be played.

In a no-trump contract (or nullo, if played), the joker is a suit by itself but is also the highest card of any suit and wins any trick to which it is legally played. The holder of the joker may not play it if he can follow suit to the suit led. If not, the joker may be played and wins the trick. If a player leads the joker in a no-trump (or nullo) contract, he must specify the suit that others must play to, but the joker wins the trick.

Scoring. If the contractor wins as many tricks as bid, he scores the number of points called for in the scoring table being used (see p. 175). There is no credit for extra tricks over the contract except that, if the contractor wins all 10 tricks, he scores a minimum of 250.

Select Scoring System. Three scoring schedules are popular for the game: the Original Schedule from 1904, the improved Avondale Schedule, and the optional Inverted Schedule. The Avondale schedule is recommended because it contains no two bids of the same numerical value, and it more nearly equalizes the value of the suits. (See chart next page.)

If the contractor fails to make the contract, the value of the bid is deducted from his score. It is possible for a player to have a negative score which is referred to as "in the hole" because of the common practice of drawing a ring around a minus score

Whether the contract is made or defeated, each opponent of the contractor scores 10 for each trick he takes

Game. The player or side that reaches a total of 500 points first wins the game. A player or side that goes 500 in the hole loses. (If one player

SCORING TABLES FOR FIVE HUNDRED

Avondale Schedule		6 Tricks	7 Tricks	8 Tricks	9 Tricks	10 Tricks
	♠ Trump	40	140	240	340	440
	♣ Trump	60	160	260	360	460
	♦ Trump	80	180	280	380	480
	♥ Trump	100	200	300	400	500
	No Trump	120	220	320	420	520

Original Schedule		6 Tricks	7 Tricks	8 Tricks	9 Tricks	10 Tricks
	♠ Trump	40	80	120	160	200
	♣ Trump	60	120	180	240	300
	♦ Trump	80	160	240	320	400
	♥ Trump	100	200	300	400	500
	No Trump	120	240	360	480	600

If reverse order of suit values is used, table of points is as follows:

Inverted Schedule		6 Tricks	7 Tricks	8 Tricks	9 Tricks	10 Tricks
	♣ Trump	40	80	120	160	200
	♠ Trump	60	120	180	240	300
	♥ Trump	80	160	240	320	400
	♦ Trump	100	200	300	400	500
	No Trump	120	240	360	480	600

NOTE: The Avondale Schedule is recommended because it contains no two bids of same numerical value and more nearly equalizes the value of the suits.

in a three-hand game becomes minus 500, he cannot win the game but continues to play until another player wins; if he happens to make 500-plus points first after scoring minus 500, no one wins the game.) If the contractor and an opponent reach 500 on the same deal, the contractor wins.

In a three-hand game, if the contractor does not reach 500, but both opponents do, the first opponent to reach 500 wins. If the contractor could not reach 500 by making the bid, the opponent who is first to reach 500 may claim the game as soon as his tricks score 500. At the time he makes the claim, the player must show his remaining cards. If he does not have the 500 points, the game continues with that player's remaining cards exposed (see Irregularities).

Another option is to require 1,000 or 1,500 for game. The scoring is speeded up by awarding points for cards won in tricks: 1 point for each ace, 10 for each face card or ten, the pip value for each lower card, and zero for the joker. These points have no bearing on whether the contractor makes the bid, which depends solely on the number of tricks that player takes.

Four-Hand Five Hundred

The four-hand game is played with fixed partnerships; the partners sit opposite each other. The pack is 42 or 43 cards, made by discarding the twos, threes, and black 4s from a standard 52-card pack, and adding a joker if desired. Many people play without a joker. Each player receives 10 cards, and the remaining cards go to the widow. If one side's score reaches minus 500, the opponents win the game. All other rules are the same as in Three-Hand Five Hundred.

Two-Hand Five Hundred

The pack and the deal are the same as in the three-hand game, except that the hand to the dealer's left is dealt face down on the table and is "dead." With these 10 cards out of play, the bidding is largely guesswork. Not to be left "at home" by a bold opponent, a player is bound to be forward in bidding and to speculate on getting the cards he needs from the widow. If a player's score reaches minus 500, his opponent wins the game.

Two-Hand Five Hundred may also be played with a 24-card pack, with the nine as the lowest card. The widow is then four cards, and no extra hand is dealt.

Five-Hand Five Hundred

Five players use a standard 52-card pack, usually with the joker added, so that each player receives 10 cards and the widow has three cards, as in the the three-hand version. After the bidding, the high bidder may select any other player to be his partner. If the player bids eight or more tricks, he may name any two partners. In some games, the high bidder selects a partner by naming a card, as in Call-Ace Euchre. (See p. 183.)

Six-Hand Five Hundred

For six players, there is a special 62-card pack available that includes spot cards numbered 11 and 12 in each suit and 13 in each of two other suits. The joker may be added, making a 63-card pack. This permits a deal of 10 cards to each player and three cards to the widow. There are two partnerships of three players on each side. The partners are seated so that each has an opponent on his left and right. *(A special deck is available from The U.S. Playing Card Company)*

EUCHRE

NUMBER OF PLAYERS	NUMBER OF CARDS	GAME PLAY	SKILL LEVEL
4 (2-7)	**32**	◇ ◇ ◆ ◇ ◇ EASY ➤ COMPLEX	◇ ◇ ◇ ◆ ◇ LUCK ➤ SKILL

Euchre is an offshoot of Juckerspiel, a game that became widely popular throughout Europe during the Napoleonic era. In the 1800s, it became one of the most popular card games in America and Australia. Euchre (and its variations) is the reason why modern card decks were first packaged with jokers, a card originally designed to act as the right and left "bowers" (high trumps). Although later eclipsed by Bridge (as with so many other games of this type), Euchre is still well known in America and is an excellent social game.

Number of Players. From two to seven people can play, but the game is best for four participants, playing two against two as partners. Therefore, the rules for the four-hand version are given first.

The Pack. Special Euchre decks are available, or the standard 52-card pack can be stripped to make a deck of thirty two cards (A, K, Q, J, 10, 9, 8, 7 of each suit), or 28 cards (7s omitted), or 24 cards (7s and 8s omitted). In some games, a joker is added.

Rank of Cards. The highest trump is the jack of the trump suit, called the "right bower." The second-highest trump is the jack of the other suit of the same color called the "left bower." (*Example*: If diamonds are trumps, the right bower is ♦J and left bower is ♥J.) The remaining trumps, and also the plain suits, rank as follows: A (high), K, Q, J, 10, 9, 8, 7. If a joker has been added to the pack, it acts as the highest trump.

The Draw. From the shuffled pack spread face down, the players draw cards for partners and first deal. The two players with the two lowest cards play against the two players with the two highest cards. The player with the lowest card deals first. For drawing, the cards rank: K (high), Q, J, 10, 9, 8, 7, A. Players drawing equal cards must draw again. Partners sit opposite each other.

The Shuffle and Cut. The dealer has the right to shuffle last. The pack is cut by the player to the dealer's right. The cut must not leave less than four cards in each packet.

The Deal. The cards are dealt clockwise, to the left, beginning with the player to the left of the dealer. Each player receives five cards. The dealer may give a round of three at a time, then a round of two at a time, or may give two, then three; but the dealer must adhere to whichever distribution plan he begins with. After the first deal, the deal passes to the player on the dealer's left.

The Turn-up. On completing the deal, the dealer places the rest of the pack in the center of the table and turns the top card face up. Should the turn-up be accepted as trump by any player, the dealer has the right to exchange the turn-up for another card in his hand. In practice, the dealer does not take the turn-up into his hand, but leaves it on the pack until it is played; the dealer signifies this exchange by placing his discard face down underneath the pack.

Making the Trump. Beginning with the player to the left of the dealer, each player passes or accepts the turn-up as trump. An opponent of the dealer accepts by saying "I order it up." The partner of the dealer accepts by saying, "I assist." The dealer accepts by making his discard, called "taking it up."

The dealer signifies refusal of the turn-up by removing the card from the top and placing it (face up) partially underneath the pack; this is called "turning it down."

If all four players pass in the first round, each player in turn, starting with the player to the dealer's left, has the option of passing again or of naming the trump suit. The rejected suit may not be named. Declaring the other suit of the same color as the reject is called "making it next"; declaring a suit of opposite color is called "crossing it." If all four players pass in the second round, the cards are gathered and shuffled, and the next dealer deals.

Once the trump is fixed, either by acceptance of the turn-up or by the naming of another suit, the turn-up is rejected, the bidding ends and play begins.

Playing Alone. If the player who fixes the trump suit believes it will be to his side's advantage to play without the help of his partner's cards, the player exercises this option by declaring "alone" distinctly at the time of making the trump. This player's partner then turns his cards face down and does not participate in the play.

Object of the Game. The goal is to win at least three tricks. If the side that fixed the trump fails to get three tricks, it is said to be "euchred." Winning all five tricks is called a "march."

The Play. The opening lead is made by the player to the dealer's left, or if this player's partner is playing alone, it is made by the player across from the dealer. If he can, each player must follow suit to a lead. If unable to follow suit, the player may trump or discard any card. A trick is won by the highest card of the suit led, or, if it contains trumps, by the highest trump. The winner of a trick leads next.

Scoring. The following table shows all scoring situations:

Partnership making trump wins 3 or 4 tricks	1
Partnership making trump wins 5 tricks	2
Lone hand wins 3 or 4 tricks	1
Lone hand wins 5 tricks	4
Partnership or lone hand is euchred, opponents score	2

Game. The first player or partnership to score 5, 7 or 10 points, as agreed beforehand, wins the game. In the 5-point game, a side is said to be "at the bridge" when it has scored four and the opponents have scored two or less.

Keeping Score with Low Card Markers. An elegant and widespread method of keeping score is with cards lower than those used in play. When game is 5 points, each side uses a three-spot and a four-spot as markers. To indicate a score of 1, the four is placed face down on the three, with one pip left exposed. For a score of 2, the three is placed face down on the four, with two pips left exposed. For a score of 3, the three is placed face up on the four. For a score of 4, the four is placed face up on the three.

Rubbers. Many Euchre games are scored by rubber points, as in Whist. The first side to win two games wins the rubber. Each game counts for the side winning; 3 rubber points if the losers' score in that game was 0 or fewer, 2 rubber points if the losers' score was 1 or 2, and 1 rubber point if the losers scored 3 or more. The winners' margin in the rubber is 2 points bonus, plus the winners' rubber points, minus the losers' rubber points.

Railroad Euchre

Railroad Euchre is the name given to any number of versions designed to speed up the scoring. Some of the features that have been added in various localities are as follows:

Joker. The joker is included and ranks as the highest trump.

Defending alone. Either opponent of a lone player may call "alone" and defend alone against the player. Euchre of a lone hand by a lone opponent counts 4.

Calling for best. A lone player or defender may discard any one card and call for his partner's best card as a replacement. The partner complies by choosing what he judges to be the most advantageous card and passes it, face down, to the lone player.

Laps. Points scored in excess of those needed to win the game are credited toward the next game.

Slam. A side is credited with two games if it reaches game before the opponents have scored a point.

Three-Hand Euchre
(Cutthroat Euchre)

This version is played like Four-Hand Euchre except that the two other hands combine in play against the player who fixes the trump. The scoring:

Maker of trump wins 3 or 4 tricks 1

Maker of trump wins 5 tricks 3

Maker of trump euchred, each opponent scores 2

In applying the laws for irregularities, the maker of trump is deemed a lone hand and the other two a partnership.

Two-Hand Euchre

The pack is reduced to 24 cards by discarding the 7s and 8s. The rules are as in the four-hand game, except that there can be no declaration of alone and the score for "march" is 2 points. Laws regarding irregularities omit penalties for errors that do not damage the opponent. For example, there is no penalty for the exposure of cards or for leading out of turn.

Auction Euchre

Number of Players. Five, six or seven people can play.

The Pack. For a five-hand game, 32 cards are used, as in Four-Hand Euchre. For six players, 36 cards are used – the usual pack with sixes added. For a seven-hand game, 52 cards are used. In each instance, the joker may be added if desired (and it will rank as the highest trump).

The Draw. The players draw cards, and the lowest card designates the first dealer. The player with the second-lowest card sits on the dealer's left, and so on.

The Deal. In five-hand and six-hand games, the deal is the same as in four-hand, except that after the first round, the dealer deals two cards face down for a widow. In a seven-hand game, each player is dealt seven cards; a round of three cards at a time, then a round of four, or vice versa. After the first round, three cards are dealt face down for a widow (or four cards if the joker is used).

The Bidding. Starting with the player on the dealer's left, each player in turn may make a bid or pass. There is only one round of bidding, and the highest bidder names the trump suit. Each bid is for a number of points, and it must be higher than the preceding bid.

The Widow. The maker of trump may take the widow into his hand and discard an equal number of cards, unless he has contracted to play without the widow.

Partners. In the five-hand game, the player who fixes the trump chooses his partners after seeing the widow. A bid of three tricks entitles him to one partner, a bid of four or five tricks, to two partners. The maker of trump may choose any player, regardless of where the player sits. The six-hand game is usually played by set partnerships of three against three, and the partners' seats alternate with their opponents'. In the seven-hand game, the maker of trump chooses partners after seeing the widow. A bid of four or five tricks entitles him to one partner; a bid of six or seven tricks, to two partners.

The Play. The play is the same as in Four-Hand Euchre.

Scoring. The following tables show the various numbers that may be bid and the obligation of each bid.

Five-Hand Euchre:

Bid	Obligation
3	Maker must win 3 tricks with help of one partner.
4	Maker must win 4 tricks with help of two partners.
5	Maker must win 5 tricks with help of two partners.
8	Maker must play alone and win 5 tricks, using the widow.
15	Maker must play alone and win 5 tricks, without the widow.

Six-Hand Euchre:

Bid	Obligation
3, 4, 5	Side making trump must win number of tricks named (widow taken by maker of trump).
8	Maker must play alone and win 5 tricks, using the widow.
15	Maker must play alone and win 5 tricks, without the widow.

Seven-Hand Euchre:

Bid	Obligation
4, 5	Maker must win number of tricks named with help of one partner.
6, 7	Maker must win number of tricks named with help of two partners.
10	Maker must play alone and win 7 tricks, using the widow.
20	Maker must play alone and win 7 tricks, without the widow.

If the side making trump wins the number of tricks bid, it scores the value given in the table. There is no credit for winning more tricks than necessary. If the side making trump is euchred, the opponents score the value of the bid. In six-hand partnership play, only two accounts need be kept, one for each side. However, with five or seven players, the full amount to which a side is entitled is credited to each member individually.

Call-Ace Euchre

In this version for four, five or six players, partnerships are determined in secret. Trump is made as in the four-hand game by acceptance of the turn-up as trump, or declaration of another trump if the turn-up is rejected. The maker of trump calls a suit, and the holder of the best card in that suit becomes his partner, but must not reveal the fact until the card is duly played.

Cincinnati Euchre

This version of Euchre borrows from many of the other Euchre games. It is for four players – two partnerships – determined by agreement among the players. Trump is made as in Auction Euchre, by bidding.

The Pack. A standard pack is used with 2s, 3s, 4s, 5s, 6s, 7s and 8s removed, or a Euchre pack is used with the 7s and 8s removed, producing a 24-card pack.

Partners. Unlike Auction Euchre, the partners are fixed for the duration of the game. Any player winning the bid plays in cooperation with his partner and all tricks taken by the partnership count toward making the bid.

The Bidding. As in Auction Euchre, the bidding starts with the player on the dealer's left, and each player in turn may make a bid or pass. The minimum starting bid is three. There is only one round of bidding, and the highest bidder names the trump suit or notrump. Each bid must be higher than the preceding bid. If no player bids (all pass), the dealer must accept a "Force bid" of three.

If any player believes he can win all six tricks he may call "Moon." A Moon, if successful (all tricks taken), scores 12 points. If the next player also believes he can win all six tricks, he may "Double Moon"; if successful he scores 24 points. Any third player believing he can also win all tricks may "Triple Moon" and, if successful, scores 32 points. If the last player to bid is equally convinced, he may bid "Quadruple Moon"; if successful, he scores 48 points. Any Moon bid won by a player is played alone. The partner of the player with the moon bid lays his hand face down, and his hand is not played.

Any bid may be unsuccessful if the number of tricks bid are not taken. When such a bid is not made, the partners are "set" and the number of tricks bid is deducted from their score.

The Play. The play is the same as in four-hand Euchre.

Scoring. The points are equal to the number of tricks successfully taken by a partnership. The partnership which first reaches 32 points wins the game. It is possible for the partnership score to become negative. *Example*: If a player "Moons" and does not make the bid (six tricks), the partnership has 12 points deducted from their score. If the partnership score was zero, their score become -12 points.

NAPOLEON
(Nap)

NUMBER OF PLAYERS	NUMBER OF CARDS	GAME PLAY					SKILL LEVEL				
2-6	**52**	◇	♦	◇	◇	◇	◇	◇	♦	◇	◇
		EASY	→		COMPLEX		LUCK	→			SKILL

Napoleon is a deceptively simple bidding and trick-taking game. Although it is relatively easy compared to more sophisticated games like Bridge or Whist, what Napoleon lacks in finesse it makes up for in fast pace and player interaction. The scoring system, using chips, also lends itself well to wagering. The delightful difference of using "Wellington" and "Blucher" in the bidding refers, of course, to other famous generals of Napoleon's day; but the card game itself is said to date back only to the late 1800s – well after the French leader's death.

The Pack. The standard 52-card pack is used.

Rank of Cards. A (high), K, Q, J, 10, 9, 8, 7, 6, 5, 4, 3, 2.

The Draw. From a shuffled pack spread face down, each of the players draws a card. The player with the lowest card deals first, the ace ranking below the two for the draw only.

The Shuffle and Cut. The dealer has the right to shuffle last. The pack is cut by the player on the dealer's right.

The Deal. Each player receives five cards, dealt in a round of three at a time, then a round of two at a time, or first two and then three.

Bidding. Each player in turn, beginning to the dealer's left, may make one bid or pass. A bid is the number of tricks, out of five, that the player thinks he can win with a particular suit as trump. A bid of all five tricks is called Nap. (Variation: A bid of Nap can be overcalled by Wellington, and that in turn by Blucher. These latter calls are also bids to win five tricks, but incur greater penalties if the bidder fails.)

The Play. The highest bidder indicates the trump suit by making the opening lead, which must be a trump. Other players must follow suit if possible. A player who cannot follow suit may trump or discard at will. A trick is won by the highest card played of the suit led, or, if it contains a trump, by the highest trump. The winner of a trick leads next.

Scoring. There is no credit for extra tricks won either by the bidder or by the opponents beyond what was needed to make or defeat the bid.

If the bidder makes the bid, he collects from all the other players. If the bidder is defeated, he pays every player.

Bid	Bidder Wins	Bidder Loses
Less than 5	1 for each trick	1 for each trick
Nap	10	5
Wellington	10	10
Blucher	10	20

The usual way of settling scores is to distribute an equal number of chips to all players before the game and then settle in chips after each deal.

Irregularities. *Misdeal*. If a misdeal is called for any of the usual causes, the same dealer redeals.

Incorrect number of cards. A player dealt the wrong number of cards must announce the error before bids or passes; otherwise he must play on with the incorrect hand. A short hand cannot win a trick on which it has no card to play. If a bidder's hand is correct and an opponent's incorrect, the bidder does not pay if he loses but collects if he wins. If the bidder's hand is incorrect and all others are correct, the bidder does not collect if he wins but pays if he loses.

Play out of turn. There is no penalty for a lead or play out of turn by bidder, but the error must be corrected on demand if noticed before the trick is completed, otherwise, it stands. If an opponent leads or plays out of turn, he must pay three chips to the bidder but collects nothing if the bidder loses.

Revoke. Failure to follow suit when possible is a revoke. If a revoke is detected and claimed before settlement for the deal, play is abandoned and settlement is made at once. A revoking bidder must pay all opponents as though he had lost. A revoking opponent must pay the bidder the full amount he would have collected had the bidder won. The other opponents pay nothing.

Pool Nap

A scoring variation is to create a "pool" (pot) of chips which is won by the first player to successfully take five tricks on a Nap bid. Each player puts in an equal number of chips to begin the pool; and thereafter, each dealer in turn adds the same number of chips each hand. The pool may be further increased by requiring a player revoking to contribute five chips, and for a lead out of turn, three chips. A player bidding Nap and failing to take five tricks must double the pool.

Peep Nap

In this version of Pool Nap, one card only is dealt to make a widow, usually on the first round. By adding one chip to the pool, any player may "peep" at this card before bidding or passing. The highest bidder may take the widow card but must discard one card to reduce his hand to five cards before play begins.

Sir Garnet

In this a popular version of Nap, an extra hand of five cards is dealt to the right of the dealer's location.

Instead of making the usual bid, each player in turn to the left may pick up the extra hand and place it with the five cards he originally had. From these ten cards, the player picks out any five and discards the others without revealing them. The player is then obliged to bid Nap, but if he fails to make the bid, that player must pay double the normal penalty.

SPOIL FIVE
(Five Fingers, Twenty-Five)

NUMBER OF PLAYERS	NUMBER OF CARDS	GAME PLAY	SKILL LEVEL
5-6 (2-10)	**52**	◇ ◇ ◇ ◆ ◇ EASY → COMPLEX	◇ ◇ ◆ ◇ ◇ LUCK → SKILL

First described in 1674 as "Five Fingers" (which, in this game, is a slang term for the five of trumps), Spoil Five is ancient and features elements that date back much further in time. The game's long popularity attests to its excellent play value. One variation, Twenty-Five, is a prominent game in Ireland. Yet another version, Forty-Five, is extremely popular in Nova Scotia.

Number of Players. While two to 10 people can play as individuals, the game is best for five or six.

The Pack. The standard 52-card pack is used.

Rank of Cards. The ace of hearts is always third-best trump. There are 13 trumps when hearts are trump, 14 when any other suit is trump. Rank of spot cards is different in red and black suits.

Rank in trump suit:

Spades and clubs: 5 (high), J, ♥A, A, K, Q, 2, 3, 4, 6, 7, 8, 9, 10.

Hearts: 5 (high), J, A, K, Q, 10, 9, 8, 7, 6, 4, 3, 2.

Diamonds: 5 (high), ♦J, ♥A, ♦A, K, Q, 10, 9, 8, 7, 6, 4, 3, 2.

Rank of cards in plain suits (no trump):

Spades and clubs: K (high), Q, J, A, 2, 3, 4, 5, 6, 7, 8, 9, 10.

Diamonds: K (high), Q, J, 10, 9, 8, 7, 6, 5, 4, 3, 2, A.

Hearts: K (high), Q, J, 10, 9, 8, 7, 6, 5, 4, 3, 2.

The rule to remember is, "Low in black, high in red." (Diagram next page)

The Shuffle and Cut. Any player shuffles the pack and deals the cards face up, one at a time to each player in rotation, beginning with the player at his left, until a jack is turned up. The player who gets the jack deals first. Thereafter, the turn to deal passes from each player to the player at his left. The dealer may shuffle last, and the player at the dealer's right cuts.

The Deal. The dealer completes the cut and deals five cards to each player clockwise – three, then two (or two, then three) in rotation, to the left, beginning with the player on his left. After the deal is completed, the next card is turned over to indicate trump.

SPOIL FIVE RANK OF CARDS

In Trump Suits

Spades (or Clubs)

Hearts

Diamonds

In Plain Suits

Spades (or Clubs)

Hearts

Diamonds

Robbing the Trump. The player holding the ace of the trump suit may exchange any card in his hand for the turned card. If the player does not choose to make this exchange, he must ask the dealer to turn down the trump card, thus announcing who holds the ace (otherwise that player's ace becomes lowest trump, even if it is the ace of hearts). If an ace is turned, the dealer may discard at once and take the ace into his hand after the first trick, or may play with his original hand, announcing this intention.

Object of The Game. The goal is to accumulate the most chips by winning tricks.

The Play. The player on the dealer's left leads any card. Each player, in turn, must follow suit if possible, or trump. If unable to follow suit, a player may play any card.

When a lower trump is led, a player is not required to follow suit with the five or jack of trumps or the ace of hearts.

A trick containing a trump is won by the highest trump played. Any other trick is won by the highest card of the suit led. The winner of each trick leads next.

Scoring. Before every hand, players put one chip each into a pot. The pot may be taken by the first player to win three tricks in any deal. However, that player also has the option of continuing to play after winning three tricks. In that case, he must win all five tricks. If he does, that player wins the pot plus one chip from each opponent. If he does not win all five tricks, the player wins nothing, and the pot "rolls over" to the next hand.

Irregularities. *Misdeal.* There is a misdeal if too many or too few cards are dealt, if the dealer exposes a card in dealing, if the deal begins with an uncut pack (provided a new deal is demanded before the deal is completed), or if the dealer counts the cards on the table or in the pack. If there is a misdeal, the deal passes to the player on the original dealer's left.

Irregular hand. A hand with an incorrect number of cards is dead, and the other players continue play. However, if a player has won three tricks with an irregular hand before it is discovered, he wins the pot.

Revoke. If there is an illegal exposure of a card after any player has won two tricks, the offender's hand is dead, and he does not receive cards until the pot in progress is won. However, he must still add to the pot when other players do.

Forty-Five

This is a variation of Spoil Five for two, four (two against two), or six (three against three) players. The game is scored by points. The side taking three or four tricks scores 5 points; five tricks, 10 points. An alternative system is that each trick counts 5 points, and the score of the side taking the fewest tricks is deducted from that of the side taking the most tricks. Thus, three tricks count 5; four tricks, 15; five tricks, 25 points; 45 points is game.

Auction Forty-Fives

This variation of Spoil Five and Forty-Five is one of the most popular games in Nova Scotia. The number 45 is no longer relevant to the game.

Number of Players. Four people playing two against two as partners, or six (three against three as partners), seated alternately.

Bidding. The player on the dealer's left bids first, and the turn passes to the left. Bids are in multiples of 5 points, and the highest bid is 30. Each bid must be higher than the preceding bid except that the dealer is allowed to beat the previous bid merely by saying, "I hold"; if he does, each player who did not previously pass gets another turn, and the dealer again may take the bid without topping it. A side that has scored 100 points or more may not bid less than 20.

Discarding and Drawing. The high bidder names the trump. Then each player discards as many cards as desired, and the dealer restores the hand to five cards from the top of the pack. The player to the left of the high bidder leads first.

Scoring. Each trick won counts 5 points, and the highest trump in play counts an additional 5, making 10 points in all for the trick it wins. If the high bidder's side makes its bid, it scores all it makes; if it fails, the amount of the bid is subtracted from that side's score. The opposing side always scores whatever it wins in tricks. A bid of 30 (for all five tricks) is worth 60 if it is made, and it loses 30 if it fails. The game is won by the first side to reach 120.

AUCTION PITCH
(All-Fours, High-Low-Jack, Set Back)

NUMBER OF PLAYERS	NUMBER OF CARDS	GAME PLAY	SKILL LEVEL
3-5 (2, 6, 7)	**52**	◇ ◇ ◆ ◇ ◇ EASY → COMPLEX	◇ ◇ ◆ ◇ ◇ LUCK → SKILL

A ll Fours is a game of English origin and dates from the 17th century. Once known to virtually every card-playing American, it survives today, principally as Auction Pitch. It is still a popular game in the United States and has also evolved into Seven-Up, Cinch, and other games. There are many versions of Auction Pitch, and while the rules have changed greatly over the years, the essential feature has always been the scoring of high, low, jack, and the game.

Number of Players. Two to seven people can play, but the game is most often played by three to five people, with four players being the most popular number of participants. Each person plays for himself.

The Pack. The standard 52-card pack is used.

Rank of Cards. A (high), K, Q, J, 10, 9, 8, 7, 6, 5, 4, 3, 2.

The Draw. From a shuffled pack spread face down, each player draws a card. The player with the highest card deals and has his choice of seats. His opponents may sit where they please, and in case of any question, the player with the next highest card has preference.

The Shuffle and Cut. Any player may shuffle, the dealer shuffles last, and the player to the dealer's right cuts, leaving at least five cards in each packet.

The Deal. The dealer completes the cut and deals three cards at a time clockwise, in rotation, beginning with the player to his left, until each player has six cards. After each hand, the deal passes to the left.

Object of the Game. The goal is to be the first player to reach a total of 7 points. Points are scored as follows:

High. One point for holding the highest trump in play.

Low. One point for being dealt the lowest trump in play, no matter who wins it in a trick. (Variation: In many games, Low counts for the player winning it.)

Jack. One point for winning the trick on which the jack of trumps was played.

Game. One point for winning tricks with cards scoring the greatest value, each ten counting 10 points, each ace 4, each king 3, each queen 2, each jack 1.

If the trump jack is not in play, no one counts it. If two or more players tie for game, no one counts the point for game.

The Bidding. The player on the dealer's left bids first. Each player in turn may either bid or pass. The lowest bid is two, and each successive bid must be higher than any preceding bid, except the dealer, who can bid and play for the amount of the preceding bid. However, if any player bids four, he is said to "smudge," and the bid cannot then be taken away from that player.

THE JACK AND THE KNAVE

Bet You Didn't Know

Auction Pitch evolved from All Fours, an English pub game that dates back to the 17th century. It is the first game that used the term "jack," which is now the name used for the third-ranking face card in a standard 52-card pack. Previously, this card was known as the "knave." As the popularity of All Fours spread, the special role of the jack in scoring usurped the term knave. Today, the term knave has been relegated to an alternate name for jack.

The Play. The "pitcher" (highest bidder, or the dealer if he assumes the contract at the highest preceding bid) leads first. The suit of the card "pitched" indicates the trump suit. On a trump lead, each player must follow suit if possible. On any other lead, a player may either follow suit or may trump. When unable to follow suit, a player may play any card. The player of the highest trump – or the highest card of the suit led if the trick contains no trump – wins the trick and leads next.

Scoring. When all six tricks have been played, the points due each player are tabulated. Usually a score is kept with pencil and paper. Each player except the pitcher scores whatever points he makes. The pitcher scores whatever points he makes if the score at least equals the bid contract. However, if the pitcher has not scored as many points as were bid, he is "set back" by the amount of the bid – that is, the number of points bid is deducted from his score. Thus, a player may have a net minus score, which is called being "in the hole." The score for a player in the hole is indicated on the score sheet as a number with a ring around it.

The first player to reach a plus score of 7 points wins the game. The pitcher's score is counted first, so that if the pitcher and another player reach 7 points on the same hand, the pitcher wins, even if the other player has a higher total score. If two players other than the pitcher are able to reach 7 points on the same hand, the points are counted in this order: High, Low, Jack, Game.

A player who smudges and who makes the bid by winning all 4 points wins the game immediately – unless he was in the hole (in which case the smudger only receives the 4 points).

The winner of the game receives one point from each player whose score is 1 point or more, and 2 points from each player whose score is zero or minus (in the hole). (*Variation:* In some games, the winner receives an additional point from each player for each time that player has been set back.)

Irregularities. *Misdeal.* It is a misdeal if an ace, jack, or deuce is exposed during the deal. Since the deal is an advantage, a misdeal loses the deal.

Revoke (failure to follow suit or trump, when possible). A play once made cannot be withdrawn, so a revoke stands and play continues to the end. If the pitcher revokes, he cannot score and is set back the amount of his bid, while all the other players scores what that player makes. If any player except the pitcher revokes, all players except the revoker score what they make (including the pitcher, even if he does not make his bid); the revoking player cannot score and has the amount of the bid deducted from his score.

Error in bidding. A bid not higher than a previous bid, or a bid out of turn, is void, and the offender must pass.

Error in pitching. Once the pitcher plays a card, the trump cannot be changed. If a player pitches before the auction closes, he is assumed to have bid 4 and play proceeds. However, any player before the pitcher who has not had a turn to bid may himself bid 4 and pitch when it is his turn, whereupon the card illegally pitched, and any card played to it, must be withdrawn. If the wrong player pitches after the auction is closed, the pitcher may require that that card and any card played to it be withdrawn. In addition, when it is the offender's turn to play first, the pitcher may require him to play the highest or lowest card of the suit led, or to trump or not to trump. Exception: If the pitcher has played to the incorrect lead, it cannot be withdrawn and the pitcher must immediately name the trump, which he must then lead the first time he wins a trick.

Pitch

(Smudge)

One of the most popular forms of Auction Pitch, this game was formerly called Smudge. Now, it is usually called Pitch by those who play it.

This version is the same as Auction Pitch, except for the following changes: winning all 4 points in one hand constitutes a smudge by any player, whether he is the pitcher or not, and it wins the game immediately regardless of that player's previous score. The dealer is not permitted to take the contract unless he bids more than any previous bid. Low is scored by the player winning it in a trick, not necessarily by the player to whom it was dealt. In case of a misdeal, the same player deals again.

It is customary for every player to start with a score of 7. When a player is set back, the points he bid are added to his score. Points a player wins are subtracted from his score, and the first player to reach zero is the winner of the game.

Auction Pitch with a Joker

An enhanced version of Auction Pitch may be played with a 53-card pack, which includes the joker. There are 5 points in play, with the joker counting as 1 point to the player who wins it in a trick. The joker is the lowest trump in the play, but does not score for Low; that point goes to the holder of the lowest natural trump card. If the joker is pitched, it is a spade. The first player to score 10 points wins the game.

In counting points to determine the winner, the order is High, Low, Jack, Joker, Game. However, the pitcher's points are always counted first.

Sellout

In one of the popular early forms of Auction Pitch, the player on the dealer's left has the right to "sell" the right to pitch. The player on the dealer's left may either assume the contract for a bid of 4, or give each player, beginning on his left, one bid as in Auction Pitch. The player on the dealer's left may then sell to the highest bidder, in which case that player becomes the pitcher, and the player on the dealer's left immediately scores the amount of the bid; or that player may become the pitcher at the highest bid made, in which case the high bidder immediately scores the amount of the bid.

A player is not permitted to make any bid high enough to put the player on the dealer's left out if he sells, and the player on the dealer's left is required to sell if he would put the high bidder out by refusing to do so. The game is to 7 points.

CINCH
(High Five, Double Pedro)

NUMBER OF PLAYERS	NUMBER OF CARDS	GAME PLAY	SKILL LEVEL
4	52	◇ ◇ ◆ ◇ ◇ EASY → COMPLEX	◇ ◇ ◆ ◇ ◇ LUCK → SKILL

Once the most popular game of the All Fours family, Cinch eventually gave way to Auction Bridge and finally to Contract Bridge among serious card players.

Number of Players. Four people can play. Each may play for himself, but Cinch is almost always played by partners, two against two, who face each other across the table.

The Pack. The standard 52-card pack is used.

Rank of Cards. In trumps, the rank A (high), K, Q, J, 10, 9, 8, 7, 6, 5 ("Right Pedro"), 5 of same color as trumps ("Left Pedro"), 4, 3, 2. In the other two suits, the rank is A (high), K, Q, J, 10, 9, 8, 7, 6, 5, 4, 3, 2.

The Shuffle and Cut. From a shuffled pack spread face down, all players draw, and in a partnership game the two high cards play against the two low. The person with the highest card has the choice of cards and seats. Any player may shuffle; the dealer shuffles last, and the player to the dealer's right cuts, leaving at least four cards in each packet. The deal passes to the left after each hand.

The Deal. The dealer completes the cut and deals three cards at a time to each player clockwise, beginning with the player on his left until each player has nine cards.

The Bidding. The player on the dealer's left bids first, and each player has one turn to bid (or pass). Each bid must top the preceding bid. The highest possible bid is 14, which represents all the points in play.

Drawing and Discarding. The high bidder names the trump, and each player then discards all cards but trumps from his hand. The dealer gives each player in rotation enough cards to fill out each hand to six cards. Then the dealer discards and "robs" the pack – that is, he looks through the undealt cards and selects any cards there to fill out his own hand to six cards.

Each player except the dealer must discard all cards but trumps (though there is no prescribed penalty for failure to do so). If a player is forced to discard a trump, due to having seven or more trumps, he must show the discarded trump to the other players, after which the card is out of play.

A player may change his discard until he has looked at any card dealt to him in the draw, but thereafter the discard may not be changed. If he has discarded a trump, it must be shown, and then becomes a dead card. (If a scoring card is discarded in error by an opponent of the high bidder, it is later scored for the high bidder's side.)

Object of The Game. The goal is to win tricks with the scoring cards, each of which counts for the side or player winning it, as follows: High, 1; Low, 1; Jack, 1; 10 of trumps (Game), 1; each pedro, 5; making a total of 14 points.

The Play. The high bidder leads first and may lead any card. Each player must follow suit to a trump lead, if possible. If unable to follow suit, a player may play any card. On any other lead, a player may follow suit or trump, as desired. Any trick containing a trump is won by the highest trump played; any other trick is won by the highest card of the suit led.

Scoring. If the bidding side wins at least as many points as it has bid, the side with the higher count scores the difference between the two counts. Thus, either the bidding or the non-bidding side may score. If the bidding side does not make its contract, the non-bidding side scores 14 plus the number of points by which the bidding side fell short. *Example*: The bid is 6, and the bidding side wins 6 points, and the opponents win 8 points. The opponents score 2 points for that hand. *Another example*: The bid is 8, and the bidding side wins 7 points, and the opponents win 7 points; in this case, the opponents score 15 points.

Game is won by the first player or side to reach 51 points.

Irregularities. *New deal*. The same dealer deals again if a card is found face up in the pack; or, on demand of an opponent, if a card is dealt face up; or if the shuffle or cut was improper, provided this is noticed before the deal is completed.

Misdeal. The dealer loses the deal, which passes to the left, if he gives too many or too few cards to any player and this is discovered before the first bid is made.

Incorrect hand. A player with too few cards must play on; a player with too many cards must offer the hand, face down, and an opponent draws out the excess cards, which are shuffled back into the pack.

Bid out of turn. Neither member of the offending side may bid thereafter, but any bid previously made stands.

Lead or play out of turn. The card must be withdrawn on demand of an opponent if neither opponent has played to the trick. If a lead out of turn was made when it was the offender's partner's turn to lead, the offender's right-hand opponent may require him to lead or not to lead a trump.

Revoke. Play continues, but the offending side may not score in that hand, and if the offender is an opponent of the bidder, the bidder cannot be set.

SEVEN-UP
(All-Fours, Old Sledge)

NUMBER OF PLAYERS	NUMBER OF CARDS	GAME PLAY	SKILL LEVEL
2-4	52	◇ ◇ ◆ ◇ ◇ EASY ➤ COMPLEX	◇ ◇ ◆ ◇ ◇ LUCK ➤ SKILL

This is an Americanized version of All-Fours, the classic English pub game.

Number of Players. Two or three people can play, or four may play as partners, two against two.

The Pack. The standard 52-card pack is used.

Rank of Cards. A (high), K, Q, J, 10, 9, 8, 7, 6, 5, 4, 3, 2.

The Draw. From a shuffled pack spread face down, each player draws a card. The player drawing the highest card deals and has his choice of seats. In a partnership game, the players with the two high cards play against those with the two low cards.

The Shuffle and Cut. Any player may shuffle, the dealer shuffles last, and the player to the dealer's right cuts, leaving at least five cards in each packet.

The Deal. The dealer completes the cut and deals three cards at a time to each player clockwise, beginning with the player on the left, until each player has six cards. The next card is turned up and placed on top of the undealt cards which form the stock. If the upcard is a jack, the dealer scores 1 point immediately.

Making the Trump. If the player on the dealer's left stands, the suit of the upcard becomes trump, and that player leads first. If he "begs" (proposes to the dealer that three additional cards be dealt to each hand and that a new card be turned up as trump), the dealer may say, "Take it," whereupon the player scores one point for "gift." The gift is always awarded to the player on the dealer's left when he begs and the dealer rejects. The other alternative for the dealer is to "run the cards," accepting the beg by giving three more cards to each player and turning up another card as trump. If this new upcard is of a different suit from the first one, it becomes trump without further option; and if it is a jack, the dealer again scores 1 point. If the second card turned up is of the same suit as the first one, that card and the three cards dealt to each player are laid aside, and the dealer runs the pack again, continuing to do so until a new suit is turned up or until there are not enough cards to go around. In the latter case, there is a new deal by the same dealer.

There may also be a new deal by the same dealer if, when the second trump is turned, any player suggests "Bunch." This means that if no other player insists that the hand be played, the present deal is abandoned, and the cards are shuffled and dealt again.

If the cards have been run, once a trump is decided, each player discards enough cards, face down near himself, to bring his hand down to the original six.

Object of the Game. The goal is to be the first player to get rid of all his chips.

The Play. The player on the dealer's left leads first. Each player, in turn, must either follow suit or play a trump if possible. The winner of each trick leads next. If unable to follow suit to subsequent leads, the player may play any card, and is not required to play a trump.

Scoring. At the start of the game, each player has seven chips, and each time the player scores a point he puts one chip in the pot. In addition to the points for turn of jack and for gift, other points are scored as follows:

High. One point for being dealt the highest trump in play.

Low. One point for being dealt the lowest trump in play.

Jack. One point for winning the trick containing the jack of trumps.

Game. One point for winning in tricks the greatest total in counting cards, each ten counting 10 points, each ace 4, each king 3, each queen 2, and each jack 1. In case of a tie for game, in two-hand play, the non-dealer scores it. In three- or four-hand play, no one scores it.

The first player to get rid of all his chips wins the game. If the winner is not determined until the end of a hand, and two or more players are able to go out, the points are counted in this order: High, Low, Jack, Game. (In some games, 10 points instead of 7 constitute game.)

Irregularities. *Misdeal.* If the dealer gives any player an incorrect number of cards, he loses the deal, which passes to the player on his left. If the dealer exposes a card, the player to whom it is dealt may decide to let the deal stand or ask for a new deal by the same dealer.

Revoke. The offender cannot score for Jack or Game; each opponent scores 1 point if the jack is not in play and 2 points if the jack is in play.

CALIFORNIA JACK

NUMBER OF PLAYERS	NUMBER OF CARDS	GAME PLAY	SKILL LEVEL
2	52	◇ ◆ ◇ ◇ ◇ EASY → COMPLEX	◇ ◇ ◆ ◇ ◇ LUCK → SKILL

This game is a variation on the All Fours theme with the following twist: players replenish their hands from the stock after each trick, and the stock, unlike virtually all other card games, is always face up instead of face down.

Number of Players. The game is designed for two players.

The Pack. The standard 52-card pack is used.

Rank of Cards. A (high), K, Q, J, 10, 9, 8, 7, 6, 5, 4, 3, 2.

The Shuffle and Cut. From a shuffled pack spread face down, each player draws a card. High card deals. The dealer shuffles the cards, and the opponent cuts.

The Deal. The dealer completes the cut and distributes the cards either one or three at a time, beginning with his opponent, until each player has six cards. The remaining cards are squared and turned face up in the center of the table, serving as a stock. The top card is the trump suit for that deal.

The Play. The player on the dealer's left leads. The card led loses the trick to a higher card of the same suit or to a trump, but wins the trick otherwise. The winner of each trick leads next. The second player to each trick must either follow suit or trump, if possible. If unable to follow suit or trump, he may play any card.

The winner of each trick draws the top card of the stock, and the loser takes the next card. Since the top card of the stock is always exposed, an object of play frequently is to win or lose a trick depending on whether the player wishes to draw the top card of the stock or take a chance on what the next card will be. When the stock is exhausted, the last six cards of each player's hand are played out until all cards have been played.

Scoring. One point each is scored for taking the tricks that contain: High (ace of trumps), Low (deuce of trumps), Jack of trumps, and Game (the greatest number of points in counting cards, each ten counting 10 points, each ace 4, each king 3, each queen 2, each jack 1).

The first player to score 10 points wins the game. If both players reach 10 in the same hand, the points count in order: High, Low, Jack, Game.

Shasta Sam

Shasta Sam is the same game as California Jack, except that the stock is kept face down so that the winner of each trick does not know what card will be drawn. Before the deal, a card is cut or turned from the pack to determine the trump suit for that deal.

Chapter VI

Pinochle
and Related
Games

PINOCHLE
(Two-Hand Pinochle)

NUMBER OF PLAYERS	NUMBER OF CARDS	GAME PLAY		SKILL LEVEL	
2	48	◇ ◇ ◇ ◆ ◇		◇ ◇ ◇ ◇ ◆	
		EASY ➜ COMPLEX		LUCK ➜ SKILL	

Pinochle is a classic two-player game developed in the United States, and it is still one of the country's most popular games. The basic game of Pinochle is Two-Hand Pinochle, which derives from the European game Bezique. It is explained first.

Enthusiastic players have since created many interesting variations of Pinochle, including good versions for three players, four players (with partners, some including bidding subtleties incorporated from Bridge), and more.

Number of Players. Two people can play. Versions for more than two players follow this description.

The Pack and Rank of Cards. A 48-card Pinochle pack is used. It consists of: A (high), K, Q, J, 10, 9 (low) in each of the four suits, with two of each card. Less frequently, a 64-card Pinochle pack is used, which includes 8s and 7s as well.

The Shuffle and Cut. From a shuffled pack spread face down, each player draws a card. The person with the highest card deals first and has his choice of seats. If both players draw cards of the same rank, they cut again. The non-dealer may shuffle, then the dealer shuffles, and the non-dealer cuts, leaving at least five cards in each portion of the pack. The dealer completes the cut.

The Deal. The dealer gives 12 cards to each player, non-dealer first, dealt three or four cards at a time. The next card is turned up and placed on the table; it is the trump card and every card of that suit is a trump. The remainder of the pack forms the stock and is placed face down so as to cover half of the trump card. (When the 64-card pack is used, each player receives 16 cards.)

Object of the Game. The goal is to win tricks, so as to score the value of counting cards taken in on tricks, and to meld certain combinations of cards having values in points (see below).

The values of cards taken in on tricks are:

| 11 points | 10 points | 4 points | 3 points | 2 points | 10 points |

Each ace 11

Each ten 10

Each king 4

Each queen 3

Each jack 2

Last trick 10

Nines (and 8s and 7s, when the 64-card pack is used) have no point value.

The values of the melds are:

Class A

A, K, Q, J, 10 of trump suit (flush, or sequence) 150

K, Q of trump (royal marriage) 40

K, Q of any other suit (marriage) 20

Dix (lowest trump; pronounced "deece") 10

Class B

♠A, ♥A, ♦A, ♣A (100 aces) 100

♠K, ♥K, ♦K, ♣K (80 kings) 80

♠Q, ♥Q, ♦Q, ♣Q (60 queens) 60

♠J, ♥J, ♦J, ♣J (40 jacks) 40

Class C

♠Q, ♦J (pinochle) 40

VALUE OF MELDS

Class A

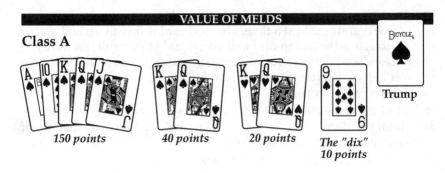

150 points   40 points   20 points   The "dix"
                                                           10 points

Trump

Class B

100 points   80 points   60 points   40 points

Class C

40 points

(The dix is the nine of trumps if the 48-card pack is used; it is the seven of trumps if the 64-card pack is used.)

The Play. Each trick consists of a lead and a play. The non-dealer leads; thereafter the winner of each trick leads next. When a trump is led, it wins the trick unless the opponent plays a higher trump. When any other suit is led, the card led wins unless the opponent plays a higher card of the same suit or a trump. The leader may lead any card, and the opponent may play any card. It is not necessary to follow suit.

After each trick, each player draws a card from the top of the stock to restore his hand to 12 cards; the winner draws first.

Melding. Upon winning a trick, and before drawing from the stock, a player may meld any one of the combinations that have value, as previously described. He makes his meld by placing the cards face up on the table, where they remain until he wishes to play them, or until the stock is exhausted. Melding is subject to the following restrictions:

1) Only one meld may be made in a turn.

2) For each meld, at least one card must be taken from the hand and placed on the table.

3) A card once melded may be melded again, only in a different class, or in a higher-scoring meld of the same class.

To illustrate these rules: A player may not put down ♠K, ♠Q, ♦J and score both for the marriage and for the pinochle; only one meld may be made in any turn. The player may put down ♠Q and ♦J for 40 points; and, after winning a subsequent trick, he may add the ♠K and score for the marriage. A player may meld the trump K, Q for 40 points and later add A, J, 10 for 150, but may not first meld ♠A, K, Q, J, 10 for 150 and later score for a royal marriage, even if he adds another king or queen of spades. A player may not meld ♦K, ♦Q and then meld another marriage in diamonds by adding another ♦K or another ♦Q. He would need a different king or queen of diamonds.

Once a card has been melded and placed on the table, it may be played to a trick as though it were in the holder's hand; however, after it has been played, it may no longer be used to form a new meld.

Melding the dix. If the dealer turns a dix (pronounced "deece") as the trump card, he scores 10 points immediately. Thereafter, a player holding a dix may count it merely by showing it upon winning a trick. He may count the dix and make another meld in the same turn. The holder of the dix has the right to exchange it, upon winning a trick, for the trump card.

The Playoff. The winner of the twelfth trick may meld if possible, and then must draw the last face-down card of the stock. He shows this card to his opponent, who draws the trump card (or the dix, if the exchange has been made). The winner of the preceding trick now leads, and the rules of the play are as follows: each player must follow suit to the card led if possible, and must try to win when a trump is led (by playing a higher trump). A player who cannot follow suit must trump if he has a trump. In this manner the last 12 tricks are played, after which the players count and score the points they have won in their tricks and melds.

Scoring. The score may be kept with pencil and paper, or chips may be used. If chips are used, there may be a central pile from which each player draws enough chips to represent the number of points he scores. Alternatively, each player may be provided with chips representing 1000, from which the appropriate chips are removed as points are scored.

Melds are scored when they are made. Scores for cards taken in tricks are added after the play is complete and the cards are counted. In this count, 7 points or more count as 10. *Example*: 87 points count as 90. If one player scores 126 and the other 124, or if each scores 125, they count only 120 each; the other 10 points are lost.

Game. Every deal may constitute a game. The player who scores the most points wins.

Alternatively, a match can be played to 1,000 points, playing a series of deals. When one player has scored 1,000 or more, and the other player less than 1,000, the former wins the game. If at the end of the play of any hand each player has 1,000 or more, play continues for a game of 1,250, even if one player has, for example, 1,130, while the other has only 1,000. If both players go over 1,250 at the end of the hand, the play continues for a 1,500-point game, and so on. However, this seldom happens because either player has the right, during the play, to "declare himself out."

Declaring Out. At any time during the play, a player may "declare out." At that point, play stops and his tricks are counted. If, in fact, the player has 1000 points or more, he wins the game – even if the opponent has more. If the claimant has fewer than 1,000 points, he loses the game. If the game has been increased to 1,250 points, 1,500 points, or a higher score, a player may declare out at that figure.

Variation 1. After declaring out, a player must win a trick before the cards are counted; and if, in the meantime, the opponent also declares out, the first player to win a trick is the one to have his cards counted and to win or lose the game, depending on his score.

Variation 2. The same as variation 1, except that the claimant's cards are not counted until he wins a trick on a lead from his own hand.

Three-Hand Pinochle

A Pinochle game on the order of the two-hand game was once played by three players, usually with a 64-card pack. Each player received 12 cards in the deal and played in turn. Game was 1,000, as in the two-hand game. This version has been superseded by Auction Pinochle (described on p. 214)

Partnership Pinochle

The basic game of Partnership Pinochle is described first. Several variations have grown in such popularity that they are also described below, including Partnership Auction Pinochle and Double-Pack Pinochle.

Number of Players. Four people can play, two against two as partners.

The Pack. The 48-card Pinochle pack is used.

Rank of Cards. A (high), 10, K, Q, J, 9. If duplicate cards are played to the same trick, the one played first ranks higher.

The Draw. The two players drawing the highest cards play as partners against the other two. If two players cut cards of identical rank, they draw again.

The Shuffle and Cut. Any player may shuffle the cards, and the dealer shuffles last. The player to the dealer's right cuts.

The Deal. The dealer distributes the entire deck, three cards at a time to each player in rotation, except that the last card is turned up to indicate the trump card. Every card of that suit is a trump for the current deal.

The Trump Card. Each player in turn, beginning with the player on the dealer's left, has the right to exchange the dix (nine of trumps) for the trump card. The trump card, or the dix exchanged for it, then becomes part of the dealer's hand, so that each player has 12 cards. If the dealer turns a dix as the trump card, he scores 10 points for it; each original holder of a dix scores 10, whether or not it was exchanged.

Melding. Following the exchange for the trump card, each player shows on the table any melding combinations he holds, and scores them in accordance with the tables and rules for basic Two-hand Pinochle. Instead of doubling the value of a single combination, the following scores are counted for double combinations:

Double pinochle	300
All 8 jacks	400
All 8 queens	600
All 8 kings	800
All 8 aces	1,000
Double flush	1,500

Having shown and scored their melds, all players pick up their hands. No meld finally counts unless the side making it wins at least one trick. If either member of that partnership wins a trick, both members score their melds.

The Play. The player on the dealer's left leads first and may lead any card. Each player in turn must follow suit if possible. Otherwise, he must play a trump. If a trump is led, each player must beat the highest card previously played. If a player is unable to play according to these requirements, he may play any card. The winner of each trick leads next. (*Variation:* In some games, each player in turn must try to win every trick, whether a trump trick or not, and must play a card higher than any previously played, even if the highest card so far was played by his partner.)

Scoring. A single score is kept for each partnership. The partnership is credited with the points both partners score in melds (provided the side wins at least one trick), plus the value of cards they have taken in tricks. Cards may be counted as in Two-Hand Pinochle (Aces, 11 points; tens, 10; kings, 4; queens, 3, and jacks, 2). However, most players simplify the count by scoring 10 for each ace or ten taken in, and 5 points for each king or queen, with jacks and nines counting nothing. Other players simplify still further by counting 10 points each for ace, ten or king and nothing for any lower card. In any of these methods, the winner of the last trick always scores 10 points, and the total points by cards are 250.

Game. The first side to score 1,000 points, in melds and cards, wins the game. Any player may claim the game ("declare out," as described for Two-Hand Pinochle) at any time he believes that his side has scored 1000 points or more. Play then stops, and the cards are counted to verify the claim. If the claimant's side has 1,000 points or more, it wins the game regardless of how many points the other side has. If the claimant's side has fewer than 1,000 points, it loses the game. The claimant's side may not count its melds in the current deal as part of its total unless it has won a trick after melding. If at the end of play in any deal, both sides have reached 1,000 or more, play continues to 1,250. If the same thing happens again, play continues to 1,500, and so on.

Partnership Auction Pinochle

Although other interesting variations follow this description, Partnership Auction Pinochle for four players is considered the classic form of the game.

The Deal. Twelve cards are dealt to each player, but a trump card is not turned.

The Play. Each player in turn, beginning on the dealer's left, may either bid or pass. The lowest bid is 100. When a player has passed, he may no longer bid; however, until then, he may bid each time it is his turn, provided the bid is higher than the last previous bid. Bids are made in multiples of 10 points.

The highest bidder names any suit as trump, and the players meld. Play then proceeds as in Partnership Pinochle, with the player on the dealer's left leading first, no matter who made the highest bid. A side that wins any trick may count the melds of both partners.

Scoring. If the bidding side, in melds and cards, scores at least the amount of its bid, it scores all the points it has made. If it scores less than its bid, the amount of the bid is deducted from its score, even if it causes that side to have a net minus score. The non-bidding side always scores all the points it makes. The first side to reach 1,000 points wins the game. There is no declaring out, since the score of the bidding side is always counted first, and both sides cannot reach 1,000 on the same hand.

The Widow. A variation is to deal only 11 cards to each player with a widow of four cards. The widow goes to the highest bidder, who looks at it, but does not show it. He then keeps one card and gives one card each, face down, to the other players.

Partnership Pinochle for Six or Eight

Six players form two partnerships of three each, sitting alternately. Eight players form two partnerships of four each, also sitting alternately. A double Pinochle pack (96 cards) is used, and the cards are dealt out four at a time, so that each player has 16 cards in the six-hand game and 12 cards in the eight-hand game.

The rules of Partnership Pinochle (with the last card turned as trump) or of Partnership Auction Pinochle (with players bidding for the trump) are followed.

Scoring. Instead of the scores for certain standard melds, as shown in the rules for Two-Hand Pinochle, multiples of these melds are scored as follows:

8 aces (2 of each suit)	1,000
8 kings (2 of each suit)	800
8 queens (2 of each suit)	600
8 jacks (2 of each suit)	400
Double pinochle	300
2 kings and 2 queens of same suit	300
Double flush	1,500
Triple pinochle	600
3 kings and 3 queens of same suit	600
Quadruple pinochle	1,200
4 kings and 4 queens of same suit	1,200
12 aces (3 of each suit)	2,000
12 kings (3 of each suit)	1,600
12 queens (3 of each suit)	1,200
12 jacks (3 of each suit)	800
Triple flush	3,000
15 of same denomination, (such as 15 aces)	3,000

Firehouse Pinochle

This is the game from which Check Pinochle was derived. It is a four-hand partnership game, with 12 cards dealt to each player and bidding for trump. The player on the dealer's left bids first, and each player has exactly one bid (or he may pass). The minimum bid is 200, and a player does not need any specific holding to bid. The high bidder names the trump and leads first. The game is won by the first side to reach 1,000 points, and the score of the bidding side is counted first.

Check Pinochle

This is a Partnership Auction Pinochle game in which special bonuses are paid in checks (chips) for unusual melds and for making or defeating the bid.

The Play. Four people play, two against two, using a regular 48-card Pinochle pack. Each player is dealt 12 cards, and no trump card is turned. The bidding begins with the player to the dealer's left. The minimum bid is 200. None of the first three players may bid unless the player holds a marriage in his hand. If all the players pass, the dealer must bid 200, and may bid more if he holds a marriage. Until he has passed once, a player may continue to bid in turn so long as he bids higher than the previous bid.

The high bidder names the trump suit. Then all the players may meld, according to the Partnership Pinochle table listed earlier on page 207. The high bidder leads any card, and the play proceeds as in Partnership Pinochle (see p. 206).

Scoring. The game is 1,000, and the score of the bidding side is counted first. Every hand is played out. A side cannot score its meld unless it has won a trick.

Check Awards. Each player collects from one of his opponents: for melding a round trip, 5 checks; flush, 2 checks; 100 aces, 2 checks; 80 kings, 60 queens, or 40 jacks, 1 check; double pinochle, 2 checks.

For making a contract of 200–240, 2 checks; for a contract of 250–290, 4 checks; 300–340, 7 checks; 350–390, 10 checks; and 5 checks more for each series of 50 points.

For defeating the opponents' contract: twice the number of checks for making a contract.

For making a slam (winning all 12 tricks): 5 checks.

For winning the game: 10 checks, plus 1 check for each 100 points (or fraction thereof) by which the winners' score exceeds the losers', plus 5 checks if the losers have a net minus score.

Irregularities. *Bidding without a marriage.* The opponents, after consultation, may elect: 1) to abandon the deal, 2) to assume the contract at the highest or lowest bid they made during the auction, or 3) to require the offending side to assume the contract at the highest bid it made.

Revoke. A revoke (failing to follow suit or trump when required and able to do so) becomes established when the offending side leads or plays to the next trick. All previous tricks stand, but all other cards go to the non-offending side.

Double-Pack Pinochle

The most popular form of Partnership Pinochle, Double-Pack Pinochle evolved during the 1940s and produced two innovations: a double pack, with no nines or lower cards, and bidding during which a player can tell his partner about the contents of his hand.

Number of Players. Four people can play, two against two as partners.

The Pack. A pack of 80 cards is used: four each of A, 10, K, Q, J (ranking in that order) in each suit. The pack is made by mixing together two regular 48-card Pinochle packs, and discarding all the 9s.

The Draw. Each player draws a card from the pack. The players with two highest cards are partners against those with the two lowest, and the highest deals. There is no rank of suits, and if two or more players draw cards of the same rank, they draw again to determine the order among themselves only. High card deals. (*Example*: A draws an ace, B and C draw kings, D draws a jack. B and C draw again; the higher will be A's partner, the lower D's partner. Player A deals.)

The Deal. The dealer shuffles the pack and offers it to an opponent, who cuts it approximately in half. The entire pack is dealt, four or five cards at a time, giving each player 20 cards. The turn to deal passes to the left.

The Bidding. Beginning with the player to the dealer's left, each player in turn may make a bid, announce a meld, or pass. Having once passed, a player may not bid again in that hand.

The minimum bid is 500. Bids are made in multiples of 10, and each bid must be higher than any previous bid. (It is customary to drop the extra zero at the end of every score and bid. *Example*: 50 instead of 500, 51 instead of 510, and so on.)

Before any player has bid, each player in turn may announce the amount of his meld, without giving any other information as to the nature of his hand, such as by announcing 100, 400 (or 10, 40). The player may announce more or less than the actual amount.

In making a bid, a player may state that it is based on a flush or on a long suit, and may also announce a meld, as by bidding 500 and announcing a flush and 100 meld. The bidder may not name a particular suit, or say that he has two long suits, or give any information as to the playing strength of the hand. If a player announces a flush or long suit before any bid has been made, he is deemed to have bid 500. If a player announces a meld in points after a bid has been made, he is deemed to have topped the previous bid by 10 points for each 100 points, or fraction of 100 points, that he announces. *Example*: The last bid was for 500; if the next player announces 100 meld, he has bid 510; if he announces 140 meld, the bid is 520. (In some games, only bids and passes are permitted, but not announcements.)

If all four players pass (or announce melds) but no one bids, the hands are thrown in and the next dealer deals.

Melding. The high bidder names the trump suit. Each player then melds, scoring as follows:

Sequences	Points
A, K, Q, J, 10 of trumps (flush)	150
K, Q of trumps (royal marriage)	40
K, Q of any other suit (marriage)	20

(There is no extra score for a duplicated sequence. A double flush counts only 300.)

Groups	Points
4 aces (one of each suit)	100
Double aces (two of each suit)	1,000
Triple aces (three of each suit)	1,500
4 kings (one of each suit)	80
Double kings (two of each suit)	800
Triple kings (three of each suit)	1,200
4 queens (one of each suit)	60
Double queens (two of each suit).	600
Triple queens (three of each suit)	900
4 jacks (one of each suit)	40
Double jacks (two of each suit)	400
Triple jacks (three of each suit)	600

A quadruple group counts simply as two doubles; sixteen aces count 2,000

Pinochle	
Pinochle (♠Q, ♦J)	40
Double pinochle	300
Triple pinochle	450
Quadruple pinochle	3,000

A card that is part of a meld under one heading may be counted as part of a meld under another heading, but not part of another meld under the same heading.

A side's melds do not count unless that side later wins a scoring trick. A worthless trick, such as four jacks, does not make the meld count.

The Play. The high bidder leads and may lead any card. Each player in turn must follow suit, if possible. If a trump is led, the player must top it if he can. If the player cannot follow suit, he must trump, if possible. If duplicate cards are played to the same trick, the one played first ranks higher. The winner of each trick leads next.

Scoring. Cards won in tricks may be scored in either of two ways, which should be agreed on before the game begins:

1) Aces, tens, and kings score 10 points each or

2) Aces and tens score 10 points each, kings and queens score 5 points each. Other cards count nothing, but the last trick counts 20. The total to be won in cards is 500.

If the bidding side makes at least the amount of its bid in melds and cards, it scores all it makes. If it makes less than the bid, the whole amount is subtracted from its score. That side's opponents always score whatever they made.

Game is 3,550, and the score of the bidding side is counted first.

(These rules are based on those prepared by Richard Setian of Philadelphia.)

Three-Hand Double-Pack Pinochle

There are two methods of dealing:

1) Twenty-five cards to each player and five to a widow; the high bidder must announce the trump before seeing the widow.

2) Twenty-six cards to each player and two to a widow; the high bidder may announce the trump after seeing the widow.

Game is 4,550. The minimum bid is 500, and if the first two players pass, the dealer must bid 500. There are no announcements of melds or suits in the bidding. Each player melds, but must win a scoring trick to make the meld count. The high bidder gets the widow and must discard an equal number of cards before picking up his meld. The discard counts, but he must still win a trick to score the meld. Any irregularity in discarding is a revoke.

The high bidder may concede defeat before leading, in which case each opponent scores his meld plus 100, while the bidder is set back the amount of his bid.

Six-Hand Triple-Pack Pinochle

Six people play in two partnerships of three each; each player has an opponent to his right and left. Three regular Pinochle packs, without the nines, are mixed together, making a pack of 120 cards. Each player is dealt 20 cards, and the rules of Double-Pack Pinochle apply, except that game is 4,550, the minimum bid is 750, and the last trick counts 30. Most of the extra melds made possible by the triple pack do not count extra; if a player should hold twenty aces, five of each suit, the value would be

2,500 (that is, 1,500 for triple aces plus 1,000 for double aces). However, a quintuple pinochle counts 4,000, and all six pinochles count 5,000 (which is more than enough for game, if the side is not 500 in the hole).

Auction Pinochle

This is the most popular form of Pinochle for three players and is played with the standard Pinochle pack.

Number of Players. Three players receive cards in the deal; these are the active players. (Four or five people can also play. If there are four players, the dealer receives no cards; if five people play, the dealer and the player second from his left receive no cards. These are the inactive players, who participate in the settlement, but not in the bidding or play.)

The Draw. The players draw to determine first deal and seats. The person drawing the lowest card deals first, the player with the next lowest sits on his left, and so on. There is no rank of suits, so players cutting equal cards cut again.

The Deal. Three or four cards at a time are dealt to each active player in turn, beginning on the dealer's left; a widow of three cards is dealt after the first round of dealing. All cards are dealt as follows: 1) either three cards, the widow, then four more rounds of three cards; or 2) four cards, the widow, two rounds of four cards, and a final round of three cards. Each active player receives 15 cards in all.

Object of the Game. The bidder seeks to score at least as many points as bid by making melds, and taking counting cards in tricks. The two opponents combine against the bidder to prevent him from making the contract.

Some Auction Pinochle Strategy Hints

As a rule the opponents should use the following methods:

1) "An ace calls for an ace." When the opponent on the bidder's left leads an ace, the other opponent is expected to play the other ace of that suit if he holds it.

2) "Smear on your partner's tricks." A player should fatten (or "schmier" in German), a trick taken by his partner by playing a high-scoring card on it, reserving the lowest cards for tricks won by the bidder.

It is understood that the typical play is not made when more points might be scored by a different play.

The Bidding. Each active player in turn, beginning with the player on the dealer's left, bids or passes. Having once passed, a player may no longer bid. The player on the dealer's left must start by bidding at least 300. Each successive bid, in multiples of 10, must be higher than any preceding bid. When two players have passed, the auction is closed; the player who made the highest bid wins the contract; and the other two players become his opponents. (*Variation:* In many games, the compulsory first bid by the player on the dealer's left is 250, not 300.)

The Widow. If the contract is for 300, the bidder may concede defeat without looking at the widow, in which case his loss is reduced (see "Concessions" below). If the bid is anything more than 300, or if the bidder of 300 does not wish to concede, he turns up the three cards of the widow so that all the players may see them and then adds them to his hand.

CHANCES OF FINDING A DESIRED CARD IN THE WIDOW		
Places open	**Chances**	**Approximate Odds**
1	961 out of 5,456	5 to 1 against
2	1,802 out of 5,456	2 to 1 against
3	2,531 out of 5,456	even
4	3,156 out of 5,456	3 to 2 for
5	3,685 out of 5,456	2 to 1 for

It must be remembered that there are two cards of every suit and denomination. With one ♦A in the hand, odds are 10 to 1 against finding the other ♦A in the widow.

Melding. The bidder names the trump suit and lays out his melds, which are scored in accordance with the following table:

Class A

A, K, Q, J, 10 of trump (flush, or sequence) 150

K, Q of trump (royal marriage) 40

K, Q of any other suit (marriage). 20

Dix (lowest trump) 10

Class B

♠A, ♥A, ♦A, ♣A (100 aces). 100

♠K, ♥K, ♦K, ♣K (80 kings) 80

♠Q, ♥Q, ♦Q, ♣Q (60 queens) 60

♠J, ♥J, ♦J, ♣J (40 jacks) 40

Class C

♠Q, ♦J (pinochle). 40

(No card may be used twice in melds of the same class, but the same card may be used in two or more melds of different classes.)

Cards count for the side winning them as follows: each ace, 11 points; each ten, 10; each king, 4; each queen, 3; each jack, 2; winning the last trick, 10. Some players simplify the count by scoring 10 points for aces and tens, 5 each for kings and queens, and zero for jacks or nines. Others simplify still further by scoring 10 points for aces, tens and kings and zero for other cards. Under any system, the total that can be scored is 250 points.

Burying. Only the bidder may meld. Then the bidder buries (discards) three cards face down in front of him, which count as a trick. The bidder may not bury any card he has used in a meld. However, he may change the trump suit, the melds, and the cards buried as often as desired before leading to the first trick.

The Play. Having melded and buried, the bidder restores the melds to his hand and leads first. He may lead any card. A trick consists of one card played by each player. The highest card of the suit led, or the highest trump if the trick contains any trump, wins the trick. When identical cards are played on the same trick, the card played first outranks the other. Each player must follow suit if possible; if a trump was led, he must try to win the trick if he can. If he cannot follow suit but has a trump, he must play a trump but need not try to win the trick if it has previously been trumped. The winner of each trick leads next.

Settlement. In Auction Pinochle, every deal is a complete game, and the players settle in full before the next deal. Settlement may be made with chips, or a score may be kept with pencil and paper. The bidder collects if his melds plus the value of the cards he has taken equal or exceed the amount of the contract. The bidder can never win more than he bid. The bidder pays if the points he scores fall short of his bid.

In settlement, the bidder pays to or collects from every other player in the game, (including the inactive fourth and fifth players, if any) and pays the kitty if the bid was 350 or more (see below).

The Kitty. A separate score is kept, and a separate pile of chips is maintained for an imaginary extra player called the kitty. The kitty collects only when a minimum bid of 300 is forfeited and pays or collects the same as an opponent does when the bid is 350 or more. Every player in the game owns an equal share of the kitty and must chip in to make up for any deficit when kitty cannot pay what it owes. Each player shares equally in any surplus remaining in the kitty when the game breaks up or when a player leaves the game.

Values of Bids. Every contract has a value in units or chips. The customary schedule of values is as follows:

Bid	Basic Values	Value if Spades Are Trump
300–340	3	6
350–390	5	10
400–440	10	20
450–490	15	30
500–540	20	40
550–590	25	50
600 or more	30	60

Variation. Several other schedules of unit values are in common use. These are:

1) The basic value doubles for each step above 350, so that 450 is worth 20; 500, 40; 550, 80 and so on. This schedule, however, tends to bring the value of an unusually big hand far out of proportion to the values of normal hands.

2) 300 is worth 1 chip; 350, 2 chips; 400, 4 chips; 450, 6 chips and so on, adding two chips for each step. These values apply when diamonds or clubs are trump. Spades count double and hearts count triple.

3) One unit or chip is added for every additional 10 points bid, so that 350 is worth 5 points, 360 is worth 6 points, 370 is worth 7 points, and so on.

Concessions. If all the players pass on the compulsory 300 bid, the bidder may forfeit without looking at the widow, in which case he pays the basic unit value (3 chips) to the kitty but nothing to the other players.

Having intentionally looked at any card in the widow, the bidder may concede defeat, in which case there is no play but the bidder pays the basic unit value of his bid to each opponent. This is called a "single bete."

The opponents, by agreement, may concede the bidder's contract without forcing him to play. In this event, the bidder collects the value of the bid from every other player.

Once the bidder leads to the first trick, the deal stands as though played out even if either side later concedes.

Deals Played Out. If the bidder makes the contract, he collects from each opponent. If he fails to make the contract, he pays every other player twice what would have been collected if he had won. This is called a "double bete."

Inactive Player. An inactive player should not look at the widow or at any active player's hand and may not give advice, or comment on any matter of judgment in bidding, play, or concession. He may, however, point out an irregularity such as a revoke or a play out of turn.

SIXTY-SIX

NUMBER OF PLAYERS	NUMBER OF CARDS	GAME PLAY	SKILL LEVEL
2	24	◇ ◇ ◆ ◇ ◇ EASY → COMPLEX	◇ ◇ ◆ ◇ ◇ LUCK → SKILL

Sixty-Six is an ancestor of Bezique and dates back to the 17th century. Played in its original form, it is still a very enjoyable game.

Number of Players. Two people can play.

The Pack. The standard 52-card pack is stripped of all cards except the A, K, Q, J, 10, and 9 of each suit, making a total of 24 cards.

Rank of Cards. A (high), 10, K, Q, J, 9.

The Deal. Each player cuts, and the player drawing the high card shuffles, offers the pack for a cut, then deals six cards each, three at a time, beginning with his opponent. The thirteenth card is turned up for trump and laid beside undealt cards which become the stock.

Object of the Game. The goal is to score 66 points as follows:

Marriage in trumps (K, Q announced)	40
Marriage in any other suit (K, Q announced)	20
Each ace (taken in on tricks)	11
Each ten (taken in on tricks)	10
Each king (taken in on tricks)	4
Each queen (taken in on tricks)	3
Each jack (taken in on tricks)	2
Winning last trick	10

The player who first reaches 66 scores 1 game point. If he reaches 66 before the opponent gets 33 (a "schneider"), he scores 2 game points; if before the opponent gets a trick (a "schwarz"), he scores 3 game points. If neither player scores 66, or each has scored 66 or more without announcing it, no one scores in that hand and 1 game point is added to the score of the winner of the next hand.

If a player "closing" (see below) gets 66 or more, he scores the same as if the game had been played out. If the player fails, the opponent scores 2 points. If a player closes before his opponent has taken a trick, but fails to score 66, the opponent scores 3 points.

The Play. The non-dealer leads first. No one is obligated to follow suit. The higher card of the suit led, or a trump played to a plain-suit lead, wins the trick. The winner of the trick draws the top card of the stock (the opponent taking the next card), and leads for the next trick.

Either player holding the nine of trumps may exchange it for a higher trump card at any time, provided he has previously won a trick, unless the nine is the last card in the stock. A "marriage" is announced by showing the appropriate king and queen and leading one of those cards. Marriages may be announced only when one of the two cards is played – unless a player by showing a marriage makes his score 66 or more.

The non-dealer may announce a marriage on his first lead and score it after he wins a trick.

After the stock is exhausted or closed, the non-leader on each trick must follow suit if possible. Marriages may still be scored.

Closing. Either player may close (end the game), when he has the lead, either before or after drawing, by turning down the trump card. Thereafter, no cards are drawn, and the last trick does not score 10 points.

If either player announces during play that his score is 66 or more, the play immediately stops and the game is "closed."

Game. Seven game points.

Three-Hand Sixty-Six

The dealer takes no cards and scores as many game points as are won on his deal by either of the other two players. If neither active player scores 66, or both score 66 or more but they fail to announce it, the dealer scores 1 game point, and active players do not score. The game is 7 game points. A dealer may not score enough to win the game; he must win his seventh point when he is an active player.

Four-Hand Sixty-Six

The A, 10, K, Q, J, 9, 8, 7 of each suit are pulled from a standard 52-card pack to form a 32-card deck. Eight cards are dealt clockwise to each player in packets of three, then two, then three, beginning with the player on the dealer's left. The last card is turned for trump and belongs to dealer.

The player on the dealer's left leads, and each succeeding player in turn not only must follow suit but must win the trick if possible. If the player cannot follow suit, he must trump or top the previous trump if he can.

The scoring is the same as in the two-hand game, except that there are no marriages. A side counting 66 or more, but less than 100, scores 1 game point; a side with more than 100 but less than 130 scores 2 points; if it takes every trick (130), the side wins 3 points. If each side has 65, neither scores, and 1 game point is added to the score of the winners of the next hand.

The game is 7 points. In some localities, the 10 of trumps counts 1 game point for the side winning it, in addition to its value as a scoring card. If one side has 6 game points and wins the 10 of trumps on a trick, that side scores game immediately.

BEZIQUE

NUMBER OF PLAYERS	NUMBER OF CARDS	GAME PLAY	SKILL LEVEL
2	64	◇ ◇ ◇ ◇ ◆ EASY → COMPLEX	◇ ◇ ◇ ◆ ◇ LUCK → SKILL

The original game of Bezique is the ancestor of American Pinochle, which, along with other versions – most notably, Rubicon Bezique and Six-Pack Bezique – have become more popular than the parent game. Three- and Four-Hand Bezique variations are described later.

Number of Players. Two people can play.

The Pack. Two standard 52-card packs are stripped to form two 32-card packs containing the Ace down through the seven of each suit. The 32-card packs are shuffled together to form a pack of 64 cards.

Rank of Cards. A (high), 10, K, Q, J, 9, 8, 7.

The Shuffle and Cut. One player shuffles. Each player lifts a portion of the pack and shows the bottom card. Low card deals first. If cards of the same rank are shown, the players cut again. Each player may then shuffle, the dealer last. The non-dealer cuts about half the pack and the dealer completes the cut.

The Deal. Eight cards are dealt in packets of three, then two, and then three, beginning with the non-dealer. The next card is turned and its suit indicates the trump suit. The undealt cards are placed face down, partly covering the trump card, and become the stock.

Object of The Game. The goal is to show and score for certain declarations, and to win tricks containing aces and tens, called "brisques."

Scoring. If the dealer turns a seven as the trump card, he scores 10. Thereafter, either player, upon winning a trick, may exchange a trump seven for the trump card, or merely declare a trump seven, and score 10.

The other declarations are:

      Marriage (K, Q of the same suit) in trumps. 40

      Marriage (K, Q) in any other suit 20

      Sequence (A, 10, K, Q, J of trumps) 250

      Bezique (♠Q, ♦J) 40

      Double Bezique. 500

      Any 4 aces. 100

      Any 4 kings. 80

      Any 4 queens 60

      Any 4 jacks 40

BEZIQUE SCORING

Trump

40 points   *20 points*   *250 points*

Bezique
40 points   *Double Bezique*
500 points

100 points   *80 points*   *60 points*   *40 points*

Each brisque (ace or 10) taken in counts 10. Winning the last trick counts 10.

All points except brisques are scored as soon as they are made, either on a scorepad or with chips. After the play ends, brisques and the last trick are counted and scored.

The Play. Non-dealer leads. Thereafter, the winner of each trick leads next. Any card may be played to the lead. The card led wins the trick unless a higher-ranking card of the same suit or a trump is played.

After winning a trick, a player may make any declaration by placing the cards face up on the table in front of him and leaving them there until he wants to play them, which he may do at any time.

After making the declaration, if any, the winner of the trick draws the top card of the stock, and the opponent draws the next card to restore each hand to eight cards.

A player may declare and show more than one declaration at a turn, but may score for only one at that time; he may score others (or a new declaration) the next time he wins a trick.

A card may not be used twice in the same declaration, but may be used in different declarations. *Example*: if spades are trump, the ♠Q may be used in a marriage, a sequence, a bezique and four queens; but if four queens were declared and one of them was played, another queen may not be added to the three still on the table to score an additional 60 points; four different queens would be required.

The K, Q of trumps may be declared as 40, and the A, J, 10 added at a later turn to score 250; but if the entire sequence is declared at once, the K, Q may no longer be declared as 40.

Likewise, a bezique may be declared as 40 and a second bezique added for 500, but if a double bezique is declared at once, it counts only 500.

When the stock contains only one face-down card, the winner of the previous trick takes it, but may not declare. His opponent takes the exposed trump. Each player picks up any cards still exposed on the table. The winner leads, and in the play of the last eight cards, each player must follow suit and try to win the trick if possible.

Game. The game is 1,500 points. If both players reach 1,500 on the same deal, the higher score wins. Some people play 1,000 points as the game, and in some games, each deal represents a full game.

Bezique Without Turning Trump

This game is like regular Bezique except that no trump card is turned. The first marriage declared establishes the trump suit, and there is no count for the seven of trumps.

Three-Hand Bezique

Three 32-card packs are shuffled together to make a 96-card deck. The player to the dealer's left leads first, and thereafter, the winner of each trick leads next. The three participants play in clockwise rotation. Only the winner of the trick may declare. A triple bezique counts 1,500; a player having counted 500 for a double bezique may add the third and count 1,500. Game is usually set at 2,000.

Four-Hand Bezique

Four 32-card packs are shuffled together to make a 128-card deck. The four players play in clockwise rotation. Participants may play as individuals or two against two as partners.

In the partnership version, partners face each other across the table, and the winner of each trick may declare, or may pass the privilege to the partner; however, if the partner cannot declare, the winner of the trick cannot then declare. Partners may not consult on who shall declare. A player may put down cards from his own hand to form declarations in combination with cards previously declared by his partner and still exposed on the table; but he may not declare any combination that the partner could not legally declare. *For example:* If one partner has declared a sequence, the other partner may not add a trump king to the queen in the sequence and score for a marriage.

After the last card of the stock has been drawn, each player in turn must beat the highest card previously played to a trick, even if that card was in his partner's hand.

A double bezique counts 500, and a triple bezique 1,500, but only if all the cards come from the hand of the same player. Game is usually set at 2,000 points.

SIX-PACK BEZIQUE

NUMBER OF PLAYERS	NUMBER OF CARDS	GAME PLAY	SKILL LEVEL
2	192	◊ ◊ ◊ ◊ ◆ EASY ➤ COMPLEX	◊ ◊ ◊ ◆ ◊ LUCK ➤ SKILL

A favorite game of Sir Winston Churchill (and one in which he was one of the earliest expert players), Six-Pack Bezique is fast, high scoring, and exciting. Many players think it is a better game than the standard Bezique.

Number of Players. Two people can play.

The Pack. Six 32-card Bezique packs are shuffled together. It does not matter if they differ in back design or color.

Rank of Cards. A (high), 10, K, Q, J, 9, 8, 7 in each suit.

The Shuffle. Both players shuffle, trading portions until all the cards are thoroughly mixed.

The Cut. Each player lifts a portion of the pack and shows the bottom card. The player cutting the high card has choice of seats and whether or not to deal. Since the deal is a disadvantage, it is customary to choose not to deal. If the players cut cards of the same rank, regardless of suit, they cut again.

The dealer then lifts off a part of the pack. If this portion contains exactly 24 cards, the dealer scores 250. The non-dealer then estimates the number of cards the dealer took off; if his guess is correct, he scores 150. The remainder of the pack is then toppled over, all cards face down, at the side of the table so that cards may easily slide off the top. This is the stock.

The Deal. Using the portion lifted off the pack, the dealer gives 12 cards to each player, one at a time, starting with his opponent. Any cards left undealt in the packet are restored to the stock. If the dealer runs out of cards before giving 12 to each player, he takes enough cards from the stock to complete the deal.

Object of the Game. The goal is to score points by showing certain declarations, sometimes called "melds," as in Pinochle, and by winning the last trick.

THE NOVEL "CUT 24" RULE

One of the most whimsical features of Six-Pack Bezique is the opportunity to score points even before play begins. If the dealer is successful in cutting exactly 24 cards from the top of the pack prior to dealing 12 cards to each player, he earns 250 points. Then the non-dealer has the chance to guess how many cards the dealer took off. If he is correct, he earns 150 points. An unusual skill element that is far removed from the traditional rules of card games, Cut 24 adds a unique twist to the already exciting game of Six-Pack Bezique.

Bet You Didn't Know

Declarations. The following combinations have scoring value:

Sequence (A, K, Q, J, 10) in trumps	250
Sequence (A, K, Q, J, 10) in any other suit	150
Marriage (K, Q) in trumps	40
Marriage (K, Q) in any other suit	20

Bezique:

♠Q, ♦J, if spades are trumps

♦Q, ♠J, if diamonds are trumps

♥Q, ♣J, if hearts are trumps

♣Q, ♥J, if clubs are trumps	40
Double bezique (2 such queens and jacks)	500
Triple bezique (3 such queens and jacks)	1,500
Quadruple bezique (4 such queens and jacks)	4,500
Any 4 aces	100
Any 4 kings	80
Any 4 queens	60
Any 4 jacks	40
4 aces of trumps	1,000
4 tens of trumps	900
4 kings of trumps	800
4 queens of trumps	600
4 jacks of trumps	400
Winning the last trick	250

Originally, the spade queen and diamond jack counted as bezique no matter what suit was trump, and no other queen and jack combination ever counted as bezique. Many players still follow this rule in playing Six-Pack Bezique.

In some games, "Carte Blanche" – which means no king, queen or jack in the 12 cards originally dealt – scores 250. The entire hand must be shown. Thereafter, each time the holder draws a card, he may show it before putting it into his hand; and if it is not a face card, the player again scores 250 for Carte Blanche. However, as soon as he draws a face card, or puts any drawn card into hand without showing it, the player may no longer score for Carte Blanche.

The Play. When the deal is completed, the non-dealer leads any card. The dealer does not have to follow suit. The card led wins unless a higher card of the same suit is played, or unless a trump is played to a plain-suit lead.

No points are scored for cards won in tricks. Therefore, the tricks are not gathered in, but are left face up in a pile.

The winner of each trick may show and score any one declaration. Then each player draws one card from the top of the stock to restore his hand to 12; the winner of the previous trick draws first and leads next.

The Trump Suit. The suit of the first marriage declared becomes trump. If a sequence is declared before a marriage, the suit of the sequence becomes trump. However, the same suit may not become trump in two consecutive deals. A marriage in the trump suit of the previous deal may be declared before the new trump is established and counts 20. (*Variation*: When it is played that ♠Q and ♦J always constitute a bezique, regardless of the trump, then the same suit may become trump in two or more consecutive deals.)

Method of Declaring. A player makes a declaration by placing the counting cards face up on the table and leaving them there; however, any such cards are available for play as though any of them were in the player's hand.

Every declaration is scored when it is made. Since the scoring is fast, special counting devices were often used for recording each player's score. Today, these devices are hard to find. Instead, players often use a pile of chips in at least three colors, representing 10, 100, and 1,000 points each. As a player scores, he takes the appropriate amount of chips from the pile.

The same card may be counted in a declaration more than once. *Example:* A player puts down ♠A, ♥A, ♦A, ♦A and counts 100. The player then plays one of the aces. If it wins a trick, or the next time the player wins a trick, he may put down another ace and score 100 again. However, no more than the cards necessary to any one declaration may be on the table at one time. *Example*: A player declares four queens of trumps, counting 600. The player holds another queen of trumps, but may not add it to the four on the table and score another 600. That player must first play one of the four queens on the table; then, if he wins that trick or a subsequent one, the queen may add the queen.

A marriage may be declared, and then A, J, 10 of the suit may be added to score a sequence. However, if the entire sequence is scored at one time, the count for the marriage is lost.

If a double bezique is declared, it counts 500. But if a single bezique is declared, it counts 40. When a second bezique is added (both cards of the first bezique being on the table), the full 500 is counted, making the total score for the two 540. Similarly, a third bezique may be added for a count of 1,500, provided that all cards of the double bezique are still on the table. Likewise, a fourth bezique may be added for 4,000, provided all cards of the triple bezique remain on the table.

Only one declaration may be scored during one turn. However, more than one declaration may be announced. *Example*: Hearts are trumps. A player who has the ♥K on the table puts down the ♥Q and ♣J, and declares, "40 for bezique, and 40 to score for the marriage of the ♥K and ♥Q." The next time that player wins a trick, he may score the additional 40. Actually a player may have several unscored declarations pending at the same time. He may select the order in which such declarations are scored, and the player does not have to score a combination unless he chooses—whether or not the necessary cards are on the table.

A player who has a declaration still unscored should announce it after every trick, whether or not that player wins the trick.

The Final Play. No declaration may be scored after the last two cards of the stock have been drawn. Each player then picks up any cards he has on the table, and the winner of the previous trick leads. In the play of the final 12 cards, the non-leader must follow suit to the card led if he can, and try to win the trick.

Game. Each deal constitutes a game, and the player with the higher score wins. The winner adds 1,000 to his score. If the loser has failed to reach 3,000, it is a "rubicon" (from the expression "failing to cross the Rubicon"), and the winner scores all the points made by both players even if his score was less than 3,000. *Example*: The winner scores 2,700; the loser 2,600. The winner scores 2,700 + 2,600 + 1,000 for game, for a total of 6,300. In computing the final scores, it is customary to disregard any fraction of 100 points.

Eight-Pack Bezique

This zany variation is exactly the same as Six-Pack Bezique, except for the greater number of cards and the following differences:

In the deal, each player receives 15 cards.

A single bezique counts 50, a double bezique 500, a triple bezique 1,500, a quadruple bezique 4,500, and quintuple bezique 9,000.

Five trump aces count 2,000, five trump tens 1,800, five trump kings 1,600, five trump queens 1,200, and five trump jacks 800.

The loser is rubiconed if he fails to reach 5,000.

Rubicon Bezique

This game is the forerunner of the Six-Pack and Eight-Pack variations.

Two people play, using four 32-card packs shuffled together, 128 cards in all. In the deal, nine cards are dealt to each player. No trump is turned; the first marriage declared is the trump suit.

A sequence in a non-trump suit (called a "back door") counts 150. A triple bezique counts 1,500, a quadruple bezique 4,500, and the last trick 50. There is no count for the seven of trumps.

Carte Blanche is scored as explained in Six-Pack Bezique (p. 225), except that it counts only 50 each time.

The same cards may be used more than once in the same declaration, as explained under Six-pack Bezique; however, there is no additional count for four of a kind in the trump suit.

Each player gathers in his tricks as they are won, but brisques are not counted except to break a tie or to permit a player to escape being rubiconed. If either player counts brisques, both count them.

Each deal constitutes a game, and the player with the higher score adds 500 for game. All fractions of 100 points are disregarded unless they are needed to determine the winner. If the player with the lower score has less than 1,000 points, including brisques, he is rubiconed; and the winner receives a bonus of 1,000 instead of 500, plus all the loser's points, plus 320 for all the brisques.

Chouette Bezique

Chouette Bezique is a variation that allows three or more people to play Rubicon, Six-Pack Bezique, or Eight-Pack Bezique. The game is similar in format to a game called Chouette, a version of Backgammon which is played when more than two players want to participate in the same game.

All three players draw a card from the shuffled packs. The player with the high card is "in the box" and has his choice of seats; the player with the next-highest card is "captain" and plays against the player in the box. The third player and any others are partners of the captain and may consult with him, but the captain makes the final decision on any play.

If the player in the box wins the game, he collects in full from every opponent and remains in the box. The captain then retires, and the next player in order of precedence becomes captain.

When the player in the box loses a game, he pays every opponent in full and retires, becoming lowest in order of precedence. The previous captain is now in the box, and the next in line becomes captain.

SKAT

NUMBER OF PLAYERS	NUMBER OF CARDS	GAME PLAY	SKILL LEVEL
3 (4, 5)	**32**	◇ ◇ ◇ ◇ ◆ EASY ➔ COMPLEX	◇ ◇ ◇ ◇ ◆ LUCK ➔ SKILL

Skat is often said to be the best three-player card game in the world. What is not mentioned nearly so often is that it is also the most complex! Whereas most three-player games are variations of games that are better-played with two or four people, Skat is actually designed with three players in mind – and works best that way.

The game was first brought to the United States and other countries by German immigrants. It peaked in popularity during the 1940s, then went into a decline. In recent years, it has become more widely played, and many players rate it among the most scientific of all card games. Players with the patience to learn its many subtleties will be well-rewarded.

Newcomers to the game will find the rules easier to grasp if they first understand that Skat has a very complex scoring system. While this broadens a player's strategic options, it also makes the game difficult to learn. In most bidding games, the winner of the bidding simply names the trump, with a few other options (such as no-trump or bidding "null.") In Skat, however, the winner of the bidding has an array of options, which can be mixed and matched to "customize" a game format that best fits his hand and (theoretically) maximizes his score. Each option has a "degree of difficulty" called a "multiplier," which is then factored into the score. A hand can be played with several such multipliers. Before jumping into the complex combinations, newcomers should try to experience a few of the many possibilities by using basic play in several practice games.

Number of Players. Three people can play. Four or five may participate, but only three people can actually play at one time.

The Pack. The standard 52-card pack is used and stripped to create a deck of 32 cards which includes the A, K, Q, J, 10, 9, 8, and 7 of each suit.

Rank of Cards. When there is a trump suit, the four jacks are always the four highest trumps, ranking as follows regardless of which suit is trump: ♣J (high), ♠J, ♥J, ♦J. The remainder of the trump suit, and also non-trump suits, rank in this order: A, 10, K, Q, 9, 8, 7. The cards in every suit rank A, K, Q, J, 10, 9, 8, 7, only when there is no trump suit.

The Draw. For games at home, the players may decide on positions at the table in any way they wish. In tournament play, seats are assigned under the direction of the *Skatmeister* (referee).

The Shuffle, Cut, and Deal. One participant is chosen to keep score. The player on the scorekeeper's left deals first. The dealer makes the last shuffle, and the pack is cut by the player on his right. The turn to deal rotates clockwise around the table. The most desirable time to end the play is when all players have dealt the same number of times.

Cards are dealt to only three players. (With four at the table, the dealer gives no cards to himself. With five people at the table, the dealer gives cards only to the first, second, and fourth players from his left. He always deals the first packet of cards to the player on his left.)

The rule of the deal is "3–skat–4–3." That is, a round of three cards at a time is dealt. Then two cards are dealt face down in the center of the table, constituting a "skat," or blind. Then a round of four cards is dealt at a time, and finally a round of three cards at a time.

Designation of Players. The player on the dealer's left is called the "Forehand" (or "Leader"), the other two players in order being "Middlehand" and "Rearhand" (or "Endhand"). The player who finally wins the bidding is called the Player, and the other two become the opponents.

Object of the Game. At all trump declarations, the primary object is to win counting cards to the total of 61; other goals are to win 91 points or win all the tricks. If the game is Null or Schwarz Announced, the Player tries to either lose or win all the tricks. At Ramsch, the object is to gather as few counting cards as possible.

It must be emphasized that the Player scores nothing, and loses the value of the game, if he fails to take in tricks the minimum number of points guaranteed by that game (see the table on p. 233) whether it is 61 points, 91 points, all the tricks, or none of the tricks, whatever the case may be.

The Play. The opening lead is always made by the player on the dealer's left, who may lead any card. All other players must follow suit if they can, remembering that at any trump declaration, all four jacks are trumps. If unable to follow suit, a player may trump or discard; no one is required to win tricks in any suit even if they are able to. A trick that contains a trump is won by the highest trump played; tricks without trumps are taken by the highest card of the suit led. The winner of each trick leads next.

Bidding Sequence. An unusual type of competitive auction is used to determine which player may declare trump and "game" (the type of play to follow).

The Leader has an advantage in bidding because he is entitled to name the trump and game unless another player makes a bid that the Leader is unwilling to equal. The Leader does not specify how high he is willing to bid.

First, the Leader competes with the Middlehand player who begins by making a bid. If the Leader wants to bid the same amount, he says, "I hold" or "Yes." To win the right to name trump, Middlehand must increase the bid to an amount that the Leader is unwilling to equal. When either player wants to drop out of the bidding, he says "Pass" or "No." Then the remaining player, or survivor, competes against the Rearhand, who may try to buy the privilege of naming trump and game using the same bidding procedure.

If both the Middlehand and Rearhand pass without bidding, the Leader names the game (without bidding any specific number of points) or passes. In the latter case, the hand must be played at "Ramsch" (each player alone, as described below). Otherwise, the winning bidder, now called the Player, declares his game.

SKAT GAMES BASE VALUES				
GAME	TRUMP			
	♦	♥	♠	♣
Tournee	5	6	7	8
	♦	♥	♠	♣
Solo	9	10	11	12
Grand	*With Jacks as the only trumps*			
Tournee	12			
Guckser	16			
Solo	20			
Ouvert	24			
Ramsch	10			
Null	*Notrump*			
Simple	20			
Ouvert	40			

Bidding. Each bid names a number of points without specifying trump or game. The lowest possible bid is 10. It is customary to bid up by increases of 2 points, such as 10, 12, 14, and so on.

Games. To the left is the list of the fifteen possible games that the Player may declare, together with their base value, which is used to determine the scoring value of each game.

Solo. On declaring Solo, the Player must also name the trump suit. The two Skat cards (blind) are left face down, and the hands are played out as dealt.

Tournee. On declaring Tournee, the Player picks up the top Skat card. He may use it to fix the trump suit, in which case it must be shown to the others, or may reject it as trump without showing it (this privilege is called "Passt mir nicht" which is German for "It does not suit me").

If the first Skat card is rejected, the second is turned face up and fixes the trump suit. The game is then known as "second turn."

If the card turned is a jack, the Player may either select that suit as trump or may declare that only jacks will be trumps, in which case the game becomes *Grand Tournee.*

Whether trump was fixed by the first or second card, the Player is entitled to put both Skat cards in his hand and discard any other two cards face down.

Grand. In all Grand games, the jacks are only trumps. *Grand Solo* is played without the use of the Skat. On announcing *Guckser*, the Player picks up the Skat cards without showing them and discards any other two cards face down, leaving 10 cards in his hand. *Grand Ouvert* is a contract to win all the tricks, with the Player's hand exposed on the table before the opening lead. *Grand Tournee* can be announced only if a jack is turned up from the Skat, following announcement of Tournee. The Player then has the option of declaring only jacks as trumps, for a Grand Tournee.

Ramsch. Played only when all three participants refuse to make a bid or name another game, Ramsch is a Grand game, with only jacks as trumps. Each player plays individually and tries to take in as few points as possible.

Null. At Null, there are no trumps, and the cards in each suit rank: A (high), K, Q, J, 10, 9, 8, 7. An announcement of Null is a contract not to win a single trick. The Skat cards are set aside unused. In *Null Ouvert,* the Player must expose his whole hand face up on the table before the opening lead.

The Skat. The two cards set aside from the play, whether they are the Skat that was dealt originally or discards from the Player's hand, are added to the Player's tricks at the end of play. Any counting cards in the Skat are reckoned in his score. At Ramsch, the Skat goes to the winner of the last trick.

Values of the Games. The point value of each game has to be computed for scoring as well as bidding purposes. The point value of Null games is always 20 or 40, as shown in the table. The point value of every other game is found by multiplying its base value, (as shown in the table), by the sum of all applicable multipliers. Following is the list of possible multipliers. An explanation follows the listing.

Multiplier

Matadors (each). 1

Game 1

Schneider 1

Schneider announced 1

Schwarz 1

Schwarz announced 1

Matadors. The term matadors refers to a hand with top trumps in an unbroken sequence from the ♣J down. A hand holding the ♣J is said to be "with" a specified number of matadors. A hand lacking the ♣J is said to be "against" as many matadors as there are trumps higher than the highest in the hand. *Examples:* A trump suit headed by ♣J, ♠J, ♦J, is "with two" because the ♥J is missing. A trump suit headed by ♦J, A, 10 is "against three."

The first item in the total of multipliers applicable to a trump declaration is the number of matadors which the hand is either "with" or "against." The skat cards, whether or not the Player used them, are counted as part of his hand in counting matadors. If the hand is "with," the skat may increase but cannot decrease the value of the Player's game. However, if the hand is "against," a matador found in the skat may decrease the value. *Example*: The Player has bid 30 and declares Heart Solo. The Player's trumps are headed by ♥J. Thus, he is "against two" and expects to make contract through "Matadors 2, game 1, total multipliers 3; 3 times 10 is 30." But the ♣J is found in the skat; now the hand is "with one," the multipliers are reduced by one, and the Player is set – unless the Player manages to make schneider when he plays.

Game. In declaring any trump game, the Player contracts to win in tricks (plus whatever is in the skat) at least a majority of the 120 points in the pack, reckoned on this count:

Each ace 11

Each ten. 10

Each king. 4

Each queen 3

Each jack 2

(No count for lower cards)

If he gathers in tricks enough cards to total 61 points or more – that is, a majority of the 120 points available – the Player earns one multiplier, called (the "point for game").

Schneider. The Player strives to reach 61 points in cards, while the opponents strive to reach 60. Failure by either side to reach half that total (31 for Player, 30 for opponents) constitutes schneider and adds one multiplier.

Schneider announced. The Player may add one multiplier by predicting, before the opening lead, that he will make schneider (gather at least 91 points in cards). This announcement is allowed only in games where the skat cards are set aside untouched.

Schwarz. The winning of all ten tricks by one side constitutes schwarz and adds one multiplier.

Schwarz announced. The Player may announce schwarz before the opening lead–that is, he may contract to win every trick, and thereby gain one additional multiplier. Schwarz may be announced only in games where the skat is not used.

Computing the Game. The table of multipliers above shows the order in which the total score must be computed, since all points beyond the count of matadors are cumulative. That is, having earned any of the subsequent multipliers, the Player is entitled to all those preceding it. *Example*: If the Player earns the point for schwarz, he also gets the points for schneider and schneider announced.

The Player is not permitted to announce a game that cannot possibly score the value of the bid. For example, the Player may not declare Null if the bid is more than 20, nor Null Ouvert if the bid is more than 40.

Scoring. The score sheet contains one column for each participant in the game. At the end of a hand, the value of the game is computed, as previously described. This value is entered as a plus quantity in the column of the Player, provided that it is at least as large as his winning bid, and as long as he has taken the minimum of points or tricks needed for the game he selected. If the Player fails in either respect, the value of the game is entered in his column as a minus quantity. Moreover, the loss is doubled if the game was Guckser or second turn in a Tournee.

The multipliers for game, schneider, and schwarz are duly applied to determine the value of the game; if the Player did not reach 61 points, the multipliers accrue to his opponents. Therefore, on reaching 60 points, the opponents need not cease play, but may demand that the game continue so that they may try to earn the multipliers for schneider or schwarz.

The value of the game may fall short of the bid if there is an unlucky skat when the Player is "against," (see Matadors, p. 235), but the loss must be at least equal to the bid. In this case, the debit is the lowest multiple of the game's base value game that equals or exceeds the

Player's bid. *Example*: The Player bid 24 and announced Spade Solo. He was originally "against two," but skat held the ♠J. Although the Player made 61 points in cards, his game was worth only 2 x 11, or 22. The loss is 33, the lowest multiple of the base value 11 that exceeds 24.

Scoring of Ramsch. Ramsch is the only skat game in which each person plays alone (without the two opponents acting as partners). The player who gathers the least points in tricks is credited with 10 for winning the game, or 20 if he takes no tricks at all, the others scoring nothing. If all three players tie in points taken in tricks, the leader is the winner and scores 10 points. If two players tie for low score, the one who did not take the last trick is the winner and scores 10. If one player takes all the tricks, he loses the game and has 30 points subtracted from his score.

Settlement. A running total is kept of the points scored or lost by each player. When play ends, each participant pays or receives according to the amount by which his final score falls below or above the average of all the scores. *Example*:

Final scores:

W	X	Y	Z
28	-75	137	82

It is convenient to first eliminate the minus signs by adding to all scores the numerical value of the largest minus score. Thus, 75 is added to each score above:

W	X	Y	Z
103	0	212	157

The total of the scores is now 472. Divide by 4, the number of players, to find the average, 118. Then the differences from average are:

W	X	Y	Z
-15	-118	+94	+39

The final plus and minus totals must, of course, balance. In this example, -113 balances +113.

Irregularities. *Revoke or misplay by Player.* If the Player misleads or neglects to follow suit, he loses the game even if he already has 61 points or more. However, any of the opponents may opt to correct the error and proceed with play in order to increase the Player's loss. If an opponent misleads or does not follow suit, the Player wins the game, and the full value of his score is deducted from the offending opponent's score.

Räuber Skat

In this variation, the Tournee game is eliminated, and the Player has the option of "handplay" – playing without the skat – or of picking up the skat and then naming the "game." In either case, he has a choice between naming a suit or only the jacks as trumps.

The increased use of the skat leads to livelier bidding and to some spectacular possibilities.

EXPECTANCY OF FINDING DESIRED CARDS IN THE SKAT			
The bidder's chance of finding at least one helpful card in the skat is shown in the following table:			
To find	**Probability for**	**Percentage for**	**Approximate odds**
Any one card	1 in 11	9%	10 to 1 against
Either of 2 cards	41 in 231	18%	5 to 1 against
Any one of 3 cards	20 in 77	26%	3 to 1 against
Any one of 4 cards	26 in 77	34%	2 to 1 against
Any one of 5 cards	95 in 231	41%	3 to 2 against
Any one of 6 cards	37 in 77	48%	even
Any one of 7 cards	6 in 11	55%	6 to 5 for
Any one of 8 cards	20 in 33	60%	3 to 2 for
Any one of 9 cards	153 in 231	66%	2 to 1 for

SCHAFKOPF
(Sheepshead)

NUMBER OF PLAYERS	NUMBER OF CARDS	GAME PLAY		SKILL LEVEL	
3 (4, 5)	**52**	◇ ◇ ◇ ♦ ◇	EASY → COMPLEX	◇ ◇ ◇ ♦ ◇	LUCK → SKILL

One of the precursors of Skat, Schafskopf is a German game that is at least 200 years old. The name comes from its original scoring system, in which marks were made on paper in the form of a sheep's head. In addition to the principal variations described here, there are many other versions for four or six actual players.

Number of Players. Three people can play. Four or five may participate, but only three can actually play at the same time.

Rank of Cards. All queens, jacks, and diamonds are trumps, ranking in the following order: ♣Q (high), ♠Q , ♥Q, ♦Q, ♣J, ♠J, ♥J, ♦J, ♦A, ♦10, ♦K, ♦9, ♦8, ♦7.

In each of the three side suits, the cards rank: A (high), 10, K, 9, 8, 7,

The Deal. The draw, shuffle, cut and deal are as in Skat. The dealer gives three cards at a time to each of the players, then two cards face down for the blind, then a round of four at a time, and finally a round of three at a time, for a total of 10 cards per player.

Determining the Player. The player on the dealer's left has first chance to pick up the blind. If he refuses, the privilege passes to the two other players in turn. Whoever picks up the blind becomes the Player and assumes a contract to win a majority of the points for cards. The Player plays alone against the other opponents. After picking up the blind, the Player discards two cards face down to restore his hand to 10 cards.

If all three players pass, the hand must be played at "least" (as described below).

Game. For purposes of determining game, the cards have point values as follows (whether trump or plain):

Each ace 11
Each ten 10
Each king 4
Each queen 3
Each jack 2
(No count for lower cards)

The total points in the pack is 120, and the Player wins game if he takes 61 points or more in tricks. If the Player gathers 91 points or more, it is a called "schneider" as in Skat: and if all the tricks are taken, it is a "schwarz."

Least. If all three players pass, the hand is played for "least." Each participant plays for himself. The object is then to take as few of the points for cards as possible. The blind is left untouched until the play is completed, when it goes to the winner of the last trick.

The Play. The player on the dealer's left makes the opening lead. The winner of each trick leads next. A player must follow suit if possible. If unable to follow suit, a player may trump or discard at will. No one is required to win a trick even if he can. The highest trump played, or the highest card of the suit led if no trump is played, wins the trick. It is important to remember that all queens, jacks, and diamonds belong to the same trump "suit."

Scoring. Individual scores are kept on paper, with a running total for each participant. If the blind is picked up, the scoring values are:

Game 2

Schneider. 4

Schwarz. 6

If the Player reaches 61 points or more, he is credited with the appropriate figure; if the Player fails to make 61, he is debited the appropriate figure
(4 if he fails to catch 31 points, or 6 if he loses all the tricks.)

Scoring the game "least," the player who gathers the fewest points scores plus 2–plus 4 if he wins no tricks at all. If one person takes all the tricks, he is debited 4. If two players tie for low, the one who did not take the last trick wins and gets 2 points. If each player gets 40 points in cards (a triple tie), the winner is the hand that passed third, and that player scores 2.

Auction Sheepshead

This is a version of Schafskopf for four people who play two against two as partners. The cards are dealt four at a time, each hand receiving eight cards. The player on the dealer's left makes first bid or pass, and each other player is allowed one bid. Bidding is by the number of points over 60 that the bidder (with the help of his partner) guarantees to win in play. The only permanent trumps are ♣J (high), ♠J, ♥J, ♦J. The winning bidder names the trump, and the player on the dealer's left makes the first lead. The rest of the rules of play are the same as in Schafskopf.

SIX-BID SOLO

NUMBER OF PLAYERS	NUMBER OF CARDS	GAME PLAY	SKILL LEVEL
3 (4)	**36**	◇ ◇ ◇ ◆ ◇ EASY → COMPLEX	◇ ◇ ◇ ◆ ◇ LUCK → SKILL

Many versions of Skat are played, including Solo, Slough, or Sluff. These are thought to derive partly from an old German game called "Frage" (pronounced like frog) which used Tarot cards. Common to all of these variations is that the point value of the cards and the object of play are the same as in Skat. How they differ is mainly in the number and types of "games" or declarations that may be bid. One of the most popular variations is Six-Bid Solo.

Number of Players. Three people can play. Four may participate, but only three people are dealt cards during any one deal.

The Pack. The standard 52-card pack is stripped to a 36-deck that includes the A, K, Q, J, 10, 9, 8, 7 and 6 of each suit

Rank of Cards. The cards in each suit rank: A (high), 10, K, Q, J, 9, 8, 7, 6.

Point Value of Cards. The point value of the high cards is as in Skat:

> Each ace counts 11
> Each ten counts 10
> Each king counts. 4
> Each queen counts 3
> Each jack counts 2
> *(No count for lower cards)*

The Deal. Only three players participate in each hand. If four people play, the dealer deals only to the other three players. The rule of the deal is "4–3–widow–4." That is, the dealer first deals a round of four at a time, beginning with the player on his left, then a round of three at a time, then three cards face down for a widow, or blind, and, finally, a round of four at a time, for a total of 11 cards dealt to each player.

Bidding. The player on the dealer's left makes the first bid or pass. Each bid consists in naming one of the six "games." If he bids and the next player bids more (names a higher-ranking "game"), these two players must first settle who can make the higher bid. Once a player passes, that player is out of the bidding. The third player settles with the survivor of the first two bidders as to who can make the higher bid. The player who wins the bidding is called the Bidder. If all three players pass, the next dealer deals a new hand.

The Games (Bids). There are six possible bids, ranking as follows:

Call Solo (highest)

Spread Misere

Guarantee Solo

Misere

Heart Solo

Solo (lowest)

Call Solo. The Bidder undertakes to win all 120 points. The widow is not used in play, but is added to the Bidder's tricks at the end. Before the opening lead, the Bidder calls for any card not in his hand, and the holder of this card must give it to the Bidder in exchange for any card that the Bidder chooses to give in return. If the called card is in the widow, there is no exchange of cards.

Spread Misere. Same as Misere, with two additions: the Bidder exposes his entire hand face up after the opening lead, which is made by the player on his left.

Guarantee Solo. The Bidder guarantees to win a certain minimum of the counting cards: 74 points if the Bidder names hearts as trumps, or 80 if he names another suit. The widow is not used during play, but is added to Bidder's cards afterward.

Misere. There are no trumps, and the Bidder undertakes to avoid taking any counting card. The widow is set aside and is neither used during play, nor counted afterward.

Heart Solo. Same as simple Solo in all respects, but hearts are trumps.

Solo. At simple solo, the Bidder names any suit other than hearts as trumps. The widow is set aside untouched, but is added to the Bidder's cards at the end of play. The Bidder does not name trump unless his bid proves to be the high one.

The Play. Except in Spread Misere, the opening lead is always made by the player on the dealer's left. Each player must follow suit if possible; if he cannot follow suit, he must trump if he can. There is no need to trump high or low. The object, if there is a trump, is to win counting cards. The object in both Misere games is to avoid taking any cards that count. The two other players combine against the Bidder.

Scoring. For convenience, most players use counters or chips to settle the score after every deal. The Bidder, if he has made the required number of points, collects the value of the game from each of the other players. If the Bidder fails, he pays a like amount to the other two players. If there are four players, all share in the gains or losses, except that in Simple Solo or Heart Solo, the winner collects only from the two other active players.

Game	Bidder Must Take	Value in Chips
Call Solo	120 points	
hearts trumps		150
another trump		100
Spread Misere	no points	60
Guarantee Solo		40
hearts trumps	70 points	
another trump	80 points	
Misere	no points	30
Heart Solo	60 points	3
		(for each point over or under 60)
Simple Solo	60 points	2
		(for each point over or under 60)

(In Simple Solo and Heart Solo, if each side wins 60 points there is no score for the deal.)

Frog

Extremely popular in Mexico and the southern United States, this variation of Solo makes an excellent introduction to both Six-Bid Solo and Skat. Essentially, it's the same as Six-Bid Solo except that only three bids are possible:

Frog (lowest). Hearts are trumps. The Bidder picks up the widow and then discards any three cards face down. The Bidder collects or pays for every point he takes in play over or under 60.

Chico has the same meaning as Simple Solo in Six-Bid Solo.

Grand (highest) has the same meaning as Heart Solo in Six-Bid Solo.

SOLO
(Ombre, Spanish Solo)

NUMBER OF PLAYERS	NUMBER OF CARDS	GAME PLAY	SKILL LEVEL
4	32	◊ ◊ ♦ ◊ ◊ EASY → COMPLEX	◊ ◊ ◊ ♦ ◊ LUCK → SKILL

Not to be confused with the variations of Skat and Whist known by the same name, Solo was once a popular game known throughout the world as Ombre or Hombre. It is also known as Spanish Solo because it is very popular in South America. It is an easy, fast-moving game free of the complexities in count and scoring found in the other variations,

Number of Players. Four people can play.

The Pack. The standard 52-card pack is stripped to create a 32-card deck comprised of the A, K, Q, J, 10, 9, 8, and 7 in each suit.

Rank of Cards. The black queens are permanent trumps. The ♣Q, called "spadilla," is the highest trump, and the ♠Q, called "basta," is the third-highest trump. The second-highest trump, called "manilla," is the seven of the trump suit. The cards in each suit, trump or plain, rank as follows: A (high), K, Q (in red suits), J, 10, 9, 8, 7 (unless promoted to "manilla").

The Draw. Any player distributes the cards face up, one at a time around the table, and the first player who receives a club becomes the first dealer.

The Shuffle and Cut. Dealer has the right to shuffle last. The pack is cut by the player on the dealer's right. The cut must leave at least five cards in each packet.

The Deal. The rule of the deal is "3-2-3." The dealer first gives a round of three cards at a time, then a round two at a time, and, finally, another round three at a time. Each player thus receives eight cards.

Object of the Game. The goal is to win at least five tricks, or to win all eight tricks, depending on the bid.

The Color. One suit is fixed as "the color" by agreement before play begins. If the players don't agree on a color, clubs becomes the color. (*Variation*: The play commences without a color, and the suit of the first game won becomes the color thereafter.)

A bid is "in color" when it names this prefixed suit as trump; a bid is "in suit" if it names any other suit. Bids in color rank higher than bids in suit.

The "Games". The possible games that may be declared, rank in bidding precedence as follows:

Tout in color (highest)

Tout in suit

Solo in color

Solo in suit

Simple Game (Frog) in color

Simple Game in suit (lowest)

If all four players pass without a bid, the hand must be played as a game in Spadilla.

Tout. This game is a Solo in which the Player undertakes to win all eight tricks.

Solo. In Solo the Player names the trump suit and then plays alone against the other three players.

Simple Game (Frog). The Player names the trump suit and then calls an ace that he does not hold himself. The holder of the called ace becomes his partner, but must say nothing to reveal the fact. The partnerships become evident when the called ace is played. The Player and partner must win at least five tricks.

If a player holds both "spadilla" and "basta" (the black queens), he may not allow the hand to be played at Simple Game. If no higher bid has been made ahead of this player, he must declare Solo or Tout. This is called *Forcée*. (If all four players pass without a bid, the holder of "spadilla" (♣Q) must announce it and must undertake a Simple Game.)

The Bidding. The player on the dealer's left bids first. He first settles with the next hand as to who will bid higher, as in Skat. The survivor settles with third hand, and so on. Once a player has passed, he is out of the bidding.

The winning bidder may either hold to the bid that won or to name any higher declaration. Each bidder, therefore, conceals his real intention as long as possible, bidding only high enough to top the previous bid.

The player on the dealer's left has the first turn to bid, and if he does not pass, that player must say "I ask" (German, *ich frage*, which sounds like the English term "frog"). This is equivalent to a bid of Simple Game. If the next hand wishes to overcall, he says "Is it in color?" If the answer is "Yes," the other may continue, "Is it a solo?" and so on. When the bidder, whose intentions are so asked passes, the questioner stands committed to play a game at least as good as the last game named.

The winning bidder becomes the Player and must at once announce the game and the trump suit.

The Play. The person on the dealer's left leads first. The other players must follow suit to the lead if possible. A player who cannot follow suit may discard or trump at will. A trick is won by the highest card of the suit led, or by the highest trump if a trump is played. The winner of a trick leads next.

Scoring. The basic values of the games are as follows:

Simple Game in Suit	2
Simple Game in color	4
Solo in suit	4
Solo in color	8
Tout in suit	16
Tout in color	32

At Simple Game, the Player and his partner each win 2 or lose 2. (If settlement is by chips, 4 chips change hands.)

At Solo or Tout, the player pays or collects the value of the game from each opponent. (*Variation*: in addition to this settlement for each hand, the dealer puts 2 chips into a pot, and the pot accumulates until it is won by the first player who makes a Solo in color or a Tout.)

Variations. There are many different variations of Solo because it has been played in so many different countries and for so many generations. Among the most popular are:

1) the Player may not call the ace of a suit he does not hold; or

2) the Player may not call the ace of a suit he does not hold unless the Player also puts a card face down on the table; that card must be played to the first trump lead but cannot win a trick.

3) In a declared Simple Game or Solo, either side may win a double game (in suit) or quadruple game (in color) by taking 8 tricks. However, if the side plays on after winning the first five tricks, and then loses a trick, it must pay the double or the quadruple value of the game.

Irregularities. A player who fails to follow suit when possible loses the game and must pay the entire loss for his side. If an opponent of the Player leads or plays out of turn, or exposes a card, the offender's side loses and the offender must pay the entire loss. There is no penalty against the Player for similar errors; the error is simply corrected if possible and play continues.

PIQUET

NUMBER OF PLAYERS	NUMBER OF CARDS	GAME PLAY	SKILL LEVEL
2	32	◇ ◇ ◇ ◆ ◇ EASY → COMPLEX	◇ ◇ ◇ ◆ ◇ LUCK → SKILL

Over 500 years old, Piquet is a classic game which originated in France where it was the dominant card game for many years. It has long been regarded as one of the best games for two players.

The Pack. The standard 52-card pack is stripped to create a 32-card deck comprised of the A, K, Q, J, 10, 9, 8, and 7 in each suit. Two packs are used alternately.

Rank of Cards. A (high), K, Q, J, 10, 9, 8, 7.

The Draw. The pack is shuffled and spread face down. Each player then draws a card. The lowest card deals first and has his choice of seats. If cards of equal rank are drawn, there must be a new draw. The turn to deal alternates.

The Shuffle and Cut. Both players may shuffle and the dealer has the option of shuffling last. The non-dealer cuts the pack. The cut must leave at least two cards in each packet.

The Deal. The dealer completes the cut and deals each player twelve cards, two at a time, face down, alternately, beginning with the non-dealer. The remaining eight cards are spread face down on the table and form the stock.

Discarding. After picking up his hand, the opponent discards at least one, and up to five, cards. He then takes an equal number of cards from the top of the stock. If the opponent leaves any of the first five cards he could have drawn, he may look at them without showing them to the dealer.

The dealer is entitled to take all of the stock left by non-dealer, after first discarding an equal number of cards. However, the dealer does not have to take cards from the stock. If he chooses to leave any or all of the cards, he may decide whether they will be turned up and viewed by both players or set aside unseen. (Some play that the dealer discards first.)

The object in discarding is to form certain scoring combinations, as described below.

Carte Blanche. A hand with no king, queen, or jack is called "Carte Blanche." If dealt such a hand, the non-dealer may expose it before the discard and score 10 points. If the dealer picks up Carte Blanche, he may wait until the non-dealer has discarded, and then show it and score 10.

Point. The player with the most cards of one suit scores 1 point for each card held in that suit. If both players hold suits of the same length, the one with the greater pip total scores the points. Scores count the ace as 11, the king, queen, jack and ten at 10 each, and lower cards at pip value. If the players tie in points, neither player scores.

Sequence. A sequence of three cards in the same suit (tierce) counts 3 points; a sequence of four (quart) counts 4; a sequence of five or more counts 10 plus the number of cards. Only the player holding the highest sequence can score in this class; having established that he has the best sequence, that player may score for all additional sequences held. Any sequence is higher than one of lesser length; and between sequences of equal length, the one headed by the higher card scores. If the players tie for best sequence, neither scores in this class.

Sets. A set comprises three or four cards of the same rank, higher than nine. The player with the highest set scores it plus any additional sets he may hold. Four-of-a-kind, counting 14, is higher than three of a kind, counting 3. If both players hold sets of an equal number of cards, the set higher in rank scores.

Declaring. After the discarding is completed, the players declare their holdings to determine the scores for point, sequence, and sets, in that order. However, the player who does not score in a class need not give more information than is necessary to establish the other's superiority. The declaration, therefore, proceeds as in the example below. The non-dealer is obliged to make the first declaration for each class:

Non-dealer: *Four.* (Naming length of suit for point.)

Dealer: *How much?* (With five or more cards of a suit, dealer would state "Five," and so on. With no suit as long as four, dealer would say "Good.")

Non-dealer: *Thirty-seven.*

Dealer: *Not good. Thirty-nine.* (This means the dealer has the high "point", and thus scores 4.)

Non-dealer: *Sequence of three.* (Or, "Tierce.")

Dealer: *How high?* (dealer also holds a tierce.)

Non-dealer: *Ace.*

Dealer: *Good.*

Non-dealer: *And another tierce. I score 6. Now for sets, I have three kings.*

Dealer: *Not good, 14 tens (four tens).* (Dealer wins the sets. Dealer now lists the total he scored.) *I start with 18.*

Non-dealer: *I start with 6.*

Proving. On demand, a player must show any combination of cards for which he has scored. Proving scores is usually unnecessary since a player can infer the suit of his opponent's point.

Sinking. A player is not obliged to declare any combination. *Example*: The non-dealer may say "No set" although he holds three queens, believing that the dealer holds three kings. However, if a player thus "sinks" a combination, he may not later declare it when he finds that it would have been high.

The Play. The declaring completed, the non-dealer leads first. The opponent must follow suit if possible. A trick is won by the higher card of the suit led. The player who wins the trick leads next.

The player scores 1 point for each card he leads higher than a 9, and 1 point each time he tops the opponent's lead with a card higher than a 9. The player who wins the last trick gets 1 extra point for it.

(In American games, it is usual to count 1 point for each lead and 1 point for each trick taken, regardless of the rank of cards.)

With each card, the players announce their cumulative score up to that juncture, including the initial count for combinations. To continue the example (see "Declaring"): the non-dealer scored 6 for two sequences. On the non-dealer's first lead (an ace) he announces "Seven." If the dealer scored 18 for combinations, then on winning his first trick (with a king), the dealer would say "Nineteen."

Tricks. The winner of seven or more of the twelve tricks scores 10. If the tricks are split, with each player having won six, neither scores. If one player wins all twelve tricks, he scores 40 for "capot" (but nothing extra for majority or for the last trick).

Pique and Repique. A player who reaches a score of 30 or more in declarations, before the opponent scores anything and before a card is led, adds 60 for "repique." A player who reaches 30 or more in declarations and play before the opponent scores anything, adds 30 for "pique."

Game. There are six deals in a game. (*Variation*: the game is four deals and the scores of the first and last game are doubled.) The player with the higher cumulative score at the end of the game wins the difference of the totals, plus 100 for game, provided that the loser scored at least 100 points. If the losing player failed to reach 100, he is said to be "rubiconed," and the winner scores the sum of both scores plus 100 for game. (The loser is rubiconed even if the winner also failed to reach 100.)

KLABERJASS
(Kalabrias, Klob, Klab, Clob, Clabber, Clobber, Clubby)

NUMBER OF PLAYERS	NUMBER OF CARDS	GAME PLAY	SKILL LEVEL
2	32	◇ ◇ ◆ ◇ ◇ EASY → COMPLEX	◇ ◇ ◇ ◆ ◇ LUCK → SKILL

K laberjass is the famous two-hand game played by the Broadway characters in Damon Runyon's stories. It is essentially the same as the French game Belotte. "Klaberjass" means "clover jack" (that is, the jack of clubs).

The Pack, The standard pack is stripped to create a deck comprised of the A, K, Q, J, 10, 9, 8, and 7 in each suit, a pack of 32 cards.

Rank of Cards. In trumps: J, 9, A, 10, K, Q, 8, 7. In other suits: A, 10, K, Q, J, 9, 8, 7.

Rank of Cards in Trump Suit

Rank of Cards Plain Suits

The Draw. The pack is shuffled and spread face down. Each player then draws a card. The lowest card deals first and has his choice of seats. If cards of equal rank are drawn, there must be a new draw. The turn to deal alternates.

The Shuffle and Cut. Both players may shuffle, and the dealer has the option of shuffling last. The non-dealer cuts the pack. The cut must leave at least three cards in each packet.

The Deal. The dealer gives six cards to each player, face down, three at a time, beginning with the non-dealer. The next card is turned up, and the remainder of the pack is placed face down next to, and partly covering, the turned up card.

Bidding. There may be one or two rounds of bidding. The non-dealer bids first and may "take it" (accept the turned-up suit as trump), may "pass" (reject that suit), or may "schmeiss" (offer either to play the turned-up suit or to throw the hand in, as his opponent may choose). If the opponent says "Yes" to a schmeiss, there is a new deal. If the opponent says "No," the turned-up suit becomes trump.

If the non-dealer passes, the dealer may take it, pass, or schmeiss. If both players pass, there is a second round of bidding: The non-dealer may name one of the other three suits as trump, or may schmeiss (offering to name one of those suits, or to let the hand be thrown in, as the dealer chooses), or may pass again. If the non-dealer passes again, the dealer has the last turn, and he may name one of the other three suits as trump or start a new deal.

As soon as either player accepts or names a trump, the bidding ends. The player who accepted or named the trump suit becomes the Maker.

Redealing. After the Maker is determined the dealer gives three additional cards to each player, one at a time, so that each has nine cards. He then turns up the bottom card of the pack and places it on top. This card is shown for the player's information only and has no part in the play. Any player holding the seven of trumps may exchange it for the card previously turned up, but scores no points for this. The seven of trumps is known as the "dix" (pronounced "deece").

Melding. Only sequences may be melded. In forming sequences, the cards rank: A, K, Q, J, 10, 9, 8, 7. The ace may be used only in the sequence A, K, Q. A four-card sequence counts 50 points, and a three-card sequence 20 points.

The non-dealer starts by announcing the point value of the best sequence he holds. Thus, with ♥Q, J, 10, he would say, "Twenty." If the dealer has no sequence as good, he says, "Good." If the dealer has a higher-ranking sequence, he says, "No good." In either case, the melding is ended, and the non-dealer leads the first trick.

When the dealer has a sequence of the same length as the non-dealer, the response to the announcement is, "How high?" The non-dealer must then name the card heading his sequence. Again, the dealer replies that it is good, or no good, or that the dealer has a sequence headed by the same card. If the latter occurs, a trump sequence outranks a sequence in any other suit. If both sequences are in non-trump suits, neither is scored. (*Variation*: If the sequences are equal in every respect, the non-dealer scores.)

The Play. The non-dealer always leads first and may lead any card. The opponent must follow suit if possible. Otherwise he must trump, if he holds a trump card, and he must try to win a trump lead. The higher trump played wins any trick containing a trump, and the higher card of the suit led wins any other trick. The winner of each trick leads next.

After both players have played the first trick, the player with the higher-ranking meld shows and scores all sequences in his hand, while the opponent may not count any sequence.

A player holding the king and queen of trumps may score 20 points for them by announcing, "Bella" as he plays the second card of this combination. Holding K, Q, J, of trumps, he may score both a sequence and a bella.

Scoring. For cards taken in tricks, each player scores:

Trump jack *(jasz)*	20
Trump 9 *(menel)*	14
Each other jack	2
Each queen	3
Each king	4
Each ten.	10
Each ace.	11
Last trick	10

The Maker must score more in melds and cards than the opponent. If the Maker does so, each player scores whatever points he makes. If the Maker is tied, he scores nothing, and the opponent scores the value of his melds and cards. If the Maker has the lower score, he is "bete" and the opponent scores all the points made by both players in that deal.

The Game. The first player to reach 500 points wins the game. If both players go over 500 points in the same deal, the higher score wins. (*Variation*: the Maker's score is counted at the outset, and the first score that reaches 500 points wins.)

Irregularities. *Misdeal.* Before bidding, the non-dealer may require either a new deal or correction 1) if any of his cards are exposed in dealing, 2) if a card is exposed in the pack, or 3) if either player has the wrong number of cards. For correction, a hand with too many cards is offered face down to the opponent, who draws the excess. A short hand is supplied from the top of the pack. An incorrect hand, if discovered after the bidding has started, must be corrected.

Revoke. A revoke is: 1) a failure to follow suit, to trump, or to play over on a trump lead, when required by the rules to do so; 2) announcing a meld not actually held (as, for example, by saying, "How high?" when not holding a sequence of equal value), or 3) having too few or too many cards after leading or playing to the first trick. The non-offender scores all points for both players melds and cards on that deal.

Belotte

Belotte is the most popular two-hand game in France. It is identical to Klaberjass, although the "schmeiss" is called "valse" (waltz). The highest-ranking melds are four of a kind, counting 200 points for four jacks and 100 points for four nines, aces, tens, kings or queens, the groups ranking in that order. A five-card sequence is worth 50 points, a four-card sequence counts 40 points, a three-card sequence 20 points. The player having the highest-ranking group scores all groups in hand, and the player having the highest-ranking sequence scores all sequences in hand. If the maker does not score more points than the opponent, the maker loses his own points, but the opponent does not score the combined totals of both players.

Darda

Darda is a variation of Klabberjass for two, three or four people. If four people play, the dealer scores against the Maker. The rank of cards in trumps is: Q, 9, A, 10, K, J, 8, 7, and the queen (not the jack as in Klaberjass) counts 20 points whereas the jack counts only 2. In non-trump suits, the rank is: A, 10, K, Q, J, 9, 8, 7. There is no "schmeiss."

After trump has been named, and the three additional cards have been dealt to each player, the undealt cards are turned face up, squared so that only the top card shows, and become the widow. As in standard Klabberjass, a player may exchange the trump 7 for the turned-up card (the trump 8 may be exchanged if the 7 was turned), and that player may take the exposed card of the widow as long as it is a trump. However, the player must discard a card from his hand each time he makes an exchange.

The Maker then leads. Each player announces his meld on the first play. Thereafter, it does not count, including the trump K, Q ("bele"). After the first trick is completed, players with melds of the same length ask and decide which is highest.

For the scoring, the Maker succeeds if neither opponent has an equally high score. If the Maker succeeds, he scores 1 if his score is less than 100 points; 2 if it is 100-149; 3 if it is 150-199; 4 if it is 200 or more. Game is 10.

If four of a kind are held, there is no play. Instead the highest four of a kind wins the hand, and the scoring is: 4 for four queens, 3 for four nines, and 2 for four aces, kings, jacks, or tens.

Chapter VII

Cribbage
and
Counting
Games

CRIBBAGE

NUMBER OF PLAYERS	NUMBER OF CARDS	GAME PLAY	SKILL LEVEL
2 (3 or 4)	52	◇ ◇ ◇ ◆ ◇ EASY → COMPLEX	◇ ◇ ◇ ◆ ◇ LUCK → SKILL

Cribbage is one of the best two-hand games – and one of the most enduring, for the game was entertaining card players as far back as the seventeenth century. It evolved from an earlier English game called "Noddy," and the man credited with inventing it is Sir John Suckling, a wealthy English poet. Cribbage affords players both the anticipation of the luck of the deal as well as ample opportunity to exercise their skills in discarding and play.

One of the novel features of Cribbage is that a Cribbage board is used for scoring rather than the usual pencil and paper. The rectangular wooden board is equipped with holes that accommodate pegs. The board speeds up scoring, and in this fast-moving game, pegging greatly reduces the chances for errors in computing scores.

Number of Players. Two or three people can play. Or four people can play two against two as partners. But Cribbage is basically best played by two people, and the rules that follow are for that number.

The Pack. The standard 52-card pack is used.

Rank of Cards. K (high), Q, J, 10, 9, 8, 7, 6, 5, 4, 3, 2, A.

Rank of Cards

The Draw, Shuffle and Cut. From a shuffled pack face down, each player cuts a card, leaving at least four cards at either end of the pack. If both players cut cards of the same rank, each draws again. The player with the lower card deals the first hand. Thereafter, the turn to deal alternates between the two players, except that the loser of the game deals first if another game is played. The dealer has the right to shuffle last, and he presents the cards to the non-dealer for the cut prior to the deal. (In some games, there is no cut at this time.)

The Deal. The dealer distributes six cards face down to his opponent and himself, beginning with the opponent.

Object of the Game. The goal is to be the first player to score 121 points. (Some games are to 61 points.) Players earn points during play and for making various card combinations.

The Crib. Each player looks at his six cards and "lays away" two of them face down to reduce the hand to four. The four cards laid away together constitute "the crib". The crib belongs to the dealer, but these cards are not exposed or used until after the hands have been played.

Before the Play. After the crib is laid away, the non-dealer cuts the pack. The dealer turns up the top card of the lower packet and places it face up on top of the pack. This card is the "starter." If the starter is a jack, it is called "His Heels," and the dealer pegs (scores) 2 points at once. The starter is not used in the play phase of Cribbage , but is used later for making various card combinations that score points (see p. 258).

The Play. After the starter is turned, the non-dealer lays one of his cards face up on the table. The dealer similarly exposes a card, then non-dealer again, and so on – the hands are exposed card by card, alternately except for a "Go," as noted below. Each player keeps his cards separate from those of his opponent.

As each person plays, he announces a running total of pips reached by the addition of the last card to all those previously played. (*Example:* The non-dealer begins with a four, saying "Four." The dealer plays a nine, saying "Thirteen".) The kings, queens and jacks count 10 each; every other card counts its pip value (the ace counts one).

CRIBBAGE INVENTOR ENDS LIFE BY TAKING POISON

The author, Douglas Anderson, of *All About Cribbage*, told his readers that Sir John Suckling, the inventor of Cribbage, "cut quite a swath in his day. He spent several years in France and Italy and returned to England in 1630 to be knighted by the King." Suckling inherited his father's fortune when he was only 18, and in addition to being a poet, he was also a soldier. Rich, handsome, and generous, Suckling was also very popular and was regarded as the best card player and bowler in Britain, if not all Europe. In 1641 he led a conspiracy to rescue a friend who was jailed in the Tower of London, and when the plot was discovered, Sir John fled to France. A year later – unable to return to his beloved England – the unhappy poet took poison and died.

Bet You Didn't Know

The Go. During play, the running total of cards may never be carried beyond 31. If a player cannot add another card without exceeding 31, he or she says "Go" and the opponent pegs 1. After gaining the Go, the opponent must first lay down any additional cards he can without exceeding 31. Besides the point for Go, he may then score any additional points that can be made through pairs and runs (described later). If a player reaches exactly 31, he pegs two instead of one for Go.

The player who called Go leads for the next series of plays, with the count starting at zero. The lead may not be combined with any cards previously played to form a scoring combination; the Go has interrupted the sequence.

The person who plays the last card pegs one for Go, plus one extra if the card brings the count to exactly 31. The dealer is sure to peg at least one point in every hand, for he will have a Go on the last card if not earlier.

Pegging. The object in play is to score points by pegging. In addition to a Go, a player may score for the following combinations:

Fifteen. For adding a card that makes the total 15. . . . . Peg 2

Pair. For adding a card of the same rank as the
card just played. . . . . Peg 2
(Note that face cards pair only by actual rank: jack with jack, but not jack with queen.)

Triplet. (also called "Threes" or "Pair Royal")
For adding the third card of the same rank. . . . . Peg 6

Four. (also called "Double Pair" or "Double Pair Royal")
For adding the fourth card of the same rank . . . . Peg 12

Run (Sequence). For adding a card that forms, with those just played:

For a sequence of three . . . . Peg 3

For a sequence of four. . . . . Peg 4

For a sequence of five. . . . . Peg 5

(Peg one point more for each extra card of a sequence. Note that runs are independent of suits, but go strictly by rank; *to illustrate:* 9, 10, J, or J, 9, 10 is a run but 9, 10, Q is not.)

It is important to keep track of the order in which cards are played to determine whether what looks like a sequence or a run has been interrupted by a "foreign card." *Example:* Cards are played in this order: 8, 7, 7, 6. The dealer pegs 2 for 15, and the opponent pegs 2 for pair, but the dealer cannot peg for run because of the extra seven (foreign card) that has been played. *Example:* Cards are played in this order: 9, 6, 8, 7. The dealer pegs 2 for fifteen when he plays the six and pegs 4 for run when he plays the seven (the 6, 7, 8, 9 sequence). The cards were not played in sequential order, but they form a true run with no foreign card.

Counting the Hands. When play ends, the three hands are counted in order: non-dealer's hand (first), dealer's hand (second), and then the crib (third). This order is important because, toward the end of a game, the non-dealer may "count out" and win before the dealer has a chance to count, even though the dealer's total would have exceeded that of the opponent. The starter is considered to be a part of each hand, so that all hands in counting comprise five cards. The basic scoring formations are as follows:

	Combination	**Counts**
Fifteen.	Each combination of cards that totals 15	2
Pair.	Each pair of cards of the same rank	2
Run.	Each combination of three or more cards in sequence *(for each card in the sequence)*	1
Flush.	Four cards of the same suit in hand *(excluding the crib, and the starter)*	4
	Four cards in hand or crib of the same suit as the starter *(There is no count for four-flush in the crib that is not of same suit as the starter)*	5
His Nobs.	Jack of the same suit as starter in hand or crib	1

Combinations. In the above table, the word combination is used in the strict technical sense. Each and every combination of two cards that make a pair, of two or more cards that make 15, or of three or more cards that make a run, count separately.

Example: A hand (including the starter) comprised of 8, 7, 7, 6, 2 scores 8 points for four combinations that total 15: the 8 with one 7, and the 8 with the other 7; the 6, 2 with each of the two 7s. The same hand also scores 2 for a pair, and 6 for two runs of three (8, 7, 6 using each of the two 7s). The total score is 16. An experienced player computes the hand thus: "Fifteen 2, fifteen 4, fifteen 6, fifteen 8, and 8 for double run is 16."

Note that the ace is always low and cannot form a sequence with a king. Further, a flush cannot happen during the play of the cards; it occurs only when the hands and the crib are counted.

Certain basic formulations should be learned to facilitate counting. For pairs and runs alone:

A. A triplet counts 6.

B. Four of a kind counts 12.

C. A run of three, with one card duplicated (double run) counts 8.

D. A run of four, with one card duplicated, counts 10.

E. A run of three, with one card triplicated (triple run), counts 15.

F. A run of three, with two different cards duplicated, counts 16.
(See diagram next page.)

Basic Formulations for Pairs & Runs

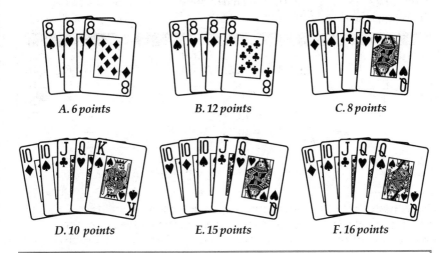

| A. 6 points | B. 12 points | C. 8 points |

| D. 10 points | E. 15 points | F. 16 points |

A PERFECT 29!

The highest possible score for combinations in a single Cribbage deal is 29, and it may occur only once in a Cribbage fan's lifetime – in fact, experts say that a 29 is probably as rare as a hole-in-one in golf. To make this amazing score, a player must have a five as the starter (upcard) and the other three fives plus the jack of the same suit as the starter – His Nobs: 1 point – in his hand. The double pair royal (four 5s) peg another 12 points; the various fives used to hit 15 can be done four ways for 8 points; and the jack plus a 5 to hit 15 can also be done four ways for 8 points. Total = 29 points.

A perfect 29 Hand

The following list includes many of the hands that may give the beginner some difficulty in counting. Note that no hand can make a count of 19, 25, 26, or 27. (In the chart below **J** stands for His Nobs, the jack of the same suit as the starter.)

CRIBBAGE SCORES

Cards					Count	Cards					Count
A—	A—	2—	2—	3	= 16	2—	6—	7—	7—	8	= 16
A—	2—	3—	3—	3	= 15	6—	7—	8—	9—	9	= 16
A—	4—	4—	4—	K	= 12	3—	3—	6—	6—	6	= 20
2—	3—	4—	4—	4	= 17	3—	3—	3—	4—	5	= 21
2—	2—	3—	3—	4	= 16	A—	A—	7—	7—	8	= 12
2—	3—	3—	3—	4	= 17	3—	3—	3—	6—	6	= 18
3—	3—	4—	4—	5	= 20	3—	3—	6—	6—	9	= 14
3—	4—	4—	4—	5	= 17	5—	5—	5—	J—	J	= 23
3—	4—	4—	5—	5	= 16	5—	5—	5—	Q—	Q	= 22
3—	6—	6—	6—	6	= 24	A—	4—	4—	J—	4	= 13
4—	4—	5—	6—	6	= 24	5—	5—	J—	Q—	K	= 18
4—	5—	5—	6—	6	= 24	2—	2—	2—	2—	9	= 20
4—	5—	6—	6—	6	= 21	3—	3—	3—	3—	9	= 24
5—	**J—**	**5—**	**5—**	**5**	**= 29**	3—	3—	3—	3—	6	= 20
5—	5—	5—	5—	K	= 28	4—	4—	4—	4—	7	= 24
5—	5—	J—	Q—	K	= 17	A—	7—	7—	7—	7	= 24
6—	6—	9—	9—	9	= 20	4—	4—	4—	7—	7	= 20
6—	9—	9—	9—	9	= 20	4—	4—	7—	7—	7	= 14
6—	6—	7—	7—	8	= 20	3—	3—	4—	5—	5	= 20
7—	7—	7—	8—	9	= 21	A—	A—	6—	7—	7	= 12
7—	7—	7—	8—	6	= 21	2—	6—	6—	7—	7	= 12
7—	7—	7—	8—	8	= 20	7—	7—	7—	A—	A	= 20
7—	8—	8—	8—	8	= 20	3—	4—	4—	4—	4	= 20
7—	7—	8—	8—	9	= 24	5—	5—	5—	4—	6	= 23
7—	8—	8—	9—	9	= 20	A—	A—	6—	7—	8	= 13
5—	5—	J—	J—	J	= 21						

Muggins (optional). Each player must count his hand (and crib) aloud and announce the total. If he overlooks any score, the opponent may say "Muggins" and then score the overlooked points for himself. For experienced players, the Muggins rule is always in effect and adds even more suspense to the game.

Game. Game may be fixed at either 121 points or 61 points. The play ends the moment either player reaches the agreed total, whether by pegging or counting one's hand. If the non-dealer "goes out" by the count of his hand, the game immediately ends and the dealer may not score either his hand or the crib.

If a player wins the game before the loser has passed the halfway mark (did not reach 31 in a game of 61, or 61 in a game of 121), the loser is "lurched," and the winner scores two games instead of one. A popular variation of games played to 121, is a "skunk" (double game) for the winner if the losing player fails to pass the three-quarter mark – 91 points or more – and it is a "double skunk" (quadruple game) if the loser fails to pass the halfway mark (61 or more points).

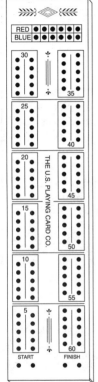

The Cribbage Board. The Cribbage board (see illustration) has four rows of 30 holes each, divided into two pairs of rows by a central panel. There are usually four (or two) additional holes near one end, called "game holes." With the board come four pegs, usually in two contrasting colors. *Note:* There are also continuous track Cribbage boards available which, as the name implies, have one continuous line of 121 holes for each player.

The board is placed to one side between the two players, and each player takes two pegs of the same color. (The pegs are placed in the game holes until the game begins.) Each time a player scores, he advances a peg along a row on his side of the board, counting one hole per point. Two pegs are used, and the rearmost peg jumps over the first peg to show the first increment in score. After another increase in score, the peg behind jumps over the peg in front to the appropriate hole to show the player's new score, and so on (see diagram next page). The custom is to "go down" (away from the game holes) on the outer rows and "come up" on the inner rows. A game of 61 is "once around" and a game of 121 is "twice around." As noted previously, continuous line Cribbage boards are available.

Standard Cribbage Board

If a Cribbage board is not available, each player may use a piece of paper or cardboard, marked thus:

Units   1, 2, 3, 4, 5, 6, 7, 8, 9, 10

Tens   10, 20, 30, 40, 50, 60

Two small markers, such as small coins or buttons, can substitute for pegs for counting in each row.

Pegging

Strategy

The Crib. If the dealer is discarding for the crib, he should "salt" it with the best possible cards, but at the same time retain good cards in his hand that can be used for high scoring. Conversely, for the non-dealer, it is best to lay out cards that will be the least advantageous for the dealer. Laying out a five would be the worst choice, for the dealer could use it to make 15 with any one of the ten-cards (10, J, Q, K). Laying out a pair is usually a poor choice too, and the same goes for sequential cards, such as putting both a six and seven in the crib. The ace and king tend to be good cards to put in the crib because it is harder to use them in a run.

The Play. As expected, the five makes for the worst lead in that there are so many ten-cards that the opponent can use to make a 15. Leading from a pair is a good idea, for even if the opponent makes a pair, the leader can play the other matching card from his hand and collect for a pair royal. Leading an ace or deuce is not a good idea, for these cards should be saved until later to help make a 15, a Go, or a 31. The safest lead is a four because this card cannot be used to make a 15 at the opponent's very next turn. Finally, when the opponent leads a card that can either be paired or make 15, the latter choice is preferred.

During the play, it is advisable not to try to make a count of 21, for the opponent can then play one of the many 10-cards and make an easy 31.

Five-Card Cribbage

Five-Card Cribbage is the original game of Cribbage, and is strictly for two players.

Cut for Deal. The players cut for deal, the higher card winning the deal, but the losing player pegs three holes to compensate him for the disadvantage that his opponent has in getting the first crib.

The Deal. Five cards are dealt to each player, and each lays down two cards for the crib. The non-dealer then cuts the remainder of the pack, and the dealer turns up the starter.

The Play. The only change, and it is an important one, is that the play ends when the first Go or 31 is reached. When play ends with a Go, the person who played the last card scores 1 for it. When play ends with a 31, the person who played the last card to make the count 31 scores 2.

Counting. Counting is done in the same way as the six-card game, but the score is considerably lower because fewer cards are involved. In this version, if the player holds three cards of the same suit in his hand, he counts 3 for flush. If the starter is of the same suit as the flush, the count is 4. To have a flush in the crib, all five cards must be in the same suit, just as in the six-card game. Game is 61 points.

Three-Hand Cribbage

Three-Hand Cribbage can be a very dynamic game. The players draw for first deal, and thereafter the deal rotates to the left.

Five cards are dealt to each player, one at a time, plus one card to the crib. Each player puts one card into the crib. Thus, the crib, is four cards, as in the two-player game. The crib belongs to the dealer. The player to the left of the dealer cuts for the starter.

When a player calls Go, the next opponent must continue play if he can. If he does play, the third opponent must also play if able. If the first player after the Go cannot play, the second player does not play. The point for Go is always won by the person who played the last card.

All other rules of play and scoring are the same as in Two-Hand Cribbage . The hands are counted in order, beginning with the player to the dealer's left, continuing left, and ending with the crib. Game is usually 61 points, although many players choose to play to 121 points.

Four-Hand Cribbage

The players draw for partners and first deal. The player with the highest card deals, and the two highest and two lowest cards designate partners. Five cards are dealt to each player, one at a time. Each player puts one card into the crib, which belongs to the dealer. The rest of the rules of play are as in Three-Hand Cribbage .

Scores made by partners are combined in a running total, and one player for each side should be appointed to keep the score. Game is 121 points.

SUBMARINES, CRIBBAGE AND THE WAHOO

During World War II, Cribbage became a traditional game for American submariners to play while passing the time on patrol for Japanese ships.

In 1943, the famous sub U.S.S. Wahoo was beginning a dangerous patrol 10 miles north of Shantung Promontory in the Yellow Sea. Waiting for action, the legendary captain "Mush" Morton played Cribbage with executive officer Richard H. O'Kane. He dealt him a "Perfect 29" hand! The superstitous crew felt the 29 was a strong omen of good fortune for the patrol, and indeed it was. After the hand, the lucky cards were signed by witnesses and saved for posterity.

Bet You Didn't Know

CASSINO
(Casino)

NUMBER OF PLAYERS	NUMBER OF CARDS	GAME PLAY	SKILL LEVEL
2-4	**52**	◇ ◇ ◆ ◇ ◇ EASY → COMPLEX	◇ ◇ ◆ ◇ ◇ LUCK → SKILL

This original Cassino can be traced back to nineteenth-century Italy. It has been a popular family game ever since, and a version called Stealing Bundles is a wonderful card game for children.

Number of Players. Two, three or four people can play. Four usually play as partners, two against two.

The Pack. The standard 52-card pack is used.

Rank of Cards. Face cards have no numerical value; an ace counts 1, any other card counts its pip value.

The Draw, Shuffle and Cut. Players draw or cut for first deal, and the player with the lowest card deals. When two people play, the winner of each hand deals the next one. When three or four people play, the turn to deal proceeds clockwise. The dealer shuffles and the person to his right cuts.

The Deal. Beginning with the opponent to the left, the dealer gives two cards at a time to each opponent face down, then two cards face up on the table, then two cards face down to himself. This round is repeated, so that each player has four cards and four cards are face up on the table. The remainder of the deck is set aside to be used in redealing. The dealer may deal the cards one at a time if preferred.

Object of the Game. The goal is for players to take in cards, which score points as follows:

Greatest number of cards taken in	3
Greatest number of spades taken in.	1
Big Cassino (♦10)	2
Little Cassino (♠2)	1
Each ace	1
Each "sweep"	1

A sweep consists of taking in all cards on the table. (This feature is not used in the two-hand version.)

In partnership play, cards, spades and counting cards taken in by both partners are counted together.

When there is a tie for cards or spades, the points do not count. *Example:* If each side has 26 cards, the 3 points for the most cards taken are not scored. If in three-hand play, two players have five spades each, the point for taking the most spades is not scored.

The Play. Beginning with the person on the dealer's left, each participant must play one card; a player has the following choice of plays:

Taking in. A player may take the card he plays plus any card or combination of cards on the table that pair with it. *Example:* With a six he may take in any six on the table, or a four and a two, or a six and a four and a two, or two or three sixes. He places any cards gathered face down in a pile in front of him.

Building. A player may add a card from his hand to a card or cards on the table, to form any combination that the player will be able to take in on the next turn. The player must announce what he is building. Example: Having a six and two in his hand, the player may add the two to a four on the table, announcing "Building six." With two fours in his hand and a four on the table, he may place a four on a four and announce, "Building fours." Builds must be left face up on the table; they may be taken by any other player in turn who has the appropriate card.

Face cards may not be combined in any way; with two jacks on the table, a player holding a jack may take in one of them but not both. He may not build jacks, queens, or kings.

Increasing a build. A player may add a card from his hand to a build already on the table, provided the player will be able to take in the increased build on the next turn. *Example:* The opponent has built a seven with a six and an ace; a player holding a nine and a two may place a two on the six and ace, building nine; another opponent in turn may place an ace on the build, increasing it to ten. A player may increase his own build as well as an opponent's (or partner's in the four-hand game).

A single combination may be increased; a multiple combination may not be. *Example:* When a player has built fours with a four, a three, and an ace, the build may not be increased to nine by adding an ace. It may be taken only by a four.

Note that a build may be increased only with a card from the hand, never from the table unless the player can combine the table card with one in his hand. (See Adding to a Build next page.) *To illustrate:* A five has been built, a deuce is on the table, and the player holds an ace and an eight. The player may not take the ace , the deuce on the table, and the cards built to increase the build to eight.

Adding to a build. A player may add a card from his hand to a build already on the table, and combine a card from his hand with a card on the table to add to that build. *Example:* There is a build of nine on the table, and a six on the table; a player may take a three from his hand and the six on the table to add to the build of nine. If the build was made by any other player, he need not have a nine in his hand to do this. That is, a partner may add to his partner's build without being able to take in the build.

At the time of taking in a build, the player may also take in any card or combination on the table that is equivalent to his card. *Example:* The player is taking in a build of seven, and sees another four and a three on the table; even though these are not part of the build, he may take them in.

A card once taken in and turned face down may not be examined by the player or side taking it, and may be examined by an opponent only before the next time he plays.

Trailing. A player who does not wish to make any other play must "trail" by playing a card face up on the table. However, he is not permitted to trail while any build he made is still on the table.

Redealing. When each player has played all four of his cards, the dealer picks up the remainder of the pack and deals four more cards to each player, but no cards to the table. After these have been played, he deals four more cards to each player, and so on until the pack has been exhausted. Before dealing the final round, the dealer must announce that it is the last deal. Cards not taken prior to any new round of dealing remain on the table. After the pack is exhausted, the last player who took in a card gets all the cards remaining on the table. However, these cards do not constitute a sweep unless they are all paired with the last card played.

In some games, if there are cards remaining in the pack when a sweep occurs, the dealer turns up four cards on the table before the game continues. In other games, the next player simply trails (puts down one card face up).

Scoring. When the game ends, the players or partners turn up the cards they have taken in and count the points they have scored. A sweep is identified at the time it is taken in by leaving one card face up in the pile, so the cards representing sweeps will be facing the other way and may be picked out easily.

There are several ways to decide the winner, and include the following:

1) In two-hand play, each complete deal usually represents a game. Sweeps do not count, and the majority of the 11 points wins (except that the game may end in a tie if each player scores 4 points and gets 26 cards).

2) Eleven points constitute the game. If a player or side scores 11 points in two deals, the score is doubled to 22 points; and if it scores 11 points in one deal, the score is redoubled to 44 points. The loser's score is deducted from the winner's to determine the margin of victory. If both sides reach 11 or more points on the same deal, the higher score wins, and if both have the same score, the game ends in a tie.

3) Twenty-one points constitute game. If both sides reach 21 on the same deal, the points are counted in this order to determine the winner: cards, spades, Big Cassino, Little Cassino, ♠A, ♣A, ♥A, ♦A, and sweeps.

Royal Cassino

In this version of Cassino, picture cards can be used in building. Jacks count 11, queens 12, kings 13 , and aces are either 1 or 14 as the holder wishes. Also, there is no restriction on combining or pairing face cards. Thus, a jack and a king may be paired. The play is exactly as in regular Cassino, and 21 points constitute game. In some regions Royal Cassino is played with a 60-card pack, which includes eight special cards: four of each suit marked 11 and four of each suit marked 12.

Draw Cassino

This version is played as in regular Cassino or Royal Cassino, whichever the players prefer. As usual, after the first round of dealing, the undealt cards are placed on the table to form a stock. But in Draw Cassino, each participant, after playing, draws a card from the stock to restore his hand to four cards.

Spade Cassino

Either regular Cassino or Royal Cassino is played, but (in addition to the count for cards, spades, Big Cassino and aces) the ace, jack and deuce of spades count 2 points each and other spades count 1 point each. Twenty-six points may be scored in each deal, exclusive of sweeps, if played. Game is 61 points, and the margin of victory is the difference between the winning score and the losing score, As in Cribbage , the winner's score is doubled if the losing score is less than 31. Spade Cassino can be conveniently scored on a Cribbage board with each point being recorded as the card is taken in.

THIRTY-ONE

NUMBER OF PLAYERS	NUMBER OF CARDS	GAME PLAY	SKILL LEVEL
4+	52	◇ ♦ ◇ ◇ ◇ EASY　→　COMPLEX	◇ ♦ ◇ ◇ ◇ LUCK　→　SKILL

This general type of game dates back some 500 years and is still seen in many forms in Europe. In the United States, the most popular games of this type are Cribbage and Blackjack.

Number of Players. Four or more people can play.

The Pack. The standard 52-card pack is used.

Rank of Cards. A (high), K, Q, J, 10, 9, 8, 7, 6, 5, 4, 3, 2 (low)

Card Values. An ace counts 11 points, face cards count 10 points, and all other cards count their face value.

The Deal. The players cut for deal and the lowest card deals, the turn to deal alternates to the left. Three cards are dealt face down to each player; then three cards are dealt face up for a "widow."

Object of the Game. The goal is to obtain a hand that totals 31 in cards of one suit; or to have a hand at the showdown whose count in one suit is higher than that of any other player.

The Play. Before play begins, all players put an equal amount of chips into a pot. The player on the dealer's left has the first turn.

On each turn, a player may take one card from the widow and replace it with one card from his hand (face up). (*Variation*: Players may exchange any number of cards with the widow in this manner.)

Players take turns, clockwise around the table, until one player is satisfied that the card values he holds will likely beat the other players. He indicates this by "knocking" on the table. All other players then get one more turn to exchange cards. Then there is a showdown in which the players reveal their hands and compare values. The player with the highest total value of cards of the same suit wins the pot.

If there is a tie for the highest score, the player with the highest-ranking card wins. *Example*: K, Q, 6 (total 26) would beat Q, 9, 7 (also total 26). If there is a tie in the highest cards, the next highest cards are compared, and so on.

Any time a player holds exactly 31, he may "knock" immediately, and he wins the pot.

If a player knocks before the first round of exchanges have begun, the showdown occurs immediately with no exchange of cards.

After the pot has been won, all the players put in chips for the next hand.

Chapter VIII

The Stops Family

T he Stops Family of games is not a large one, but all the games have one thing in common: Participants play their cards in a certain order, and the action is often interrupted – "stopped" – by the absence of a suitable card. These games lend themselves to gambling, usually for small stakes. However, strictly speaking they are not considered casino games.

FAN TAN
(Parliament, Sevens, Card Dominoes, Stops)

NUMBER OF PLAYERS	NUMBER OF CARDS	GAME PLAY	SKILL LEVEL
3-8	**52**	◆ ◇ ◇ ◇ ◇ EASY → COMPLEX	◇ ◆ ◇ ◇ ◇ LUCK → SKILL

F an Tan was once very popular. As with other games of the Stops group, it is easy to play and the action is very fast.

Number of Players. From three to eight people can play.

The Pack. The standard 52-card pack is used.

Rank of Cards. The cards in each suit rank: K (high), Q, J, 10, 9, 8, 7, 6, 5, 4, 3, 2, A.

The Draw. Any player distributes the cards one at a time, face up, around the table; the player who receives the first jack deals first.

The Ante. Each player puts one chip in the pot before each deal.

The Shuffle and Cut. The dealer has the right to shuffle last. The player on his right cuts. The cut must leave at least five cards in each packet.

The Deal. The dealer completes the cut and deals the cards one at a time clockwise, face down, beginning with the player on his left. All the cards are dealt, and some players may receive fewer cards than others. It is customary for each player with fewer cards to ante one additional chip.

Object of the Game. The goal is to be the first player to get rid of all his cards.

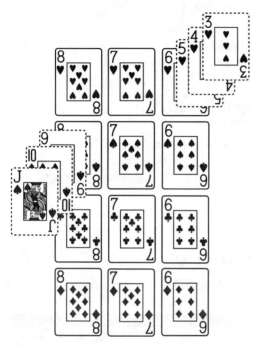

On each eight, build up: *nine, ten, jack, queen and king* – following suit.

On each six, build down: *five, four, three, two and ace* – following suit

The Play. Beginning with the player to the left of the dealer, each person must play a card if possible. All cards played remain face up on the table, arranged in four rows of the four suits. The plays that may be made are: 1) any seven or 2) any card in suit and sequence to a card previously played. As the sevens are played, they are placed in a row in the center of the table. The sixes are placed in another row to the right, and the eights on the left of the sevens in their respective suits. The fives and lower cards in sequence are piled on the sixes, while the nines and higher cards in sequence are piled on the eights.

Each player must play a card during his turn if possible; if the person cannot play, he puts one chip in the pot and the turn passes to the left. The game ends when one player gets rid of all his cards. Each opponent then pays the pot one chip for each card remaining in his hand, and the winner takes the pot.

Irregularities. If a player passes when he could have played, the offender must pay three chips into the pot. If the player passed when he was able to play a seven, he must pay an additional five chips to the players holding the six and the eight of the same suit.

Five or Nine

In this variation, played like Fan Tan, the first player able to play either a five or a nine may set the denomination of the foundations. The foundations are then built up on one side, and down on the other, as in Fan Tan.

Snip Snap Snorem

(Earl of Coventry)

In this version, the first player may play any card. Whatever card he plays calls for the other three cards of the same rank. The turn to play moves to the left. The player who plays the fourth card may then choose any card in his hand for the next series. If a player cannot play, he passes and puts one chip in the pot. If a player fails to play when he can, there is no additional penalty.

Play or Pay

This game is yet another version of Fan Tan. The first player may play any card. The sequence in the suit must be built up until all thirteen cards are played, and the sequence in the suit is continuous. For example: J, Q, K, A, 2, and so on. The turn to play rotates to the left and if a person is unable to play in turn, he puts one chip in the pot. Whoever plays the thirteenth card of a suit may choose any card from his hand to begin the next series. The first player to get rid of all his cards wins the pot.

MICHIGAN
(Boodle, Newmarket, Chicago, Saratoga, Stops)

NUMBER OF PLAYERS	NUMBER OF CARDS	GAME PLAY		SKILL LEVEL	
3-8	56	♦ ◇ ◇ ◇ ◇ EASY → COMPLEX		◇ ♦ ◇ ◇ ◇ LUCK → SKILL	

A novice can learn to play Michigan after just a brief explanation. This makes the game ideal for groups in which no one game is familiar to all members.

Number of Players. Three to eight people can play.

The Pack. The standard 52-card pack is used, plus the four "boodle" cards from another pack. (See "layout" below.)

Rank of Cards. The cards in each suit rank: A (high), K, Q, J, 10, 9, 8, 7, 6, 5, 4, 3, 2.

The Draw. Players may take seats at random, and any player distributes the cards one at a time around the table face up. The person who receives the first jack deals first.

The Layout. The ♥A, ♣K, ♦Q, and ♠J are taken from another pack. These four cards, called "boodle" or "money cards," are placed in the center of the table and remain there throughout the game.

(Boodle Cards)

The Ante. Before the deal, each player except the dealer places one chip on each boodle card; the dealer places two chips on each. (In some regions, each player antes a fixed number of chips, placing them where he wishes on the layout.)

The Shuffle and Cut. The dealer has the right to shuffle last, and the player on his right cuts. The cut must leave at least five cards in each packet.

The Deal. The dealer completes the cut and deals the cards one at a time, face down. One extra hand is dealt immediately to the left of the dealer. No player may see the extra hand except the player, if any, who exchanges for it. The cards are dealt out as far as they will go, even though all players may not receive the same number of cards.

Object of the Game. The object in play is twofold: to be the first player to get rid of all his cards and to collect chips from the layout by playing one of the four boodle cards.

The Play. Each card played is placed face up in front of the owner, separate from all other hands, and the player names its rank and suit.

The person to the left of the dealer plays first. He may lead any suit, but must play the lowest card he holds in that suit. Whichever player holds the next higher card in sequence in the same suit plays it, and so on. The sequence in the suit is continued until it is stopped by a card in the dead hand or by the ace. The player who played last before the stop has the next turn. He must play a new suit, and it must be the lowest card in that suit. If the player has no new suit, the turn passes to the left.

Any time a player can play a card that duplicates one of the four boodle cards, he takes all the chips from that card.

Any chips that are still on the layout after the hand ends remain there until they are won in a subsequent hand.

Settlement. Play ends as soon as any player plays his last card. The winner collects one chip from each opponent for every card remaining in that player's hand.

Irregularities. If a player starts a suit without using the lowest card held in the suit, he must pay one chip to each opponent and cannot collect for any boodle cards played after that.

If a player causes a stop by failing to play a card when possible, play continues as usual, even though the card withheld may later enable the offender to get a stop. However, the offender may not collect for any boodle cards played after the error. If at the end of the hand there are still chips on the boodle card of the suit of the card the offender withheld, he must pay the same number of chips to any player who held the duplicate of the boodle card. If the offender is first to get rid of his cards, he does not win the hand, and play continues to determine the eventual winner.

ELEUSIS

NUMBER OF PLAYERS	NUMBER OF CARDS	GAME PLAY	SKILL LEVEL
4-8+	104 (156)	◇ ◇ ◆ ◇ ◇ EASY → COMPLEX	◇ ◇ ◇ ◇ ◆ LUCK → SKILL

A modern classic, Eleusis is one of the most unusual card games ever devised. It is a game that makes people think in reverse as the players actually create the rules! A new "secret rule" is created by the dealer for each round, which the other players must try to discover. Playing Eleusis requires a peculiar mental approach which may not appeal to everyone.

Eleusis was invented in 1956 by *Robert Abbott*. The rules presented below feature his latest edition of the official Eleusis rules, copyright 1977, and are used with his permission.

THE CARD GAME STUDIED BY SCIENTISTS!

Eleusis gained recognition in 1959 when it was featured in Scientific American magazine and has been an object of study by scientists. Why? Because, as with scientific inquiry, the game involves inductive rather than deductive reasoning. In most card games, the players start with certain known rules and deduce which card would be the best to play during each turn. But in Eleusis, the players must figure out a secret rule as the goal of the game, based upon what they observe happening when they play a card, similar to the way scientists try to figure out how nature works by observing the results of an experiment. In scientific papers such as "Simulating Scientific Inquiry with the Card Game Eleusis" (1979, H. Charles Romesburg, Utah State University), an effort was made to study the thought processes involved in playing the game. Investigators hoped to discover hidden patterns that might lead to breakthrough solutions: for example, how to avoid drawing hasty conclusions, among others. As yet, there is no evidence that good Eleusis players become good scientists, but the game has been described as "...a training ground for bringing science concepts relegated to the blackboard into action."

Number of Players. Usually, four to eight players participate. Although it is possible for more than eight to play, it is best for a large group to split into two separate games.

The Pack. There should be enough cards so that the stock does not run out. Initially, two standard 52-card packs are shuffled together to form the stock. If the stock is reduced to four or fewer cards, another 52-card deck is added immediately. Three decks will usually be enough, but if more cards are needed, a fourth 52-card deck is added.

Choosing the Dealer. The dealer plays a special role in Eleusis. The choice of dealer is usually made informally. It is often the first player to have a good idea for a secret rule (explained below). If inexperienced players are involved, an experienced player should be the first dealer. In formal play, players can draw for high card to determine the first dealer.

Rounds of Play. A game consists of one or more rounds of play. A different player is chosen as the dealer of each new round.

The Central Layout. All plays are made to a central layout which grows as the round progresses, beginning from an initial "starter card." A layout consists of a horizontal "mainline" of cards that follow a certain pattern. Below this are vertical "sidelines" of cards that are exceptions to the pattern.

Eleusis is normally played on a large table or the floor because the central layout often becomes too large for a standard card table.

Object of the Game. The person who deals a round does not play during that round; instead he is responsible for creating and controlling a "secret rule." His score as the dealer is based on the scores of the other players.

Players score points by getting rid of the cards in their hands, usually by playing cards that are accepted on the mainline of the layout. Players may also score by acting as the "Forecaster."

The Secret Rule. Each round has a different rule that determines which cards are accepted on the mainline and which are rejected. At the beginning of a round, no player knows this rule.

This secret rule is devised by the dealer. He does not tell the rule, but, when a card (or string of cards) is played, the dealer announces whether it is accepted or rejected.

Cards that are accepted are added to the right of the mainline, beginning with the starter card and forming a sequence. As more and more cards are accepted, the pattern involved becomes clearer, and players are better able to make more accurate guesses as to the secret rule. Cards that are rejected are put below the mainline.

Players try to figure out the rule by observing the pattern that emerges on the layout. The closer a player gets to understanding the rule, the more easily he is can take advantage of this knowledge to score points.

Examples of Secret Rules. The secret rule can be simple or clever and is most easily understood by analyzing some examples:

Rule: If the last card is an odd-numbered card (ace, 3, 5, etc.), play a black card; if the last card is even, play a red card.

Rule: If the last card was black, play a card higher than or equal to that card; if the last was red, play lower or equal.

Rule: If the last card was a spade, play a heart; if the last card was a heart, play a diamond; if the last card was a diamond, play a club; and if the last card was a club, play a spade.

Rule: The card played must be one point higher or one point lower than the last card.

In all these rules, "last card" refers to the last card accepted on the mainline, or, if no card has yet been accepted, it refers to the starter card.

When numbers are involved, ace is usually 1, jack is 11, queen is 12, and king is 13.

The dealer should write the secret rule on a piece of paper which is put aside to be examined later. Before play begins, the dealer may, if desired, offer a "hint" about the rule. However, once play begins, no hints should be given.

The rule should be straightforward and involve one basic concept that is easily written in one sentence. The scoring system does not reward the dealer for overly complex rules, but does reward the dealer for "interesting" rules. (See Scoring, p. 279)

The Deal. The dealer shuffles the stock and deals 14 cards to each of the other players. The dealer receives no cards. He then places one card, face up, in the center of the playing area. This is the starter card and the first card of the mainline.

The Play. The player who goes first is chosen by the following method: Starting with the player to the left of the dealer, count around the table (skipping the dealer) up to the number value shown on the starter card. The player on whom the the count stops takes the first turn. Thereafter, the turn passes to the left. Play continues until the round ends, at which time scores are counted.

During each turn, a player may:

1) Play one card.

2) Play a string of cards.

3) Declare no play.

Playing One Card. To play a single card, the player takes the card from his hand and shows it to the dealer. The dealer then says "Right" or

"Wrong," depending on whether the card is playable at that point under the secret rule.

If "right," the card is put on the layout to the right of the last mainline card.

If "wrong," the card is put below the last card played (it either starts a sideline or continues one) and the dealer gives the player two cards from the stock. Thus, a right play will decrease a player's hand, and a wrong play will increase his hand.

Playing a String of Cards. A string consists of two, three, or four cards, which, if correct, will extend the mainline pattern. To play a string, the player takes the cards from his hand, overlaps them slightly to indicate their exact order, and shows them to the dealer.

A string of, say, three cards is the same as three consecutive plays of a single card each. The dealer calls this string "right" only if all three cards would be right. If one or more of the cards in the string are wrong, the dealer declares the entire string wrong. The dealer does not reveal which individual cards in the string are wrong.

When a string is called right, it is placed to the right of the last mainline card. Thus, a correct string of four cards would look the same as four correct plays of a single card each. If a string is called wrong, its cards remain overlapped, and the entire string is placed below the last card played. The overlapping is necessary to retain the information that these cards were played as a string and to show the order that the player gave to the string.

As penalty for a string wrongly played, the player is given cards from the stock equal to twice the number of cards in the string.

Declaring No Play. A player has the option of declaring that he has no correct card to play. A player who declares "no play" must show his hand to everyone, and the dealer says whether the player is right or wrong.

If the player is right (that is, there was no correct card to play), and his hand is down to four cards or less, the cards are returned to the stock and the round ends at that point.

If the player is right but still holds five or more cards, the cards are counted and put on the bottom of the stock. The player is then dealt a fresh hand from the top of the stock, but the player's reward is to receive four cards less than the number he held previously. (*For example:* If the player originally had six cards, he would be given only two.)

If the player was wrong (i.e., at least one of his cards could have been played correctly), the dealer takes one of these correct cards and puts it on the layout to the right of the last mainline card. The player who was wrong keeps his cards, and as a penalty, is dealt five more cards from the stock.

Becoming a Forecaster. Once a player believes he has discovered the secret rule, he has the opportunity to prove his assumption, and score higher by forecasting how the dealer will speak. In other words, he becomes the Forecaster.

The new Forecaster does not state what he believes the secret rule to be. Instead he calls "right" or "wrong" when others play, and takes over other functions of the dealer, as explained below.

A player becomes a Forecaster simply by declaring, "I am the Forecaster." However, the player can make this declaration only if:

1) He has just played (right or wrong) and the next player has not yet played.

2) There is not already an existing Forecaster.

3) There are at least two other players still in this round (besides himself and the dealer).

4) The player has not been the Forecaster before in this round.

When a player declares he is the Forecaster, he puts a marker (a poker chip) on the layout on the last card of the mainline. This records the point where the player became the Forecaster. The Forecaster keeps his hand but will play no more cards from it unless he is "overthrown."

The Forecaster will receive a bonus score if he succeeds in remaining the Forecaster until the end of the round without being overthrown.

Acting as Forecaster. After a player has declared he is the Forecaster, the play continues as usual, but the Forecaster does not take a turn.

When a player plays a single card, the Forecaster says "Right" if he thinks the card is playable under the dealer's secret rule, or says "Wrong" if he thinks the card is not playable. The dealer then confirms whether the Forecaster made the correct call. If the dealer says "Correct," the Forecaster completes the play, putting the card on the mainline or sideline, and giving the player cards from the stock if the play was wrong.

Similarly, if a player plays a string of cards, the Forecaster calls the string right or wrong, and the dealer reveals whether the Forecaster is correct or not.

Overthrown. If the dealer says the Forecaster is incorrect, the Forecaster is overthrown and suffers a penalty described in the next section. But first, the turn is completed by the dealer, according to special rules:

The dealer completes the play as usual, except that the initial player is not given any penalty cards. (This exception to the normal procedure has a purpose: It makes it more likely that a player will attempt a tricky play, even a deliberately wrong play, in hopes of overthrowing the Forecaster.)

There is a rare case with a special rule. If a player declares a "no play" and the Forecaster incorrectly says the no play was wrong, the dealer challenges The Forecaster to pick one correct card from the player's hand and play it on the mainline. If the dealer says that the Forecaster is "Right," the Forecaster then deals the player the five penalty cards as usual. But if the Forecaster plays a wrong card, the dealer steps in, returns the card to the player's hand, and picks the correct card. This card is put on the mainline. The player who originally declared "no play" is not given any penalty cards.

After a Forecaster is Overthrown. When a Forecaster is overthrown, he is given five cards from the stock as a penalty. The ex-forecaster (or "false Forecaster") then resumes his normal place in the game. He may not become Forecaster again during that round, and his marker is removed from the layout. Other players are now free to declare themselves Forecaster, subject to the usual restrictions.

Expulsion. After a round has lasted for a specified time, players may be expelled from the round when they make incorrect plays. (An incorrect play is either a card or string played wrong or an incorrect declaration of "no play.") If all the players (or all players except the Forecaster) have been expelled, the round ends.

If there is no Forecaster, a player is expelled if he makes an incorrect play and there are 40 or more cards on the layout before the play. If there is a Forecaster, a player is expelled if he makes an incorrect play when there 30 or more cards after the Forecaster's marker. However, no one is expelled during a turn in which a Forecaster is overthrown. (When there is a possibility of expulsion, the marker makes it easy to keep count.)

An expelled player makes no further play during the round (and may not become Forecaster). However, he is given the penalty cards for his last incorrect play and retains his hand for scoring purposes.

Scoring. When one player gets rid of all his cards, the round ends. It also ends if all players, or all players besides the Forecaster, are expelled. The players, including any who were expelled, now receive scores based on the number of cards in their hands.

Player Scores. First, determine the "high count," the greatest number of cards in any one player's hand (including the Forecaster's). Each player (including the Forecaster but not the dealer) then scores this high count minus the number of cards in his own hand. If a player had eliminated all of his cards, that player receives a 4-point bonus. *Example:* Player A has four cards, Player B has 10, Player C has six, and Player D has zero. The high count is 10. Therefore, Player A scores 6 points (10 - 4), Player B scores 0 (10 - 10), Player C scores 4 points (10 - 6), and Player D scores 10 (10 - 0) plus 4 bonus points for a total of 14 points.

Dealer's Score. The dealer's score equals the highest score in the round, with one exception: If there is a Forecaster, count the number of cards (mainline and sideline) that precede the Forecaster's marker and multiply this number by two. If the resulting number is smaller than the highest score, the dealer scores that smaller number. (The dealer is thus rewarded for creating a secret rule that is "just right"– difficult enough so it won't be quickly discovered, but easy enough so it won't stump the players for too long.)

Forecaster Bonus. The Forecaster receives 1 point for every card played correctly after he became Forecaster, plus 2 points for every card played incorrectly. This amount is added to the points the Forecaster scored as a player.

One player should keep a running total of scores in each round. Participants play as many rounds as there are players to determine an overall winner. Alternatively, if there is not enough time to play that many rounds, 10 points is added to the total score of any player who has not been the dealer.

CRAZY EIGHTS

(Eights, Crazy Jacks, or Swedish Rummy)

NUMBER OF PLAYERS	NUMBER OF CARDS	GAME PLAY	SKILL LEVEL
2-8	**52**	◆ ◇ ◇ ◇ ◇ EASY ➤ COMPLEX	◇ ◇ ◆ ◇ ◇ LUCK ➤ SKILL

The game of Crazy Eights offers a better chance than other Stops games for the player to overcome poor cards through skillful play. Crazy Eights is a popular game for both children and adults.

Number of Players. From two to eight people can play. The game is best for two or three individual players, or four people playing two against two as partners.

The Pack. The standard 52-card pack is used. With six or more players, two packs are shuffled together.

The Draw. Any player distributes the cards, face up, one at a time around the table, and the player who receives the first ace deals first.

The Shuffle and Cut. The dealer has the right to shuffle last, and the pack is cut by the player on his right. The cut must leave at least five cards in each packet.

The Deal. The dealer completes the cut and distributes the cards clockwise one at a time, face down, beginning with the player to his left. If there are two players, seven cards are dealt to each; with more players, each person receives five cards. The balance of the pack is placed face down in the center of the table and forms the stock. The dealer turns up the top card and places it in a separate pile; this card is the "starter." If an eight is turned, it is buried in the middle of the pack and the next card is turned.

Object of the Game. The goal is to be the first player to get rid of all the cards in his hand.

The Play. Beginning with the player to the dealer's left, each participant in turn must place one card face up on the starter pile. If unable to play, the participant must draw cards from the top of the stock until he can play, or until the stock is exhausted. If unable to play when the stock is exhausted, the player must pass. A player may draw from the stock if he wishes, even though he can play a card in his hand.

Each card played (other than an eight) must match the card showing on the starter pile, either in suit or in denomination. Thus, if the ♣Q is the starter, any club may be played on it or any queen.

All eights are wild! That is, an eight may be played at any time in turn, and the player need only specify a suit for it (but never a number). The next player must play either a card of the specified suit or an eight.

Winning. The player who is the first to have no cards left wins the game. He collects from each other player the value of the cards remaining in that player's hand as follows:

Each eight 50

Each K, Q, J or 10 10

Each ace 1

Each other card . . . . pip value

If the game ends in a "block" (no participant can play and the stock is exhausted), the player with the lowest count in his remaining cards collects from each other player the difference of the counts. Players who tie divide the winnings.

A four-hand partnership game does not end until both partners on a side go out. When a partner goes out, the other three players continue to play. If the game ends in a block, the total counts of the two sides are compared to determine the winner.

Irregularities. If the dealer gives any player too many cards, another player draws the excess cards from that hand and restores them to the middle of the pack. If the dealer gives a player too few cards, that player draws the appropriate number of additional cards from the stock. After the stock is exhausted, a player who passes when able to play may be forced to play on the demand of another player. If the score of a game ending in a block has been agreed upon, it stands, even if it is found that a player could have continued.

Hollywood Eights

This game is a variation of two-hand Crazy Eights, except that the scoring formate is like Gin Rummy (see p. 125 - Hollywood Scoring). The standard 52-card pack is used and the cards count as follows: each eight, 20 points; ace, 15 points; face cards, 10 points; lower cards, pip value. The first player to reach 100 points wins a game. The score sheet is set up for three simultaneous games. The first hand won by each player is scored only in Game 1. The second hand won is scored in Games 1 and 2. The third and all subsequent wins are scored in all three games. When any of these games ends, Game 4 may be opened up, and so on.

Chapter IX

Children's
Card
Games

Teaching Card Games to Children

Familiarity with playing cards and card games can provide children with entertainment, social interaction, and educational benefits. Even at a very early age, children are naturally attracted to the bright colors, shapes and pretty designs found on most playing cards, and these can help stimulate a child's recognition of letters, symbols, and numbers.

Best of all, playing card games is a pastime that offers immediate pleasure, as well as many advantages that will last into adult life. The fact that grown-ups enjoy playing with cards is a gratifying discovery for a child, and most children will want to play cards too. This is a great opportunity for adults to teach timeless favorites such as Go Fish or Old Maid.

Often, card games are best taught by demonstration along with an explanation. A child can be helped to play the first few rounds or hands with cards exposed while the card play is explained as the game progresses. Alternatively, children can watch a few games being played before actually participating.

In the description for each game there is a suggested age range and the skills that might be developed or enhanced. However, these are just guidelines. Children are individuals, and readiness to learn a particular game will vary from child to child.

What is most important is to demonstrate how much fun it is to play cards. Also, when families play card games together, it can be one of the most rewarding of all indoor recreational activities.

SLAPJACK

NUMBER OF PLAYERS	NUMBER OF CARDS	GAME PLAY	SKILL LEVEL
3-4 (2-8)	**52**	◆ ◇ ◇ ◇ ◇ EASY → COMPLEX	◆ ◇ ◇ ◇ ◇ LUCK → SKILL

Slapjack is a very simple game, and it is often a child's first introduction to playing cards. The memories of playing this often noisy, and always fun pastime are never forgotten!

Suggested Ages. 5 to 12.

Skills Developed. Visual alertness and quick responses.

The Pack. The standard 52-card pack is used.

Number of Players. Two to eight people, playing individually.

The Deal. Any player may deal first. The dealer shuffles the cards and then deals them out, one at a time face down, to each player in rotation, until all the cards have been dealt. The hands do not have to come out even. Without looking at any of his cards, each player squares up his hand into a neat pile in front of him.

Object of the Game. The goal is to win all the cards, by being first to slap each jack as it is played to the center.

The Play. Beginning on the dealer's left, each player lifts one card from his pile and places it face up in the center of the table. In doing this, the player must turn up the card away from himself so that he does not see it sooner than anyone else. However, the player should turn his card up quickly enough so that the other players do not see the face of the card before he does.

When the card played to the center is a jack, the fun begins! The first player to slap his hand down on the jack takes it, as well as all the cards beneath it. The player winning these cards turns them face down, places them under his pile of cards, and shuffles them to form a new, larger pile. He then places the pile in front of him as before.

When more than one player slaps at a jack, the one whose hand is lowest (directly on top of the jack) wins the pile. If a player slaps at any card in the center that is not a jack, he must give one card, face down, to the player of that card.

When a player has no more cards left, he remains in the game until the next jack is turned. He may slap at the jack in an effort to get a new pile. If he fails to win that next pile, he is out of the game.

Play continues until one player has won all the cards. That player is the winner.

Irregularities. If a card is exposed in dealing, the recipient's cards must be shuffled before he places them face down in a pile and plays.

I DOUBT IT

NUMBER OF PLAYERS	NUMBER OF CARDS	GAME PLAY	SKILL LEVEL
3-13	**52** (104)	◆ ◇ ◇ ◇ ◇ EASY → COMPLEX	◇ ◇ ◆ ◇ ◇ LUCK → SKILL

I Doubt It is excellent for children – and even for adults or for mixed groups – because it is easy to learn and can be played either haphazardly or scientifically. It can also be hilarious, especially when eight or ten players are participating in the same game.

Suggested Ages. 6 and up.

Skills Developed. Counting and number sequencing.

The Pack. Four or fewer players should use one standard 52-card pack. Five players may use either a single or a double pack. Six or more players should use a double pack – two standard 52-card decks (104 cards) shuffled together.

The Shuffle and Cut. The players draw cards from a shuffled pack spread face down. The player with the highest card deals first. Anyone may shuffle, and it does not matter whether the cards are cut or not.

The Deal. The dealer gives two or three cards at a time to each player in rotation beginning on his left. On the last round of dealing, the cards are dealt out one at a time as far as they will go.

Rank of Cards. Cards have no actual value but are played in sequence with aces first, then twos, then threes, and so on.

Object of the Game. The goal is to be the first player to get rid of all his cards.

The Play. The player on the dealer's left places from one to four cards, face down on the table. As he puts them down, the player announces that he is putting down as many aces as the number of cards. For example, the player may put down three cards, saying, "Three aces." However, the cards need not be aces; the player does not have to tell the truth!

Any player at the table may then say "I doubt it," in which case the cards must be turned up. If the player's statement was true (if, as in this case, <u>all</u> three cards were actually aces), the doubter must take up those three cards and all other cards that have been played on the table previously, into his hand. If the announcement was false in any respect, the player who didn't tell the truth must take all the cards on the table, including those just put down, into his hand. If two or more players doubt the announcement, the one who spoke first is the official doubter. If two players doubt simultaneously, the one nearest to the player's left is the official doubter.

When an announcement is not doubted, the cards remain face down in front of the player until, by the rules of the game, some player is compelled to pick them up and add them to his hand.

After the first player's announcement either has been doubted or not, the player on his left must put down one to four cards and announce that he is putting down that many twos. Next, the player to his left must put down and announce so many threes, and so on around the table. When a player in turn has announced kings, the next player starts over with aces again.

When a double pack is being used, a player may lay down any number of cards from one to eight. The principle is that a player must be permitted to put down every card of a group if he holds it: four of a kind with a single pack or eight of a kind with a double pack.

It is quite ethical to make false statements. *For example:* When it is someone's turn to play sevens, saying "No sevens," is a normal part of the game, even if that player has one or more sevens.

Game. When a player puts his last card on the table and either is not doubted or, upon being doubted, is shown to have announced correctly, he wins the game. If the game was played for points or chips, the other players pay the winner 1 point or 1 chip for each card remaining in their hands.

Irregularities. There is no penalty for a misdeal. Any irregularity in dealing should be corrected by adjusting the number of cards in the respective hands, even if the players have looked at them.

WAR

NUMBER OF PLAYERS	NUMBER OF CARDS	GAME PLAY	SKILL LEVEL
2	52	◆ ◇ ◇ ◇ ◇ EASY → COMPLEX	◆ ◇ ◇ ◇ ◇ LUCK → SKILL

This game is a favorite with even the youngest age group. The rules are very simple, and the game, while pure luck, can be very exciting. It is all a matter of chance because only the denomination of the cards matters.

Suggested Ages. 5 to 12.

Skills Developed. Counting and the card values.

Number of Players. Two people can play.

The Pack. The standard 52-card pack is used.

Rank of Cards. K, Q, J, 10, 9, 8, 7, 6, 5, 4, 3, 2, A. (In some games aces are high.)

The Deal. The deck is divided evenly, with each player receiving 26 cards, dealt one at a time, face down. Anyone may deal first. Each player places his stack of cards face down, in front of him.

Object of the Game. The goal is to be the first player to win all 52 cards.

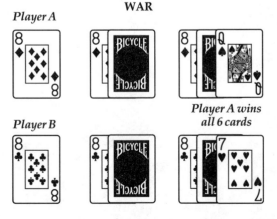

WAR

Player A

Player B

Player A wins all 6 cards

The Play. Each player turns up a card at the same time and the player with the higher card takes both cards and puts them, face down, on the bottom of his stack. If the cards are the same rank, it is War. Each player turns up one card face down and one card face up. The player with the higher cards takes both piles (six cards). If the turned-up cards are again the same rank, each player places another card face down and turns another card face up. The player with the higher card takes all 10 cards, and so on. The game ends when one player has won all the cards.

Quadruple War

In this version, when there is a War, each player counts out four cards face down, instead of one, and the next card turned face up by each player determines the winner of all the cards. Quadruple War is even more exciting than regular War, and in many regions, it has become more popular than the standard game.

Stealing Bundles
(Steal the Old Lady's Bundle)

This is a children's version of Cassino (see page 264).

Suggested Ages. 6 and up.

Skills Developed: Identifying cards and pairing.

The game is best for two to four players and the rules are the same as Cassino except for the following:

1) Players may win cards from the middle of the table only by pairing, not by building or adding numbers in any way.

2) Cards won are stacked in a pile face up, and, for his turn, a player can capture an opponent's pile by matching its top card. If he does, the player takes the entire pile and places it face up on top of any cards he has already taken. However, his pile may be recaptured by any opponent as long as the card on top is matched.

The object of the game is to win more than half the cards. When a player has done this, the game ends, and he is the winner.

GO FISH
(Fish, Go Fishing)

NUMBER OF PLAYERS	NUMBER OF CARDS	GAME PLAY	SKILL LEVEL
2-5	52	◆ ◇ ◇ ◇ ◇ EASY → COMPLEX	◇ ◆ ◇ ◇ ◇ LUCK → SKILL

Go Fish is a fun game that will amuse and entertain even the youngest card players.

Suggested Ages. 4 to 10.

Skills Developed. Matching and pairing.

Number of Players. The game is best for two to five players.

The Pack. The standard 52-card pack is used. There are also special decks available for the game of Authors (see p. ••), which has very similar rules to Go Fish.

Rank of Cards. The cards rank from ace (high) to two (low). The suits are not important, only the card numbers are relevant, such as two 3s, two 10s, and so on.

The Draw. Any player deals one card face up to each player. The player with the lowest card is the dealer.

The Shuffle and Cut. The dealer shuffles the cards, and the player on his right cuts them.

The Deal. The dealer completes the cut and deals the cards clockwise one at a time, face down, beginning with the player to his left. If two or three people are playing, each player receives seven cards. If four or five people are playing, each receives five cards. The remainder of the pack is placed face down on the table to form the stock.

Object of the Game. The goal is to win the most "books" of cards. A book is any four of a kind, such as four kings, four aces, and so on.

A "book" of tens

The Play. The player to the left of the dealer looks directly at any opponent and says, for example, "Give me your kings," usually addressing the opponent by name and specifying the rank he wants, from ace down to two. The player who is "fishing" must have at least one card of the rank he asked for in his hand. The player who is addressed must hand over all the cards requested. If he has none, he says, "Go fish!" and the player who made the request draws the top card of the stock and places it in his hand.

If a player gets one or more cards of the named rank he asked for, he is entitled to ask the same or another player for a card. He can ask for the same card or a different one. So long as he is succeeds in getting cards (makes a catch), his turn continues. When a player makes a catch, he must reveal the card so that the catch is verified.

If a player gets the fourth card of a book, he shows all four cards, places them on the table face up in front of him, and plays again.

If the player goes fishing without "making a catch" (does not receive a card he asked for), the turn passes to his left.

The game ends when all thirteen books have been won. The winner is the player with the most books.

During the game, if a player is left without cards, he may (when it's his turn to play), draw from the stock and then ask for cards of that rank. If there are no cards left in the stock, he is out of the game.

Authors

This game is similar to Go Fish, but there is more to learn and remember.

Suggested Ages. 8 and up.

Skills Developed. Counting, matching, and recognizing suits.

It is best for four or five players. The whole pack is dealt out, as nearly evenly as possible. Each player requests a desired card, not only by rank but also by suit. *For example:* he says to an opponent "Give me the queen of diamonds." If the opponent has the card, he must hand it over. The player's turn continues so long as the player receives the card requested. If not, the turn passes to the left

As soon as a player collects four cards of the same denomination such as four 3s or four queens, he lays them face down. The game continues until all cards have been laid down in books.

Irregularities. These apply to both Go Fish and Authors.

Misdeal. The dealer must deal again if he exposes a card while dealing, or if any player receives too few cards and calls attention to this mistake before looking at his hand.

Exposed card. When a player drops or otherwise exposes a card, there is no penalty. He simply restores the card to his hand.

Playing out of turn. If a player asks for cards when it is not his turn, he may not score a book in that rank for the rest of the game.

Failure to show a book. If a player fails to show a book he has formed before the end of his turn, he cannot count that book in his score.

Illegal call. If a player asks for a rank when holding no card of that rank (or, in Authors, asks for a card that he already holds), he misses his next turn.

Failure to give up card. If a player has a card in his hand that he fails to hand over when properly asked for, that player may not score a book in that rank and also misses his next turn.

Pig

This is a really easy game to play. Adults, as well as children, find it very humorous.

Suggested Ages. 6 and up.

Skills Developed. Counting, matching, and recognizing suits.

Number of Players. 3 to 13.

The Pack. The standard 52-card pack is used. The number of cards in the pack varies: four cards represent any one rank for each player in the game. Thus, four players would use a 16-card pack consisting of four aces, four kings, four queens, and four jacks. Five players would use a 20-card pack, with 10s added. Six players would use a 24-card pack, with nines added, and so on.

The Shuffle and Deal. Any player shuffles the pack thoroughly and deals four cards, one at a time, to each player.

Object of the Game. The goal is to be the first player to make a group of four of a kind in his hand, or not to be the last player to notice when someone else has done so.

The Play. The players look at their hands; then each player passes one card to the left and picks up the card passed by the player on his right. This passing continues as rapidly as possible so that players have a difficult time keeping up the pace. As soon as a player assembles four cards of one denomination, such as four jacks, he stops passing or picking up cards and puts a finger to his nose. The other players must immediately stop passing, and they, too, must put their fingers to their noses. The last person to do this is the Pig!

OLD MAID

NUMBER OF PLAYERS	NUMBER OF CARDS	GAME PLAY	SKILL LEVEL
2-12	**51**	◆ ◇ ◇ ◇ ◇ EASY → COMPLEX	◇ ◆ ◇ ◇ ◇ LUCK → SKILL

Old Maid is a constant favorite with children and lots of fun for families playing cards together. Colorful decks made specially for the game are popular, but regardless of the playing cards used, the rules are the same.

Suggested Ages. 4 to 10.

Skills Developed. Matching, pairing, and recognizing numbers.

The Pack. The standard 52-card pack is used, however, one of the four queens is removed, leaving a total of 51 cards.

The Deal. Any player shuffles the pack and deals them around, one at a time to each player, as far as they will go. The cards need not come out even.

Object of the Game. The goal is to form and discard pairs of cards, and not to be left with the odd card (a queen) at the end.

OLD MAID

One of the remaining Queens is the Old Maid

Remove one queen from the deck

The Play. Each player removes all pairs from his hand face down. If a player has three of a kind, he removes only two of those three cards. The dealer then offers his hand, spread out face down, to the player on his left, who draws one card from it. This player discards any pair that may have been formed by the drawn card. He then offers his own hand to the player on his left. Play proceeds in this way until all cards have been paired except one – the odd queen, which cannot be paired – and the player who has that card is the Old Maid!

Irregularities. If any player is found to have discarded two cards that are not a pair, (thus causing three unpaired cards instead of one to remain at the end), the player who made the mistake loses and becomes the Old Maid.

CONCENTRATION
(Memory)

NUMBER OF PLAYERS	NUMBER OF CARDS	GAME PLAY	SKILL LEVEL
2-12	51	♦ ◇ ◇ ◇ ◇ EASY → COMPLEX	◇ ◇ ◇ ♦ ◇ LUCK → SKILL

This is an excellent game for virtually any number of players, and can be played competitively or just for fun.

Suggested Ages. 7 and up.

Skills Developed. Matching, pairing, and memorizing.

The Pack. The standard 52-card pack is used.

The Deal. Any player shuffles the pack and spreads all the cards out, face down all over the table, one at a time, so that no two cards touch or overlap at the corners. The entire surface of the table is usually needed to make room for all the cards.

Object of the Game. The goal is to collect pairs of cards of the same rank, such as two sixes or two queens.

The Play. The first player may be decided in any way. He turns up any two cards on the table, leaving the first card face up until he has turned the second. If the two cards form a pair, the player takes them and puts them them face down in front of him in a pile, and then he turns up t wo more cards. Whenever the two cards turned up do not form a pair, the player, after a pause of at least five seconds, turns both cards face down again, leaving them in exactly the same position on the table. It is then the next player's turn (the player to the left). Play proceeds in the same manner. The player who takes in the greatest number of pairs is the winner.

Go Boom

This game is of the same family as Crazy Eights (see p. 281). Both games are favorites for children as well as grownups.

Suggested Ages. 8 and up.

Skills Developed. Matching, how to follow suit, and counting the values of cards.

Number of Players. Virtually any number of people can play, from two up.

The Pack. The standard 52-card pack is used. Up to six players use the 52-card pack. Seven or eight players may opt to use a double pack (two 52-card packs shuffled together). More than eight players should use a double pack.

Rank of Cards. A (high) K, Q, J, 10, 9, 8, 7, 6, 5, 4, 3, 2.

The Draw, Shuffle and Cut. From a shuffled pack spread out face down, each player draws a card. Lowest card deals. The dealer shuffles, and the player on his right cuts.

The Deal. The dealer completes the cut and then gives seven cards to each player, clockwise one at a time, starting with the player to the left. The remainder of the pack is placed face down in the center of the table to form the stock.

Object of the Game. The goal is to be the first player to get rid of all the cards in his hand.

The Play. The player to the left of the dealer leads and may play any card. Each player in turn must either follow suit or play a card of the same rank as the card led. Thus, if the jack of diamonds is led, each player must play a diamond or any jack. If a player cannot follow suit or play a card of the same rank, he must draw from the stock until he can. When the stock is exhausted and the player cannot play, he simply does not play to the trick. The highest card of the suit led wins each trick. If, in the two-deck game, cards of identical rank are played, the one played first outranks the other. The winner of each trick leads next.

Scoring. The first player to get rid of all his cards wins the game. The winner collects from each other player the pip value of the cards remaining in that player's hand. Aces count 1 point each, face cards 10 points each, and other cards their pip value.

Game. Each deal may constitute a game, or play may continue until one player has scored 200 points.

Snap

This is an amusing, and often very noisy game!

Suggested Ages. 8 and up.

Skills Developed. Matching, improving alertness, attention span, and speed of visual and verbal responses.

Number of Players. Two or more people can play.

The Pack. The standard 52-card pack is used.

Rank of Cards. Because this is a matching type of card game, the rank of cards is not important.

The Deal. Any player can deal the cards. All of the cards are dealt clockwise, face down and one at a time, beginning with the player on the dealer's left. It does not matter if some players have more cards than others. Each player puts his cards in a pile, face down in front of him.

Object of the Game. The goal is to win all of the cards.

The Play. The player on the dealer's left turns over the top card of his pile and puts it face up and starts another face up pile of cards next to his face down cards. The next player to the left does the same and so on around the table.

Snap. When someone turns up a card that matches a card already face up on another player's pile, the first person to notice the two matched cards (two kings, two 10s, two 3s, and so on) calls out "Snap!" and he wins both piles. This player adds the cards to the bottom of his face-down pile. When two players shout "Snap!" at the same time, the two piles are combined and placed in the center of the table face down. These cards form a "Snap Pot." Play continues where it left off with the player to the left of the last player who turned over a card. If a player spots a card that matches the card on top of the Snap Pot, he shouts "Snap Pot!" and wins all of those cards. During the game, if a player runs out of cards in his face-down pile, he turns his face up cards down and continues to play. Play continues until one player has won all of the cards. The game ends and that player is the winner.

Irregularities. A player who calls out "Snap!" at the wrong time, must give up his top card to the player who just played.

ROLLING STONE

NUMBER OF PLAYERS	NUMBER OF CARDS	GAME PLAY	SKILL LEVEL
4-6	**32** (40, 48)	◇ ♦ ◇ ◇ ◇ EASY ➔ COMPLEX	◇ ♦ ◇ ◇ ◇ LUCK ➔ SKILL

T his exciting game is similar to Crazy Eights and Go Boom.

Suggested Ages. 8 and up.

Skills Developed. Learning card values and how to follow suit.

Number of Players. Four, five or six people can play.

The Pack. The standard 52-card pack is used as follows: for four players, the sixes down through twos are removed, leaving a 32-card pack. For five players, the fours, threes, and twos are removed, leaving 40 cards. For six players, only the twos are removed.

Rank of Cards. A (high) K, Q, J, 10, 9, 8, 7, 6, 5, 4, 3.

(Rank of cards in a six-player game)

The Draw, Shuffle and Cut. From a pack that is shuffled and spread out face down, each player draws a card. Lowest card deals. The dealer shuffles and the player on his right cuts.

The Deal. The dealer completes the cut and gives eight cards to each player, dealt one at a time clockwise, starting with the player to the left. Thus, regardless of whether there are four, five, or six players, all of the cards are dealt out.

Object of the Game. The goal is to be the first player to get rid of all his cards.

The Play, The player to the dealer's left leads first and may play any card. The next player must follow suit if possible. A player who cannot follow suit must pick up all the cards played so far and add them to his hand. That player then leads any card to start a new round.

If everyone follows suit, the player who played the highest card collects the trick, but places it in a waste pile. These cards do not count as part of the cards in his hand, so, the only advantage in winning a trick is that the player may lead the suit of his choice next. The player who succeeds in getting rid of all his cards first, wins the game.

SPIT

NUMBER OF PLAYERS	NUMBER OF CARDS	GAME PLAY	SKILL LEVEL
2	**52** (x2)	♦ ◇ ◇ ◇ ◇ EASY ➔ COMPLEX	◇ ♦ ◇ ◇ ◇ LUCK ➔ SKILL

This wild and crazy game is all about speed and quickness!

Suggested Ages. 8 and up.

Skills Developed. Counting, sequencing and manual dexterity.

Number of Players. Any number can play. The more players there are, the wilder the game gets.

The Pack. One standard 52-card pack for each player. Each pack should have a different color cardback.

Rank of Cards. A (high) K, Q, J, 10, 9, 8, 7, 6, 5, 4, 3, 2.

The Shuffle. Each player shuffles his own deck thoroughly.

Layout. Each player has his own deck and begins by placing the top four cards from his deck face up in front of him in a row. There should be lots of empty space in the middle of the table between the two players. (In fact it is best to play on the floor, since cards often go flying once play starts.) Players hold the remainder of their deck in one of their hands during play.

Object of the Game. The winner is the first player to get rid of all his cards.

The Play. There are no turns taken in this game, everyone plays at the same time. When both players are ready, one of them says "spit" and immediately each player takes the top card from his deck and plays it to the center of the table. These first cards should be far away from each other, forming two play piles between the players *(see diagram)*. Then, the players immediately begin playing their cards, as fast as they can, from their layout onto one of the piles in the center. A card can be played only if it is one higher or one lower than the card on the top of the pile. The card's suit does not matter, and an ace can be played high or low (so that the sequence can "wrap around" between kings, aces and deuces).

Example:

1) In the illustration below, one could play the ♦9 (from layout) on the ♣10 (pile) since it is one lower in sequence.

2) Then one could play the ♦10 (layout) on the ♦9 (pile) just played, and so on.

A player may only use one hand to move a card and may only play one card at a time. Many times both players can play a card on the same pile. In that case the player who gets there first gets the play and the other player must take back his card. This race to play out the cards can get very exciting!

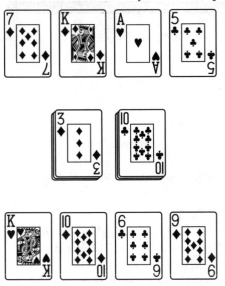

Spit Layout

Cards played from the layout row may immediately be replaced by a new card from the top of the deck.

Players cannot exceed four cards in their layout rows.

The players continue to rapidly play cards to the center and replace cards in their rows until all players get "stuck" and cannot make a play. Often several dozen cards can be played before all players get stuck. When all players are stuck, they say "Ready, Spit," and again deal new starter cards to the top of each pile in the center. Play then continues as before.

Going Out. When a player has played all the cards in his deck, he must continue play using only the cards left in his layout (even though he will not have a card to "Spit" with if all players get stuck). When that player "goes out" by playing the last card from his layout row, he wins. If both players have run out their decks and get stuck before going out, the player with the fewest cards left wins.

Scoring. One can play a series of rounds, scoring 1 point for each card each player has remaining at the end of each round. When one player reaches 100 points, the game is over and the player who then has the smallest score is the overall winner.

TOSSING CARDS IN A HAT

NUMBER OF PLAYERS	NUMBER OF CARDS	GAME PLAY		SKILL LEVEL	
1-13	52	◆ ◇ ◇ ◇ ◇ EASY → COMPLEX		◇ ◇ ◇ ◇ ◆ LUCK → SKILL	

This is a simple but popular pastime, and it is one of the few card games that requires physical skill! In addition to one or two packs of cards, a hat with a brim is required. If no hat is available, a bowl, or wastebasket can be substituted.

Suggested Ages. 4 and up.

Skills Developed: How to judge distances, and improve accuracy in tossing.

Number of Players. Virtually any number of people can play.

The Pack. The standard 52-card pack is used.

The Deal. Anyone can deal and the cards are distributed evenly among the players, either face up or face down – it does not matter. If there are any cards left over, they are set aside.

Object of the Game. The goal is to land the most cards inside the hat.

The Play. The hat should be placed with brim up so it can receive the tossed cards. It is placed at the far end of the room, either on the floor or on a low table. Players sit or stand at the other end of the room, away from the hat. If very young children are playing, they are allowed to position themselves closer. In the game, each player in turn flips one card toward the hat, and tries to land the card inside it.

Each player keeps track of the number of cards that land inside, with one point being scored for each, and half a point if a card lands on the brim. However, if another player succeeds in knocking in a card resting on the brim, it counts as a full point for that player.

Solitaire Play. If only one person plays, he keeps score by keeping track of how many cards out of 52 he tossed in the hat. Victory is awarded if the player scores 20 or more points in a round. Thirty points or more scores a double-victory, and 40 or more points scores a triple-victory.

Chapter X

Solitaire
Games

Solitaire is one of the most pleasurable pastimes for one person. Often called, "Patience," more than 150 Solitaire games have been devised. A few of the most popular are presented here, as well as some new ones.

Many Solitaire games can be played on areas smaller than a card table. Others require a larger playing area, and these games are often played on the floor or on a bedspread. Alternatively, in order to play with large layouts on a card table, miniature playing cards are available. These are usually half the size of standard playing cards.

General Guidelines

Virtually all Solitaire games are played with one or more standard 52-card packs. Most of the games proceed in the following way:

Some or all of the cards are distributed face up in some distinctive array, forming the "tableau." The tableau, together with any other cards dealt at the outset are often called the "layout."

The initial array may be changed by "building" – transferring cards among the face–up cards in the tableau. Certain cards of the tableau can be played at once, while others may not be played until certain blocking cards are removed.

The first objective is to release and play into position certain cards called "foundations." In most Solitaire games, the four aces are the bottom card or base of the foundations, and the objective is usually to build up each foundation, in sequence and in suit, from the ace through the king. The ultimate objective is to build the whole pack onto the foundations, and if that can be done, the Solitaire game is "won."

If the entire pack is not laid out in a tableau at the beginning of a game, the remaining cards form the stock (or "hand") from which additional cards are brought into play according to the rules. Cards from the stock that have no place in the tableau or on foundations are laid face up in a separate pile called the "talon" or "waste pile."

In some games, the layout includes a special packet of cards called the "reserve," which the player attempts to use by turning up and playing one card at a time. In many games, a vacancy in the tableau created by the removal of cards elsewhere is called a "space," and it is of major importance in manipulating the tableau. In some games, a space can only be filled in with a king.

The rank of cards in Solitaire games is: K (high), Q, J, 10, 9, 8, 7, 6, 5, 4, 3, 2, A.

Klondike
(Solitaire)

The most popular version of Solitaire is also the best! The official name is Klondike, but most people know it as just plain Solitaire. Mistakenly called Canfield by many (which is another popular Solitaire game), Klondike is fast, has plenty of card play, and features a classic, elegant layout. While it is one of the most difficult Solitaire games to win, it is likely that Klondike will remain one of the most frequently played versions of the game for generations to come.

The Pack. The standard 52-card pack is used.

Tableau. The tableau is created by dealing out 28 cards in seven piles as follows: The first pile is one card; the second pile has two cards, and so on up to seven in the last pile. The top card of each pile is face up; all others are face down.

To set the tableau, the player deals seven cards cross-wise from left to right. In the first deal, one card is placed face up and six are placed face down. In the second deal, one card is placed face up on the second pile, and one face down on each other pile; and so on (see diagram next page).

Foundations. The four aces form the foundations. As it becomes available, each ace must be played to a row above the tableau. Cards in the appropriate suit are then played on the aces in sequence – the two, then the three, and so on – as they become available.

Object of the Game. The goal is to get the four suits built onto the foundations from aces up through kings.

Building. Any movable card (from tableau, stock or talon) may be placed on a card next-higher in rank if it is of opposite color. *Example:* A black five may be played on a red six. If more than one card is face up on a tableau pile, all such cards must be moved as a unit. *Example:* the ♦3, ♣4, ♥5 may be moved as a unit onto ♠6 or ♣6. When there is no face-up card left on a pile, the top face-down card is turned up and becomes available.

Spaces. Only a king may fill an open space in the layout.

Stock. After the tableau is dealt, the rest of the pack forms the stock. The player turns up cards from the top of the stock in groups of three, and the top card of the three may be used for building on the tableau or, if possible, played on a foundation. If a card is used in this manner, the card below it becomes available for play. If the upcard cannot be used, the one, two, or three cards of the group are placed face up on the talon (waste pile), and the next group of three cards is turned up. When the stock is exhausted, the talon is turned upside down (without shuffling) to form a stock, and groups of three cards are again turned up. This process is repeated until no further plays are possible. The top card of the talon is always available for play, provided that the next three cards of the stock have not been turned.

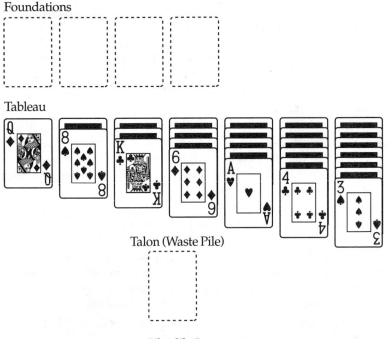

Klondike Layout

Las Vegas Solitaire

The play is the same as in Klondike, but with the following rule change: Instead of turning up cards from the stock three at a time indefinitely, the player turns the cards one at a time, but goes through the stock only once.

Settlement. In some casinos, Las Vegas Solitaire is a gambling game. A player pays to play, and once the game ends, the house pays the player for each card on the foundations. *For example:* A player pays $50 to play and the house pay $5 for each card on the foundation. Thus 10 cards "upstairs" (on the foundations) would break even; 11 or more would win. Getting all 52 cards onto the foundations pays a jackpot that varies from casino to casino.

Joker Solitaire

This game was created by *Joli Quentin Kansil* and is played in the same way as Klondike, but with a wild twist: Two jokers are added to the pack, and they serve as limited wild cards. Of all Klondike variations, this game probably requires the most skill because it demands that the player make many calculated decisions. Joker Solitaire is played Las Vegas-style: The cards of the stock are turned up one card at a time, rather than three at a time, and the player goes through the stock only once.

Jokers. The two jokers must be different from each other as one represents any black card, and the other is any red card. If the two jokers in the pack are different, the more ornate one can serve as the black joker, and the other one can be the red joker. (In packs of cards where the jokers are identical, use the extra advertising card that often comes with the pack as the red joker, or mark the face of one of the two jokers with a felt pen.)

How the Jokers Function. When the black joker appears in the tableau, it may be designated as any black card, such as a black queen or a black three. The player does not have to specify the particular suit. When the black joker is designated as a black king, it may be placed on an open space. When it is selected to be an ace, it is placed above to form one of the four foundations, though the player does not have to designate whether the joker is the club ace or spade ace. This joker will become either of these aces once the club deuce or spade deuce is played on it.

When a black joker is turned up from the stock, or when it appears as the top card of the talon (waste pile), it may be played as any needed black card on to the tableau as long as both such black cards are not in the tableau or foundations already. *Example:* A player would not be permitted to use a black joker as a black six, if both the spade six and club six were already in the tableau or foundations. When a black joker is the top card of the talon and cannot be played on to the tableau because only black cards are the top cards of the piles, it is not played, and the next card of the stock is turned up. All of these same rules apply in the same way for red jokers and red cards.

Tableau Rule. One important regulation is that when a joker is turned up from the stock, or when it is the top card of the talon, it may not be played directly to the foundations – it must first be played to the tableau before being placed in the foundations. *Example:* If the red joker is the top card of the talon and the player wishes to use it as a red ace, it must be placed on a black deuce in the tableau before then being played to the foundations as a red ace. Thus, the player should take care not to automatically play a black deuce onto a matching black ace in the foundations, as he may wish to keep open the option of using the black deuce in the tableau for the possible play of a red joker as a red ace.

Exchanging. When a joker is used for a specific card, and that card is later turned up in the stock or tableau, the player must use that card to exchange it with the matching joker. The card is placed where the joker was, either in the talon, tableau, or foundations. After the exchange, the player is permitted to use the joker for another card, and this process can later be repeated so that during the game, a joker may be used for several different cards. *To illustrate:* The red joker is a red seven in the tableau and is on top of a black eight, with a black six on top of the red joker. If the diamond seven is turned up from the stock, it is exchanged with the red joker, which is placed as the top card of the talon. This red joker can now be used as another playable red card. *Another example:* The black joker is the club three in the foundations, and the club three is turned face up from one of the face-down piles in the tableau. The club three is exchanged with the black joker in the club foundation pile, and the joker is put on top of the pile in the tableau where the club three used to be. The joker can now be used as another black card, or the player can just leave the joker in the tableau and declare what card it will be at a later time.

Once a joker is declared, the player cannot change the decision and select a different card unless the joker is exchanged, as already described.

If a player cannot play a joker when it becomes available, he continues play by turning up cards from the stock. A player always has the option of removing the joker from the game by placing it out of play. Once a player does so, the joker cannot be used again.

Winning. If the player succeeds in playing 15 or more cards to the foundations, it is a win; 25 or more cards "up top" is a double victory, and all cards up top is a triple victory.

Double Solitaire

In this variation, two people can participate. The players sit across from each other, and each has his own pack of cards. The two packs must be of different colors or designs. All foundations may be played on by both players, but players cannot play to each other's tableaus. The first player is determined by the low card on the one-card piles; if these cards are the same, the two-card piles decide, and so on. A player's turn ends when he puts a card face up on his talon and cannot play it; then, the opponent's turn begins. A player's turn also ends if he makes another play when able to start a foundation pile with an ace, provided the opponent notices the error and stops him. The winner is the player who has played the most cards to the foundations at the time the game becomes blocked. If one player gets all 52 cards upstairs, he "goes out," and immediately wins.

Canfield
(Fascination, Demon)

Closely related to Klondike, the game of Canfield is probably the second most popular Solitaire game.

The Pack. The standard 52-card pack is used.

The Layout. The player counts off 13 cards face down, squares them up, and places them face up horizontally to the left to form the reserve. He turns up the next (14th) card as the first foundation card and places it above the reserve, to the right. Beside the reserve, and directly below the first foundation card, the player deals a row of four cards face up to the right. This forms the tableau.

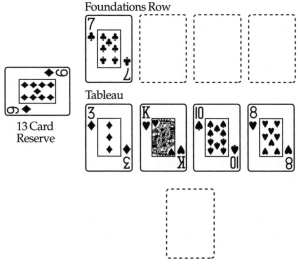

Canfield Layout

Foundations. As they become available, the other three cards of the same rank as the first foundation card are added in a row to the right of the first foundation. The player builds up on each foundation in suit and sequence, going "around the corner." *Example:* If a queen is the first foundation, each other queen, as it becomes available, forms a foundation and is built up as follows: ♦Q, ♦K, ♦A, ♦2, ♦3 and so on, up to ♦J.

Object of the Game. The goal is to build all four foundations up to the 13th card in each suit.

Stock. After the layout is dealt, the rest of the pack forms the stock (or "hand"). Cards are turned over three at a time, and the top card of each packet is available for building. The cards underneath are available once the top card is played.

Talon. The player places each packet of three cards, as they are turned up from the stock, on a talon (waste pile) below the layout. The top card of the talon is always available for building. When all of the stock is played onto the talon, the player turns it face down to make a new stock and goes through it again, three cards at a time. The stock may be run through any number of times until no more plays are possible, or until the game is won.

Building. Any movable card or cards (from tableau, reserve, or stock) may be placed only on a card next-higher in rank and of opposite color in the tableau. *Example:* The ♥8 may be placed on ♣9 or ♠9. An entire pile of the tableau must be moved as a unit.

Spaces. A space in the tableau must be filled by the top card of the reserve, which must always be kept squared up so that only the top card can be identified. After the reserve has been exhausted, spaces may be filled from the stock and talon.

Thirteen-Up
(Storehouse)

This game is the same as Canfield, but is easier to win because the four aces are removed from the pack prior to play. They are then placed above the reserve to start the four foundations. All the foundations are built up from the ace through the king, in sequence and in suit.

There are two other differences:

1) Cards from the stock are turned up one at a time, instead of three at a time.

2) The player may go through the stock three times only. That is, no more than two "redeals" are permitted.

Seahaven Towers

A relatively new version of Solitaire, Seahaven Towers was invented by *Art Cabral* in 1988. It may be one of the greatest solitaire card games ever devised because there is very little luck involved – the outcome depends almost entirely on the player's skill. With clever card manipulation, a player should be able to win the game more than three-quarters of the time. An average player, though, will win about once in three times.

The Pack. The standard 52-card pack is used.

Tableau. The cards are dealt face up into ten columns of five cards each, and all cards should overlap so that they remain visible. The remaining two cards are placed above the tableau to form two of the four "Towers." It is on these four towers where most essential card play takes place. Well to the left of the towers are two spaces for the ♠A and ♥A when they become available. Well to the right of the towers are two more spaces, where the ♦A and ♣A are placed when they become available. The four aces form the foundations.

Object of the Game. The goal is to build up each suit onto the foundations from ace through king.

The Play. With the cards overlapping, the lowest card in each column serves as the top (first) card and is the only one in each column that is available for play. Any top card can be moved to an empty tower space; but the player should be careful, because Tower spaces are needed as places to put cards which block vitally needed cards.

The player can play a card onto a top card in the tableau only if the top card is the next-higher card of the same suit. Thus, the ♣3 can be placed on the ♣4. When cards are moved in this manner, a column can grow much longer than the original five cards.

Spaces. When all of the cards of a column have been placed elsewhere in the tableau, onto a tower space, or onto the foundations, the empty space can be filled in only with a king.

Foundations. In the foundations, a higher card is placed on a lower card of the same suit, as in many Solitaire games. *For example:* The ♦2 may be placed on the ♦A or the ♥10 may be placed on the ♥9 if the ♥9 is the top card in the hearts foundation pile at the time.

Accordion

Players should not doubt their card-playing skills if they do not succeed in playing all the cards in this Solitaire game. It has been estimated that the chances of winning in Accordion are about one in a hundred!

The Pack. The standard 52-card pack is used.

Tableau. The player deals out the cards one by one face up, in a row from left to right, as many at a time as space allows. (Dealing may be interrupted at any time if the player wishes to make a move. After making a move, the deal is then resumed).

Object of the Game. The goal is to get all the cards in one pile, by building.

Building. Any card may be placed on top of the next card at its left, or the third card at its left, if the cards are of the same suit or of the same rank. *Example:* Four cards, from left to right, are: ♥6, ♥J, ♣9. ♥9. The ♥9 may be placed either on the ♣9 or on the ♥6. It may not be played on the jack of the same suit because the jack is not to the immediate left, or third from the left. (see diagram below)

When the movement of one or more cards has formed a pile, the entire pile is moved with the top card. In the example above, when the ♥9 is put on the ♣9, the two may be put on the ♥J and then all of these cards on the ♥6. However, it is not obligatory to make a particular move if the player prefers not to do so.

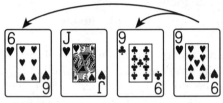

Accordion

Napoleon at St. Helena
(Forty Thieves)

After his final exile to the island of St. Helena, Napoleon often played Solitaire. This is probably the version he played. Also known as Forty Thieves, it was once one of the most popular two-deck Solitaire games. It is still frequently played.

The Pack. Two standard 52-card packs are used and they are shuffled together.

Tableau. Ten piles of four cards each, dealt by rows, all face up. The cards should overlap so that the player can see them all.

Foundations. All aces are placed above the tableau as soon as the player can release them from the tableau. (See diagram next page)

Building. Only the top card of a pile may be moved. The removal of a card releases the one below it. A card may be placed only on another of the same suit and next-higher in rank. *Example:* A ♠7 may be placed only on ♠8. A king may not be built on an ace, and aces must be placed as foundations as soon as possible. Foundations are built up in suit and sequence from ace through king.

Object of the Game. The goal is to get all eight foundations built up from ace through king.

Spaces. When any of the ten tableau piles is entirely cleared away, any movable card may be placed in the space.

Stock. Cards are turned up one at a time from the top of the stock and may be placed on the tableau or foundations.

Foundations Row

Tableau

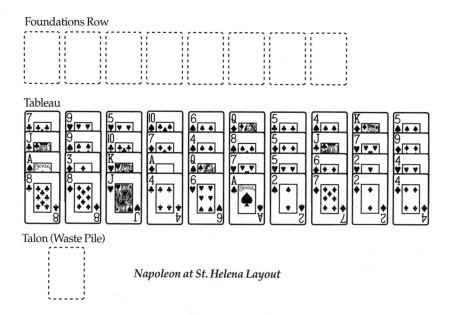

Talon (Waste Pile)

Napoleon at St. Helena Layout

Talon. Cards from the stock that cannot be used are placed face up in a pile below the tableau to form the talon (waste pile). The top card of the talon is always available for building onto the tableau or foundations. The player may overlap the talon cards so that all of them can be seen.

Emperor

The rules are the same as for Napoleon at St. Helena, with the following exceptions (which make the game easier to win): For the layout, the player deals the first three rows face down, and the last row face up. On the tableau piles, he builds down using alternate colors. Also, face-up cards on a pile may be moved as a unit, and cards on foundation piles may be removed and built on the tableau.

Spider

The Pack. Two standard 52-card packs are used, and they are shuffled together.

Tableau. Ten piles of five cards each are dealt by rows. The first four cards of each pile are dealt face down, the top cards face up. All play is made on the tableau. There are no foundations and no talon.

Building. The top card of a pile may be moved, together with all face-up cards below it that follow in ascending suit and sequence. A sequence of available cards may be broken at any point by leaving some cards behind. *Example:* If a pile from top down shows ♥4, ♥5, ♥6, ♣7, either the first one, two, or three cards may be moved as a unit, but the ♣7 may not be moved until the covering three cards are removed.

When all face-up cards on a pile are removed, the next card below is turned face up and becomes available.

A movable unit of cards may be placed either in a space or on a card of the next-higher rank to the bottom card of the unit, regardless of color or suit. *Example:* If the bottom card of a unit is the ♦J, it may be moved onto any one of the four queens.

A king can be moved only onto a space. Alternatively, the spaces may be filled with any movable unit.

Object of the Game. The goal is to assemble 13 cards of a suit, in ascending sequence from ace through king, on top of a pile. Whenever a full suit of 13 cards is so assembled, it is lifted off and discarded from the game. The game is won if all eight suits are played out.

Stock. When all possible or desired moves on the tableau come to a standstill, the player deals another row of ten cards face up on the tableau piles. However, before such a deal may be made, all spaces in the tableau must be filled. The final deal consists of only four cards, which are placed on the first four tableau piles.

Streets and Alleys

The Pack. The standard 52-card pack is used.

The Layout. A column of four cards is dealt to the center of the table, slightly to the left. A column of four cards is then dealt to the right of center, leaving room between these two columns for another column. All cards are dealt face up. The player continues dealing the cards in columns of four alternately to the left and right, overlapping outward from the center with the cards already dealt. The entire pack is dealt out, so that each row on the left will contain seven cards and each row on the right, six cards. These rows form the "wings" of the tableau.(See diagram next page)

Foundations. The four aces form the foundations. As each ace is released, it is moved into the center between the left and right wings of the tableau. The foundations are built up in suit and sequence.

Building. Only the outermost card of each row is available for transfer. A card may be moved onto the outer end of a row, provided that it is in descending sequence with the card there, regardless of suit. *Example:* The ♦5 may be placed on ♦6, ♥6, ♣6, or ♠6. Any available card may be placed on a space.

Object of the Game. The goal is to get all cards built onto the foundations.

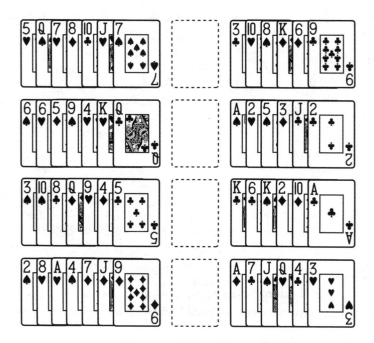

Streets and Alleys Layout

Beleaguered Castle

This game is the same as Streets and Alleys except that the four aces are removed from the pack prior to play and are placed in the center column. Each row of the tableau, left and right, will then contain six cards.

Poker Solitaire

The Pack. The standard 52-card pack is used.

Tableau. From the shuffled pack, the player turns up the first 25 cards one by one, placing them in a square (grid) that is five cards wide and five cards deep. Each card, as it is turned up, may be placed anywhere with reference to those previously placed, so long as all remain within the five-by-five limits. Once placed, a card may not be moved.

Object of the Game. The goal is to score as high a count as possible in the ten Poker hands formed by the five rows and five columns of the tableau.

Scoring. There are several systems of scoring; the two shown below are the most popular. The American system follows the ranking of hands in standard Poker, while the English system is based on the actual difficulty of forming the hands in Poker Solitaire.

Hand	American Score	English Score
Royal Flush	100	30
Straight Flush	75	30
Four of a Kind	50	16
Full House	25	10
Flush	20	5
Straight	15	12
Three of a Kind	10	6
Two Pair	5	3
One Pair	2	1

One common variation is to deal all 25 cards face up quickly in the five-by-five grid and then the cards are moved by the player to come up with the 10 highest-scoring poker hands within the grid.

Calculation

The Pack. The standard 52-card pack is used.

Foundations. Remove from the pack and lay in a row any ace, any two, any three, and any four.

Object of the Game. The goal is to build 12 cards on each foundation in arithmetical sequence (regardless of suit). The sequences on the four piles must be:

A, 2, 3, 4, 5, 6, 7, 8, 9, 10, J, Q, K.

2, 4, 6, 8, 10, Q, A, 3, 5, 7, 9, J, K.

3, 6, 9, Q, 2, 5, 8, J, A, 4, 7, 10, K.

4, 8, Q, 3, 7, J, 2, 6, 10, A, 5, 9, K.

Stock. The 48 remaining cards of the pack are the stock. Cards are turned up one by one from the stock and played either on a foundation or a talon (waste pile).

Talon. Cards from the stock may be placed on any of four talons below the foundations. The top card of a talon is always available for play on a foundation, but may not otherwise be moved once it is placed.

Devil's Grip

Devil's Grip has a touch of Calculation in it, and the deck for the game is rather unusual.

The Pack. Two standard 52-card packs are stripped of all the aces, leaving a deck of 96 cards.

Tableau. After the pack is shuffled, 24 cards are dealt face up in three rows of eight columns. At any time, cards may be moved within this three-by-eight grid by changing places with one another. The remainder of the pack is placed face down to form the stock.

The Play. Cards may be placed on top of one another if they are of the same suit and adhere to one of the following bottom-to-top orders:

2, 5, 8, J

3, 6, 9, Q

4, 7, 10, K

The order may seem random, but it makes sense visually on the grid: deuces in the top row, threes in the middle, fours on the bottom row, then in the top row, fives, middle row sixes, and so on.

Object of the Game. The goal is to place the entire deck into the piles on the grid, winding up with jacks on top in the top row, queens on top in the middle row, and kings on top in the bottom row.

Spaces. When an empty space appears as a result of moving one card on top of another, the top card of the stock is drawn to replace it. This is the only way that the base cards (deuces, threes and fours) can make it onto the grid. If there are no empty spaces, cards are turned up in the traditional Solitaire manner – groups of three – and these cards are left face up in a pile to form the talon. Cards of the correct suit may be taken and placed on top of appropriate cards already on the grid. Thus, the ♠8 may be placed on the ♠5. It is not necessary for the five to already be on top of a ♠2.

Ending the Game. Play continues until no more cards can enter the grid. Usually, every pile will have a picture card on top. The cards left in the talon are counted to become the player's score – the lower the better. It is rare to play out the entire deck. A score of 10 or fewer cards left in the talon is "good"; a score of five cards or under is "excellent"; and 2 or fewer cards is "brilliant."

BICYCLE®

Glossary

Card Game Terms

Above the Line. *Bridge.* The place on the score sheet where premium points are scored.

Adversary. Any opponent; someone playing against the highest bidder.

Advertise. *Poker.* Make a bluff with the intention of being caught, so that future bets or raises will more likely be called.

Against. *Skat.* See Without.

Age. 1) See First Hand. 2) *Poker.* The right to bet last after the draw

Alone. *Euchre family.* A bid to play without the help of a partner.

Alternate Straight. See Skip Straight.

Anchor. *Duplicate Bridge.* In pivot or Progressive play, the player who retains his seat throughout the contest.

Announce. 1) Name a trump suit. 2) Show melds. 3) Predict a Schneider or Schwarz. (See also, Schneider or Schwarz.)

Ante. 1) A bet made before the deal or before drawing cards. 2) Contribution, usually cash or chips, to a pot which, at the start, belongs equally to all players.

Ask. 1) *Whist.* Signal one's partner to lead trumps. 2) *Skat family.* Inquiry by the "First hand" whether the next hand wishes to compete in the bidding.

Assist. *Euchre.* Order one's partner to take up trump.

Auction. An initial period of bidding before cards are played.

Authorized Opponent. *Bridge.* One solely entitled to assess a penalty.

Available Card. *Solitaire.* A card that is not blocked and may be transferred elsewhere in the layout.

Avondale Schedule. The recommended table for scoring of the game Five Hundred.

Back Door. *Bezique.* A sequence in a plain suit.

Back Hand. The top-ranking 5-card hand in Pai-Gow or Pusoy.

Back In. *Poker.* Come into the betting after checking

Back to Back. *Poker.* The hole card and first upcard when they are a pair.

Bait. 1) *Rummy family.* A discard intended to influence an opponent's later discard. 2) See Bete.

Balanced Hand. A hand with no void, singleton, or very long suit. (See also Void; Singleton.)

Balking Cards. *Cribbage.* Cards unlikely to produce a score, which are given to the opponent's crib.

Banco. *Chemin-de-fer.* A bet equal to the entire bank

Bank. The Casino or house in a gambling game such as Black Jack or Chemin de Fer; the dealer in a gambling game.

Banker. 1) Dealer against whom all others bet. 2) *Poker.* The player who keeps the supply of chips.

Barred. Stopped from bidding by a legal penalty.

Base. *Canasta.* The number of natural cards required in a canasta.

Basto, or Basta. The queen of spades.

Bate. See Bete.

Beg. *All Fours.* A proposal by the player on the dealer's left to the dealer that three additional cards be dealt to each hand and that a new card be turned up for trump.

Bela, or Bella. *Klaberjass.* The king and queen of trumps.

Below the Line. *Bridge.* The place on the score sheet where the trick score is entered.

Best. Highest-ranking.

Best Bower. The joker, when it is the highest trump, as in Five Hundred.

Bet Blind. Bet without looking at the hand.

Bete (pronounced bate). 1) Beaten. 2) A forfeit paid by a loser or by a transgressor of a rule of correct procedure.

Bet the Pot. Bet as many chips as there are in the pot at the moment.

Betting Interval. *Poker.* Period in which each player may bet or drop out.

Bicycle. *Poker.* The lowest hand in Lowball.

Bid. An offer to contract to win a certain number of tricks or points in play; to make a bid.

Bidder. 1) Any player who makes a bid. 2) The player who makes the highest bid and assumes the contract.

Bid Over. Overcall; bid higher than the last previous bid.

Big Cassino. *Cassino.* The ten of diamonds.

Big Dog. *Poker.* A hand consisting of ace-high and nine-low but no pair.

Big Joker. The higher of the two jokers, which, in a game with trumps, ranks as the highest trump.

Big Tiger. *Poker.* A hand consisting of king-high and eight-low but no pair.

Blackjack. *Black Jack.* An ace and any ten-card.

Black Lady. The queen of spades, also called the Black Maria.

Blackwood Convention. *Contract Bridge.* A system of cue-bidding to reach slams, invented by Easley Blackwood.

Blank. 1) Holding no cards of (a suit); void. 2) To discard all cards of a suit or all low cards from a card.

Blaze. *Poker.* A hand composed entirely of face cards.

Blind. 1) A compulsory bet or ante made before the cards are dealt. 2) The widow, as in Skat. (See also Ante; Widow.)

Blind Lead. A card led made before certain cards are disclosed.

Blitz. See Shutout.

Block. A situation in which the player in turn is unable to play, or no player is able to play.

Blocking a Suit. Playing a card so that a partner with the longer of two partnership holdings in a suit cannot obtain the lead in that suit.

Blue Peter. *Whist.* The signal for a trump lead.

Bluff. *Poker.* A bet on a hand not believed to be the best.

Board. 1) *Stud Poker.* The exposed cards of all active players. 2) A deal in Duplicate Bridge.

Bobtail. *Poker*. A Four Flush or Double-Ended Straight, (Which see).

Bonus. A score given for holding certain cards or completing a high contract.

Booby Prize. A prize for the lowest score.

Booby Table. In progressive play, the table of highest number, to which losers move from table No. 1) (See also Progression.)

Boodle Card. *Stops family*. Extra cards placed in a layout on which bets are laid.

Book. *Whist family*. The number of tricks (usually six) that a side must win before it can score by winning subsequent tricks; usually, six tricks.

Bower. See Left Bower, Right Bower.

Box. 1) *Gin Rummy*. The score for winning a deal. 2) An apparatus from which cards are dealt, as in Faro. Also known as a shoe, which see.

Break. 1) To divide in a specified way, such as the cards or a particular suit held by one's opponents. 2) *Rummy*. The point at which the stock contains too few cards for everyone to have another draw. 3) *Rummy*. The act of making the first meld.

Break Contract. *Spades*. To take fewer than the number of tricks contracted for.

Breaks. Distribution of the adverse cards between the two hands.

Bridge. *Euchre*. A score of 4 when one's opponents have not more than 2 tricks.

Brisque. Bezique. Any ace or ten.

Buck. *Poker*. A token used as a reminder of the order of precedence in dealing, exercising any privilege or duty, etc.

Buck the Tiger. *Faro*. Play against the bank.

Bug. *Poker*. The joker, when it may be used only as an ace or as a wild card in filling a flush. a straight, or a low hand.

Build. 1) *Cassino*. Combine two or more cards to be taken in later. 2) *Solitaire*. Transfer cards among the tableau or layout.

Bull. Ace. Also called bullet.

Bunch. 1) Abandon the deal; gather cards preparatory to shuffling. 2) *Auction Pitch*. An offer to play a contract of 2 or to have a new deal, at the opponent's option.

Burn a Card. Expose and bury a card, or place it on the bottom of the pack.

Bury a Card. 1) Place a card in the middle of the pack or among the discards, so that it cannot be readily located. 2) *Pinochle*. Lay aside for future counting.

Business Double. *Bridge*. A double made for the purpose of exacting increased penalties.

Bust. 1) A hand devoid of trick-taking possibilities. 2) *Black Jack*. A hand totaling more than 21.

Buy. Draw from the widow or stock; cards so received.

Buy-in. See Stack (2).

By Me. A declaration meaning "Pass."

Call. 1) Declare, bid, or pass. 2) *Bridge*. Any pass, double, redouble or bid. 3) *Poker*. Make a bet exactly equal to the last previous bet.

Canasta. *Canasta*. A meld of seven or more of the same rank, with or without wild cards.

Cards. *Cassino*. The score of 3 for winning a majority of the cards.

Carte Blanche. A hand without a face card.

Case Card. The last card of a rank remaining in play.

Cash. Lead and win tricks with cards that are sure winners.

Cash Points. *Cassino.* The scores for Big and Little Cassino and aces.

Cat. See Big Tiger, Little Tiger.

Catch. Find valuable cards in the widow or in drawing from the stock.

Cat-hop. *Faro.* Two cards of the same rank among the last three.

Center. *Solitaire.* The foundation piles.

Check. 1) A counter or chip. 2) *Poker.* A nominal bet; usually one that does not require any chip to be put in the pot.

Chicane. Void of trumps.

Chip. 1) A token used in place of money, 2) Placing chips in the pot.

Chouette. A method by which three or more players can participate in a two-hand game.

Cinch Hand. *Cinch.* Play a trump higher than the five to prevent an opponent from winning with a Pedro. (See also Pedro.)

Cinch Hand. A hand that is sure to win.

Clear. 1) *Hearts.* Having taken in tricks with no counting cards. 2) To establish a suit; to draw trumps.

Close Cards. See Near Cards.

Coffee Housing. Attempting to mislead opponents as to one's cards by speech or manner.

Cold Hands. *Poker.* Hands dealt face up, as for determining the winner of extra chips in dividing the pot.

Colon. *Bridgette.* One of the three extra cards that separate the pack into groups and which, when discarded, force the opponent to lead a different suit.

Column. *Solitaire.* A line of cards extending toward the player; a part of the tableau used for building.

Come In. Enter the betting.

Come-on. *Bridge.* A signal to one's partner to continue leading a suit. (See Echo.)

Command. The best card of a suit; master card; control.

Commoquer. *Panguingue.* Any card but an ace or king.

Condition. A meld that has extra value, as in Panguingue.

Condone. Waive penalty for an irregularity.

Contract. The obligation to win a certain minimum number of tricks or points.

Contractor. The high bidder.

Conventions. Advance agreement between partners on how to exchange information by bids and plays.

Copper. *Faro.* A token placed on a bet, indicating that it is a bet on a card to lose.

Counter. 1) Chip, a token used in place of money. 2) A card that has scoring value when won in a trick.

Count Out. Go for game, especially by accumulation of points during the play of a hand.

Coup. 1) A brilliant play. 2) A winning play or bet.

Court Card. See Face Card.

Cover. Play a card higher than the highest previously played to the trick.

Crib. *Cribbage.* The extra hand formed by the players' discards, belonging to the dealer.

Cribbage Board. *Cribbage.* A device for scoring utilizing pegs.

Cross-ruff. *Whist family.* Alternate trumping of each other's plain-suit leads by the two hands of a partnership.

Cross the Suit. *Euchre.* Name as trump a suit of the opposite color from that of the rejected turn-up card.

Cue-bid. 1) *Contract Bridge.* One that systemically shows control of a suit, especially by possession of the ace or a void. 2) *Bridgette.* An artificial bid to ask one's opponent about short suits or high cards.

Curse of Scotland. The nine of diamonds.

Cut. 1) Divide the pack into two sections and reverse their order. (See Draw (1).)

Cutthroat. Three-Hand; applied also to any game in which each person plays for himself.

Cut the Pot. Take a percentage from the pot.

Dead Card. A card that cannot be used in play.

Dead Hand. A player or hand barred from further participation.

Dead Man's Hand. A poker hand, with two aces and two eights. (Said to have been held by Wild Bill Hickok when he was shot and killed.)

Deadwood. 1) *Poker.* The discard pile. 2) *Rummy.* Unmatched cards in a hand.

Deal. 1) Distribute cards to the players; the turn to deal. 2) The complete period from one hand to the next, including the scoring. 3) The cards dealt to the players respectively; a layout of the hands of all players.

Dealer. 1) The player who distributes the cards in preparation for play. 2) Banker.

Deal Off. Make the first deal in the last round after which the session ends.

Deal Out. Omit giving a card or cards to a hand in regular turn during the deal.

Deck. See Pack.

Declaration. Call; bid; naming of a trump suit or game. 2) The trump suit or game as named in a bid.

Declare. 1) Call; bid; name the trump. 2) Announce; meld.

Declare Out. See Count Out.

Declarer. 1) *Bridge.* The player who plays both his own hand and the dummy. 2) See Bidder (2).

Defender. *Contract Bridge.* An opponent of the declarer.

Defense. *Bridge.* 1) The opponents of the opening bidder during the auction or of the declarer. 2) During the play, their acts and tactics.

Demand Bid. *Bridge.* A strong bid that the partner must respond to by bidding himself.

Denial Bid. *Bridge.* A bid showing lack of support for a partner's declaration.

Denomination. 1) Rank. 2) *Contract Bridge.* The suit or notrump as named in a bid.

Deuce. A card with two pips.

Dis. See Dix.

Discard. 1) Lay aside excess cards in exchange for others from the stock or the widow; a discarded card or cards. 2) Play a plain-suit card not of the same suit as the lead.

Discard Pile. 1) *Rummy.* Cards previously discarded. 2) *Solitaire.* (See Talon.)

Distribution. Division of cards among the hands, especially as to the number of each suit held by each hand.

Dix. *Pinochle.* The lowest trump. Also, called "dis."

Dog. See Big Dog, Little Dog.

Double. *Bridge.* A call that has the effect of increasing the trick values and penalties if the last preceding bid becomes the contract.

Double Bete. *Pinochle.* The penalty suffered by a bidder who has elected to play the hand and has lost.

Double Dummy. *Whist family.* A game or situation in which a player knows the location of all cards.

Double-Ended Straight. *Poker.* Four cards in sequence that can be filled to a straight by the draw of a card of next-higher or next-lower rank.

Double Pair Royal. Four of a kind.

Double Run. *Cribbage.* A hand comprising a run of three cards with one rank duplicated, such as 4, 5, 5, 6.

Double Skunk. *Cribbage.* An award of a quadruple victory for holding the opponent to 60 or fewer points in a 121-point game.

Doubleton. *Whist family.* A holding of two cards in a suit.

Down. Defeated; having failed to make a contract; set back.

Downtown. *Bid Whist.* The Format of having the cards rank in reverse, A, 2, 3, 4, 5, 6, 7, 8, 9, 10, J, Q, K(low). (See also Format.)

Draw. 1) Pull cards from a pack spread face down to determine seats, first deal, and the like. 2) Receive cards from the stock to replace discards.

Drop. Withdraw from a current deal or pot.

Duck. *Bridge.* Fail to Cover when able. (See also Cover.)

Dummy. *Bridge.* Declarer's partner; the hand laid down by that player and played by declarer.

Duplicate. A form of Bridge or Whist in tournament play in which all contestants play the same series of deals, which are kept in their original form by the use of duplicate boards.

Dutch Straight. See Skip Straight.

Eagles. A fifth suit, green in color, at one time added to the standard deck.

Easy Aces. *Auction Bridge.* A round of play during which each side holds two aces.

Echo. *Whist family.* The play, for signaling purposes, of a higher card before a lower card of the same suit.

Endhand. *Skat family.* The active player who is third in order of bidding.

End Play. Any of several stratagems (especially a throw-in) that can usually be executed only in the last few tricks of the play. (See also Throw-in.)

Entry. A card with which a hand can eventually win a trick and so gain the lead.

Escalera. *Bolivia.* A canasta of cards in sequence rather than of the same denomination.

Establish. See Clear (2).

Euchre. *Euchre.* Failure of the maker to win the number of tricks he contracted for.

Exacto. *Bridgette.* In the six-deal version, the bonus scored for fulfilling the contract exactly, with no overtricks.

Exchange. *Bridgette.* The period prior to the bidding during which cards are drawn and switched so as to improve one's original hand.

Exit. Get out of the lead; compel another hand to win a trick.

Exposed Card. A card played in error, inadvertently dropped, or otherwise shown in an illegitimate manner and therefore (in most games) subject to penalty.

Face Card. Any king, queen, or jack. Also called "picture card."

Faced. A card lying with its face exposed.

False Card. A card selected for play, when there is a choice, to mislead opponents as to the contents of the hand.

Fatten. 1) *Poker.* See Sweeten. 2) *Pinochle.* See Smear.

Fifteen. *Cribbage.* A combination of cards totaling 15 in pip values; the score of 2 for such a combination.

Fill. *Poker.* Draw cards that improve one's original hand.

Finesse. *Whist family.* An attempt to make a card serve as an equal to a higher-ranking card held by an opponent.

First Hand. 1) The leader to a trick. 2) The first player in turn to call. 3) The player to the left of the dealer.

Fish. *Go Fish.* Draw cards from the stock.

Five-Card Charlie. *Black Jack.* In the changing bank version, a hand of five cards that total 21 or less and entitle the holder to a bonus payment.

Five Fingers. The five of trumps.

Flag Flying. *Bridge.* Assuming a losing contract to prevent the opponents from winning a game.

Flash. Expose a card, as in dealing.

Flush. 1) *Poker, Cribbage.* A hand with all cards in one suit. 2) *Pinochle.* A meld of the A, K, Q, J, 10 of trumps. 3) *Loo.* A three-card hand containing all trumps.

Fold. *Stud Poker.* Withdraw from the current deal, as signified by turning one's cards face down.

Follow Suit. Play a card of the same suit as the lead.

Forecaster. *Eleusis.* the term used for players who think they have discovered the secret rule.

Force. 1) Compel a player to trump if he wishes to win the trick. 2) *Contract Bridge.* By a conventional call, demand that one's partner bid. 3) *Rummy.* Discard a card that the next player is required to take.

Forehand. *Skat family.* The active player who is first in order of bidding. (See First Hand.)

Format. *Bid Whist.* The determination of whether the cards rank ace down to deuce, or, in reverse, ace down to king.

Foul Hand. *Poker.* One of more or less than the legal number of cards.

Foundation. *Solitaire.* A card on which a whole suit or sequence must be built up.

Four Flush. *Poker.* Four cards of the same suit.

Four of a Kind. Four cards of the same rank, such as four aces.

Fourth-best. *Whist family.* The fourth-highest card of a suit in one's hand.

Freak. 1) *Bridge.* A hand of extraordinary pattern. 2) *Poker.* A wild card.

Free Bid. *Bridge.* A bid made voluntarily, not compelled by a rule of the game.

Free Double. *Bridge.* The double of an adverse contract which is sufficient for game if made undoubled.

Free Ride. *Poker.* Playing in a pot without having to ante or bet.

Freeze. *Canasta.* Discard a wild card to make it more difficult for opponents to take the discard pile.

Freezeout. Any variation of a game in which a player must drop out when his original stake is exhausted.

Frog. *Skat family.* The bid of lowest value. Also called "frage."

Front Hand. 1) The 2-card hand in Pai-Gow. 2) The 3-card hand in Pusoy.

Full Hand. See Full House.

Full House. *Poker.* A hand comprising three of a kind and a pair.

Game. 1) A pastime, in the general sense, as Bridge, Poker. 2) The specific number of points that determines the winner of a contest, as 121 points in Cribbage. 3) The specific number of tricks or points that must be won in play to fulfill contract, as 61 or more in Skat. 4) A declaration, as in Skat. 5) A variation of the basic game named by the dealer to be played in that deal, as in Dealer's Choice Poker. 6) A certain card, as the ten of trumps in some versions of All Fours. 7) A system of play.

Gate. The pay-off card, as in Monte Bank.

Gift. *All Fours.* The point scored by the "First hand" when he begs and the dealer rejects.

Gin. *Gin Rummy.* A hand completely formed in sets, with no deadwood.

Go. *Cribbage.* A call signifying that the player cannot play another card without exceeding 31; the score of 1 point to an opponent when Go is called.

Go Down. *Rummy.* Meld, especially when the act terminates play.

Go Out. 1) Get rid of all cards in one's hand, as in Michigan Rummy. 2) Reach the cumulative total of points needed to win the game, as in All Fours. 3) Count out, as in Cribbage.

Go Over. Bid higher.

Goulash. *Bridge.* A deal of unshuffled cards, three or more at a time, to produce unusual hands.

Grand. *Skat family.* A declaration in which only the jacks are trumps. Also called "grando."

Grand Coup. *Bridge.* A stratagem of play; the trumping of partner's winning plain card in order to shorten a trump holding to advantage.

Grand Slam. *Whist family.* The winning of all 13 tricks by one side.

Group. 1) *Rummy.* A meld of cards of the same rank. 2) *Bridgette.* One of three categories: aces and the grand colon, picture cards and the royal colon, and spot cards and the little colon.

Guarded. *Bridge.* Accompanied by as many small cards of the same suit as there are higher cards outstanding.

Guckser. *Skat.* A declaration in which jacks are trumps and the bidder picks up the skat. Also called "gucki."

Guide Card. *Duplicate Bridge.* A large sheet that indicates to which table partnerships must move after each round of play.

Hand. l). The cards dealt to or held by any player; 2) Any player. 3) See Deal (2). 4) *Solitaire.* An undealt remainder of the pack after the tableau is laid out.

Handplay. Playing without use of the widow.

High. *All Fours family.* The ace of trumps, or the highest trump dealt; the score for holding such a card.

High Low. 1) *Bridge.* See Echo. 2) *Poker.* Designating a pot that the highest and lowest hands divide.

High Value. *Cribbitaire.* Combinations of cards that are too valuable to be discarded in the crib.

Hinterhand. See Endhand.

His Heels. *Cribbage.* 1) A jack turned as starter card; 2) the score of 2 to the dealer for turning up a jack.

His Nobs. *Cribbage.* 1) A jack of the same suit as the starter card, in one's hand or in the crib. 2) The score of 1 point for such a jack.

Hit Me. *Black Jack.* A player's request for an additional card

Hoc. *Faro.* The last card in a deal. Also called "hock", "hockelty."

Holding. The cards in a player's hand.

Hold Up. *Bridge.* Refuse to win a trick with a sure winning card, preferring to wait until a subsequent trick.

Hole Card. *Stud Poker.* The first card, dealt face down, received by a player.

Honors. 1) High cards, especially if they have scoring value. 2) *Bridge.* The five highest trumps, or, if there is no trump, the four aces.

Honor-tricks. *Bridge.* High cards, in the evaluation of a hand.

Immortal Hand. See Cinch Hand.

Improve. Draw cards that increase the value of a hand.

Index. The small number or letter and suit symbol printed near the corner of a card, used to read the card when it is held in a fan with others.

Informatory Double. *Bridge.* A double in some bidding systems made primarily to give information to a player's partner.

Initial Bid. See Opening Bid.

Inside Straight. *Poker.* Four cards needing a card of interior rank to make a straight, such as 9, 8, 6, 5.

Insufficient Bid. A call that is not legally high enough to overcall the preceding bid.

Intermediates. *Bridge.* Cards, such as nines and 10s, that are not high enough to be valued but affect the strength of a hand.

In the Hole. A minus score, named after the practice (as in Euchre) of marking a score as minus by drawing a ring around it.

Irregularity. Any departure from a rule of correct procedure.

Jack. 1) *All Fours family.* The score for winning the jack of trumps in play. 2) *Hearts.* A pool not won because no hand is clear, and therefore held intact for the next deal.

Jackpot. *Poker.* A deal in which everyone antes; usually, in such a deal a pair of jacks or better is required to open.

Jambone. *Railroad Euchre.* A bid to play alone and with the entire hand face up on the table.

Jamboree. *Railroad Euchre.* A hand holding the five highest trumps which, when shown and scored, cancels the necessity to play.

Jass, Jasz. *Klaberjass.* The jack of trumps.

Jink It. *Spoil Five.* Play for all five tricks.

Joker. An extra card furnished with the standard 52-card pack and used in some games as the highest trump or as a wild card. See also Bug.

Jump Bid. *Bridge.* A bid of more tricks than are legally needed to overcall the previous bid, such as Three Spades after a bid of Two Hearts.

Junior. See Younger.

Kibitzer. A spectator; one who watches a game but does not otherwise participate.

Kicker. *Draw Poker.* An extra card kept with a pair for a two-card draw, such as a single ace kept with a pair of sixes.

Kilter. *Poker.* A hand nine-high with no pair, straight, or flush.

Kitty. 1) A percentage taken out of the stakes to defray expenses or pay admission fees; a pool to which bets are paid and from which royalties are collected. 2) The Widow in Bid Whist and other card games. (See also Widow.)

Knave. The jack of a suit.

Knock. 1) *Rummy family.* Signify termination of play by laying down one's hand. 2) *Poker.* Showing one does not want to cut the pack, or to bet, by knocking on the table.

Laps. Excess points that are carried foward, from one game to the next.

Last. Points scored for winning the last trick, as in Pinochle.

Lay Away. 1) *Cribbage.* Give cards to the crib. 2) *Pinochle.* See Bury (2).

Lay-down. See Cinch Hand.

Lay Off. *Rummy.* Get rid of one's cards on an opponent's meld.

Layout. *Solitaire.* The array of cards first dealt out, comprising the tableau and possibly a stock and foundations. (See also Foundation; Tableau.)

Lead. 1) Play first to a trick; 2) the card so played.

Least. *Schafskopf.* The format played if all players pass, the object being to take as few counting cards as possible.

Left Bower. *Euchre.* The other jack of the same color as the jack of the trump suit.

Light. In debt to the pot.

Limit. *Poker.* The maximum amount by which a player may increase a previous bet.

Line. *Gin Rummy.* See Box.

Little Cassino. *Cassino.* The two of spades.

Little Dog. *Poker.* A special hand, consisting of seven-high and deuce-low but no pair.

Little Joker. The lower of the two jokers, which, in a game with trumps, ranks as the second highest trump.

Little Slam. See Small Slam.

Little Tiger. *Poker.* A special hand, consisting of eight-high and three-low but no pair.

Live Card. A card still in the hands or stock, or otherwise available; a card that is not Dead.

Lock. A sure thing; a cinch.

Lone Player. One who elects to play without the help of his partner's hand; solo player.

Long Card. A card left in one's hand after all opponents no longer have cards in that suit.

Long Game. A game in which all cards are dealt out originally and no stock remains, as in Bridge.

Long Suit. *Whist family.* 1) A holding of more than four cards in a suit. 2) The longest holding in any suit in a hand.

Loo. *Loo.* Failure to win one of the three tricks, which exposes the player to increased payments in the next round.

Look. See Call (2).

Losing Card. A card that cannot be expected to win a trick. Also called Loser.

Love. Score of zero.

Low. *All Fours family.* 1) The two of trumps, or the lowest trump dealt. 2) The score for holding or winning such card.

Lurch. Winning a game before an opponent has passed the half-way mark, as in Cribbage.

Make. 1) Fulfill a contract. 2) Name the trump suit or game.

Make Good. *Poker.* Add enough chips to meet the previous bet.

Maker. Player who names the trump suit or game.

Make Up. Gather and shuffle the pack for the next deal.

Manille, or Manilla. The lowest card of a trump suit in games where it ranks as the second-best trump.

March. *Euchre.* The winning of all five tricks by one player or one side; the score for winning all the tricks.

Marriage. *Bezique family.* A meld of the king and queen of a suit.

Master Card. The highest card of a suit remaining live or unplayed.

Matador. Any of an unbroken sequence of trumps from the highest down; any high trump.

Matched Set. *Rummy family.* (See Set (1).)

Matchpoint. *Duplicate Bridge.* A unit of scoring awarded to a partnership in comparison with one or more other scores.

Meld. 1) A combination, set, or group of cards that either scores or helps a player to get rid of cards in his hand; 2) to show or announce such a combination.

Menel. *Klaberjass.* The nine of trumps.

Middlehand. *Skat family.* The active player who is second in order of bidding.

Middle Hand. *Pusoy.* The second five-card hand, which ranks between the first and last of three poker hands set up for play.

Milking. A method of shuffling, by drawing cards simultaneously from the top and bottom of the pack and piling them on the table.

Misdeal. Any departure from the laws of correct procedure in dealing.

Misere or Misery. See Nullo.

Mixed Pair. In tournament play, a partnership of a man and a woman.

Mouth Bet. A bet announced by a player who puts no chips in the pot.

Muggins. *Cribbage.* The right of a player to take points overlooked by his opponent.

Multipliers. *Skat.* Amounts by which the base value of the trump suit is multiplied to determine the value of a game.

Natural. 1) A hand without any wild card. 2) A combination that wins without further play or contest except from another natural.

Near Card. *Cribbage.* A card consecutive with another card, or nearly so.

Negative Double. See Informatory Double.

Nest. *Euchre.* The other suit of the same color as the rejected turn-up card.

Notrump. A declaration that offers to play the hand without a trump suit.

Nullo. A declaration in which the object of play is to avoid winning tricks or points.

Odd Trick. *Bridge.* Any trick won by the declarer in excess of six tricks.

Off, Offside. *Bridge.* Not in position to be captured by a finesse. (See Finesse.)

Official. *Pinochle.* Validated by the winning of a trick; said of the score for a meld.

One-ender. *Poker.* A, K, Q, J or A, 2, 3, 4.

Open. 1) Make the first declaration or the first bid. 2) *Poker.* Make the first bet. 3) A declaration that offers to play with the entire hand face up on the table. 4) *Stud Poker.* Cards face up on the table. 5) Make the first lead of a suit.

Open-ender. *Poker.* See Double-Ended Straight.

Openers. *Poker.* A holding that entitles a player to make the first bet.

Opening Bid. The first bid of the auction.

Order Up. *Euchre.* A declaration by an opponent of the dealer, accepting the turn-up card for trump.

Original Bid. See Opening Bid.

Ouvert. See Open (3).

Overbid. 1) Overcall. 2) A bid that cannot be expected to be fulfilled.

Overcall. Make a bid high enough to supersede the preceding bid.

Overhand Shuffle. A shuffle executed by holding the pack in one hand and dropping packets from the top into the other hand.

Overtrick. *Bridge.* Any trick won by declarer in excess of the contract.

Pack. Deck of cards; the aggregation of all cards used in a game.

Packet. A portion of the pack; refers especially to shuffling and cutting.

Paint. 1) *Hearts.* Discard a heart on a trick won by another player.
2) *Lowball Poker.* Deal a face card to a player who is drawing to low cards.

Pair. 1) Two cards of the same rank.
2) A partnership of two players.

Pair Royal. *Cribbage.* Three of a kind.

Pam. The jack of clubs in some card games.

Part score. *Bridge.* A trick score total of less than game, also, called "partial."

Pass. 1) A declaration signifying that a player does not wish to bid or bet, or that he withdraws from the current deal. 2) *Hearts family.* Cards exchanged among the original hands after the deal.

Passt Mir Nicht. *Skat.* The second turn.

Pat Hand. *Draw Poker.* 1) A hand requiring no discard and no draw.
2) A player who draws no cards.

Pattern. *Whist family.* A group of four integers, as 4-4-3-2, expressing the way in which a given suit is divided among the four hands or a given hand is divided into suits.

Pedro. *Cinch.* The five of trumps or the other five of the same color.

Peg. *Cribbage.* 1) A marker used for scoring on a cribbage board. 2) To win points, especially during the play.

Penalty Card. *Contract Bridge.* An exposed card that must be played at the first legal opportunity.

Penalty Double. See Business Double.

Penny Ante. *Poker.* A game in which the ante or limit is one cent.

Pianola. *Bridge.* A lay-down hand, one that is sure to win all the tricks.

Picture Card. See Face Card.

Pigeon. *Poker.* A card drawn that greatly improves one's hand.

Pinochle. *Pinochle.* A meld of the queen of spades and jack of diamonds.

Pip. Any of the large suit symbols ♠, ♥, ♦, ♣ printed on the face of a card (excluding index marks).

Pip Value. The numerical or index value of a card.

Pique. *Piquet.* 1) The winning of 30 points before the opponent scores a point. 2) The bonus of 30 points awarded to this win. Also called "pic".

Pitch. *Auction Pitch.* The opening lead that fixes the trump suit.

Pivot. 1) A schedule for four players whereby each person plays with each other player as his partner. 2) The player who remains in the same seat while the others progress.

Places Open. *Pinochle.* Available cards that will improve a hand.

Plain Suit. Cards of a suit that are not the trump suit.

Player. 1) A participant in a game. 2) *Skat.* The highest bidder, who then plays alone against the two others in partnership. 3) A card that may legally be played.

Playing to the Score. Modifying normal strategy of bidding or play when one side is close to game.

Play Off. *Cribbage.* Play a card of rank far enough from that of previous cards so that opponent cannot use it to make a run.

Play On. *Cribbage.* Play a card that may enable an opponent to make a run.

Point. 1) A unit of scoring. 2) *Piquet.* A scoring combination; the holding in a suit that totals the greatest number of pips; the score for such a holding.

Point Count. *Bridge.* A method of evaluating a player's hand by assigning a relative number of points to each high card held.

Pone. The player on the dealer's right; in two-hand play, the non-dealer.

Pool. See Pot.

Post mortem. Discussion of the merits of the bidding and play after the hand is over.

Pot. The aggregate of chips or money at stake in a deal, consisting usually of contributions from each active player.

Predict. *Skat.* See Announce (3).

Preemptive Bid. *Bridge.* A high opening bid made to shut out competition.

Premiums. 1) See Royalties. 2) *Bridge.* All scores other than for odd tricks.

Progression. Movement of players or of boards from table to table in Progressive or Duplicate Bridge.

Psychic Bid. *Bridge.* A bid made without the cards to support it for the purpose of misleading opponents.

Punter. One who plays against the bank.

Puppy foot. The ace of clubs; any club.

Pure Canasta. See Natural Canasta (1).

Quart. *Piquet* A sequence of four cards in the same suit.

Quatorze. *Piquet.* Four of a kind (10s or higher), counting 14.

Quick Tricks. See Honor-Tricks.

Quint. *Piquet.* A sequence of five cards in the same suit.

Quitted Trick. A trick that has been taken and turned face down.

Raise. 1) *Poker.* Put more chips in the pot than are needed to meet the previous bet. 2) *Bridge.* Bid an increased number of tricks in a declaration previously bid by one's partner.

Rake off. The percentage of the stakes taken by the house or club, usually by means of a kitty.

Ramsch. *Skat.* A nullo game, which is played if all players pass.

Rank. The ordinal position of a card in its suit.

Rearhand. See Endhand.

Rebid. *Bridge.* A bid made by a player who has previously bid.

Receiver. *Bridgette.* The opponent of the dealer.

Renege. See Revoke.

Renig. *Bid Whist.* See Revoke.

Renounce. Play a card not of the suit led.

Repique. *Piquet.* 1) The winning of 30 points in hand, without play, before the opponent scores a point. 2) A bonus of 60 points awarded for such a win. Also called "repic".

Reserve. *Solitaire.* A special packet of cards dealt out at the beginning, which is used, one card at a time, during the play.

Response. *Bridge.* A bid made in reply to a bid by one's partner.

Revoke. Failure to follow suit when possible; failure to play a card as required by a law of correct procedure, or by a proper penalty.

Riffle. A way of shuffling, primarily with the thumbs of both hands, allowing the cards to drop alternately.

Right Bower. *Euchre.* The jack of the trump suit.

Robbing. Exchanging a card in the hand for the card turned up for trump.

Rob the Pack. *Cinch.* Select any desired cards from the stock (the privilege of the dealer).

Roodles. *Poker.* Any special pot with increased ante or stakes.

Rotation. Progression of the turn to deal, to receive cards, to bid, or to play.

Rough. *Poker.* Relatively bad.

Round. 1) Any division of the dealing, bidding, or play in which each player participates once. 2) A trick.

Round Game. One in which there are no partnerships.

Round House. *Pinochle.* A meld comprising a king and a queen of each suit, also called "round trip".

Round-the-Corner. Circular sequence of rank, the highest card being deemed adjacent to the lowest, such as Q, K, A, 2, 3 a round-the-corner straight in Poker.

Royal Flush. *Poker.* An ace-high straight flush.

Royal Marriage. *Bezique family.* A meld of the king and queen of trumps.

Royal Sequence. *Pinochle.* See Flush.

Royalties. Payments collected by a player who holds any of certain high hands, given in addition to whatever the player may win in regular play.

Rubber. *Bridge.* The winning of the first two out of three games by one side or of a series of deals in Four deal Bridge.

Rubber Bridge. *Bridge.* A form of play in which rubbers are scored (as opposed to duplicate play).

Rubicon. *Pique.* Failure of the loser of a game to reach 100 points.

Ruff. Play a trump on a plain-suit lead.

Rummy. *Rummy family.* 1) To get rid of the last card in a player's hand; lay down a hand completely formed in sets. 2) To call attention to a play overlooked by an opponent.

Run. A sequence of three or more cards of the same suit as in Cribbage or Rummy.

Run the Cards. *All Fours.* Deal additional cards and make a new turn-up, when a beg is accepted. (See also Beg.)

Sacrifice Bid. *Bridge.* A call made without the expectation that the contract will be fulfilled, in order to avoid a greater loss.

Samba. *Samba.* A canasta of cards in sequence in the same suit rather than in the same denomination.

Sandbagging. Withholding action on a good hand in order to trap an opponent into greater loss.

Schmeiss. *Klaberjass.* A declaration that is a proposal to accept the turn-up card for trump or abandon the deal.

Schmier. See Smear.

Schneider. 1) *Skat family.* Failure of one side to win 31 or more points in a play. 2) *Gin Rummy.* See Shutout.

Schwarz. *Skat family.* The winning of all the tricks by one player or one side.

Scoop. *High-Low Poker.* To win both the high and low portions of the pot by having both the highest and lowest hands.

Score. 1) The counting value of specific cards or tricks. 2) The accumulated total of points won by a player or a side. 3) Score sheet.

Second Hand. Second in turn to call or play.

Second Turn. *Skat.* Turning up the second skat card for trump.

See. *Poker.* Meet a bet; Call (2).

Senior. See First Hand.

Sequence. Two or more cards of adjacent rank. as 8, 9, 10; in Rummy, such cards in the same suit.

Serve. Deal cards, especially additional cards in Draw Poker.

Set. 1) A combination of melding or scoring value, as in Rummy. 2) Defeat the contract, as in Bridge.

Set Back. 1) A deduction from a player's accumulated score. 2) An alternative name for certain games, such as Cutthroat Euchre.

Sextette. *Piquet.* A sequence of six cards in the same suit.

Shoe. A dealing box used in Chemin de Fer, Baccarat and other casino games.

Short Game. Any round of play in which not all the cards of the pack are used during a deal.

Short Suit. 1) *Whist family.* A holding of fewer than four cards in a suit. 2) *Bridgette.* A holding of fewer than three cards in a suit.

Show. 1) Meld; expose. 2) *Cribbage.* Count the hand.

Showdown. *Poker.* Turning the cards of all active hands face up to determine the winner of a pot.

Shuffle. Mix the cards in the pack in preparation for dealing.

Shutout. 1) *Gin Rummy.* The winning of a game before a player's opponent has scored a point. 2) *Bridge.* A preemptive bid.

Shy. Short, as said of a pot to which additional antes are due, or of a player who owes chips to the pot.

Side Card. 1) Any of a plain suit. 2) *Poker.* The highest card in the hand aside from a pair or two pairs, used to in determine the higher hand between two players that hold one or two pairs of the same rank.

Side Money. A bet in a side pot.

Side Pot. *Table Stakes Poker.* One separate from the main pot, made by continued betting after one player has put all his chips in the main pot.

Side Strength. High cards in plain suits.

Side Suit. See Plain Suit.

Sight. The right to compete for the main pot in the showdown.

Signal. *Whist family.* Any convention of play whereby one partner properly informs the other of his holdings or desires.

Simple Game. *Skat family.* The lowest declaration that may be bid.

Simple Honors. *Auction Bridge.* The holding of three honors by one side; the score thereof.

Sign-off. A bid that asks a player's partner to pass.

Singleton. *Whist family.* A holding of one card in a suit.

Sink. *Piquet.* Omit announcement of a scoring combination (for possible advantage in play).

Skat. *Skat family.* The widow.

Skeet. *Poker.* A special hand, consisting of 2, 5, 9 and two other cards lower than 9, but no pair

Skip Bid. See Jump Bid.

Skip Straight. *Poker.* A special hand, consisting of a sequence of odd or even cards, such as J, 9, 7, 5, 3.

Skunk. *Cribbage.* A doubling of the winner's score for holding the opponent to 90 or fewer points in a 121-point game.

Skunked. Beaten without having scored a point.

Slam. The winning of all the tricks by one side.

Sluff . Dispose of an unwanted card by discarding. Also called Slough. (See Discard (2)).

Small Slam. *Whist family.* The winning of twelve tricks by one side.

Smear. Discard a counting card on a trick won by a player's partner, thereby adding to its value. Also called "Schmier".

Smoke Out. *Hearts family.* Force out the queen of spades by repeated leads of lower denominations of spades.

Smooth. *Poker.* Relatively good.

Smudge. *Auction Pinch.* A bid to win all four points.

Sneak. *Whist family.* A plain suit singleton. (See Singleton.)

Soda. *Faro.* The first card the dealer turns up from the deck after dealing the hands.

Soft Hand. *Black Jack.* An ace with a number card making two different possible counts, in that the ace counts 1 or 11. Thus, A, 4 may count 5 or 15.

Solo. *Skat.* A bid to play without using the widow.

Space. *Solitaire.* A vacancy in the tableau created by the removal of all cards of one pile.

Spadille. The queen of clubs. Also called Spadilla.

Split. 1) *Faro.* The appearance of two cards of the same rank in one turn. 2) See Break.

Splitting Openers. *Poker.* In a jackpot, discarding part of the combination that qualified the hand to open (in an effort to better the chances of improvement).

Spot Card. Any of rank 10, 9, 8, 7, 6, 5, 4, 3, 2.

Spread. 1) Open; show. 2) Meld. 3) A contract that can be fulfilled without playing.

Squeeze. 1) Look at one's cards by slightly separating them at one corner to see the indexes. 2) *Bridge.* Compel other hands to discard; an end-play dependent upon compelling adverse discards. (See also Throw-In.)

Stack. Pile of chips; quota of chips assigned to each player.

Stand. 1) *All Fours.* A declaration by "First hand" that he is satisfied with the turn-up card for trump. 2) Decline to draw additional cards.

Stand off. A tie or draw.

Stand Pat. Decline to draw additional cards; play with one's original hand.

Starter. *Cribbage.* The card cut by a non-dealer and turned up by the dealer prior to the play.

Stay. *Poker.* Remain in the pot without raising; meet a bet; call.

Stiff Card. See Long Card.

Still Pack. The deck that is not being used in a game for which two packs are used in rotation.

Stock. An undealt portion of the pack, which may be used later in the same deal.

Stop. 1) *Stops family.* Interruption of play caused by absence of the next card in sequence; the card so missing. 2) *Russian Bank.* A call upon an opponent to cease play because of an irregularity in the order of play.

Stop Card. *Canasta.* A card, such as a black three, that prevents a player from taking the discard pile.

Stopper. A holding by which a hand can eventually win a trick in a suit led by an opponent.

Straddle. *Poker.* Raise the previous player's blind or the previous player's straddle by doubling it. (See also Blind.)

Straight. *Poker.* A hand of five cards in sequence, but not all in the same suit.

Straight Flush. *Poker.* A hand of five cards the same suit in sequence.

Stringer. See Sequence.

Strip. Remove low cards from the pack to reduce the number of cards, as required by a particular game, such as Pinochle or Skat.

Support. Cards that are of assistance to a partner. (See Raise (2).)

Sweep. *Cassino.* Taking in all cards on the table; the score of 1 point for doing so.

Sweepstake. *Hearts.* A method of settlement in which the pot is won only by a player who is clear (has taken no counting cards).

Sweeten. *Poker.* Ante again to a jackpot not opened on the previous deal.

Switching. *Bid Whist.* Placing a joker in the kitty in exchange for another card.

System. *Bridge.* An agreement between partners on the requirements for various bids, and on tactical procedures in various situations.

Tableau. 1) *Solitaire.* That part of the layout, excluding foundations, on which builds are made. 2) In some games, the entire layout.

Table Stakes. *Poker.* The placing of a limit on betting.

Take-All. *Hearts.* The winning of all the counting cards by one player. Sometimes called "shoot the moon".

Take In. Gather cards from the table, as in Cassino.

Takeout. 1) *Bridge.* A bid, over one's partner's bid, in a different denomination. 2) *Poker.* (See Stack (2).)

Take the Lead. *Stud Poker.* Make the first bet in a round.

Take Up. *Euchre.* Accept the first card turned face up after the hands are dealt, as trump.

Tally. Score sheet, especially as used in progressive play.

Talon. *Solitaire.* Waste pile; cards laid aside as unplayable on being turned up from the stock or hand.

Tap. *Poker.* Bet all the chips in one's possession.

Tenace. *Whist family.* A holding of two cards in a suit, lacking one or more cards of intervening rank, as A, J. The Major Tenace is A, Q; the Minor Tenace is K, J.

Ten Card. *Black Jack.* The ten, jack, queen or king, each of which has a count of 10.

Tenth Card. Any of pip value 10, as a face card in Cribbage.

Third Hand. Third in turn to call or play.

Three of a Kind. Three cards of the same rank, such as three aces.

Threes. See Three of a Kind.

Throw-In. An end-play dependent on compelling an opponent to win a trick and then lead to his disadvantage.

Throw Off. Discard; smear.

Tierce. *Piquet.* A sequence of three cards of the same suit.

Tiger. See Big Tiger, Little Tiger.

Tops. Highest cards of a suit.

Total Point Scoring. *Bridge.* A method of scoring in duplicate play.

Touching. Adjacent in rank.

Tournee. *Skat.* A declaration that offers to turn up a card from the skat to fix the trump suit.

Trail. *Cassino.* Play a card to the table without building or taking in.

Traveling Score Slip. *Duplicate Bridge.* A small piece of paper that is used to record the score of a hand for each set of two partnerships that play a duplicate hand, and for tallying the results and awarding the correct matchpoint score. (See also Matchpoint.)

Trey. Any three-spot (playing card with three pips).

Trick. A round of cards during which one card is contributed by each active player; the packet of such cards when gathered.

Trick Score. *Bridge.* Points made by declarer for odd tricks; the part of the score sheet where such points are entered.

Triplets. Three of a kind.

Trump Card. 1) Any card of the trump suit. 2) A card designated as a trump by the rules of the game.

Trump Suit. A suit selected, under the rules of the game, which then ranks higher than any other (non-trump) suit in winning tricks. Any card of the trump suit is higher than any other card of a non-trump suit.

Turn. 1) A player's opportunity, in rotation, to deal declare, play, and so on. 2) A play that decides how certain bets shall be settled.

Turn It Down. *Euchre.* Reject the first turned up card as trump.

Turn-up. A card turned face up, after the deal, to fix or propose the trump suit.

Two-suiter. *Bridge.* A hand containing five or more cards in each of two suits.

Unblock. *Bridge.* Avoid or resolve a blocked suit by cashing or discarding high cards. (See also, Blocking a Suit; Cash.)

Undercut. *Gin Rummy.* Show a hand that counts the same or less than the opponent's, after the opponent has knocked.

Under the Gun. *Poker.* The first player in turn to bet.

Undertrick. *Bridge.* Any trick by which the declarer falls short of making the contract.

Unlimited Poker. A game in which the players have agreed not to limit the size of the bets and the number of raises.

Unload. Get rid of the dangerous cards in one's hand.

Unmatched Card. *Rummy family.* Any card that is not part of a set; deadwood.

Up. *Poker.* A term used, such as "aces up," to designate the higher pair in a two-pair hand.

Upcard. 1) *Stud Poker.* A card properly dealt face up. 2) The first card turned up from the stock after the deal.

Uppercut. *Bridge.* Play a high trump to force out a higher trump in an opponent's hand.

Uptown. *Bid Whist.* The format of having the cards rank from ace (high) down to deuce (low). (Compare Downtown.)

Vigorish. The fee or percentage accruing to the banker of a game.

Void. See Blank.

Vulnerable. *Contract Bridge.* Designating a side that has won a game toward the rubber.

Waste Pile. *Solitaire.* Talon; a pile of discards; cards laid aside as unwanted or as unplayable.

Wheel. See Bicycle.

Whipsawed. *Faro.* Condition of a player who loses two bets on the same turn.

Wide Cards. *Cribbage.* Two cards separated in rank by two or more cards

Widow. Extra cards dealt at the same time as the hands, and which usually become the property of the highest bidder. Also called, "blind" or "skat".

Wild Card. A card that may be specified by the holder to be of any rank and suit its holder designates.

With. *Skat.* Holding the specified number of top trumps in unbroken sequence from the jack of clubs down.

Without. *Bridge.* 1) A call meaning "Notrump." 2) *Skat.* Lacking the specified number of top trumps, all higher than the best held in the hand.

X. A symbol representing any card lower than the lowest specified card of the same suit, as ♠J, x, x.

Yarborough. *Whist family.* A hand containing no card higher than a nine.

Younger Hand. In two-hand play, the player who does not lead first.

BICYCLE

Index